THIS ITEM 2 WEEKS ONLY
NO RENEWALS

DATE DUE

Mathematics Today

SECOND EDITION

Curriculum and Instruction

Janet S. Abbott
Coordinator of Mathematics
Chula Vista City School District
Chula Vista, California

David W. Wells
Formerly Director of Instruction
  and Mathematics Education
Oakland Schools
Pontiac, Michigan

Consulting Educators

Patricia J. Baker
Mathematics Instructional Specialist
Detroit Public Schools, Area D
Detroit, Michigan

Robert Elder
Director of Program Planning
Medford Township Public Schools
Medford, New Jersey

Rosalie Fisher
District Resource Teacher
San Diego Unified School District
San Diego, California

Dr. Dennis W. Nelson
Director of Basic Skills
Mesa Public Schools
Mesa, Arizona

Sharon Owens
Teacher
Metropolitan-Nashville Public
  Schools
Nashville, Tennessee

Fred Rectanus
Mathematics Resource Teacher
Portland Public Schools
Portland, Oregon

Mary Ann Shields
Teacher
Tecumseh Middle School
Tecumseh, Oklahoma

Rodney Thompson
Principal
Snow Hill Elementary School
Ooltewah, Tennessee

Sara Tune
Mathematics Program Assistant
Metro Nashville Public Schools
Nashville, Tennessee

Mathematics Today

SECOND EDITION

 Harcourt Brace Jovanovich, Publishers

Orlando   San Diego   Chicago   Dallas

PICTURE CREDIT LIST

Key: (t) top, (b) bottom, (l) left, (r) right.

COVER: HBJ Photo/John Petrey
Page 1 (tl), Vito Palmisano/PHOTOUNIQUE: 1(br), E. R. Degginger; 2, NASA; 3, Tom Burton/Skyline Features; 4, Culver Pictures, Inc.; 6 (tr), NASA; 6 (br), NASA/Jet Propulsion Laboratories; 7, Helmut Wimmer; 8 (tr), Jim Brandenburg/Frozen Images; 8 (cr), Milt and Joan Mann/Cameramann Int'l; 9, Photo Researchers; 10, Matthew Rosenzweig/Nawrocki/J.S.; 11, The Bettmann Archive, Inc.: 12, E. R. Degginger; 14, The Photosource, Inc.; 15 (tr), Vito Palmisano/PHOTOUNIQUE; 19 (tl), HBJ Photo; 19 (tc), The Granger Collection; 19 (tr), Ben Kocivar; 19 (bl), Ben Kocivar; 19 (bc), Tom Stack & Associates; 19 (br), Mary Evans Picture Library; 21 (tr), Blaise Zito Associates, Inc.; 21 (lc), Joseph Nettis/Photo Researchers, Inc.; 21 (rc), Blaise Zito Associates, Inc.; 21 (b), Chuck O'Rear/West Light; 23 (bl), Jeff Foott/Tom Stack & Associates; 25, Artstreet; 26, Grant Heilman/Grant Heilman; 29, Bob Glander/Shostal Associates; 31, John Meany; 35, Michael Melford/The Image Bank; 36, Jeff Foott/Tom Stack & Associates; 37 (r) Animals, Animals/Robert Maier; 37 (l), Ann Duncan/Tom Stack & Associates; 38 (l), E. R. Degginger; 38 (r), David Stoecklein/PHOTOUNIQUE; 39, Chuck O'Rear/Woodfin Camp & Associates; 40 (t), George E. Jones III/Photo Researchers; 40 (b), Roy W. Hankey, Jr./Photo Researchers; 41 (t), George E. Jones III/Photo Researchers; 43, John Bateman; 47, Blaise Zito Associates, Inc.; 49 (tl), Michal Heron; 49 (br), Suzanne J. Englemann/Shostal Associates; 50, Shostal Associates; 51, B. Krueger/Photo Researchers; 52, Michal Heron; 53, Ganges, Halley; 59, NASA; 62 (tr), Suzanne J. Engelmann/Shostal Associates; 62, HBJ Photo/Gerald Ratto; 65, NASA; 71, M. Timothy O'Keefe/Tom Stack & Associates; 73 (tr), Tom McHugh/Photo Researchers; 73 (bl), Nick Nicholson/The Image Bank; 74, FPG; 76, HBJ Photo/b.b. Steel; 77 (t), Timothy Eagan/Woodfin Camp & Associates; 77 (b), Treat Davidson/Photo Researchers; 84, Tom McHugh/Photo Researchers; 86, HBJ Photo; 87, George Hall/Woodfin Camp & Associates; 100, Nick Nicholson/The Image Bank; 101, Roy Morsch; 105, Ewing Galloway; 109 (l), Animals, Animals/Mickey Gibson; 109 (r), E. R. Degginger; 111, Jeff Rotman; 112, Russ Kinne/Photo Researchers; 113, Ed Robinson/Tom Stack & Associates; 114, Animals, Animals/Marty Stouffer; 115, E. R. Degginger; 118 (t), Four By Five; 118, Animals, Animals/Mickey Gibson; 123, Andrew Rakoczy; 129 (tr), E. M. Bordis/Leo de Wys, Inc.; 129 (bl), Focus on Sports; 130 (l), Don Graham/Leo de Wys; 130 (r), Focus on Sports; 131, Tony Duffy/Sports Illustrated; 132, Focus on Sports; 135, Daytona International Speedway; 136 (t), Ronand C. Modra/Sports Illustrated; 136 (lc), Focus on Sports; 136 (rc), Eric Schweikardt/Sports Illustrated; 138, UPI/Bettmann; 140, Warren Morgan/Focus on Sports; 141 (t), John McGrail/Wheeler Pictures; 141 (b), Focus on Sports; 148 (t), E. M. Bordis/Leo de Wys; 148 (b), E. M. Bordis/Leo de Wys; 149, Focus on Sports; 152, Walter Iooss/Sports Illustrated; 157, (l), PHOTRI, Inc.; 157 (r), Karen R. Preuss/Taurus Photos; 161, The Bettmann Archive; 164 (t), Earth Scenes/C. C. Lockwood; 164 (b), Jack Fields/Photo Researchers; 166, PHOTRI, Inc.; 167 (tr), PHOTRI, Inc.; 167 (bl), Mary Evans Picture Library; 170 (t), Jim Amos/Photo Researchers; 170 (b), Terry Domico/Earth Images; 171, Karen R. Preuss/Taurus Photos; 172, Animals, Animals/Lynn Stone; 173, Jeff Rotman; 174, Jim McNee/Tom Stack & Associates; 175, Terry Domico/Earth Images; 176, Van Bucher/Photo Researchers; 176 (b), Timothy O'Keefe/Tom Stack & Associates; 178, Philippe Gontier; 179 (tr), HBJ Photo/P. Menzel; 179 (bl), HBJ Photo/Frank Wing; 189 (tr), Fred Haynes/ARTSTREET; 189 (bl), The Photosource, Inc.; 192, The Photosource, Inc.; 194, Mark Newman/Tom Stack & Associates; 195, David Barnes/Aperture-Photobank; 196, Fred Haynes/ARTSTREET; 198, Stewart M. Green/Tom Stack & Associates; 199 (br), Earth Scenes/Breck P. Kent; 199 (inset), Robert Perron/Photo

Picture credits continued on page 443.

ART CREDITS

Key: Top (t); Center (c); Bottom (b); Left (l)

Bill Anderson: 336, 341, 342, 344, 345, 350, 359. Wendy Biggins: 214 (t), 351. Jan Brett: 223. Shirley Breuel: 54, 85, 180, 181, 184, 256, 257, 263, 297, 318, 319, 416, 417. Penny Carter: 98, 362. Jesse B. Clay: 387. Tom Dunnington: 41, 143, 310 (b). Len Ebert: 75, 92, 93. Ruth Gordon: 361. Konrad Hack: 153. Thomas Hamilton, Jr.: 210, 211, 212, 213, 214 (b). John Killgrew: 243, 363. Robert Korta: 23, 24, 34, 58, 61, 63, 64, 111, 121, 124, 134, 144, 146, 397, 398, 399, 402, 407, 409, 414, 415. Larry Mikec: 272, 280, 281, 284, 288, 377. Verlin Miller: 386. Michael O'Reilly: 95. John Rice: 82. Gail Roth: 31. Dennis Schofield: 90, 96. Dan Siculan: 160, 162, 172, 190, 200, 206, 209, 219, 298, 300, 305, 308, 310 (t), 311, 316, 322. Jim Spence: 97. Judy Sutton: 158, 159. Lane Yerkes: 78, 79, 80, 81. Sara Mintz Zwicker: 69, 91, 380.

Technical art, charts, graphs and maps: Graphic Concern, Inc./Dave Hannum: 15, 28, 205, 323 Dimensions and Directions/Vantage Art, Inc.: 30, 44

CONTENTS

UNIT IV: **Chapters 12–14**

Chapter **12**   Geometry   **329**

Chapter **13**   Ratio and Percent   **361**

Opposites • Mental Math **398**
Integers **400**
Adding with Like Signs **402**
Adding with Unlike Signs **404**
Problem Solving • Graphs and Estimation **406**
Subtracting with Like Signs **410**
Subtracting with Unlike Signs **412**
Graphing Ordered Pairs of Integers **414**
Non-Routine Problem Solving **416**

FEATURES
Thinker's Corner **399**
Calculator **405**
Career: Meteorologist **409**
Enrichment: Square Root **421**

REVIEW AND TESTING
Mid-Chapter Review **408**
Chapter Review **418**
Chapter Test **420**
Additional Practice **422**
Common Errors **423**
Cumulative Review **424**
Maintenance • Mixed Practice **408**

TABLE OF MEASURES **426**
TABLE OF SYMBOLS **427**
GLOSSARY **428**
INDEX **435**

Numeration

An airline company plans to buy additional planes. It needs planes that can carry between 125 and 150 passengers and that can travel at a speed greater than 570 miles per hour.

● Use the table at the left below to find which planes they might consider.

U.S. COMMERCIAL AIRPLANES

Airplane	Number of Passengers	Maximum Speed (mph)
707	181	600
727	131	610
737	112	586
747	442	640
DC 8	176	610
DC 9	125	576
DC 10	345	610
L 1011	400	625

Double outrigger canoes have been used for voyages of up to 1,000 miles. The platform connecting two canoes is used to carry supplies.

● Write 1,000 in exponent from.

Expanded Form

We use only ten digits to name numbers because we group by tens.
This system is called the **decimal numeration system**.

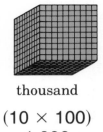
thousand
(10 × 100)
1,000

hundred
(10 × 10)
100

ten
(10 × 1)
10

one
1
1

Jacques Charles and Nicolas Robert made the
first flight in a hydrogen balloon in 1783.
They rose to a height of 2,174 feet above
Paris, France.

● Write 2,174 in **expanded form**.

Think There are four digits in 2,174.
The place of each digit tells
you the value of that digit.

Place	thousands	hundreds	tens	ones
Digit	2	1	7	4
Expanded form	(2 × 1,000) 2,000	+ (1 × 100) 100	+ (7 × 10) 70	+ (4 × 1) 4

Read: **two thousand, one hundred seventy–four**

Write the **standard form: 2,174** ◀ **A comma separates the thousands
from the hundreds.**

PRACTICE • Write the numbers.

1.

2.
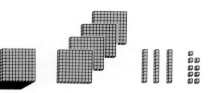

3. eight thousand, seven hundred sixty ‒ five

4. 2,000 + 500 + 40

5. 7,000 + 20 + 9

Write the expanded forms.

6. 672   **7.** 807   **8.** 3,459   **9.** 1,923   **10.** 2,006

EXERCISES • Write the numbers.

11. four thousand, six hundred forty-eight

12. nine thousand, three hundred seven

13. seven thousand, ninety-five

14. 5,000 + 400 + 30 + 8

15. 3,000 + 600 + 60 + 2

16. 1,000 + 900 + 70 + 6

17. 6,000 + 800 + 50 + 4

18. 2,000 + 10 + 8

19. 9,000 + 100 + 80 + 9

Write the expanded forms.

20. 357   **21.** 841   **22.** 6,044   **23.** 3,340   **24.** 7,058

25. 1,960   **26.** 3,456   **27.** 2,123   **28.** 2,738   **29.** 8,621

Write the numbers in words.

30. 396   **31.** 760   **32.** 1,037   **33.** 8,986   **34.** 3,002

Mental Math   Name 1000 more.

35. 4,619   **36.** 7,345   **37.** 8,090   **38.** 5,153   ★ **39.** 9,096

PROBLEM SOLVING • APPLICATIONS

Write each underlined number in standard form and in expanded form.

40. Shortly after the American Revolutionary War, two Frenchmen made the first free flight in a balloon. They reached a height of about <u>three hundred and fourteen</u> feet.

41. Three American balloonists became the first to cross the Atlantic Ocean in 1978. They covered a distance of <u>three thousand, two hundred and thirty-three</u> miles.

Solve. Write each answer in standard form and in expanded form.

42. In 1931, Auguste Piccard and Paul Kipfer rode a balloon to a height of 51,775 feet. In 1932, Piccard and another man rode a balloon to a height of 53,125 feet. How much higher was the 1932 flight?

43. In 1859, John Wise set a world distance record for balloons. He traveled 1,120 miles. In 1980, the record for a balloon flight across North America was 2,800 miles. What is the difference in miles between the records?

Place Value

In 1914, Henry Ford developed his "Model T" car for a price most people could afford. Using the first assembly line, Ford's factory mass produced *two hundred thirty thousand, seven hundred eighty-eight* cars.

● Show this amount in **standard form**.

hundred thousands 10 × 10,000 100,000	ten thousands 10 × 1,000 10,000	thousands 10 × 100 1,000	hundreds 10 × 10 100	tens 10 × 1 10	ones 1
					8
				8	0
			7	0	0
		0	0	0	0
	3	0	0	0	0
2	0	0	0	0	0
2	**3**	**0 ,**	**7**	**8**	**8**

◀ Standard form

In the ones place, the digit 8 names the number 8.
In the tens place, the digit 8 names the number 80.
In the hundreds place, the digit 7 names the number 700.

PRACTICE • What number does the 7 name?

	hundred thousands	ten thousands	thousands	hundreds	tens	ones
1.			3	7	5	8
2.	4	7	6	0	3	2
3.		1	8	4	7	6
4.	2	5	7	3	9	4
5.	7	9	8	6	0	2

In what place is each underlined digit?

6. 11,1<u>3</u>0   **7.** 2<u>6</u>8,272   **8.** <u>7</u>,136   **9.** 86,2<u>0</u>5   **10.** 266,4<u>7</u>9

EXERCISES • In what place is each underlined digit?

11. 2<u>3</u>4   **12.** 3,<u>2</u>19   **13.** 1<u>7</u>4,057   **14.** 35,27<u>6</u>

15. <u>3</u>12,407   **16.** 659,<u>8</u>07   **17.** 32,49<u>6</u>   **18.** 9<u>2</u>0,703

19. 462,<u>5</u>03   **20.** <u>8</u>64,217   **21.** 14<u>3</u>,067   **22.** 309,2<u>1</u>6

What number does each underlined digit name?

23. 2<u>3</u>4   **24.** 3,<u>2</u>19   **25.** 1<u>7</u>4,057   **26.** 35,27<u>6</u>

27. <u>3</u>12,407   **28.** 659,<u>8</u>07   **29.** 324,9<u>6</u>2   **30.** 9<u>2</u>0,703

31. 545,<u>3</u>78   **32.** <u>6</u>94,132   **33.** 135,<u>6</u>29   **34.** 387,5<u>6</u>9

Look at each pair of numbers. Write the one in which the 7 names the greater number.

35. 7,286 or 2,786   **36.** 11,974 or 12,715   **37.** 34,720 or 67,543

38. 1,742 or 3,907   **39.** 27,892 or 24,765   **40.** 86,017 or 18,711

41. 567,920 or 576,920   **42.** 407,643 or 740,529   **43.** 173,296 or 837,492

Mental Math   Name 10,000 more.

44. 46,891   **45.** 18,025   **46.** 884,302   ★ **47.** 992,174

PROBLEM SOLVING • APPLICATIONS

Use the table to answer the questions.

48. In which year were fifty-three thousand, four hundred eighty-eight "Model T" cars produced?

49. In which year were three hundred ninety-four thousand, seven hundred eighty-eight cars manufactured?

★ **50.** Which year's production total added to 53,488 equals a sum of eight hundred seventy-seven thousand, nine hundred seventy-six?

"MODEL T" PRODUCTION	
Year	Number of Cars
1911	53,488
1913	189,088
1915	394,788
1917	824,488

Millions and Billions

The Voyager II was launched to study Saturn. It took about 3 years for the space probe to travel a distance of *one billion, one hundred forty-five million, six hundred thousand kilometers.*

● Write this distance in standard form.

Billions Period			Millions Period			Thousands Period			Ones Period		
hundred billions 10 × 10,000,000,000	ten billions 10 × 1,000,000,000	billions 10 × 100,000,000	hundred millions 10 × 10,000,000	ten millions 10 × 1,000,000	millions 10 × 100,000	hundred thousands 10 × 10,000	ten thousands 10 × 1,000	thousands 10 × 100	hundreds 10 × 10	tens 10 × 1	ones 1
		1	1	4	5	6	0	0	0	0	0

Read: **1 billion, 145 million, 600 thousand**

Write in standard form: **1,145,600,000**

◀ **Large numbers are separated by commas.**

Here is another large number.

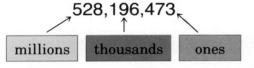

Read: → 528 million, 196 thousand, 473

PRACTICE • Write the numbers in standard form.

1. 7 million, 602 thousand, 567

2. 86 billion, 127 million, 400 thousand, 265

3. 550 billion, 336 million, 942 thousand, 466

Write the digits that are in the millions period.

4. 62,480,172   5. 164,327,430   6. 8,372,197,806

Write the digits that are in the billions period.

7. 155,674,000,162   8. 9,205,372,428   9. 42,567,332,531

EXERCISES • Write the numbers in standard form.

10. 5 million, 364 thousand, 298

11. 2 billion, 900 thousand

12. 68 billion, 435 million, 703 thousand, 264

13. 15 billion, 502

Write the digits that are in the millions period.

14. 2,496,158,370   **15.** 3,012,798,654   **16.** 46,269,800,355

17. 8,086,908,726   **18.** 6,967,444,210   **19.** 77,100,264,993

Write the digits that are in the billions period.

20. 45,301,276,489   **21.** 3,012,798,654   **22.** 2,496,158,370

23. 6,500,000,362   **24.** 9,605,867,300   **25.** 316,249,527,348

Mental Math   Name 1,000,000 more.

26. 2,674,385   **27.** 3,496,582,718   ★ **28.** 49,999,562,180

PROBLEM SOLVING • APPLICATIONS

Write each underlined number in standard form.

29. When Voyager II was <u>thirteen million, five hundred two thousand</u> kilometers from Saturn, it took a picture of Saturn's two moons.

30. Voyager II used the boost of Saturn's gravity to travel to Uranus. This planet is <u>two billion, nine hundred thirty-seven million</u> kilometers from Earth.

Use the table for Exercises 31–32.

31. Which planet is about seven hundred seventy-eight million, four hundred thousand kilometers from the sun?

32. Which planet is less than two hundred million kilometers from the sun?

Space Probe	Planet	Distance from Sun
Mariner	Venus	108,230,000 km.
Viking	Mars	228,000,000 km.
Pioneer	Jupiter	778,400,000 km.

PROJECT   Find the definition of **launch vehicle** and **thrust**.
Find the take off thrust of the following launch vehicles: Titan III C, Vanguard, Space Shuttle System and the Saturn V.
Write the thrust in words and expanded form.

Comparing and Ordering Numbers

Every major country in the world has thousands of miles of railroad tracks to provide transportation. In 1985, China had 21,750 miles of track and France had 21,645 miles of track.

● Which country has more miles of railroad tracks?

Think Compare 21,750 and 21,645.
Each has the same number of ten thousands.
Each has the same number of thousands.
Compare the hundreds. **7 > 6**

Therefore, 21,750 **is greater than** 21,645.

China has more miles of railroad tracks than France.

● Write these lengths of track in order from least to greatest.

    40,753   70,716   29,786

Think   29,786 < 40,753   ◄ **Compare the**
            40,753 < 70,716   **ten thousands.**

So 29,786 < 40,753 < 70,716.

PRACTICE • Write > (greater than), < (less than), or =.

1. 8,234 ● 8,324

2. 9,301 ● 8,469

3. 5,468 ● 5,468

4. 42,697 ● 42,679

5. 86,014 ● 87,601

6. 38,824 ● 38,284

Write in order from least to greatest.

7. 672; 736; 689

8. 2,061; 2,601; 2,016

9. 56,172; 56,672; 56,217; 56,127

10. 496,784; 496,748; 469,874; 469,784

EXERCISES • Write >, <, or =.

11. 6,024 ● 6,204

12. 5,196 ● 5,196

13. 4,926 ● 4,962

14. 21,825 ● 22,824

15. 330,467 ● 303,764

16. 273,461 ● 274,641

17. 566,723 ● 566,723

18. 666,562 ● 559,999

19. 1,141,014 ● 1,114,114

20. 1,000,000 ● 1,999,999

21. 9,908,800 ● 9,909,900

22. 4,670,900 ● 4,670,900

Write in order from least to greatest.

23. 4,826; 4,286; 4,682

24. 1,255; 5,125; 1,552

25. 34,622; 43,632; 24,262

26. 478,002; 474,200; 784,400

★ **27.** 500,000; 600,000; 650,000; 560,500

★ **28.** 1,264,563; 1,246,634; 1,264,536; 1,426,346

PROBLEM SOLVING • APPLICATIONS

Use the table to answer Exercises 29–34.

29. Which country has more railroad track, Australia or China?

30. Write a true sentence to compare the lengths of track in Australia, Brazil, and China.

31. Which country has the least length of railroad track? the greatest length?

32. Write a true sentence to compare the lengths of track in the United States and in Argentina.

★ **33.** Write the lengths of track from the chart in order from least to greatest.

★ **34.** Which country has about twice as much railroad track as Brazil?

Railroad Track	
Country	Length of Track in Kilometers
Argentina	39,782
Australia	40,753
Brazil	29,786
Canada	70,716
China	48,000
India	60,357
Soviet Union	138,500
United States	560,052

Rounding Numbers

The Brooklyn Bridge was built in 1883.
It was hailed as the eighth wonder of the world.
It was the largest suspension bridge in the
world, with a main span of 1,595 feet.

● About how long is the Brooklyn Bridge
   to the nearest thousand feet?

Think   Is 1,595 closer to 1,000 or 2,000?
Use a number line.

1,595
↓

1,000   1,500   2,000

Since 1,595 is closer to 2,000 than
to 1,000, round to 2,000.

To the nearest thousand, the Brooklyn
Bridge is **2,000 feet** long.

You can round a number without using a number line.

To round a number, look at the first digit to the right of the place to which you are rounding.
● *If that digit is less than 5, round down.*
● *If that digit is 5 or more, round up.*

● Round 23,535 to the nearest ten thousand.

Think   The ten thousands digit is 2.   23,535
The digit to the right is 3. Round down.

23,535 ⟶ **20,000**   ◀ Rounded to the
nearest ten thousand.

● Round 784,500 to the nearest hundred thousand.

Think   The hundred thousands digit is 7.   784,500
The digit to the right is 8. Round up.

784,500 ⟶ **800,000**   ◀ Rounded to the
nearest hundred thousand.

PRACTICE • Round to the nearest ten.

1. 57   **2.** 32   **3.** 89   **4.** 75

Round to the nearest hundred.

5. 3,247   **6.** 4,596   **7.** 2,351   **8.** 7,449

Round to the nearest thousand.

9. 6,896   **10.** 14,261   **11.** 17,500   **12.** 52,733

EXERCISES • Round to the nearest ten.

13. 63   **14.** 186   **15.** 732   **16.** 3,455

Round to the nearest hundred.

17. 8,639   **18.** 7,555   **19.** 52,649   **20.** 13,614

Round to the nearest thousand.

21. 4,875   **22.** 3,900   **23.** 856,104   **24.** 977,648

Round to the nearest ten thousand.

25. 64,372   **26.** 58,512   **27.** 27,350   **28.** 411,469

Round to the nearest hundred thousand.

29. 764,372   **30.** 458,512   **31.** 6,327,350   **32.** 2,858,295

Round to the nearest million.

33. 4,434,433   **34.** 4,444,976   **35.** 6,906,421   **36.** 15,569,200

Round to the nearest billion.

★ **37.** 7,896,050,321   ★ **38.** 14,095,621,484   ★ **39.** 46,724,641,312   ★ **40.** 816,432,151,029

PROBLEM SOLVING • APPLICATIONS

41. The twin towers of the Brooklyn Bridge stand 276 feet above the East River. Round this number to the nearest hundred feet.

43. The approach to the Brooklyn Bridge on the New York side is 1,592 feet long. Round this number to the nearest thousand feet.

44. Steel wire was used to make cable for the Brooklyn Bridge. Each of the four main cables was made from fourteen thousand, three hundred sixty-one miles of steel wire.
  a. Write this number in standard form.
  b. Round this number to the nearest thousand miles.

42. The oldest surviving bridge in the world is the slab stone bridge over the River Meles in Turkey. This single-arch bridge is two thousand, eight hundred thirty-four years old.
  a. Write this number in standard form.
  b. Round this number to the nearest thousand years.

Powers and Exponents

The Polynesians used double outrigger canoes for voyages as far as 1,000 miles. The canoes carried supplies on a platform connecting the two canoes.

Look at this number sentence.

Each 10 is a **factor.**
1,000 is the **product.** $10 \times 10 \times 10 = 1,000$
1,000 is a **power** of 10.

You can use an **exponent** to tell how many times 10 is used as a factor.

exponent
$10^3 = 10 \times 10 \times 10 = 1,000$

Read 10^3 as **ten to the third power.**

Look for a pattern in the chart. Compare the number of zeros in the **Number**-column with the exponent in the **Exponent Form**-column.

Number	Factor Form	Exponent Form	Read
100	10×10	10^2	ten to the second power or ten squared
1,000	$10 \times 10 \times 10$	10^3	ten to the third power or ten cubed
10,000	$10 \times 10 \times 10 \times 10$	10^4	ten to the fourth power

These all name five thousand.

$5,000$ $5 \times 1,000$ $5 \times 10 \times 10 \times 10$ 5×10^3

In the expression 2^4, the 2 is the **base** and the 4 is the exponent.
Read 2^4 as **two to the fourth power.**

$2^4 = 2 \times 2 \times 2 \times 2 = 16$

PRACTICE • Mental Math   Name the exponent forms.

1. 10×10
2. $10 \times 10 \times 10$
3. $10 \times 10 \times 10 \times 10$
4. $2 \times 2 \times 2$
5. 5×5
6. $3 \times 3 \times 3 \times 3 \times 3$

Write the standard form.

7. 10^5
8. 10^6
9. 10^7
10. 2^5
11. 6^2
12. 3^4
13. $6 \times 10 \times 10$
14. $9 \times 1,000$
15. 3×10^4

EXERCISES • Write the exponent forms.

16. $10 \times 10 \times 10$ **17.** $10 \times 10 \times 10 \times 10$ **18.** $10 \times 10 \times 10 \times 10 \times 10$

19. $3 \times 3 \times 3 \times 3 \times 3 \times 3$ **20.** $9 \times 9 \times 9$ **21.** $7 \times 7 \times 7 \times 7$

Write the standard form.

22. $10 \times 10 \times 10$ **23.** $10 \times 10 \times 10 \times 10$ **24.** $10 \times 10 \times 10 \times 10 \times 10$

25. 10^3 **26.** 10^4 **27.** 10^5

28. 8^2 **29.** 4^3 **30.** 2^5

31. 3^2 **32.** 7^2 **33.** 5^3

34. 5×100 **35.** $8 \times 1,000$ **36.** $6 \times 10,000$

37. $5 \times 10 \times 10$ **38.** $8 \times 10 \times 10 \times 10$ **39.** $6 \times 10 \times 10 \times 10 \times 10$

40. 5×10^2 **41.** 8×10^3 **42.** 6×10^4

Write the powers of ten in exponent form.

★ **43.** $(2 \times 10,000) + (5 \times 1,000) + (6 \times 100) + (8 \times 10) + (7 \times 1)$

★ **44.** $(6 \times 100,000) + (4 \times 10,000) + (3 \times 1,000) + (9 \times 100) + (8 \times 10) + (3 \times 1)$

PROBLEM SOLVING • APPLICATIONS

Rewrite the exponent form in standard form.

45. Some outrigger canoes could hold as many as 2^5 people.

46. Polynesian fishermen returned to shore with 10^2 crabs and 4^2 tuna.

Rewrite the standard form in exponent form.

★**47.** Asian peoples may have traveled as far as 8,000 miles by land, bridges, and canoes to settle the islands of Polynesia.

★**48.** Archeologists believe that some island civilizations have used canoes for over 2,000 years.

CALCULATOR • Exponent Forms

Use a calculator to find the standard form of 4^6.

Press: ④ ⊗ ④ ⊗ ④ ⊗ ④ ⊗ ④ ⊗ ④ ⊜   ⟨ 4096. ⟩

On some calculators you can use the ⊜ key to find the standard form.

Press: ④ ⊗ ⊜ ⊜ ⊜ ⊜ ⊜ ⊜   ⟨ 4096. ⟩

EXERCISES • Write the exponent form in standard form.

1. 5^8 **2.** 3^{12} **3.** 9^5 **4.** 11^7 **5.** 14^4 **6.** 36^3 **7.** 135^2

PROBLEM SOLVING · STRATEGIES

Using a Table

When solving problems, you must first find the necessary information. Sometimes you can use a table to find the information you need.

U.S. COMMERCIAL AIRPLANES				
Airplane	Number of Passengers	Maximum Speed (mph)	Usual Loaded Weight (lbs)	Length (ft)
707	181	600	251,466	144
727	131	610	169,642	135
737	112	586	110,770	89
747	442	640	731,478	322
DC 8	176	610	314,336	151
DC 9	125	576	120,758	125
DC 10	345	610	570,812	184
L 1011	400	625	465,036	177

Example

An airline company is planning to purchase additional airplanes. It needs planes which carry between 125 and 150 passengers and can fly over 570 miles per hour (**mph**).

● Using the table, which planes might they consider?

Think   You know the airline is interested in speed and number of passengers. So you use those two columns on the table.

Step 1.
Look at the **Number of Passengers** column. Find the planes which carry between 125 to 150 passengers.

The 727 and the DC 9

Step 2.
Look at the **Maximum Speed** column. Does either airplane fly over 570 mph?

Both the **727** and the **DC 9** can fly over 570 mph.

The airplane can use either the **727** or the **DC 9**

PROBLEMS • Use the table to solve each problem.

1. Which airplanes travel at less than 600 mph and carry fewer than 120 passengers?

2. The first commercial jet used by the U.S. airlines was the 707. Was it faster or slower than the DC 8?

3. If an airline planned to carry no more than 100 passengers on a single flight, which plane would they choose?

Use the heading at the top of each column to find the correct information.

4. What is the weight of the heaviest plane to the nearest thousand?

5. An airline purchased a 747. They have one large hanger which measures 210 feet long. Will the 747 fit in the hanger?

6. If you round the length to the nearest ten, which planes would have the same length?

7. An airline needs a plane which travels over 600 mph and carries about 175 passengers. Which one should they choose?

8. Suppose an airport's runways are unable to support any weight over 300,000 pounds. Which airplanes would not be allowed to land?

A table organizes information clearly.

9. List the three heaviest airplanes from the heaviest to the lightest.

10. An airline wants to purchase one plane which can carry over 350 passengers. They also want the fastest plane available. Which one would they select?

11. An airline company is considering buying a DC 9. What other airplane would be similar in speed and number of passengers?

12. There is one plane which is not only the fastest, but also is the heaviest. This plane can carry the largest number of passengers. Name the plane.

Write Your Own Problem

A flight from Orlando to Boston had reservations for 175 people. The same plane then returned to Orlando with 325 passengers.

Make up a problem using the information and information from the table.

CHAPTER REVIEW

Part 1 • VOCABULARY

For Exercises 1–6, choose from the box at the right the word that completes the sentence.

expanded
exponent
greater than
less than
millions
standard

1. A number written as 27,620 is ___?___ form. (Page 2)

2. In the sentence $2^3 = 2 \times 2 \times 2 = 8$, the number 3 is called an ___?___. (Page 12)

3. In the sentence 256 < 1,400, the sign < means ___?___. (Page 8)

4. In the sentence 1,475 > 1,471, the sign > means ___?___. (Page 8)

5. In the number 9,283,655, the 9 is in the ___?___ place. (Page 6)

6. We can write the number 3,056 as 3000 + 50 + 6. This is called the ___?___ form. (Page 2)

Part 2 • SKILLS

Write the standard form. (Pages 2–3)

7. 6,000 + 400 + 90 + 5   8. 9,000 + 50 + 3   9. three thousand, six hundred two
10. 3,000 + 50 + 6   11. 1,000 + 10   12. four thousand, eighty-three
13. 1,000 + 10 + 9   14. 5,000 + 600 + 20 + 1   15. nine thousand, one hundred twelve

Write the number in expanded form. (Pages 2–3)

16. 4,198   17. 6,052   18. 3,005
19. 6,422   20. 7,919   21. 4,024
22. 8,999   23. 2,004   24. 1,101

Write the number in words. (Pages 2–3)

25. 3,582   26. 87,029   27. 470,603
28. 4,015   29. 40,625   30. 165,017
31. 9,240   32. 99,005   33. 301,499

Write the number. (Pages 4–7)

34. 16 million, 453 thousand, 615   35. 32 billion, 821 million, 253
36. 14 million, 320 thousand, 295   37. 15 billion, 214 million, 685 thousand, 18
38. 329 million, 17 thousand, 2   39. 266 billion, 246 thousand, 820

Use 603,247,118,329. Write the digits that are in the (Pages 6–7)

40. ones period   **41.** thousands period   **42.** millions period

43. billions period

Write >, <, or =. (Pages 8–9)

44. 5,263 ⬤ 5,623   **45.** 284,215 ⬤ 284,125   **46.** 7,680,793 ⬤ 7,860,793

47. 3,010 ⬤ 3,010   **48.** 499,999 ⬤ 500,000   **49.** 1,717,118 ⬤ 1,711,118

Write in order from least to greatest. (Pages 8–9)

50. 5,786; 5,678; 5,687   **51.** 632,283; 623,283; 632,238

52. 12,352; 12,532; 12,325   **53.** 398,002; 498,002; 398,020

Round 56,425,891 as indicated. (Pages 10–11)

54. nearest hundred   **55.** nearest thousand   **56.** nearest ten thousand

57. nearest hundred thousand   **58.** nearest million   **59.** nearest ten million

Write the exponent forms. (Pages 12–13)

60. $10 \times 10 \times 10 \times 10$ **61.** $7 \times 7 \times 7$ **62.** $2 \times 2 \times 2 \times 2 \times 2 \times 2$

63. 9×9 **64.** $4 \times 4 \times 4 \times 4 \times 4$ **65.** $5 \times 5 \times 5 \times 5 \times 5$

Write the standard forms. (Pages 12–13)

66. 10^3 **67.** 2^4 **68.** 9^2

69. 10^4 **70.** 3^3 **71.** 5^3

Part 3 • *PROBLEM SOLVING* • *APPLICATIONS*

Use the table for Exercises 72–75.

72. Which bridge is one thousand one hundred fifty-two feet long? (Pages 14–15)

73. Write a true sentence to compare the lengths of the Brooklyn Bridge and the Sciotoville Bridge. (Pages 14–15)

74. Round the length of the Bayonne Bridge to the nearest thousand feet. (Pages 14–15)

75. In one minute, 9^2 cars pass through the toll booth of the Golden Gate Bridge. Write the exponent form in standard form. (Pages 12–13)

Modern Bridges	
Name	**Length (feet)**
Brooklyn Bridge	1,595
Golden Gate Bridge	4,200
Sciotoville Bridge	1,550
Bayonne Bridge	1,152

76. An airline needs a plane that can carry a load of at least 400,000 pounds and has a speed of at least 600 miles per hour. Which plane(s) can they choose? Refer to the table on page 14. (Pages 14–15)

CHAPTER TEST

Write the standard form.

1. eight thousand, seven hundred sixty-two
2. $5,000 + 600 + 3$

Write the number in expanded form.

3. 4,106
4. 780
5. 3,529

What number does each underlined digit name?

6. 5<u>7</u>8,103
7. 924,135

Use 105,623,955,477. Write the digits that are in the

8. billions period.
9. thousands period.
10. millions period.

Write in order from least to greatest.

11. 724; 429; 742
12. 3,027; 3,702; 3,072
13. 80,318; 80,831; 80,338; 80,813

Write >, <, or =.

14. 5,714 ● 5,741
15. 310,642 ● 301,642
16. 72,590 ● 72,590

Round 3,784,601 to the nearest

17. thousand.
18. hundred thousand.
19. million.

Write the exponent forms.

20. $9 \times 9 \times 9 \times 9$
21. $5 \times 5 \times 5$

Write the standard forms.

22. 5^4
23. 10^8

Use the table for Exercises 24–25.

24. Which kind of transportation has an average speed of 6×10^2 mph?

25. Round the average speed of the intercity bus to the nearest ten.

Kind of Transportation	Average Speed (Miles per Hour)
Walking	3–4 mph
Bicycle	10 mph
Ocean Liner	33 mph
Intercity bus	53 mph
Electric train	80 mph
Jet airliner	600 mph

ENRICHMENT

Roman Numerals

The ancient Romans used these symbols to name numbers.

I	V	X	L	C	D	M
1	5	10	50	100	500	1,000

The Roman system was not a place-value system. The values of the symbols are added or subtracted.

When the symbols are the same or decrease in value from left to right, the values are added.

When a symbol with a smaller value is written before a symbol with a larger value, the values are subtracted.

Symbol	Operation	Decimal Number
VII	5 + 1 + 1	7
XXVI	10 + 10 + 5 + 1	26
MDLX	1,000 + 500 + 50 + 10	1,560
IV	5 − 1	4
XC	100 − 10	90
MCMXL	1,000 + (1,000 − 100) + (50 − 10)	1,940

Write the decimal numbers.

1. MCCMXXCVII

2. CCMLXX

3. MCMXXIX

Write the Roman numeral for each year.

4. 1968

5. 1956

6. 1829

PROJECT   Roman numerals are still used today. You may see them on clocks and buildings. Find ten places where Roman numerals are used. Make a poster. Show a picture of the place, the Roman numeral, and the equivalent decimal number for each.

ADDITIONAL PRACTICE

SKILLS

Write the standard number. (Pages 2–3)

1. 8,000 + 600 + 90 + 3   **2.** 5,000 + 20 + 7   **3.** Two thousand, four hundred eight

4. 2,000 + 100 + 10 + 8   **5.** 9,000 + 9   **6.** three thousand, five

Write each number in expanded form. (Pages 2–3)

7. 8,137   **8.** 6,034   **9.** 2,009

Write each number in words. (Pages 2–3)

10. 4,951   **11.** 7,068   **12.** 4,006

In what place is each underlined digit?   (Pages 4–5)

13. $\underline{5}$,682   **14.** $\underline{2}$6,901   **15.** 174,3$\underline{4}$6   **16.** $\underline{2}$06,452

Write the numbers in standard form.   (Pages 6–7)

17. 3 million, 612 thousand, 206   **18.** 12 billion, 300 thousand

Write >, <, or =. (Pages 8–9)

19. 3,925 ⬤ 3,295   **20.** 406,823 ⬤ 406,832   **21.** 5,954,614 ⬤ 5,945,614

Round 42,821,752 as indicated.   (Pages 10–11)

22. nearest hundred   **23.** nearest thousand   **24.** nearest ten thousand

Write the exponent form.   (Pages 12–13)

25. $10 \times 10 \times 10$ **26.** $4 \times 4 \times 4 \times 4 \times 4$ **27.** 6×6

28. $2 \times 2 \times 2 \times 2$ **29.** 10×10 **30.** $3 \times 3 \times 3$

Write the exponent form in standard form.   (Pages 12–13)

31. 8^2 **32.** 2^3 **33.** 10^4

34. 9^2 **35.** 10^2 **36.** 5^3

PROBLEM SOLVING • APPLICATIONS

37. Find the year the Mariner 2 was launched. Write this number in expanded form. (Pages 14–15)

38. List the years in order from earliest to latest. (Pages 14–15)

Space Probe	Year launched
Mariner 10	1973
Mariner 2	1962
Mariner 4	1964
Viking	1975
Pioneer 10	1972

COMPUTER APPLICATIONS

Computer Basics

A computer can do many things—play chess, solve mathematics problems, write letters, and so on. To do these things, a computer needs a set of instructions to follow. This set of instructions is called a **program.**

1. You first type the instructions (program) on a keyboard. This is the **input.**

2. What you type goes into the computer's **memory.** The computer's memory is the **storage.**

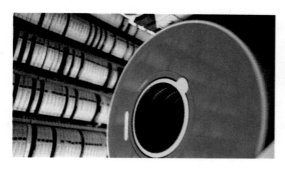

Tapes and diskettes are also used to input information.

What is in memory is lost when the computer is turned off. Because of this, **magnetic tape** or a **diskette (disk)** is used to store what was in the memory.

3. Once a program is in memory, the **central processing unit (CPU)** carries out (<u>executes</u>) what the program says to do. The CPU is a tiny chip that can fit on your thumb.

4. The **output** (answer) from a program is shown on a display screen called a **cathode ray tube** (CRT), or the output can be printed.

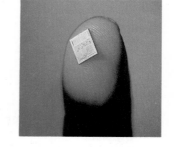

EXERCISES • Answer these questions about a computer.

1. The instructions is called a _?_.
2. What carries out the instructions?
3. What is the display screen called?
4. What part stores the instructions?
5. Name three ways of saving input.

This *one-chip computer* is smaller than a paper clip. The chip contains everything it needs to store and process data.

Mixed Practice • Choose the correct answers.

1. Round 48 to the nearest ten.

   A. 40   **B.** 50
   C. 60   **D.** not here

2. Round 4,362 to the nearest hundred.

   A. 4,000 **B.** 5,000
   C. 4,400 **D.** not here

3. Round 3,795 to the nearest thousand.

   A. 4,000 **B.** 5,000
   C. 4,400 **D.** not here

4. $8 + 7 = \underline{\quad?\quad}$

   A. 17   **B.** 15
   C. 13   **D.** not here

5. $9 + 7 = \underline{\quad?\quad}$

   A. 15   **B.** 12
   C. 16   **D.** not here

6. $9 + 8 = \underline{\quad?\quad}$

   A. 17   **B.** 16
   C. 19   **D.** not here

7. $7 + 5 = \underline{\quad?\quad}$

   A. 14   **B.** 11
   C. 10   **D.** not here

8. $9 + 6 = \underline{\quad?\quad}$

   A. 16   **B.** 15
   C. 14   **D.** not here

9. $8 + 5 = \underline{\quad?\quad}$

   A. 13   **B.** 12
   C. 14   **D.** not here

10. $17 - 8 = \underline{\quad?\quad}$

    A. 7   **B.** 8
    C. 10   **D.** not here

11. $16 - 7 = \underline{\quad?\quad}$

    A. 8   **B.** 7
    C. 9   **D.** not here

12. $15 - 9 = \underline{\quad?\quad}$

    A. 5   **B.** 6
    C. 7   **D.** not here

13. $13 - 6 = \underline{\quad?\quad}$

    A. 7   **B.** 9
    C. 6   **D.** not here

14. $12 - 7 = \underline{\quad?\quad}$

    A. 4   **B.** 6
    C. 5   **D.** not here

15. $14 - 9 = \underline{\quad?\quad}$

    A. 7   **B.** 4
    C. 6   **D.** not here

16. To prepare the land for planting, Mark plowed 9 acres. His brother plowed 7 acres. How many acres in all did the boys plow?

    A. 15   **B.** 16
    C. 13   **D.** not here

17. A farmer has 14 acres suitable for crops. There are 6 acres irrigated. How many acres are not irrigated?

    A. 8   **B.** 9
    C. 12   **D.** not here

CHAPTER 2

Addition and Subtraction

The bathyscaph enables oceanographers to explore the depths of the oceans. The average depth of the Atlantic Ocean is 3,677 meters. The deepest point in the Atlantic Ocean is the Puerto Rico Trench which is 8,648 meters deep.

● How much deeper is the Puerto Rico Trench than the average depth of the Atlantic Ocean?

Wildlife conservation protects plants and animals from becoming extinct. In 1880, there were 2,751 California gray whales. In 1960, there were 5,000 of these whales.

● How many more gray whales were there in 1960?

Addition and Subtraction Facts

Each ring in the trunk of a tree shows one year's growth. The pine tree trunk in the picture has 9 rings. The tree has lived for 9 years. Suppose the tree had 6 more rings.

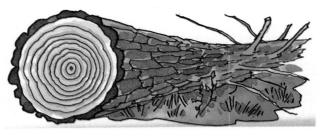

● How old would it be?

Think	You can add 9 + 6 or 6 + 9.

$$9 + 6 = 15 \leftarrow \text{Sum} \rightarrow \begin{array}{r} 9 \\ +6 \\ \hline 15 \end{array} \qquad \text{Check:} \begin{array}{r} 6 \\ +9 \\ \hline 15 \end{array}$$

This example shows the
Commutative Property of Addition.

A tree has 15 rings.

> **You can add two numbers in either order. The sum is always the same.**

● How old would it have been 6 years earlier?

Think	The word "earlier" suggests subtraction.

$$15 - 9 = 6 \leftarrow \text{Difference} \rightarrow \begin{array}{r} 15 \\ -9 \\ \hline 6 \end{array} \qquad \text{Check:} \begin{array}{r} 6 \\ +9 \\ \hline 15 \end{array}$$

The **Associative Property** of **Addition** will help you to add more than one number.

You can group addends differently. The sum is always the same.	$(3 + 4) + 6 = 3 + (4 + 6)$ $7 \quad + 6 = 3 + \quad 10$ $13 = 13$

As you know, adding zero to a number does not change the number.

Property of Zero for Addition	
When you add zero to any addend, the sum equals the addend.	$0 + 18 = 18$ $0 + 0 = 0$ $18 + 0 = 18$

PRACTICE • Add.

1.	2.	3.	4.	5.	6.	7.
9 +3	3 +9	9 +7	8 +9	4 +0	4 +5	8 +6

Subtract.

8. 9 −9	**9.** 16 −8	**10.** 16 −9	**11.** 14 −5	**12.** 13 −7	**13.** 11 −8	**14.** 9 −7

EXERCISES • Add or subtract.

15. 9 +8	**16.** 6 +5	**17.** 10 −4	**18.** 4 +7	**19.** 13 −4	**20.** 14 −9	**21.** 8 +6
22. 11 −7	**23.** 12 −7	**24.** 8 +7	**25.** 17 −9	**26.** 6 +7	**27.** 5 +8	**28.** 13 −9
29. 9 +7	**30.** 9 +5	**31.** 12 −3	**32.** 8 +7	**33.** 16 −9	**34.** 7 +4	**35.** 6 +5
36. 15 −8	**37.** 17 −9	**38.** 8 +5	**39.** 7 +5	**40.** 18 −9	**41.** 9 +8	**42.** 15 −9

Mental Math When parentheses are used with addition and subtraction, do the operation inside the parentheses first.

43. $(3 - 3) + 8 = \underline{\ ?\ }$

44. $(6 + 3) - 5 = \underline{\ ?\ }$

45. $4 + (11 - 2) = \underline{\ ?\ }$

46. $(14 - 7) + 6 = \underline{\ ?\ }$

47. $(13 - 4) - 1 = \underline{\ ?\ }$

48. $8 + (15 - 7) = \underline{\ ?\ }$

PROBLEM SOLVING • APPLICATIONS

CHOOSE • mental math • pencil and paper • calculator SOLVE

49. A silver maple tree was 8 feet tall when it was planted. It grew 3 feet. How tall is the tree now?

50. Miguel planted a 14–year–old birch tree in his yard. How many rings did the tree have 8 years ago?

51. Evelyn plants a 3–year–old elm tree in her yard. After 6 years she moves and transplants the tree to her new yard. She lives at this house for 7 years. How many rings does the tree have now?

★ **52.** The California Redwood tree holds the record for being the tallest tree in the world. One redwood tree is 348 feet tall. If it grows at the rate of 3 feet per year, how tall will it be in 10 years?

Estimating Answers • Mental Math

By conserving topsoil, a farmer may increase the number of crops produced. A farmer harvested 488 bales of cotton from a certain piece of land. After practicing soil conservation methods, the farmer harvested 232 more bales of cotton from the same piece of land.

● **Estimate** how many bales of cotton the farmer harvested after practicing soil conservation.

Think There were 488 bales before conservation and 232 **more** bales after conservation. You need to find how many bales **in all**. So you add.

$$488 + 232 = ?$$

Estimate to find the answer.

Step 1
Round numbers to nearest hundred.

$$488 \longrightarrow 500$$
$$+232 \longrightarrow +200$$

Step 2
Add.

$$500$$
$$+200$$
$$\overline{700 \textbf{ bales}}$$

E PRACTICE • Estimate. Round to the nearest ten. Then add or subtract.

1. 42 +39	2. 17 +68	3. 39 +21	4. 75 +33	5. 89 +43	6. 17 +52
7. 59 −14	8. 76 −22	9. 32 −19	10. 88 −49	11. 91 −27	12. 63 −37

E EXERCISES • Estimate. Round to the nearest hundred. Then add or subtract.

13. 645 +178	14. 237 +593	15. 839 +478	16. 587 +785	17. 348 +279
18. 463 −267	19. 643 −196	20. 391 −293	21. 835 −189	22. 709 −123

Estimate. Round to the nearest thousand. Then add or subtract.

23. 3,909 +1,855	24. 4,366 +8,585	25. 2,782 +1,354	26. 7,087 +1,219	27. 1,174 +8,809
28. 5,981 −2,653	29. 7,319 −2,986	30. 4,793 −2,081	31. 8,172 −2,887	32. 3,041 −1,119

Estimate. Round to the nearest ten thousand. Then add or subtract.

33. 84,929 +19,076	34. 52,741 +25,559	35. 20,596 +33,971	36. 46,358 +12,977	37. 27,835 +58,987

38. 52,891 −19,246	39. 69,877 −34,959	40. 31,649 −19,762	41. 84,006 −17,188	42. 49,736 −16,918

Estimate. Round to the nearest hundred thousand. Then add or subtract.

★ 43. 675,091 +229,634	★ 44. 425,099 +259,683	★ 45. 631,492 +187,406	★ 46. 709,874 −354,012	★ 47. 850,092 −329,684

PROBLEM SOLVING • APPLICATIONS

E Estimate the answers. Round to the nearest hundred. Then add or subtract.

48. A farmer uses contour plowing on 658 acres of land. On 196 acres, the same farmer uses terracing. How many more acres does the farmer contour plow than terrace?

49. A farmer harvests 286 bushels of wheat from the north field, 133 bushels from the south field, and 387 bushels from the west field. How many bushels does the farmer harvest on his land?

★ 50. Ben harvests 408 bushels of corn from his land. After using crop rotation, Ben is able to harvest 596 bushels. He sells each bushel for $14.98. How many more bushels does he harvest after using crop rotation?

★ 51. A farmer ordered 880 bags of fertilizer. He used 193 bags in the north field and 324 bags in the east field. How many bags of fertilizer did he have left for the south field?

CALCULATOR • Estimation Addition/Subtraction

When using the calculator to add or subtract:
a. Estimate the answer with paper and pencil.
b. Find the exact answer on the calculator.
c. Compare the estimate with the exact answer.

4,276 + 7,861 = ?

The answer is reasonable.

Estimate: 4,000 + 8,000 = 12,000 ←

Press: ④ ② ⑦ ⑥ ⊕ ⑦ ⑧ ⑥ ① ⊜ ⟮ 12137. ⟯

EXERCISES

1. 3,798 +6,269	2. 6,328 −4,896	3. 9,071 +8,972	4. 1,788 +7,253	5. 22,375 −13,762

Addition with Regrouping

Alaska and Hawaii have coastlines along the Pacific Ocean. The length of Alaska's coastline is 8,978 kilometers. The length of Hawaii's coastline is 1,207 kilometers.

● What is the total length of these coastlines?

Think You know the length of Alaska's coastline and Hawaii's coastline. So add.

$$8,978 + 1,207 = ?$$

Step 1	Step 2	Step 3	Step 4
Add the ones. Regroup.	Add the tens.	Add the hundreds. Regroup.	Add the thousands.
$\begin{array}{r} 1 \\ 8,978 \\ + 1,207 \\ \hline 5 \end{array}$	$\begin{array}{r} 1 \\ 8,978 \\ + 1,207 \\ \hline 85 \end{array}$	$\begin{array}{r} 1\ \ 1 \\ 8,978 \\ + 1,207 \\ \hline 185 \end{array}$	$\begin{array}{r} 1\ \ 1 \\ 8,978 \\ + 1,207 \\ \hline 10,185 \end{array}$

The total length is **10,185 kilometers.**

PRACTICE • Add.

1. $\begin{array}{r} 69 \\ +40 \\ \hline \end{array}$
2. $\begin{array}{r} 44 \\ +78 \\ \hline \end{array}$
3. $\begin{array}{r} 932 \\ + 43 \\ \hline \end{array}$
4. $\begin{array}{r} 197 \\ +204 \\ \hline \end{array}$
5. $\begin{array}{r} 56 \\ +987 \\ \hline \end{array}$

6. $\begin{array}{r} 876 \\ +392 \\ \hline \end{array}$
7. $\begin{array}{r} 2,406 \\ + 729 \\ \hline \end{array}$
8. $\begin{array}{r} 674 \\ +1,467 \\ \hline \end{array}$
9. $\begin{array}{r} 6,982 \\ +3,706 \\ \hline \end{array}$
10. $\begin{array}{r} 7,067 \\ +9,245 \\ \hline \end{array}$

EXERCISES • Add.

11. $\begin{array}{r} 21 \\ +83 \\ \hline \end{array}$
12. $\begin{array}{r} 86 \\ +25 \\ \hline \end{array}$
13. $\begin{array}{r} 21 \\ +357 \\ \hline \end{array}$
14. $\begin{array}{r} 824 \\ + 56 \\ \hline \end{array}$
15. $\begin{array}{r} 375 \\ +386 \\ \hline \end{array}$

16. $\begin{array}{r} 6,082 \\ +5,359 \\ \hline \end{array}$
17. $\begin{array}{r} 7,443 \\ + 545 \\ \hline \end{array}$
18. $\begin{array}{r} \$93.76 \\ + 64.43 \\ \hline \end{array}$
19. $\begin{array}{r} \$49.27 \\ + 84.05 \\ \hline \end{array}$
20. $\begin{array}{r} \$61.43 \\ + 48.17 \\ \hline \end{array}$

21. $\begin{array}{r} 61 \\ 32 \\ +14 \\ \hline \end{array}$
22. $\begin{array}{r} 73 \\ 28 \\ + 6 \\ \hline \end{array}$
23. $\begin{array}{r} 217 \\ 406 \\ +994 \\ \hline \end{array}$
24. $\begin{array}{r} \$71,88 \\ 48.56 \\ + 7.73 \\ \hline \end{array}$
25. $\begin{array}{r} \$49.27 \\ 19.89 \\ + 84.05 \\ \hline \end{array}$

26. 176,239	27. 332,896	28. 92,503	29, 53,024	30. 27,543
341,950	62,328	431,887	662,987	867
255,464	768,015	29,171	16	55,985
+ 6,133	+864,234	+ 827	+ 4,927	+ 2,100

Another Method • Mental Math

$$
\begin{array}{rcl}
234 & = & 200 + 30 + 4 \\
+ 8,679 & = & 8,000 + 600 + 70 + 9 \\
\hline
& & 8,000 + 800 + 100 + 13 = \mathbf{8,913}
\end{array}
$$

◄ Expanded form

Add. Use the method you prefer.

31. $3,692 + 756 =$ ___?___   **32.** $63 + 78 + 91 + 6 =$ ___?___   **33.** $859 + 16 + 249 =$ ___?___

34. $167 + 8,249 =$ ___?___   **35.** $9 + 36 + 40 + 18 =$ ___?___   **36.** $204 + 156 + 4 =$ ___?___

What are the next two numbers in each pattern?

★ **37.**

4	37	70	?	?

★ **38.**

56	199	342	?	?

PROBLEM SOLVING • APPLICATIONS

Five states in the United States have coastlines along the Gulf of Mexico.

39. What is the total length of the coastlines of Louisiana and Texas?

40. What is the total length of the five coastlines along the Gulf of Mexico?

★ **41. a.** Name the two states with the longest coastlines.
   b. What is the total length of their coastlines?

★ **42. a.** Name the states with coastlines shorter than the coastline of Texas.
   b. What is the total length of their coastlines?

State	Length of Coastline (kilometers)
Alabama	85
Florida	1,239
Louisiana	639
Mississippi	71
Texas	591

THINKER'S CORNER

Two states with long coastlines decide to start a coastline development organization. It was decided to add one new state with a coastline each month. Once a month each member state would send a state progress report to every member state of the organization. How many progress reports were mailed after six months?

Addition and Subtraction • **29**

PROBLEM SOLVING · STRATEGIES

Reading Maps

The Sullivans are going to visit a natural resources exhibit in DeWitt. They must know how to read a map in order to find their destination.

This section of a highway map shows the city of Syracuse and some of the surrounding area.

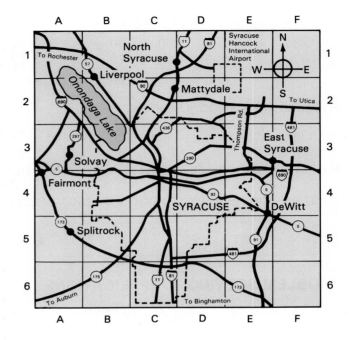

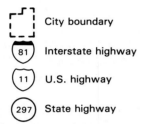

City boundary

81 Interstate highway

11 U.S. highway

297 State highway

To help you locate places, the map is marked off in squares. Each square can be identified by a letter and a number (letter-number).

Example 1

What town is located in A-3?

Step 1 Locate the letter A either above or below the map.

Step 2 Move up or down to the square opposite the number 3 at the right or left.

Step 3 Find the black dot representing the town.

The town of Solvay is located in **square A-3.**

Example 2

In which square is DeWitt located?

Step 1 Locate DeWitt on the map.

Step 2 Using the letters above or below DeWitt, identify the letter for the square.

Step 3 Using the numbers on the right or left of DeWitt, identify the number for the square.

DeWitt is located in **square E-4.**

PROBLEMS • Refer to the map on page 30.

1. What town is located in B-1?

2. What town is located in A-5?

3. In which square is East Syracuse located?

4. Give the location of Mattydale.

5. What road is located in E-2 and E-3?

6. Which four square give the location of Lake Onondaga?

Be sure you understand all the symbols on the map.

---

7. In which direction would you go to travel from North Syracuse to Mattydale?

8. In which direction would you go to travel from East Syracuse to Utica?

9. In which direction would you go to travel from East Syracuse to Fairmont?

10. Identify two different highways you could use to travel from Syracuse to Binghamton.

11. Suppose you want to drive to Auburn from Syracuse. What state highway should you take?

★ 12. You want to drive from Mattydale to Liverpool. You want to take the shortest route. Name the highways you would take.

★ 13. What two routes could you take to travel from DeWitt to Splitrock? Name the highways in the order they are traveled.

★ 14. You want to drive from Splitrock to Solvay. Name the highways you would take. Also name the direction in which you would be traveling on each highway.

MID-CHAPTER REVIEW

Add. (Pages 24–25)

1. $9 + 9 = \underline{\ ?\ }$

2. $(5 + 6) + 2 = \underline{\ ?\ }$

3. $2 + (5 + 5) = \underline{\ ?\ }$

4. $(7 + 8) + 4 = \underline{\ ?\ }$

5. $(8 + 3) + 9 = \underline{\ ?\ }$

6. $6 + (7 + 9) = \underline{\ ?\ }$

Subtract. (Pages 24–25)

7. $11 - 7 = \underline{\ ?\ }$

8. $12 - 3 = \underline{\ ?\ }$

9. $(15 - 7) - 2 = \underline{\ ?\ }$

10. $(13 - 9) - 2 = \underline{\ ?\ }$

11. $(18 - 9) - 4 = \underline{\ ?\ }$

12. $(17 - 8) - 9 = \underline{\ ?\ }$

Estimate. Round to the nearest thousand. Then add or subtract. (Pages 26–27)

13.	14.	15.	16.	17.
3,241	7,725	6,408	8,691	5,322
+5,980	−2,850	+1,124	−4,760	+3,578

Add. (Pages 28–29)

18.	19.	20.	21.	22.
68	345	2,843	24,802	642,824
+291	+ 86	+4,807	459,659	259,432
			+ 13	+140,256

23. $56 + 27 + 13 = \underline{\ ?\ }$

24. $128 + 6,953 = \underline{\ ?\ }$

25. $\$4.05 + \$39.38 + \$3.00 = \underline{\ ?\ }$

Refer to the map on page 30.

26. Give the location of the airport. (Pages 30–31)

27. In which square is Fairmont located? (Pages 30–31)

28. You want to drive from East Syracuse (F–3) to Mattydale (C–2). What would be the shortest route? Which route would allow you to travel on interstate highways for most of the trip? (Pages 30–31)

29. Mr. Spencer has to drive to Rochester (A–1) from DeWitt (F–4). What route would he use if he did not want to go through Syracuse and he wanted to travel on interstate highways? (Pages 30–31)

MAINTENANCE • MIXED PRACTICE

Write the exponent forms.

1. $8 \times 8 \times 8$

2. 10×10

3. $7 \times 7 \times 7 \times 7$

Write in order from the least to greatest.

4. 356, 348, 357, 342

5. 345,756; 345,567; 354,757; 354,775

CONSUMER APPLICATIONS

Writing Checks

Many people pay for purchases with checks. Using a check saves time. Checks also make record keeping easier. On a check, the amount being paid is written in both **decimals** and **in words.**

EXAMPLE:

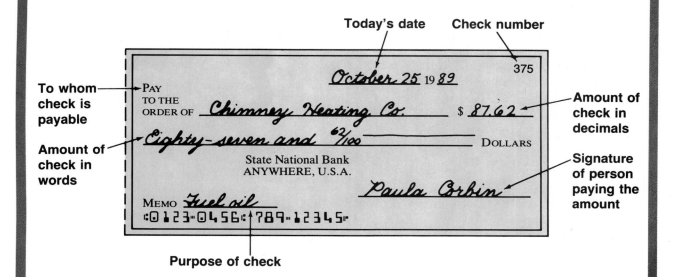

Today's date

Check number

To whom check is payable

Amount of check in words

Amount of check in decimals

Signature of person paying the amount

Purpose of check

EXERCISES

1. Who is going to receive this check?

2. How many times is the amount of money written on the check?

3. When the amount of money is written in words, what word is used to show the decimal place?

For Exercises 4–15, write the amount in words as it would appear on a check.

4. $25.12	**5.** $36.72	**6.** $14.00	**7.** $118.00
8. $325.75	**9.** $481.29	**10.** $19.08	**11.** $206.05
12. $500.35	**13.** $1,725.00	**14.** $2,042.00	**15.** $3,005.00

Subtraction with Regrouping

August Piccard designed the bathyscaph so oceanographers can explore the depths of the oceans. The Atlantic Ocean is one of the worlds largest bodies of water. It has an average depth of 3,677 meters. The Puerto Rico Trench, at a depth of 8,648 meters, is the deepest part of the Atlantic Ocean.

● How much deeper is the Puerto Rico Trench than the average depth of the Atlantic Ocean?

Think The average depth is 3,677 meters. The greatest depth is 8,648 meters. To find the difference, you subtract.

$$8,648 - 3,677 = ?$$

Step 1
Subtract the ones.
Regroup.
Subtract the tens.

$$
\begin{array}{r}
5\ 14 \\
8,6\,4\,8 \\
-\ 3,6\,7\,7 \\
\hline
7\,1
\end{array}
$$

Step 2
Regroup.
Subtract the hundreds.

$$
\begin{array}{r}
15 \\
7\ 5\ 14 \\
8,6\,4\,8 \\
-\ 3,6\,7\,7 \\
\hline
9\,7\,1
\end{array}
$$

Step 3
Subtract the thousands.

$$
\begin{array}{r}
15 \\
7\ 5\ 14 \\
8,6\,4\,8 \\
-\ 3,6\,7\,7 \\
\hline
4,9\,7\,1
\end{array}
$$

The Puerto Rico Trench is **4,971 meters** deeper.

Another Method • Mental Math

● Subtract: 832 − 198

Think Subtracting 198 is the same as subtracting 200 and then adding 2.

$$832 - 198 = 832 - 200 + 2$$
$$= 632 + 2 = \mathbf{634}$$

PRACTICE • Subtract. Use the method you prefer.

1. 96 −27	2. 75 −28	3. 815 − 72	4. 711 −269	5. 217 −196
6. 5,531 − 264	7. 4,284 − 693	8. 3,924 −1,897	9. 2,176 −1,998	10. 9,642 −3,906

EXERCISES • Subtract.

11. 87
−29

12. 93
−64

13. 813
− 77

14. 719
− 94

15. 476
− 43

16. 813
−626

17. 914
−518

18. 665
−280

19. 352
−141

20. 857
−781

21. 5,918
− 653

22. 3,884
−1,907

23. 5,419
−2,815

24. 4,375
−1,264

25. 8,276
−4,987

26. 36,527
− 982

27. 46,151
− 9,806

28. $598.37
−181.25

29. $816.43
−268.98

30. $415.72
− 68.51

31. 444,870
− 98,980

32. 897,394
−294,100

33. 59,813
−18,125

34. 382,132
−190,756

35. 135,764
− 78,349

36. 532 − 78 = ?

37. 5,980 − 987 = ?

38. 2,254 − 865 = ?

39. 33,474 − 8,765 = ?

40. 62,473 − 996 = ?

41. $4,587.67 − $329.89 = ?

42. 597,680 − 46,982 = ?

43. 971,324 − 615,817 = ?

44. 682,414 − 309,985 = ?

PROBLEM SOLVING • APPLICATIONS

45. A bathyscaph descends 8,225 meters. A research submarine descends 1,196 meters. How much deeper did the bathyscaph go?

46. The submarine Trieste II shares the record for the deepest dive. It reached a depth of 11,987 feet. On one research dive it reached a depth of 8,196 feet. How many more feet could it have gone?

47. When the Trieste dove 10,910 meters into the Marianna Trench, it was 120 meters from the bottom. How deep is the trench?

48. In 1960, the Triton made the first underwater voyage around the world. It traveled 41,500 miles. Suppose the Triton travels 3,458 miles in one week and 4,211 miles the following week. How much further did it travel the second week?

Zeros in Subtraction

Wildlife conservation is necessary to protect plants and animals from becoming extinct. In 1880 there were as few as 2,751 California gray whales. Then whaling nations agreed to prohibit the killing of all whales. By 1960 there were about 5,000 gray whales.

● About how many more gray whales were there in 1960 than in 1880?

Think You know how many whales there were in 1880 and in 1960. To find the difference, you subtract.

$$5,000 - 2,751 = \underline{\ ?\ }$$

Step 1
Regroup.
Subtract the ones.

```
      9 9
  4 10 10 10
  5,0 0 0
 -2,7 5 1
        9
```

Step 2
Subtract the tens.

```
      9 9
  4 10 10 10
  5,0 0 0
 -2,7 5 1
      4 9
```

Step 3
Subtract the hundreds.

```
      9 9
  4 10 10 10
  5,0 0 0
 -2,7 5 1
    2 4 9
```

Step 4
Subtract the thousands.

```
      9 9
  4 10 10 10
  5,0 0 0
 -2,7 5 1
  2,2 4 9
```

There were about **2,249** more gray whales in 1960 than 1880.

PRACTICE • Subtract.

1. 460 −381	2. 800 −372	3. 470 − 93	4. 900 −518	5. 506 −159
6. 2,091 − 936	7. 8,009 − 705	8. 4,000 −2,176	9. 9,082 − 765	10. 6,040 −1,858

EXERCISES • Subtract.

11. 590 − 77	12. 400 −164	13. 860 − 41	14. 300 −295	15. 702 −576
16. 1,000 − 68	17. 7,002 − 756	18. $20.10 − 8.65	19. $30.46 − 10.96	20. $60.91 − 18.24

21. 5,000	22. 8,000	23. 4,060	24. 3,704	25. 3,011
$-1,354$	$-2,674$	$-\ \ 995$	$-\ \ \ \ 92$	$-1,763$

26. 25,090	27. 30,946	28. 65,006	29. 99,400	30. 80,149
$-\ \ 8,164$	$-26,295$	$-\ \ \ 642$	$-64,500$	$-70,032$

31. 333,007	32. 904,209	33. 500,000	34. 406,921	35. 900,000
$-297,457$	$-\ 62,194$	$-386,593$	$-\ \ \ 4,734$	$-826,542$

36. $600 - 456 = \underline{\ ?\ }$

37. $\$40.00 - \$26.45 = \underline{\ ?\ }$

38. $\$20.60 - \$9.95 = \underline{\ ?\ }$

39. $94,002 - 3,670 = \underline{\ ?\ }$

40. $26,000 - 998 = \underline{\ ?\ }$

41. $447,006 - 38,695 = \underline{\ ?\ }$

42. $396,001 - 48,762 = \underline{\ ?\ }$ ★ 43. $1,000,000 - 82,683 = \underline{\ ?\ }$ ★ 44. $1,000,000,000 - 987,654,321 = \underline{\ ?\ }$

PROBLEM SOLVING • APPLICATIONS

45. In Mongolia, there are only 25 wild horses living free. There are 200 of these animals in captivity in local zoos. How many more horses live in zoos than in the wild of Mongolia?

46. Seventy years ago, only 18 Pere David deer were alive. Today there are 600 of these deer in existence. How many more deer are alive today than seventy years ago?

★ 47. The saguaro cactus should reach a height of 50 feet and live 250 years. A 70-year-old saguaro is 16 feet tall. How much taller should it grow?

★ 48. Bombay Hook Wildlife Refuge is a 15,000 acre site. 9,500 acres are salty marsh and 1,185 acres are fresh water pools. How many acres of the refuge are not salty marsh or fresh water pools?

Equal to, Greater Than, or Less Than

Forest resources can be managed to supply the demand for wood and its products. Foresters plant 38 spruce trees and 41 pine trees in Field A. They plant 86 fir trees in Field B.

● Are there more, fewer, or the same number of trees planted in Field A than in Field B?

Think   Find whether =, >, or < makes this a true sentence.

$38 + 41$ ⬤ 86

Which of these sentences is true?

$38 + 41 = 86$	$38 + 41 > 86$	$38 + 41 < 86$
Since 79 is not equal to 86, the sentence is FALSE.	Since 79 is not greater than 86, the sentence is FALSE.	Since 79 is less than 86, the sentence is TRUE.

Since $38 + 41 < 86$, there are **fewer** trees planted in Field A.

● If two numbers are not equal, then we can write two sentences showing how they are related.

86 is **greater than** 79.   79 is **less than** 86.
$86 > 79$ $79 < 86$

PRACTICE • Write >, <, or = to make a true sentence.

1. $32 + 61$ ⬤ 93
2. $46 + 71$ ⬤ 120
3. $148 + 375$ ⬤ 520
4. $43 - 14$ ⬤ 41
5. $92 - 54$ ⬤ 38
6. $680 - 326$ ⬤ 194

EXERCISES • Write >, <, or = to make a true sentence.

7. $26 + 43$ ⬤ 65
8. $42 + 91$ ⬤ 133
9. $54 + 18$ ⬤ 71
10. $46 + 42$ ⬤ 90
11. $841 + 131$ ⬤ 976
12. $640 + 130$ ⬤ 768
13. $763 + 144$ ⬤ 911
14. $327 + 432$ ⬤ 750
15. $84 - 16$ ⬤ 68

16. 76 − 38 ● 34

17. 32 − 15 ● 16

18. 81 − 29 ● 52

19. 236 − 147 ● 89

20. 916 − 420 ● 200

21. 742 − 416 ● 326

22. 546 − 192 ● 355

23. 653 + 139 ● 792

24. 246 − 178 ● 86

25. 95 − 26 ● 87 − 19

26. 539 − 216 ● 487 − 164

★**27.** 116 + 211 + 47 ● 463 − 98

★**28.** 3,482 − 987 ● 1,554 + 187 + 763

PROBLEM SOLVING • APPLICATIONS

Write a true sentence for each.

29. Foresters planted 54 pine trees and 27 fir trees in Field A. They planted 71 fir trees in Field B. Are there more, fewer, or the same number of trees planted in Field A than in Field B?

30. Foresters plan to leave 62 trees in Field C. There are 96 trees in the field. They remove 28 trees. Have they left more, fewer, or exactly the number of trees planned?

31. There are 14 pine trees and 38 spruce trees tagged for cutting in the north lot. There are 29 fir trees and 24 pine trees tagged for cutting in the south lot. Are there more, fewer, or the same number of trees tagged for cutting in the north lot as in the south lot?

★**32.** A forester plans to have the same number of trees in Field D as in Field E. Field D contains 752 trees. Foresters remove 78 of them. Field E contains 184 trees. Foresters plant 265 spruce trees and 229 pine trees in Field E. Are there the same number of trees in Field D as in Field E?

PROJECT Find the number of acres of forest land in your state. Find the number of acres of forest land for each state which borders your state. How much more, or less, acreage does your state have compared with each of the states bordering it?

NON-ROUTINE PROBLEM SOLVING

Melissa would like to play the trombone in the school marching band. To play in the band, Melissa will need a trombone of her own. She will also need a one–hour music lesson each week for four months.

Melissa and her mother found that music lessons will cost $9 an hour.

They listed these choices for obtaining a trombone.

CHOICE 1

Buy a trombone.
Pay $35 a month
for 12 months.

CHOICE 2

Rent a trombone.
Pay $30 a month for
the first 4 months.
Pay $25 a month after
4 months.

CHOICE 3

Use a rent–buy plan.
Pay $25 a months for
the first 4 months.
If they decide to buy,
pay $40 a month for the
next 8 months.

FINDING THE COST

1. What will be the cost of music lessons for a month having 4 weeks?

Find the total cost for music lessons and the trombone for each of the first 4 months. Assume there are 4 weeks in a month.

2. Choice 1   **3.** Choice 2   **4.** Choice 3

Find the cost per month of each choice for the fifth month.

5. Choice 1   **6.** Choice 2   **7.** Choice 3

MAKING A CHOICE

8. Which is the least expensive choice for the first 4 months?

9. Which is the most expensive choice for the first 4 months?

10. What is one advantage of Choice 1?

11. What is a disadvantage of Choice 2?

12. Name one advantage of Choice 3 over Choice 2.

13. Name one advantage of Choice 2 over Choice 1.

14. Which is the least expensive choice for 12 months?

15. If you were Melissa, which choice would you make? Give a reason for your answer.

CHAPTER REVIEW

Part 1 • VOCABULARY

For Exercises 1–7, choose from the box at the right the word that completes the sentence.

1. The answer in a subtraction problem is called the ? .
   (Page 24)
2. The answer in an addition problem is called the ? . (Page 24)
3. The sentences 2 + 3 = 5 and 3 + 2 = 5 show the ? property of addition. (Page 24)
4. The numbers you add together to solve a problem are called ? . (Page 24)
5. The sentences (2 + 3) + 4 = 9 and 2 + (3 + 4) = 9 show the ? property of addition.   (Page 24)
6. Adding ? to a number does not change the number. (Page 24)
7. To solve the problem 149 − 82, the ? place must be regrouped.   (Page 34)

addends
associative
commutative
difference
sum
tens
zero

Part 2 • SKILLS

Add.   (Pages 24–25)

8. $9 + 8 = $?
9. $0 + 7 = $?
10. $8 + 4 = $?
11. $(3 + 6) + 4 = $?
12. $3 + (2 + 8) = $?
13. $(6 + 8) + 5 = $?
14. $(9 + 2) + 5 = $?
15. $9 + (8 + 7) = $?
16. $(2 + 7) + 8 = $?
17. $(4 + 8) + 7 = $?
18. $5 + (5 + 8) = $?
19. $(9 + 5) + 3 = $?

Subtract.   (Pages 24–25)

20. $18 − 9 = $?
21. $15 − 7 = $?
22. $12 − 5 = $?
23. $13 − 7 = $?
24. $16 − 7 = $?
25. $(14 − 8) − 3 = $?
26. $(15 − 8) − 6 = $?
27. $(13 − 4) − 2 = $?
28. $(16 − 9) − 7 = $?
29. $(13 − 7) − 4 = $?
30. $(18 − 9) − 9 = $?
31. $(11 − 4) − 1 = $?

Estimate. Round to the nearest ten thousand. Then add or subtract.   (Pages 26–27)

32. $\begin{array}{r} 21,364 \\ +39,350 \\ \hline \end{array}$
33. $\begin{array}{r} 83,497 \\ -28,316 \\ \hline \end{array}$
34. $\begin{array}{r} 65,620 \\ +24,133 \\ \hline \end{array}$
35. $\begin{array}{r} 54,811 \\ -44,709 \\ \hline \end{array}$
36. $\begin{array}{r} 19,850 \\ +71,423 \\ \hline \end{array}$

| **37.** 33,450
+62,195 | **38.** 65,000
−19,038 | **39.** 19,820
+45,000 | **40.** 34,618
−16,482 | **41.** 44,409
+56,327 |

Add. (Pages 28–29)

| **42.** 67
+385 | **43.** 298
+623 | **44.** $35.27
+ 52.97 | **45.** 67,028
416,542
+ 814 | **46.** 330,542
147,295
+452,725 |

47. $61 + 46 + 20 + 5 = \underline{?}$ **48.** $329 + 8,714 = \underline{?}$ **49.** $$62.60 + $25.58 = \underline{?}$$

50. $38 + 2 + 108 + 90 = \underline{?}$ **51.** $645 + 9,982 = \underline{?}$ **52.** $42 + 346 + 8,095 = \underline{?}$

Subtract. (Pages 34–37)

| **53.** 594
− 67 | **54.** 6,256
−1,729 | **55.** $407.00
− 54.25 | **56.** 135,402
− 49,197 | **57.** 412,720
−234,815 |

58. $629 − 86 = \underline{?}$ **59.** $30,902 − 6,248 = \underline{?}$ **60.** $$250.12 − $198.65 = \underline{?}$$

Write >, <, or =. (Pages 38–39)

61. $814 + 253$ ● 910 **62.** $649 − 327$ ● 320 **63.** $459 + 223$ ● $989 − 253$

64. $625 + 892$ ● $907 + 610$ **65.** $300 − 199$ ● $83 + 17$ **66.** $39 + 496$ ● $900 − 332$

67. What city is located in D–2? (Pages 30–31)

68. Give the location of Waterbury. (Pages 30–31)

Part 3 • PROBLEM SOLVING • APPLICATIONS

69. Martha Samuelson has to drive from Torrington (A–2) to Hartford (D–2). She must stop in Bristol on the way. What highways will she use? (Pages 30–31)

70. The Cawleys live in Middletown (D–4). They own a farm in Torrington (A–2). What are the two routes they could use to travel to their farm? (Pages 30–31)

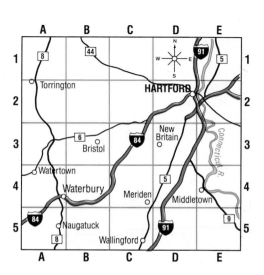

CHAPTER TEST

Add.

1. 1,742
        +2,486

2. $856.31
        + 62.97

3. 192,847
        346,512
        + 83,955

4. 4,796 + 389 = ___?___

5. $63.70 + $17.40 + $2.05 = ___?___

Subtract.

6. 658
        −169

7. $74.61
        − 28.47

8. 16,294
        − 8,986

9. 20,605
        − 1,821

10. 106,407
         − 54,822

11. 800,726
         −132,559

12. 23,437 − 1,721 = ___?___

13. $462.75 − $13.90 = ___?___

Write >, <, or =.

14. 284 − 96 ● 160

15. 96 + 545 ● 741

16. 801 − 178 ● 623

Estimate. Round to the nearest hundred. Then add or subtract.

17. 764
         +130

18. 827
         −473

19. 912
         +378

20. 627
         +250

21. 537
         −179

22. Name the four squares which locate Quabbin Reservoir.

23. Which two cities are located in B–5?

24. Fred Donnelly delivers gasoline on Mondays to gas stations in Amherst, Northampton, Holyoke and Springfield. He lives in Ware. What is his most direct route?

25. Lester Rawling lives in Palmer. He often fishes at the north end of Quabbin Reservoir. What highways could he travel?

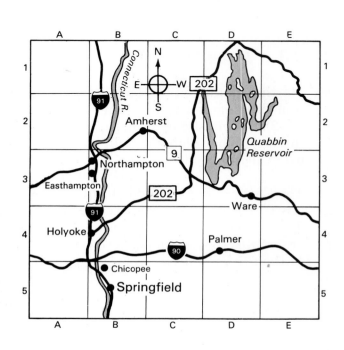

ENRICHMENT

Venn Diagrams

You can use Venn diagrams to solve problems.

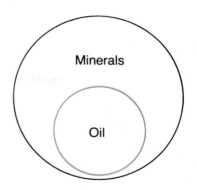

Oil is a mineral.
Some minerals are oil
A can contains oil.

● Is the contents of the can a
   mineral?

Think The diagram shows:
  a. Oil is a mineral   *"all* oil is a mineral"
  b. Not all minerals are oil   *"some* minerals are oil"

Because the contents of the can is oil, it must be a mineral.

Use the diagram. Write T or F for each statement.

1.

All wheat is grain.
All grain is wheat.
Some wheat is grain.

2.

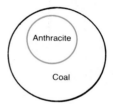

Anthracite is coal.
Some anthracite is coal.
Some coal is anthracite.

Write correct statements for each diagram.

3.

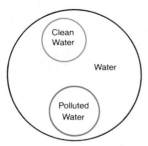

4.

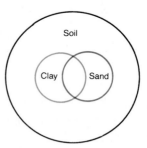

Draw a Venn Diagram for each statement.

5. All pine trees are
   evergreens.
   Some evergreens are
   white cedar.

6. Hematite is an iron ore.
   Some iron ores are iron
   oxide.
   Some iron oxides are
   hematite.

ADDITIONAL PRACTICE

SKILLS

Add.   (Pages 28–29)

1. $4 + 9 = \underline{\;?\;}$

2. $8 + 8 = \underline{\;?\;}$

3. $(7 + 5) + 3 = \underline{\;?\;}$

4. $(9 + 8) + 6 = \underline{\;?\;}$

5. $(3 + 8) + 9 = \underline{\;?\;}$

6. $6 + (7 + 8) = \underline{\;?\;}$

Subtract.   (Pages 34–37)

7. $18 - 9 = \underline{\;?\;}$

8. $16 - 7 = \underline{\;?\;}$

9. $(15 - 8) - 5 = \underline{\;?\;}$

10. $(13 - 4) - 7 = \underline{\;?\;}$

11. $(16 - 9) - 2 = \underline{\;?\;}$

12. $(14 - 5) - 9 = \underline{\;?\;}$

Estimate. Round to the nearest thousand. Then add or subtract.   (Pages 26–27)

13. $8{,}942 + 2{,}156 = \underline{\;?\;}$

14. $3{,}645 - 1{,}860 = \underline{\;?\;}$

15. $5{,}527 + 5{,}466 = \underline{\;?\;}$

16. $6{,}124 + 3{,}702 = \underline{\;?\;}$

17. $9{,}481 - 6{,}624 = \underline{\;?\;}$

18. $5{,}500 - 1{,}946 = \underline{\;?\;}$

Add.   (Pages 28–29)

19.
```
  627
+ 385
```

20.
```
  2,299
+ 5,456
```

21.
```
$380.48
+  79.65
```

22.
```
421,843
 19,607
+     21
```

23.
```
 561,294
 208,517
+154,607
```

24. $449 + 592 = \underline{\;?\;}$

25. $14{,}927 + 36{,}628 = \underline{\;?\;}$

26. $\$1{,}475.10 + \$368.77 = \underline{\;?\;}$

Subtract.   (Pages 34–37)

27.
```
  623
- 398
```

28.
```
  7,194
- 2,537
```

29.
```
$304.00
-  63.99
```

30.
```
168,250
- 49,716
```

31.
```
 700,235
-291,608
```

32. $624 - 199 = \underline{\;?\;}$

33. $56{,}012 - 38{,}291 = \underline{\;?\;}$

34. $\$5{,}268.67 - \$43.19 = \underline{\;?\;}$

Write $>$, $<$, or $=$.   (Pages 38–39)

35. $258 + 301$ ⬤ 360

36. $785 - 413$ ⬤ 372

37. $285 + 114$ ⬤ $598 - 201$

PROBLEM SOLVING • APPLICATIONS

Refer to the map on page 30.

38. Mack Smith lives in DeWitt. He works in Liverpool. He travels on interstate highways to go to work. What is his most direct route?
(Pages 30–31)

39. On her way from Utica to Rochester, Susan Lewis stops to see customers in DeWitt and Solvay. What would be her most direct route?   (Pages 30–31)

COMPUTER APPLICATIONS

Print Commands: + and −

You can use a **PRINT** command to add and subtract numbers. **PRINT** commands are part of the **BASIC** programming language. Type this command on the keyboard. This is the input.

PRINT 8592+4067 Press the SPACE BAR to make this space.

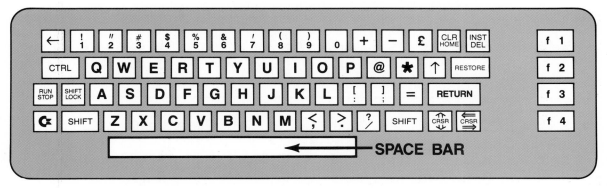

To make the + sign, hold down the **SHIFT** key and press the + key. If you have a Commodore computer, you only have to press the + key.

After you have typed **PRINT 8592+4067**, press the key marked **RETURN**, or **ENTER**, or ⟵⎮ . This will produce the output, **12659**, on the **CRT**.

EXERCISES • Find the output.

1. PRINT 3579+987   **2.** PRINT 6096−428   **3.** PRINT 7724+986

4. PRINT 9768−4029   **5.** PRINT 20895+6705   **6.** PRINT 9008−999

Write a PRINT command that you would use to solve each problem. Then solve the problem.

7. The greenhouse has 967 planters in stock. They need 2,010 to complete several new orders. How many more planters are needed?

8. The length of the Florida coastline is 1,239 kilometers. Alabama's is 85 kilometers and Louisiana's is 639 kilometers. What is the total length?

Mixed Practice • Choose the correct answers.

1. Round 74 to the nearest ten.

   A. 70   **B.** 80
   C. 100   **D.** not here

2. Round 883 to the nearest hundred.

   A. 800   **B.** 880
   C. 900   **D.** not here

3. $8 \times 6 = $ _____?_____

   A. 49   **B.** 54
   C. 48   **D.** not here

4. $6 \times 9 = $ _____?_____

   A. 52   **B.** 54
   C. 56   **D.** not here

5. $7 \times 7 = $ _____?_____

   A. 47   **B.** 64
   C. 49   **D.** not here

6. $8 \times 7 = $ _____?_____

   A. 54   **B.** 64
   C. 60   **D.** not here

7. $8 \times 4 = $ _____?_____

   A. 32   **B.** 28
   C. 36   **D.** not here

8. $7 \times 9 = $ _____?_____

   A. 63   **B.** 64
   C. 64   **D.** not here

9. $7 \times 6 = $ _____?_____

   A. 45   **B.** 43
   C. 52   **D.** not here

10. $7 \times 4 = $ _____?_____

    A. 32   **B.** 24
    C. 28   **D.** not here

11. $6 \times 4 = $ _____?_____

    A. 32   **B.** 24
    C. 28   **D.** not here

12. $9 \times 8 = $ _____?_____

    A. 72   **B.** 64
    C. 81   **D.** not here

13. $8 \times 8 = $ _____?_____

    A. 72   **B.** 65
    C. 68   **D.** not here

14. $8 \times 3 = $ _____?_____

    A. 28   **B.** 32
    C. 24   **D.** not here

15. $7 \times 8 = $ _____?_____

    A. 54   **B.** 56
    C. 60   **D.** not here

16. Pretend you are an Arctic explorer using dog sleds for travel. You estimate that you can cover 9 miles in 1 day. How far can you travel in 8 days?

    A. 72 miles   **B.** 81 miles
    C. 64 miles   **D.** not here

17. Suppose an astronaut will visit your classroom. The room has 7 rows of seats with 6 seats in each row. How many people can be seated?

    A. 38   **B.** 48
    C. 42   **D.** not here

Multiplication

One tent at the state fair showed a three-dimensional movie about mountain climbing. An expedition that climbed Mount Everest carried 235 spools of rope. Each spool held 375 feet of rope.

● How many feet of rope were there altogether?

One tent at the state fair exhibited stamp collections. One display board contains 249 stamps.
● How many stamps can there be on 7 display boards?

Multiplication

People are buying tickets to the state fair.
There are 3 lines, and 7 people are in each line.

● How many people are in the line?

Think You are *joining groups* of the
same size, so you *multiply.*

factor ⟶ 7   3
factor ⟶ ×3 or ×7
$3 \times 7 = 21$ ← product ⟶ 21   21

There are **21 people** in line.

These properties of multiplication will help you.

Commutative Property of Multiplication You can multiply two numbers in either order. The product is always the same.	$2 \times 5 = 10$ $5 \times 2 = 10$
Associative Property of Multiplication You can group factors differently. The product is always the same.	$(4 \times 2) \times 3 = 4 \times (2 \times 3)$ $8 \times 3 = 4 \times 6$ $24 = 24$
Property of One for Multiplication When one of two factors is 1, the product equals the other factor.	$1 \times 9 = 9$ $9 \times 1 = 9$
Property of Zero for Multiplication When a factor is 0, the product is 0.	$0 \times 7 = 0$ $7 \times 0 = 0$ $0 \times 0 = 0$

Practice • Multiply.

1. 5   2. 3   3. 4   4. 8   5. 2   6. 4   7. 5
   ×3   ×5   ×0   ×1   ×4   ×2   ×4

8. $6 \times 8 = $ __?__   9. $8 \times 6 = $ __?__   10. $7 \times 1 = $ __?__

11. $6 \times 5 = $ __?__   12. $7 \times 6 = $ __?__   13. $9 \times 4 = $ __?__

EXERCISES • Multiply

14. $\begin{array}{r} 3 \\ \times 3 \\ \hline \end{array}$ **15.** $\begin{array}{r} 6 \\ \times 1 \\ \hline \end{array}$ **16.** $\begin{array}{r} 6 \\ \times 3 \\ \hline \end{array}$ **17.** $\begin{array}{r} 2 \\ \times 9 \\ \hline \end{array}$ **18.** $\begin{array}{r} 4 \\ \times 3 \\ \hline \end{array}$ **19.** $\begin{array}{r} 7 \\ \times 4 \\ \hline \end{array}$ **20.** $\begin{array}{r} 6 \\ \times 7 \\ \hline \end{array}$

21. $\begin{array}{r} 9 \\ \times 9 \\ \hline \end{array}$ **22.** $\begin{array}{r} 7 \\ \times 8 \\ \hline \end{array}$ **23.** $\begin{array}{r} 8 \\ \times 9 \\ \hline \end{array}$ **24.** $\begin{array}{r} 6 \\ \times 6 \\ \hline \end{array}$ **25.** $\begin{array}{r} 7 \\ \times 5 \\ \hline \end{array}$ **26.** $\begin{array}{r} 4 \\ \times 8 \\ \hline \end{array}$ **27.** $\begin{array}{r} 8 \\ \times 5 \\ \hline \end{array}$

28. $5 \times 9 = \underline{\ ?\ }$ **29.** $3 \times 8 = \underline{\ ?\ }$ **30.** $5 \times 5 = \underline{\ ?\ }$

31. $4 \times 1 = \underline{\ ?\ }$ **32.** $3 \times 7 = \underline{\ ?\ }$ **33.** $7 \times 3 = \underline{\ ?\ }$

34. $(3 \times 3) \times 2 = \underline{\ ?\ }$ **35.** $3 \times (3 \times 2) = \underline{\ ?\ }$ **36.** $(8 \times 0) \times 4 = \underline{\ ?\ }$

37. $(5 \times 6) \times 1 = \underline{\ ?\ }$ **38.** $5 \times (6 \times 1) = \underline{\ ?\ }$ **39.** $(2 \times 2) \times 4 = \underline{\ ?\ }$

Find the missing factors.

40. $7 \times \underline{\ ?\ } = 42$ **41.** $8 \times \underline{\ ?\ } = 16$ **42.** $9 \times \underline{\ ?\ } = 54$

43. $\underline{\ ?\ } \times 6 = 0$ **44.** $\underline{\ ?\ } \times 9 = 63$ **45.** $\underline{\ ?\ } \times 3 = 27$

Complete. Multiply inside the parentheses first.

★ **46.** $(8 \times 7) + 6 = \underline{\ ?\ }$ ★ **47.** $(9 \times 6) - 8 = \underline{\ ?\ }$ ★ **48.** $9 + (4 \times 9) = \underline{\ ?\ }$

★ **49.** $(5 \times 4) + 35 = \underline{\ ?\ }$ ★ **50.** $(4 \times 7) - 12 = \underline{\ ?\ }$ ★ **51.** $86 + (7 \times 2) = \underline{\ ?\ }$

PROBLEM SOLVING • APPLICATIONS

52. This week 6 people bring pies to sell at the fair. Each person brings an apple pie, a blueberry pie, a peach pie, and a cherry pie. How many pies are for sale?

53. At the fair 5 groups take part in the animal exhibit. Each group can enter 8 small animals. How many small animals can be entered in the exhibit?

54. There are 7 divisions for the art exhibit. In each division 4 prize ribbons will be awarded. How many ribbons will be awarded at the art exhibit?

★ **55.** Everyone in line buys 8 tickets. They buy 64 tickets altogether. How many people are in line?

Multiplying by One-Digit Numbers

One of the tents at the state fair exhibited stamp collections. One display board contains 249 stamps.

● How many stamps can be displayed on 7 boards?

Method 1 • Mental Math Use the **distributive property.**

$$7 \times 249 = 7 \times (200 + 40 + 9)$$
$$= (7 \times 200) + (7 \times 40) + (7 \times 9)$$
$$= 1{,}400 + 280 + 63$$
$$= 1{,}743$$

Method 2:

Step 1	**Step 2**	**Step 3**
Multiply the ones by 7. Regroup 63 as 6 tens 3 ones.	Multiply the tens by 7. Add 6 tens. Regroup 34 as 3 hundreds 4 tens.	Multiply the hundreds by 7. Add 3 hundreds.

```
   6           3 6          3 6
 2 4 9        2 4 9        2 4 9
×    7       ×    7       ×    7
     3          4 3      1,7 4 3
```

◀ **1,743 stamps can be displayed.**

More Examples:

```
    2          43         4 3 2        2 1 1 2
   48       1,065         7,8 6 4      2 5,3 4 6
  × 3       ×    7        ×     5      ×       4
  ───       ──────        ───────      ─────────
  144        7,455        3 9,3 2 0    1 0 1,3 8 4
```

PRACTICE • Multiply. Use the method you prefer.

1. $\begin{array}{r} 86 \\ \times\ 8 \\ \hline \end{array}$
2. $\begin{array}{r} 34 \\ \times\ 2 \\ \hline \end{array}$
3. $\begin{array}{r} 836 \\ \times\ 6 \\ \hline \end{array}$
4. $\begin{array}{r} 9{,}312 \\ \times\ 6 \\ \hline \end{array}$
5. $\begin{array}{r} 2{,}478 \\ \times\ 9 \\ \hline \end{array}$

EXERCISES • Multiply

6. $\begin{array}{r} 63 \\ \times\ 5 \\ \hline \end{array}$
7. $\begin{array}{r} 77 \\ \times\ 4 \\ \hline \end{array}$
8. $\begin{array}{r} 702 \\ \times\ 4 \\ \hline \end{array}$
9. $\begin{array}{r} 200 \\ \times\ 5 \\ \hline \end{array}$
10. $\begin{array}{r} 401 \\ \times\ 8 \\ \hline \end{array}$

11. $\begin{array}{r} 4{,}623 \\ \times\ 9 \\ \hline \end{array}$
12. $\begin{array}{r} 1{,}982 \\ \times\ 6 \\ \hline \end{array}$
13. $\begin{array}{r} 3{,}746 \\ \times\ 7 \\ \hline \end{array}$
14. $\begin{array}{r} 5{,}924 \\ \times\ 3 \\ \hline \end{array}$
15. $\begin{array}{r} 3{,}874 \\ \times\ 5 \\ \hline \end{array}$

16. $\begin{array}{r} 40{,}865 \\ \times\ 8 \\ \hline \end{array}$
17. $\begin{array}{r} 45{,}360 \\ \times\ 3 \\ \hline \end{array}$
18. $\begin{array}{r} 65{,}635 \\ \times\ 9 \\ \hline \end{array}$
19. $\begin{array}{r} 64{,}502 \\ \times\ 4 \\ \hline \end{array}$
20. $\begin{array}{r} 73{,}201 \\ \times\ 3 \\ \hline \end{array}$

21. 406,395	**22.** 578,900	**23.** 120,000	**24.** 131,402	**25.** 942,347
× 6	× 8	× 7	× 2	× 3

26. 5 × 23 = __?__   **27.** 6 × 42 = __?__   **28.** 2 × 346 = __?__

29. 5 × 608 = __?__   **30.** 9 × 8,607 = __?__   **31.** 8 × 4,529 = __?__

32. 3 × 53,084 = __?__   **33.** 7 × 64,876 = __?__   **34.** 6 × 79,084 = __?__

Write >, <, or = to make a true sentence.

35. 6 × 79 ⬤ 474   **36.** 3 × 67 ⬤ 271   **37.** 3 × 789 ⬤ 2,367

38. 4 × 265 ⬤ 1,040   **39.** 9 × 244 ⬤ 6 × 132   **40.** 8 × 2,067 ⬤ 4 × 4,136

Complete the tables.

★**41. Rule: Multiply by 9.**

INPUT	OUTPUT
18	162
54	?
73	?
89	?
62	?

★**42. Rule: Multiply by 6.**

INPUT	OUTPUT
21	126
27	?
65	?
38	?
92	?

★**43. Rule: Multiply by 7.**

INPUT	OUTPUT
434	3,038
656	?
283	?
2,967	?
8,595	?

PROBLEM SOLVING • APPLICATIONS

44. Lita has 275 foreign stamps in her collection. Maria has 4 times as many. How many stamps does Maria have in her collection?

45. Brian has 203 foreign stamps. He needs 185 more to complete the album. How many stamps does the album hold?

★**46.** Ralph and Leroy collect stamps and baseball cards. Ralph has 16 pitcher cards and 18 catcher cards. Leroy has twice as many of each. How many pitcher and catcher cards does Leroy have in all?

★**47.** Maria buys 3 new stamp albums. Each album has 3 pages for British stamps. Each of these pages holds 28 stamps. How many British stamps can the albums hold?

Multiplying by 10's, 100's, 1000's · Mental Math

Each turnstile at the state fair has a device for counting. In one minute, about 23 people can pass through a turnstile.

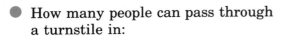

● How many people can pass through a turnstile in:

10 minutes? 20 minutes?
30 minutes? 40 minutes?

Look for a pattern.

23	23	23	23
×10	×20	×30	×40
230	460	690	920

> **When multiplying by tens, write a 0 in the ones place. Then multiply the number of tens.**

● How many people can pass through a turnstile in:

100 minutes? 200 minutes? 300 minutes? 400 minutes?

Look for a pattern.

23	23	23	23
×100	×200	×300	×400
2,300	4,600	6,900	9,200

> **When multiplying by hundreds, write a 0 in the ones place and a 0 in the tens place. Then multiply by the number of hundreds.**

● How many people can pass through a turnstile in:

1,000 minutes? 2,000 minutes? 3,000 minutes? 4,000 minutes?

Look for a pattern.

23	23	23	23
×1,000	×2,000	×3,000	×4,000
23,000	46,000	69,000	92,000

> **When multiplying by thousands, write a 0 in the ones place, the tens place, and the hundreds place. Then multiply by the number of thousands.**

PRACTICE • Multiply the numbers by 10.

1. 84   **2.** 73   **3.** 27   **4.** 432   **5.** 607

Multiply the numbers by 100.

6. 62   **7.** 29   **8.** 54   **9.** 793   **10.** 865

Multiply the numbers by 1,000.

11. 25   **12.** 69   **13.** 52   **14.** 906   **15.** 332

EXERCISES • Multiply.

16. 46
       ×70

17. 73
       ×30

18. 24
       ×50

19. 838
       × 90

20. 68
       ×400

21. 20
       ×800

22. 416
       ×700

23. 594
       ×600

24.   53
       ×5,000

25.   62
       ×6,000

26.   420
       ×3,000

27.   751
       ×2,000

28. $20 \times 45 =$ ___?___

29. $40 \times 65 =$ ___?___

30. $800 \times 92 =$ ___?___

31. $300 \times 647 =$ ___?___

32. $4,000 \times 86 =$ ___?___

33. $9,000 \times 256 =$ ___?___

Study the pairs of INPUTS and OUTPUTS.
Then write the rules.

★ **34.**

Rule?

INPUT	OUTPUT
3	90
27	810
65	1,950
358	10,740

★ **35.**

Rule?

INPUT	OUTPUT
520	520,000
865	865,000
1,430	1,430,000
4,760	4,760,000

PROBLEM SOLVING • APPLICATIONS

At the technology exhibit, engineers demonstrated the use of
various instruments, such as the **tachometer.** It is used to count
the number of revolutions per minute (**rpm**) of an engine.
Read the number on each dial. Multiply this reading by 100 to
find the rpm.

36.

37.

38.

39.

40.

41.

Multiplying by Two-Digit Numbers

Demonstrations of how clothes are made were held in a tent at the state fair. The last step showed how the clothes are packed. One box of sweaters, for example could hold 42 sweaters.

● How many sweaters are in a shipment of 59 boxes?

Think   First *estimate* the answer.

	Nearest Tens
Round 42 to 40.	$42 \longrightarrow 40$
Round 59 to 60.	$59 \longrightarrow \times 60$
Multiply.	$2{,}400$

There are about 2,400 sweaters in the shipment. Use your estimate to see if the answer is reasonable.

Step 1
Multiply by 9.

Step 2
Multiply by 50.

Step 3
Add. Compare the answer with your estimate.

$$\begin{array}{r} 42 \\ \times 59 \\ \hline 378 \end{array} \qquad \begin{array}{r} 42 \\ \times 59 \\ \hline 378 \\ 2\,100 \end{array} \qquad \begin{array}{r} 42 \\ \times 59 \\ \hline 378 \\ 2\,100 \\ \hline 2{,}478 \end{array}$$

$60 \times 40 = 2{,}400$
↑
The answer ← is reasonable.

The estimate is 2400. Therefore, **2478 sweaters** is reasonable.

More Examples:

$$\begin{array}{r} 196 \\ \times 48 \\ \hline 1\,568 \\ 7\,840 \\ \hline 9{,}408 \end{array} \qquad \begin{array}{r} 607 \\ \times 35 \\ \hline 3\,033 \\ 18\,210 \\ \hline 21{,}245 \end{array} \qquad \begin{array}{r} 65{,}483 \\ \times 47 \\ \hline 458\,381 \\ 2\,619\,320 \\ \hline 3{,}077{,}701 \end{array}$$

 PRACTICE • Estimate the answer. Then find the exact answer. Compare each answer with the estimate.

1. $\begin{array}{r} 82 \\ \times 19 \end{array}$	**2.** $\begin{array}{r} 38 \\ \times 72 \end{array}$	**3.** $\begin{array}{r} 677 \\ \times\ 29 \end{array}$	**4.** $\begin{array}{r} 548 \\ \times\ 56 \end{array}$	**5.** $\begin{array}{r} 62 \\ \times 46 \end{array}$
6. $\begin{array}{r} 312 \\ \times\ 45 \end{array}$	**7.** $\begin{array}{r} 34{,}497 \\ \times\ \ \ 21 \end{array}$	**8.** $\begin{array}{r} 7{,}335 \\ \times\ \ 66 \end{array}$	**9.** $\begin{array}{r} 42{,}107 \\ \times\ \ \ 86 \end{array}$	**10.** $\begin{array}{r} 3{,}290 \\ \times\ \ 37 \end{array}$

EXERCISES • Multiply.

11. $\begin{array}{r} 28 \\ \times 38 \end{array}$	**12.** $\begin{array}{r} 39 \\ \times 49 \end{array}$	**13.** $\begin{array}{r} 257 \\ \times\ 18 \end{array}$	**14.** $\begin{array}{r} 47 \\ \times 53 \end{array}$	**15.** $\begin{array}{r} 452 \\ \times\ 89 \end{array}$

16. 366 $\times$ 57	17. 1,841 $\times$ 26	18, 673 $\times$ 45	19. 2,759 $\times$ 34	20. 6,117 $\times$ 68
21. 32,783 $\times$ 32	22. 53,619 $\times$ 57	23. 618,578 $\times$ 74	24, 74,306 $\times$ 45	25. 391,234 $\times$ 21

26. $66 \times 18 =$ ___?___   27. $24 \times 98 =$ ___?___   28. $37 \times 45 =$ ___?___

29. $52 \times 564 =$ ___?___   30. $37 \times 2,061 =$ ___?___   31. $82 \times 5,169 =$ ___?___

32. $38 \times 32,409 =$ ___?___   33. $44 \times 68,224 =$ ___?___   34. $59 \times 785,436 =$ ___?___

Write the factor forms and the numbers.

★ 35. 5^3 ★ 36. 3^5 ★ 37. 2^6 ★ 38. 6^2 ★ 39. 9^3 ★ 40. 7^2

★ 41. Complete the table.

Exponent Form	10^3	2^3	4^3	3^4	5^4	2^8
Factor Form	$10 \times 10 \times 10$	$2 \times 2 \times 2$	$4 \times 4 \times 4$	?	?	?
Number	1,000	8	?	?	?	?

PROBLEM SOLVING • APPLICATIONS CHOOSE • mental math • pencil and paper • calculator SOLVE

42. Cardiss orders 72 cartons of umbrellas. There are 12 umbrellas in each carton. How many umbrellas does Cardiss order?

43. A machine can pack 42 sweaters in only one minute. How many sweaters can it pack in
   a. 100 minutes?
   b. 200 minutes?
   c. 150 minutes?

44. A machine can pack 112 towels in 2 minutes. How many towels can it pack in
   a. 4 minutes?
   b. 8 minutes?
   c. 32 minutes?
   d. 64 minutes?

★ 45. Cardiss bought 20 boxes of stuffed toy bears and 25 boxes of stuffed toy rabbits. Each box held 24 stuffed animals. How many stuffed animals did Cardiss buy?

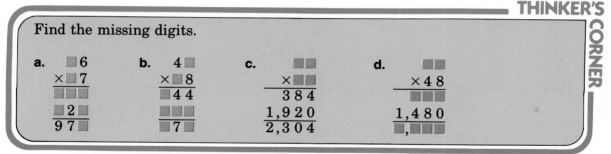

THINKER'S CORNER

Find the missing digits.

a.
```
   ■6
 ×■7
  ■■■
 ■2■
 97■
```

b.
```
   4■
 ×■8
  ■44
 ■■■
 ■7■
```

c.
```
   ■■
 ×■■
  384
 1,920
 2,304
```

d.
```
   ■■
 ×48
  ■■■
 1,480
 ■,■■■
```

PROBLEM SOLVING · STRATEGIES

Using Estimation

The National Aeronautics and Space Administration (NASA) had an exhibit at the fair. A NASA scientist illustrated the use of the distance formula.

$$d = r \times t$$ *d* = distance
r = rate of speed
t = time

Example 1 A satellite is orbiting the earth at a speed of 292 miles per minute.

● To the nearest hundred miles, how far does it travel in one hour?

Think One hour = 60 seconds and 292 rounded to the nearest 100 is 300.

$$d = r \times t \longrightarrow d = 300 \times 60 = \textbf{18,000 miles}$$

The satellite has traveled **about 18,000 miles** in one hour.

Estimation: Clustering

Example 2 **Estimate** the sum: 3,900 + 4,113 + 4,005

Think Each of the three numbers is close to 4,000.

Estimate: 3 × 4,000, or **12,000**

E PRACTICE • Choose the best estimate. Choose **a, b,** or **c.**

1. 36 + 41 + 39	**a.** 30 + 40 + 30	**b.** 40 + 40 + 20	**c.** 40 + 40 + 40
2. 185 × 357	**a.** 200 × 300	**b.** 200 × 400	**c.** 100 × 300
3. 7,362 − 4,891	**a.** 7,300 − 4,800	**b.** 7,300 − 5,000	**c.** 7,400 − 4,900
4. $32.36 + $28.74	**a.** 2 × $30	**b.** 2 × $20	**c.** 2 × $25
5. 7,271 − 3,479	**a.** 3,700	**b.** 3,800	**c.** 3,900
6. 379 × 415	**a.** 120,000	**b.** 160,000	**c.** 140,000
7. $181.25 − $28.78	**a.** $150	**b.** $160	**c.** $170
8. 988 + 1,170	**a.** 1,800	**b.** 3,000	**c.** 2,000

E PROBLEMS

9. The sixth-grade class is planning a trip to the NASA space center in Florida. It costs $151.20 to fly one way per student. Estimate the cost for 48 students.

   a. $160 × 50
   b. $150 × 50
   c. $150 × 40

10. The space shuttle travels at a speed of 17,500 miles per hour after the main engine is shut off. Estimate the number of miles it travels in 4 days.

    a. 17,500 × 4
    b. 17,500 × 100
    c. 17,500 × 90

11. Harry bought souvenirs of the trip to Florida. He bought 2 packs of slides at $9.90 per pack, 3 shirts at $14.75 each, and 12 postcards at $0.95 each. Estimate the amount he spent.

    a. $10 + $15 + $1
    b. $10 + $45 + $12
    c. $20 + $45 + $12

12. The cost of a hotel room for one student is $29.50 per night. It costs $34.50 for two students in one room. Alice and Sue plan to share a room for 5 nights. Estimate how much they will save.

    a. $35 − 30
    b. $300 − $175
    c. $200 − $150

13. A lunar expedition collected three bags of moon rocks. The bags weighed 45, 76, and 54 pounds. Estimate the total weight.

    a. 150   b. 180
    c. 210   d. 140

14. The sixth-grade class sold corsages to raise money for the trip to Florida. They charged $5.20 for each corsage and sold 289 of them. Estimate the amount they collected.

    a. $1000   b. $1800
    c. $1500   d. $1200

15. A satellite was launched by the space shuttle at an altitude of 177 kilometers. The satellite is then propelled 627 kilometers higher in order to reach its orbit altitude. Estimate the altitude of the orbit.

    a. 700   b. 800
    c. 400   d. 900

16. The bus that travels between hotels and Cape Canaveral can carry 42 passengers. Estimate the number of passengers it can carry in 28 trips to Cape Canaveral.

    a. 800   b. 1200
    c. 1500   d. 70

MID-CHAPTER REVIEW

Multiply. (Pages 50-51)

1. $\begin{array}{r} 8 \\ \times 2 \\ \hline \end{array}$ **2.** $\begin{array}{r} 3 \\ \times 7 \\ \hline \end{array}$ **3.** $\begin{array}{r} 8 \\ \times 9 \\ \hline \end{array}$ **4.** $\begin{array}{r} 6 \\ \times 6 \\ \hline \end{array}$ **5.** $\begin{array}{r} 7 \\ \times 8 \\ \hline \end{array}$

6. $8 \times \underline{?} = 64$ **7.** $(3 \times 2) \times 9 = \underline{?}$ **8.** $4 \times (1 \times 8) = \underline{?}$

Multiply. (Pages 52-53)

9. $\begin{array}{r} 52 \\ \times 3 \\ \hline \end{array}$ **10.** $\begin{array}{r} 75 \\ \times 5 \\ \hline \end{array}$ **11.** $\begin{array}{r} 408 \\ \times 3 \\ \hline \end{array}$ **12.** $\begin{array}{r} 694 \\ \times 7 \\ \hline \end{array}$ **13.** $\begin{array}{r} 2,680 \\ \times 6 \\ \hline \end{array}$

14. $3 \times 5,082 = \underline{?}$ **15.** $7 \times 22,430 = \underline{?}$ **16.** $5 \times 362,954 = \underline{?}$

17. $6 \times 3,050 = \underline{?}$ **18.** $5 \times 18,946 = \underline{?}$ **19.** $8 \times 250,146 = \underline{?}$

Multiply. (Pages 54–55)

20. $\begin{array}{r} 743 \\ \times 20 \\ \hline \end{array}$ **21.** $\begin{array}{r} 48 \\ \times 500 \\ \hline \end{array}$ **22.** $\begin{array}{r} 249 \\ \times 300 \\ \hline \end{array}$ **23.** $\begin{array}{r} 614 \\ \times 4,000 \\ \hline \end{array}$ **24.** $\begin{array}{r} 372 \\ \times 9,000 \\ \hline \end{array}$

Multiply. (Pages 56–57)

25. $36 \times 75 = \underline{?}$ **26.** $18 \times 461 = \underline{?}$ **27.** $87 \times 91,284 = \underline{?}$

28. Four pieces of equipment were placed on the space shuttle. The pieces weighed 79, 83, 46, and 94 pounds. Estimate the total weight of the equipment. (Pages 58–59)
a. 280 **b.** 290 **c.** 300

29. Each student spent about the same amount for food. Janet spent $21.35 the first day. Estimate the amount spent by 48 students in one day. (Pages 58–59)
a. $800 **b.** $1000 **c.** $900

MAINTENANCE • MIXED PRACTICE

Add or subtract.

1. $\begin{array}{r} 146 \\ + 28 \\ \hline \end{array}$ **2.** $\begin{array}{r} 258 \\ +362 \\ \hline \end{array}$ **3.** $\begin{array}{r} 475 \\ -168 \\ \hline \end{array}$ **4.** $\begin{array}{r} 3,602 \\ -1,957 \\ \hline \end{array}$ **5.** $\begin{array}{r} 14,820 \\ + 7,999 \\ \hline \end{array}$

6. $\$482.67 + \$19.78 = \underline{?}$ **7.** $\$6,525.00 - \$47.99 = \underline{?}$ **8.** $\$4,287.20 + \$95.00 = \underline{?}$

9. $\$3,005.99 + \$38.99 = \underline{?}$ **10.** $\$2,999.50 - \$45.99 = \underline{?}$ **11.** $\$8,000.00 - \$58.99 = \underline{?}$

Use the table for Exercises 12 and 13.

12. What is the total rainfall for all four months?

13. Write a problem using the information for September and December.

Monthly Rainfall

Month	Rain (centimeters)
Sept	5
Oct	25
Nov	21
Dec	18

CONSUMER APPLICATIONS

Ordering by Mail

People who attended the fair could place orders for items.
To order camping supplies, Clyde completed this mail-order form.

Procedures:

1. Find the total price for each item.

2. Find the total price of all items.

3. Find the total cost of the order, including any additional charges such as tax, postage, and so on.

W. W. Cross and Sons				
Catalog Number	Quantity	Name of Item	Price Each	Total price
H-442	1	Sleeping Bag	59.95	?
K-529	3	Cook Kits	7.60	?
K-708	12	Sterno Cans	4.35	?
B-146	2	Saw Blades	6.99	?
Postage Chart			Total for Goods	?
Orders up to $3.00 . . . .$.95			Tax	7.45
Orders from $3.01 to $5.00 . . . . . .$1.35 Orders from $5.01 to $9.00 . . . . . .$1.95			Postage	?
Orders from $9.01 to $15.00 . . . . .$2.55 Orders over $15.00 add only $3.25			Total Cost	?

EXAMPLE: Find the total price for the cook kits.

Clyde bought 3 cook kits, and each cost $7.60.

$7.60 \times 3 = $ **$22.80** ◄ **Total price for 3 cook kits**

EXERCISES

1. Find the total price of the sleeping bag.

2. Find the total price for the saw blades.

3. Find the total price for the sterno cans.

4. What is the total for the goods?

5. Use the Postage Chart to find the postage cost.

6. What is the total cost of the order?

PROJECT   Get a copy of a mail-order catalog. Pretend you have $50.00 to spend. Fill out the order form. Then find the amount of money that must be enclosed with the order.

Multiplying by Three-Digit Numbers

The photography and movie-making tent showed a three-dimensional movie about mountain climbing. An expedition that climbed Mt. Everest carried 235 spools of climbing rope. Each spool held 375 feet of rope.

● How many feet of rope were available for the climb?

Think Each spool contains an equal length of rope. So you multiply to find the total length of rope.

$375 \times 235 = ?$

Step 1 Multiply by 5.	Step 2 Multiply by 30.	Step 3 Multiply by 200.	Step 4 Add.
375 ×235 <u>1 875</u>	375 ×235 1 875 <u>11 250</u>	375 ×235 1 875 11 250 <u>75 000</u>	375 ×235 1 875 11 250 <u>75 000</u> 88,125

There were **88,125 feet** of climbing rope available.

More Examples:

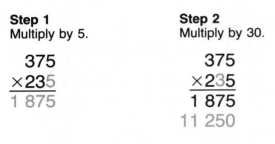

$$\begin{array}{r} 3,657 \\ \times\ 248 \\ \hline 29256 \\ 146280 \\ 731400 \\ \hline 906,936 \end{array}$$

$$\begin{array}{r} \$4.89 \\ \times\ 607 \\ \hline 3423 \\ 293400 \\ \hline \$2,968.23 \end{array}$$

PRACTICE • Multiply.

1. 265
×337

2. 803
×376

3. 985
×504

4. 961
×340

5. 897
×562

6. 4,514
× 662

7. 6,134
× 475

8. 9,843
× 162

9. 2,621
× 734

10. 3,501
× 660

EXERCISES • Multiply.

11. 473
    ×542

12. 850
    ×162

13. 929
    ×273

14. 7,243
    × 254

15. 6,474
    × 309

16. 5,143
    × 523

17. 82,913
    ×   641

18. 26,198
    ×   423

19. 13,672
    ×   608

20. $13.48
    ×   174

21. $574.92
    ×   283

22. $263.75
    ×   502

23. $179.95
    ×   459

★ 24. 634,604
      ×   206

★ 25. 292,763
      ×   913

★ 26. 915,768
      × 4,235

27. 212 × 586 = ___?___

28. 633 × 702 = ___?___

29. 297 × 5,752 = ___?___

30. 305 × 2,460 = ___?___

31. 219 × 43,762 = ___?___

32. 349 × 92,562 = ___?___

PROBLEM SOLVING • APPLICATIONS

33. Hillary took part in the first coast to coast crossing of Antarctica. Suppose that 155 crates of dried foods were packed for this expedition. Each crate held 230 pounds. How many pounds of dry food did they plan to use?

34. By climbing 27,000-foot Mt. Makalu I, Sir Edmund Hillary proved that mountaineers could survive without bottled oxygen. If the expedition had used oxygen, suppose they required 110 tanks. Each tank weighs 124 pounds. How much additional weight would they have carried?

35. Hillary's expedition to Mt. Makalu I searched for the Abominable Snowman. The adventure was recorded on film. Suppose they carried 105 cans of film. Each can contains 175 feet of film. How much footage did they shoot?

CALCULATOR • Distributive Property

(876 + 958)75 = ___?___

First find the sum. Then find the product.

⟨8⟩ ⟨7⟩ ⟨6⟩ ⟨+⟩ ⟨9⟩ ⟨5⟩ ⟨8⟩ ⟨×⟩ ⟨7⟩ ⟨5⟩ ⟨=⟩ ⟨ 137550 ⟩

1. (45 − 39)52

2. (94 + 133)5

3. (672 + 886)76

4. (1,258 + 9,355)25

5. (24,856 − 19,072)9

6. (12,804 + 9,496)129

PROBLEM SOLVING · STRATEGIES

Guess and Check

Some word problems contain conditions.

1. **Guess** an answer that meets the first condition.
2. **Check** your guess to see if it meets the second condition.

Example

An Arctic expedition used 52 dogs
to pull their sleds. There were 8 more
huskies than malamutes.

- How many of the dogs were huskies?
- How many of the dogs were malamutes?

Think   There are two conditions:

> **Condition 1:** huskies + malamutes = 52 dogs
> **Condition 2:** huskies − malamutes = 8

Guess 1	Huskies	32	**Check: Use Condition 2.**
	Malamutes	20	Does 32 − 20 = 8? **No**
	Sum	52	

◀ Since 32 − 20 = 12, 32 and 20 are too far apart.

Guess 2	Huskies	30	**Check: Use Condition 2.**
	Malamutes	22	Does 30 − 22 = 8? **Yes**
	Sum	52	

There are **30 huskies** and **22 malamutes.**

PROBLEMS • Use the two conditions to find the numbers.

1. Sum of two numbers = 14
   Difference of the numbers = 2

2. Sum of two numbers = 9
   Product of the numbers = 18

3. Sum of two numbers = 17
   Difference of two numbers = 1

4. Sum of two numbers = 15
   Difference of the numbers = 3

5. Sum of two numbers = 10
   Product of two numbers = 24

6. Sum of two numbers = 16
   Product of two numbers = 60

The first condition is given.
Write the second condition. Solve.

7. Two astronauts explore the dark side of the moon in a lunar vehicle. In two trips they cover a total of 37 kilometers. The first trip covered 5 more kilometers than the second trip. How many kilometers did each trip cover?

Condition 1: Trip 1 + Trip 2 = 37

Condition 2: ___?___

8. A mountain climber eats rice and oat bars for energy. He carries a total of 60 bars. The climber has twice as many oat bars than rice bars. How many bars does he have of each kind?

Condition 1: Rice bars + Oat bars = 60

Condition 2: ___?___

9. A pilot places two boxes of spare parts on his airplane. The boxes weigh a total of 138 pounds. One box is 34 pounds heavier than the other box. How much does each box weigh?

Condition 1: Box A + Box B = 138

Condition 2: ___?___

Use the guess and check strategy to solve each problem.

10. Alice bought two different souvenir shirts at the fair. The total cost for both was $18. The difference in the cost of the two shirts was $2. What was the cost of each shirt?

What are the conditions?

11. Sarah Como explored the African jungle with a camera. In one week she photographed 43 lions and tigers. She took pictures of 11 more lions than tigers. How many pictures are there of each animal?

12. There was a total of 40 reporters and photographers covering the fair. There were 16 more reporters than photographers. How many reporters were there?

Use your first guess to help you make your second guess

13. A reporter surveyed 80 people to find whether they preferred the NASA exhibit or the sports exhibit. Three times as many preferred the NASA exhibit. How many preferred the NASA exhibit?

Write Your Own Problem

Write a word problem about the fair. Use these two conditions.

Sum of two numbers = 15
Product of the numbers = 56

CHAPTER REVIEW

Part 1 • VOCABULARY

For Exercises 1–7, choose from the box at the right the word that completes the sentence.

associative
commutative
estimate
factors
product
regrouped
rounding

1. The answer in a multiplication problem is called the $\underline{?}$. (Page 50)

2. The numbers you multiply to solve a problem are called $\underline{?}$. (Page 50)

3. The sentences $2 \times 5 = 10$ and $5 \times 2 = 10$ show the $\underline{?}$ property of multiplication. (Page 50)

4. An answer close to the exact answer of a mathematics problem is called an $\underline{?}$. (Page 56)

5. The number 46 can be $\underline{?}$ as 4 tens 6 ones. (Page 52)

6. The sentences $(3 \times 2) \times 1 = 6$ and $3 \times (2 \times 1) = 6$ show the $\underline{?}$ property of multiplication. (Page 50)

7. In the sentence 55×24, you can estimate the answer by first $\underline{?}$ the factors to 60×20. (Page 56)

Part 2 • SKILLS

Multiply. (Pages 50-51)

8. $\begin{array}{r} 6 \\ \times 2 \\ \hline \end{array}$ 9. $\begin{array}{r} 4 \\ \times 5 \\ \hline \end{array}$ 10. $\begin{array}{r} 9 \\ \times 1 \\ \hline \end{array}$ 11. $\begin{array}{r} 0 \\ \times 6 \\ \hline \end{array}$ 12. $\begin{array}{r} 8 \\ \times 7 \\ \hline \end{array}$

13. $9 \times \underline{?} = 72$ 14. $(2 \times 4) \times 3 = \underline{?}$ 15. $6 \times (5 \times 2) = \underline{?}$

16. $5 \times \underline{?} = 40$ 17. $(3 \times 2) \times 8 = \underline{?}$ 18. $9 \times (7 \times 1) = \underline{?}$

19. $6 \times \underline{?} = 24$ 20. $(5 \times 1) \times 9 = \underline{?}$ 21. $3 \times (5 \times 4) = \underline{?}$

Multiply. (Pages 52-53)

22. $\begin{array}{r} 41 \\ \times 8 \\ \hline \end{array}$ 23. $\begin{array}{r} 52 \\ \times 6 \\ \hline \end{array}$ 24. $\begin{array}{r} 705 \\ \times 5 \\ \hline \end{array}$ 25. $\begin{array}{r} 547 \\ \times 4 \\ \hline \end{array}$ 26. $\begin{array}{r} 1,430 \\ \times 5 \\ \hline \end{array}$

27. $9 \times 2,072 = \underline{?}$ 28. $6 \times 31,423 = \underline{?}$ 29. $7 \times 638,305 = \underline{?}$

30. $5 \times 6,008 = \underline{?}$ 31. $3 \times 95,507 = \underline{?}$ 32. $4 \times 248,199 = \underline{?}$

33. $6 \times 3,284 = \underline{?}$ 34. $8 \times 29,005 = \underline{?}$ 35. $3 \times 942,012 = \underline{?}$

Multiply. (Pages 54–55)

36. $200 \times 34 = \underline{?}$ 37. $600 \times 853 = \underline{?}$ 38. $7,000 \times 582 = \underline{?}$

39. $500 \times 65 = \underline{?}$ 40. $400 \times 359 = \underline{?}$ 41. $2,000 \times 984 = \underline{?}$

42. $700 \times 39 = \underline{?}$ 43. $300 \times 560 = \underline{?}$ 44. $4,000 \times 629 = \underline{?}$

Estimate the product. (Pages 56–57)

45. $38 \times 51 = \underline{?}$

46. $75 \times 94 = \underline{?}$

47. $352 \times 865 = \underline{?}$

48. $64 \times 86 = \underline{?}$

49. $35 \times 55 = \underline{?}$

50. $261 \times 946 = \underline{?}$

51. $15 \times 94 = \underline{?}$

52. $83 \times 38 = \underline{?}$

53. $450 \times 449 = \underline{?}$

Multiply. (Pages 56-57)

54. $\begin{array}{r} 48 \\ \times 24 \\ \hline \end{array}$

55. $\begin{array}{r} 97 \\ \times 86 \\ \hline \end{array}$

56. $\begin{array}{r} 213 \\ \times \ 54 \\ \hline \end{array}$

57. $\begin{array}{r} 456 \\ \times \ 37 \\ \hline \end{array}$

58. $\begin{array}{r} 5{,}029 \\ \times \ \ \ 54 \\ \hline \end{array}$

59. $48 \times 8{,}299 = \underline{?}$

60. $79 \times 70{,}452 = \underline{?}$

61. $25 \times 420{,}812 = \underline{?}$

62. $53 \times 4{,}052 = \underline{?}$

63. $84 \times 62{,}047 = \underline{?}$

64. $33 \times 518{,}975 = \underline{?}$

Multiply. (Pages 62-63)

65. $\begin{array}{r} 309 \\ \times 824 \\ \hline \end{array}$

66. $\begin{array}{r} 678 \\ \times 593 \\ \hline \end{array}$

67. $\begin{array}{r} 2{,}423 \\ \times \ \ 264 \\ \hline \end{array}$

68. $\begin{array}{r} 3{,}089 \\ \times \ \ 725 \\ \hline \end{array}$

69. $\begin{array}{r} 26{,}537 \\ \times \ \ \ \ 243 \\ \hline \end{array}$

70. $234 \times 314{,}562 = \underline{?}$

71. $617 \times 807{,}329 = \underline{?}$

72. $\$436.82 \times 503 = \underline{?}$

73. $\$456.99 \times 204 = \underline{?}$

74. $\$650.35 \times 428 = \underline{?}$

75. $\$899.99 \times 250 = \underline{?}$

Part 3 • PROBLEM SOLVING • APPLICATIONS

76. A dog sled team travels about 85 miles in one day. At that rate, estimate how many miles they will travel in 21 days. (Pages 58–59)

    a. 1,600   **b.** 1,800   **c.** 2,400

77. An astronaut collects rock samples in collection bags. Each bag of rocks weighs 32 kilograms. Estimate the weight in kilograms of 13 collection bags. (Pages 58–59)

    a. 500   **b.** 300   **c.** 400

78. An explorer began a voyage with 43 men. Only 32 made the entire trip. Estimate the number who did not complete the trip. (Pages 58–59)

    a. 10   **b.** 20   **c.** 70

79. The length of an orbit on one flight of the space shuttle was 25,905 miles. Estimate the length in miles of 8 orbits. (Pages 58–59)

    a. 50,000   **b.** 100,000   **c.** 300,000

Use the guess and check strategy to solve.

80. A desert exploration team uses 28 trucks. Some have 4 wheels. Others have 6 wheels. There are 128 wheels in all. How many trucks of each type are there? (Pages 64–65)

81. A moon mission returns with 24 bags of moon samples. There are 2-kilogram bags and 6-kilogram bags. There are 3 times as many 2-kilogram bags as 6-kilogram bags. How many of each size are there? (Pages 64–65)

CHAPTER TEST

Multiply.

1. $8 \times (3 \times 3) = \underline{\quad ? \quad}$

2. $(7 \times 2) \times 3 = \underline{\quad ? \quad}$

3. $4 \times (6 \times 5) = \underline{\quad ? \quad}$

4. $\begin{array}{r} 73 \\ \times\ 6 \\ \hline \end{array}$

5. $\begin{array}{r} 37 \\ \times\ 8 \\ \hline \end{array}$

6. $\begin{array}{r} 464 \\ \times\ 5 \\ \hline \end{array}$

7. $\begin{array}{r} 928 \\ \times\ 3 \\ \hline \end{array}$

8. $\begin{array}{r} 42 \\ \times 50 \\ \hline \end{array}$

9. $\begin{array}{r} 36 \\ \times 800 \\ \hline \end{array}$

10. $\begin{array}{r} 192 \\ \times 700 \\ \hline \end{array}$

11. $\begin{array}{r} 365 \\ \times 6,000 \\ \hline \end{array}$

12. $\begin{array}{r} 409 \\ \times\ 24 \\ \hline \end{array}$

13. $\begin{array}{r} 2,365 \\ \times\ 47 \\ \hline \end{array}$

14. $\begin{array}{r} 89,257 \\ \times\ 63 \\ \hline \end{array}$

15. $\begin{array}{r} 210,698 \\ \times\ 16 \\ \hline \end{array}$

16. $\begin{array}{r} 128 \\ \times 416 \\ \hline \end{array}$

17. $\begin{array}{r} 896 \\ \times 492 \\ \hline \end{array}$

18. $\begin{array}{r} 4,275 \\ \times\ 621 \\ \hline \end{array}$

19. $\begin{array}{r} 63,540 \\ \times\ 184 \\ \hline \end{array}$

Choose the best estimate. Choose a, b, or c.

20. 289×305 **a.** 50,000   **b.** 60,000   **c.** 90,000

21. $\$172.75 - \$39.05$ **a.** \$130   **b.** \$140   **c.** \$150

22. A movie about ancient Indian tribes is being shown at the fair. One children's ticket costs \$1.95. Estimate the cost of 9 children's tickets.

23. Each poster in the souvenir booth costs \$1.95. Banners cost \$2.30 each. Estimate to the nearest dollar the cost of 5 posters and 3 banners.

24. A reporter asked 90 people if they preferred the Indian exhibit or the space exhibit. Twice as many people preferred the Indian exhibit to the space exhibit. How many preferred the Indian exhibit?

25. Tania took a total of 48 photographs at the Fair. She took 12 photographs more in the morning than in the afternoon. How many did she take in the afternoon?

ENRICHMENT

Combinations

The fair has an exhibit of antique cars and new cars. The new cars come in two models: two-door and four-door. A buyer also has a choice of colors: red, blue, green, yellow, or brown.

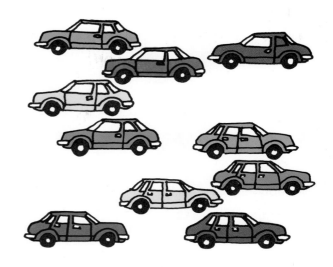

● How many choices are there?

Think There are 2 choices of models and 5 choices of color. Thus, there are $5 \times 2 = \textbf{10 choices.}$

EXERCISES • Solve.

1. Hathleen is going to a baseball game. She can enter the stadium through any one of 4 gates. She can leave by any one of 9 gates. How many ways can Hathleen get in and out of the stadium?

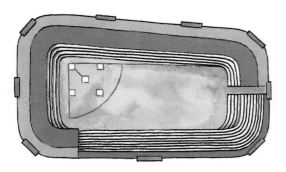

2. Cora wants to buy a bicycle. It can be a three-speed, five-speed, or ten-speed. It can be blue, red, green, yellow, or white. How many choices does she have?

3. These buttons are on a jukebox. You push them to play a record. First you push a letter. Then you push a digit. How many choices can you make?

4. Each place on the counter can show any one of the ten digits. How many numbers can be named?

ADDITIONAL PRACTICE

SKILLS

Multiply.   (Pages 50–51)

1. 6
   ×8

2. 4
   ×9

3. 0
   ×5

4. 9
   ×9

5. 8
   ×7

Multiply.   (Pages 52–53)

6. 62
   × 4

7. 82
   × 5

8. 306
   × 9

9. 249
   × 8

10. 3,560
    × 5

Multiply.   (Pages 54–55)

11. 48
    ×200

12. 165
    ×300

13. 927
    ×600

14. 1,492
    × 500

15. 423
    ×6,000

Estimate the product.   (Pages 56–57)

16. $48 \times 62 =$?

17. $85 \times 23 =$?

18. $648 \times 550 =$?

19. $51 \times 65 =$?

20. $34 \times 66 =$?

21. $250 \times 751 =$?

Multiply.   (Pages 56–57)

22. 37
    ×42

23. 65
    ×99

24. 515
    × 26

25. 308
    × 92

26. 2,680
    × 56

27. $28 \times 56 =$?

28. $23 \times 872 =$?

29. $34 \times 5,044 =$?

Multiply.   (Pages 62–63)

30. 621
    ×432

31. 805
    ×245

32. 1,476
    × 604

33. 2,589
    × 724

34. 7,973
    × 428

35. $249 \times 536 =$?

36. $306 \times 295 =$?

37. $540 \times 3,999 =$?

PROBLEM SOLVING • APPLICATIONS

38. Gail wants to buy 8 record albums. Each album costs $6.79. Estimate the total cost to the nearest dollar.   (Pages 58–59)

39. Bus fare to the fair grounds costs $1.15 for adults and $0.85 for children under 12. Estimate the total cost for 2 adults and 6 children.   (Pages 58–59)

40. Together, Seth and Marty have $36 to spend at the fair. Marty has 3 times as much money as Seth. How much money does Marty have?   (Pages 64–65)

41. The total weight of two boxes stored on the space shuttle is 156 pounds. One box is 24 pounds heavier than the other. How much does the lighter box weigh? (Pages 64–65)

PROBLEM SOLVING MAINTENANCE

Chapters 1 through 3

Use the table to solve Problems 1–4.
(Page 14)

Ocean	Greatest Depth
Arctic	17,800 ft
Atlantic	28,374 ft
Indian	25,344 ft
Pacific	36,198 ft

1. Write the depth of the Atlantic Ocean to the nearest thousand.

2. Write the ocean depths in order from least to greatest.

3. How much greater is the depth of the Atlantic Ocean than the depth of the Arctic Ocean?

4. What is the difference between the depth of the deepest ocean and the depth of the shallowest ocean?

Assuming a grid that is similar to the one in the map on page 30, solve Problems 5–7.   (Page 30)

5. Jim travels from Waterford (A-1) to Steelville (A-5). In which direction does he travel?

6. Annabelle travels from Baxter (D-1) to Princetown (A-1). In which direction does she travel?

7. Roberto travels from Chiefton (B-5) to Regisburg (B-1). In which direction does he travel?

8. On Monday one supermarket sold 465 pounds of baking apples and 321 pounds of McIntosh Apples. Estimate how many pounds of apples they sold in all.   (Page 58)

   a. 780   **b.** 790   **c.** 770

9. An Arctic explorer packed dog food in 22 large crates. Each crate weighed 136 pounds. Estimate how many pounds the crates weighed altogether.   (Page 58)

   a. 2,800 lbs.   **b.** 2,600 lbs.
   c. 4,200 lbs.

10. A commercial jet airplane travels at about 515 miles per hour when traveling westward. The same plane travels about 595 miles per hour when traveling eastward. Estimate the difference in speeds. (Page 58)

    a. 110mph   **b.** 80mph   **c.** 100mph

11. Sara and Mark are collecting coins. Together they have 75 coins. Sara has twice as many coins as Mark. How many coins does Sara have? (Page 64)

12. The National Park Service removes 17 bears from a camping area. There are 3 fewer brown than black bears. How many brown and black bears are there? (Page 64)

MAINTENANCE

Mixed Practice • Choose the correct answer.

1. $6\overline{)54}$

   A. 9   **B.** 7
   C. 8   **D.** not here

2. $9\overline{)81}$

   A. 8   **B.** 9
   C. 6   **D.** not here

3. $7\overline{)56}$

   A. 8   **B.** 7
   C. 9   **D.** not here

4. $72 \div 8 = \underline{\ ?\ }$

   A. 7   **B.** 8
   C. 9   **D.** not here

5. $63 \div 7 = \underline{\ ?\ }$

   A. 6   **B.** 9
   C. 8   **D.** not here

6. $42 \div 6 = \underline{\ ?\ }$

   A. 6   **B.** 9
   C. 8   **D.** not here

7. $100 + 89 + 94 = \underline{\ ?\ }$

   A. 283   **B.** 273
   C. 285   **D.** not here

8. Round 83 to the nearest ten

   A. 100   **B.** 80
   C. 90   **D.** not here

9. Round 16 to the nearest ten

   A. 10   **B.** 15
   C. 20   **D.** not here

10. $54 \times 3 = \underline{\ ?\ }$

   A. 162   **B.** 157
   C. 152   **D.** not here

11. $78 \times 6 = \underline{\ ?\ }$

   A. 488   **B.** 474
   C. 468   **D.** not here

12. $908 \times 7 = \underline{\ ?\ }$

   A. 6,348   **B.** 6,354
   C. 956   **D.** not here

13.
   381
  -156

   A. 235   **B.** 225
   C. 125   **D.** not here

14.
   824
  -398

   A. 426   **B.** 536
   C. 526   **D.** not here

15.
   7,000
  $-2,437$

   A. 5,437   **B.** 4,663
   C. 4,563   **D.** not here

16. King Midas has 72 gold coins. If he gives each of his 8 friends the same number, how many gold coins will each friend get?

   A. 8   **B.** 9
   C. 7   **D.** not here

17. Arachne wove 28 pieces of fabric in one month, 26 the next month, and 33 the third month. How many did she weave in all?

   A. 87   **B.** 77
   C. 86   **D.** not here

Division

The sixth grade at Carlton Middle School sold popcorn to raise money for the native American exhibit at the museum. They sold 84 packages at $1.25 per package.

● How much did they collect in all?

In one day, Hal's Hat Shop in the new Carlton Shopping Mall sold 192 tie pins at $3 each, 47 ties at $19 each, and 82 hats at $19 each.

● How much did they collect selling hats?

● What information was not needed to solve the problem?

73

Division

Carlton is a fast-growing community because it has a wide variety of job opportunities. Because of its climate, raising fruit is one of its industries. Harry planted 27 orange trees in three equal rows.

● How many trees are in each row?

Think   You need to separate 27 trees into 3 <u>equal</u> rows. So divide.

$$27 \div 3 = ?$$

When a group is separated into smaller groups of the same size, use **division**.

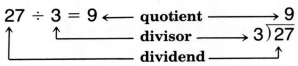

He planted **9 trees** in each row.

● Sometimes there is a remainder. Divide: $14 \div 3$

Step 1
How many threes in 14?

$$\begin{array}{r} 4 \\ 3{\overline{)14}} \end{array}$$

Step 2
Multiply:
$4 \times 3 = 12$

$$\begin{array}{r} 4 \\ 3{\overline{)14}} \\ 12 \end{array}$$

Step 3
Subtract.
Show the remainder in the answer.

$$\begin{array}{r} 4\ r2 \\ 3{\overline{)14}} \\ -12 \\ \hline 2 \end{array}$$

◀ The remainder must be less than the divisor.

● Is it possible to divide by zero?

Problem: $6 \div 0 = ?$ **Think** $? \times 0 = 6$ ◀ There is no number that will make this sentence true.

Conclusion: You cannot divide by zero.

PRACTICE • Find the quotients and the remainders.

1. $2{\overline{)19}}$ 2. $6{\overline{)36}}$ 3. $5{\overline{)29}}$ 4. $8{\overline{)34}}$ 5. $9{\overline{)68}}$ 6. $3{\overline{)16}}$

7. $4{\overline{)10}}$ 8. $7{\overline{)51}}$ 9. $2{\overline{)5}}$ 10. $4{\overline{)19}}$ 11. $6{\overline{)34}}$ 12. $5{\overline{)33}}$

EXERCISES • Divide

13. $9{\overline{)50}}$ 14. $8{\overline{)46}}$ 15. $3{\overline{)25}}$ 16. $7{\overline{)49}}$ 17. $2{\overline{)7}}$ 18. $5{\overline{)49}}$

19. $3\overline{)28}$ **20.** $6\overline{)46}$ **21.** $9\overline{)26}$ **22.** $5\overline{)45}$ **23.** $7\overline{)66}$ **24.** $8\overline{)60}$

25. $8\overline{)52}$ **26.** $3\overline{)20}$ **27.** $6\overline{)53}$ **28.** $4\overline{)35}$ **29.** $9\overline{)35}$ **30.** $7\overline{)44}$

31. $9\overline{)61}$ **32.** $3\overline{)22}$ **33.** $7\overline{)25}$ **34.** $5\overline{)36}$ **35.** $8\overline{)65}$ **36.** $4\overline{)25}$

37. $3\overline{)11}$ **38.** $7\overline{)53}$ **39.** $4\overline{)30}$ **40.** $9\overline{)75}$ **41.** $5\overline{)24}$ **42.** $8\overline{)39}$

43. $2\overline{)9}$ **44.** $6\overline{)44}$ **45.** $4\overline{)23}$ **46.** $6\overline{)50}$ **47.** $9\overline{)84}$ **48.** $8\overline{)18}$

49. $80 \div 9 =$?   **50.** $17 \div 9 =$?   **51.** $50 \div 8 =$?

52. $61 \div 8 =$?   **53.** $47 \div 9 =$?   **54.** $19 \div 4 =$?

Multiplication and division are **inverse operations**. Use one to check the other.

$$5\overline{)45}^{\,9} \qquad \begin{array}{r} 9 \\ \times 5 \\ \hline 45 \end{array}$$

Mental Math   Use the inverse operation to check your answers.

55. $7\overline{)21}$ **56.** $4\overline{)32}$ **57.** $9\overline{)63}$ **58.** $3\overline{)24}$ **59.** $2\overline{)18}$

60. 9×5 **61.** 8×7 **62.** 5×7 **63.** 6×9 **64.** 5×5

Mental Math   Do the operation inside the parenthesis first.

★ **65.** $(48 \div 6) \times 3 =$?   ★ **66.** $(72 \div 9) \div 4 =$?   ★ **67.** $6 + (35 \div 7) =$?

★ **68.** $(18 \times 3) \div 6 =$?   ★ **69.** $107 \times (28 \div 7) =$?   ★ **70.** $9 \times (63 \div 7) =$?

PROBLEM SOLVING • APPLICATIONS   CHOOSE • mental math • pencil and paper • calculator   SOLVE

71. It takes 3 meters of ribbon to make one bow for a large fruit basket.

    a. How many bows can be made using 29 meters of ribbon?

    b. How much ribbon will be left?

★ **73.** Harry planted 48 fruit trees. He planted 10 more orange trees than grapefruit trees.

    a. How many orange trees were planted?

    b. How many grapefruit trees were planted?

72. Lillian wanted to plant 8 orange trees in each row. She received a shipment of 54 trees from the nursery. How many more trees must she order to plant 7 rows?

Two-Digit Quotients

When Carlton was a small town, its main industry was producing honey.

A customer ordered 320 jars of honey. The shipping clerk estimated that 7 large cartons are needed to pack the jars of honey.

● How many jars can be packed in each carton? How many jars are left over?

 You need to separate 320 jars into 7 equal parts. So divide.

$$320 \div 7 = ?$$

Step 1 Decide where to place the first digit in the quotient.
There is one digit in the divisor.
Draw a line after the first digit in the dividend.

$$7 \overline{)3|2\ 0}$$

Since 7 > 3, draw a new line. ⟶ $7 \overline{)3\ 2|0}$ with an **X** above

Since 7 < 32, the first digit goes over the 2.

Step 2
Divide the tens.
Think: 7)32.

$$\begin{array}{r} 4 \\ 7\overline{)320} \\ -28 \\ \hline 4 \end{array}$$

⟵ 4 × 7
⟵ 32 − 28

Step 3
Divide the ones.
Think: 7)40.
Show the remainder.

$$\begin{array}{r} 45\ r5 \\ 7\overline{)320} \\ -28 \\ \hline 40 \\ -35 \\ \hline 5 \end{array}$$

⟵ 5 × 7
⟵ 40 − 35

Check
Multiply the quotient by the divisor. ⟶
Add the remainder. ⟶
Should equal the dividend. ⟶

$$\begin{array}{r} 45 \\ \times\ 7 \\ \hline 315 \\ +\ \ 5 \\ \hline 320 \end{array}$$

The clerk can pack **45 jars** in each carton.
There are **5 jars** left over.

More Examples:

$$\begin{array}{r} 12\ r2 \\ 5\overline{)62} \\ -5 \\ \hline 12 \\ -10 \\ \hline 2 \end{array} \qquad \begin{array}{r} 71 \\ 6\overline{)426} \\ -42 \\ \hline 6 \\ -6 \\ \hline 0 \end{array} \qquad \begin{array}{r} 29\ r3 \\ 9\overline{)264} \\ -18 \\ \hline 84 \\ -81 \\ \hline 3 \end{array}$$

PRACTICE • Divide. Check your answers.

1. $7\overline{)150}$
2. $5\overline{)274}$
3. $4\overline{)178}$
4. $5\overline{)225}$
5. $3\overline{)112}$

6. $4\overline{)84}$
7. $3\overline{)96}$
8. $8\overline{)616}$
9. $9\overline{)714}$
10. $7\overline{)503}$

EXERCISES • Divide.

11. $9\overline{)225}$ **12.** $9\overline{)273}$ **13.** $3\overline{)229}$ **14.** $9\overline{)412}$ **15.** $6\overline{)324}$

16. $9\overline{)327}$ **17.** $5\overline{)450}$ **18.** $4\overline{)147}$ **19.** $6\overline{)104}$ **20.** $9\overline{)620}$

21. $2\overline{)183}$ **22.** $8\overline{)111}$ **23.** $7\overline{)506}$ **24.** $8\overline{)89}$ **25.** $6\overline{)518}$

26. $3\overline{)29}$ **27.** $7\overline{)93}$ **28.** $7\overline{)427}$ **29.** $5\overline{)27}$ **30.** $9\overline{)265}$

31. $9\overline{)381}$ **32.** $4\overline{)107}$ **33.** $2\overline{)157}$ **34.** $4\overline{)153}$ **35.** $5\overline{)40}$

36. $84 \div 7 =$ ___?___   **37.** $218 \div 9 =$ ___?___   **38.** $313 \div 5 =$ ___?___

39. $92 \div 8 =$ ___?___   **40.** $402 \div 6 =$ ___?___   **41.** $191 \div 4 =$ ___?___

42. $69 \div 5 =$ ___?___   **43.** $196 \div 3 =$ ___?___   **44.** $137 \div 2 =$ ___?___

Do the operation inside the parentheses first.

★ **45.** $648 \div (3 \times 3) =$ ___?___   ★ **46.** $(525 - 169) \div 4 =$ ___?___   ★ **47.** $(264 \div 8) + 49 =$ ___?___

★ **48.** $576 \div (4 \times 2) =$ ___?___   ★ **49.** $(349 + 295) \div 7 =$ ___?___   ★ **50.** $(35 \times 6) \div 5 =$ ___?___

PROBLEM SOLVING • APPLICATIONS

51. It takes 6 bees a lifetime to collect enough nectar to make 270 grams of honey. If each bee collects the same amount of nectar, how many grams of honey does each bee make?

52. There are 774 bumblebees in 9 colonies. There are the same number of bees in each colony. How many bumblebees are in one colony?

53. In one week 8 colonies of honeybees gather 504 kilograms of nectar. Each colony gathers the same amount of nectar. How much nectar is gathered by one colony in one day?

★ **54.** A honeycomb measuring 78 square centimeters has 300 cells. Each cell is about the same size. How many cells are in a 13-square-centimeter section of the honeycomb?

Dividing Greater Numbers

Carlton's population growth means that many new homes must be built. Fortunately, there are large forests nearby.

In one month, 3,247 logs had been cut. These logs were then stored in 5 equal piles.

● How many logs are in each pile?

● How many logs are left over?

Think You need to separate 3,247 logs into 5 equal groups. So divide.
3,247 ÷ 5 = ?

Step 1 Decide where to place the digit in the quotient.
There is 1 digit in the divisor. Draw a line after 3.

$5\overline{)3,247}$

Since 5 > 3, draw a new line.

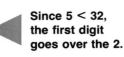
$5\overline{)3,247}$

Since 5 < 32, the first digit goes over the 2.

Step 2	**Step 3**	**Step 4**
Divide the hundreds.	Divide the tens.	Divide the ones.
Think: $5\overline{)32}$	**Think:** $5\overline{)24}$	**Think:** $5\overline{)47}$

$$
\begin{array}{r}
6 \\
5\overline{)3,247} \\
-30 \quad \leftarrow 6\times5 \\
\hline
2 \quad \leftarrow 32-30
\end{array}
$$

$$
\begin{array}{r}
64 \\
5\overline{)3,247} \\
-30\downarrow \\
\hline
24 \\
-20 \quad \leftarrow 4\times5 \\
\hline
4 \quad \leftarrow 24-20
\end{array}
$$

$$
\begin{array}{r}
649 \text{ r2} \\
5\overline{)3,247} \\
-30\downarrow \\
\hline
24 \\
-20\downarrow \\
\hline
47 \\
-45 \quad \leftarrow 9\times5 \\
\hline
2 \quad \leftarrow 47-45
\end{array}
$$

There are **649 logs** in each pile.
There are **2 logs** left over.

● Divide: 9,107 ÷ 4

Sometimes there are thousands in the quotient.

$$
\begin{array}{r}
2,276 \text{ r3} \\
4\overline{)9,107} \\
-8 \\
\hline
11 \\
-8 \\
\hline
30 \\
-28 \\
\hline
27 \\
-24 \\
\hline
3
\end{array}
$$

PRACTICE • Divide.

1. $4\overline{)2{,}536}$ 2. $6\overline{)3{,}175}$ 3. $9\overline{)1{,}903}$ 4. $5\overline{)9{,}721}$ 5. $8\overline{)3{,}563}$

6. $3\overline{)963}$ 7. $2\overline{)842}$ 8. $9\overline{)2{,}263}$ 9. $8\overline{)9{,}873}$ 10. $6\overline{)7{,}630}$

EXERCISES • Divide.

11. $6\overline{)5{,}935}$ 12. $4\overline{)3{,}811}$ 13. $7\overline{)1{,}599}$ 14. $6\overline{)7{,}036}$ 15. $4\overline{)9{,}089}$

16. $9\overline{)1{,}760}$ 17. $5\overline{)8{,}321}$ 18. $5\overline{)2{,}555}$ 19. $8\overline{)3{,}376}$ 20. $4\overline{)3{,}502}$

21. $8\overline{)3{,}956}$ 22. $7\overline{)988}$ 23. $6\overline{)2{,}888}$ 24. $3\overline{)399}$ 25. $7\overline{)5{,}500}$

26. $8\overline{)649}$ 27. $7\overline{)5{,}007}$ 28. $7\overline{)23{,}394}$ 29. $9\overline{)13{,}600}$ 30. $6\overline{)49{,}307}$

31. $166 \div 4 =$ ___?___   32. $2{,}853 \div 8 =$ ___?___   33. $2{,}714 \div 7 =$ ___?___

34. $2{,}209 \div 5 =$ ___?___   35. $12{,}316 \div 5 =$ ___?___   36. $21{,}478 \div 9 =$ ___?___

PROBLEM SOLVING • APPLICATIONS

CHOOSE • estimation • mental math • pencil and paper • calculator SOLVE

37. The logging company plants the same number of new trees each year. They planted 2,512 new trees over the last four years. How many trees did they plant each year?

38. The cook at the logging camp says that each worker eats about 3 potatoes at dinner. There are 4,452 potatoes in storage. How many workers can be fed?

39. The logging company ships about 290 logs each week. Estimate the number of logs they ship in one year.

★ 40. A truck can hold about 6 logs depending on the size of the logs. About 4 logs can be cut from one tree. How many trucks are needed for 12 trees?

THINKER'S CORNER

Use the digits 1, 2, 3, 4, and 5.

a. Arrange the digits to get the largest quotient possible. Use each digit only once. $\square\overline{)\square\square\square\square}$

b. Arrange the digits to get the smallest quotient possible. Use each digit only once. $\square\overline{)\square\square\square\square}$

Zero in the Quotient

The discovery of oil in the ocean near Carlton contributed to its growth. The new oil refinery can process 5,430 barrels of oil in 6 days. It processes the same amount each day.

● How many barrels does it process in 1 day?

 Think To separate 5,430 into 6 equal parts, you divide.

$5,430 \div 6 = ?$

Step 1
Divide the hundreds.
Think: 6)$\overline{54}$

$$
\begin{array}{r}
9 \\
6\overline{)5,430} \\
-54 \longleftarrow 9 \times 6
\end{array}
$$

Step 2
Divide the tens.
Think: 6)$\overline{3}$

$$
\begin{array}{r}
90 \\
6\overline{)5,430} \\
-54\downarrow \\
\hline
3 \\
-0 \longleftarrow 0 \times 6 \\
\hline
3
\end{array}
$$

Step 3
Divide the ones.
Think: 6)$\overline{30}$

$$
\begin{array}{r}
905 \\
6\overline{)5,430} \\
-54\downarrow| \\
\hline
3 | \\
-0\downarrow \\
\hline
30 \\
-30 \\
\hline
0
\end{array}
$$

It processes **905 barrels** in 1 day.

More Examples:

$$
\begin{array}{r}
370\ \mathrm{r}\,3 \\
8\overline{)2,963} \\
-24 \\
\hline
56 \\
-56 \\
\hline
3 \\
-0 \\
\hline
3
\end{array}
\qquad
\begin{array}{r}
4,058\ \mathrm{r}\,3 \\
7\overline{)28,409} \\
-28 \\
\hline
4 \\
-0 \\
\hline
40 \\
-35 \\
\hline
59 \\
-56 \\
\hline
3
\end{array}
\qquad
\begin{array}{r}
2,006\ \mathrm{r}\,2 \\
4\overline{)8,026} \\
-8 \\
\hline
0 \\
-0 \\
\hline
2 \\
-0 \\
\hline
26 \\
-24 \\
\hline
2
\end{array}
$$

PRACTICE • Divide.

1. 2)$\overline{1,618}$ 2. 8)$\overline{883}$ 3. 9)$\overline{1,807}$ 4. 7)$\overline{7,700}$ 5. 4)$\overline{1,840}$

6. 3)$\overline{1,202}$ 7. 6)$\overline{1,922}$ 8. 5)$\overline{1,504}$ 9. 2)$\overline{1,816}$ 10. 3)$\overline{9,270}$

EXERCISES • Divide.

11. 3)$\overline{1,050}$ 12. 6)$\overline{6,240}$ 13. 5)$\overline{3,000}$ 14. 8)$\overline{3,272}$ 15. 6)$\overline{624}$

16. $7\overline{)4,928}$ **17.** $5\overline{)2,854}$ **18.** $8\overline{)3,247}$ **19.** $9\overline{)810}$ **20.** $6\overline{)1,239}$

21. $7\overline{)1,542}$ **22.** $8\overline{)3,720}$ **23.** $3\overline{)7,042}$ **24.** $5\overline{)2,250}$ **25.** $7\overline{)6,048}$

26. $9\overline{)2,886}$ **27.** $8\overline{)4,885}$ **28.** $2\overline{)2,012}$ **29.** $8\overline{)5,624}$ **30.** $9\overline{)9,850}$

31. $6\overline{)12,537}$ **32.** $5\overline{)26,340}$ **33.** $8\overline{)24,000}$ **34.** $9\overline{)18,279}$ **35.** $3\overline{)19,491}$

36. $5\overline{)10,376}$ **37.** $3\overline{)16,211}$ **38.** $7\overline{)35,638}$ ★**39.** $8\overline{)320,720}$ ★**40.** $4\overline{)2,243,604}$

41. $2,882 \div 8 = \underline{\quad?\quad}$ **42.** $3,039 \div 5 = \underline{\quad?\quad}$ **43.** $63,128 \div 9 = \underline{\quad?\quad}$

44. $1,265 \div 6 = \underline{\quad?\quad}$ **45.** $1,855 \div 7 = \underline{\quad?\quad}$ **46.** $10,010 \div 2 = \underline{\quad?\quad}$

47. $1,808 \div 2 = \underline{\quad?\quad}$ ★**48.** $303,300 \div 5 = \underline{\quad?\quad}$ ★**49.** $39,204 \div 3 = \underline{\quad?\quad}$

When you divide by 5, the remainder can be 0. It can also be 1, 2, 3, or 4. It cannot be 5. Why?

What remainders can you get when you divide by

50. 2?   ★**51.** 3?   ★**52.** 4?   ★**53.** 6?   ★**54.** 7?   ★**55.** 8?   ★**56.** 9?

PROBLEM SOLVING • APPLICATIONS

57. The PNO Refinery can process 30,048 barrels of oil in 6 days. This large refinery processes the same number of barrels each day. In one day how many barrels does it process?

59. Pipes that are 9 meters long were used in drilling an oil well. It was estimated that 864 pipes would be needed. Estimate the depth of the well to the nearest hundred meters.

★**60.** A barge carrying 15,000 barrels of oil makes 5 stops along the way. The same number of barrels are removed at each stop. At the end of the trip, 5,000 barrels remain on the barge. How many barrels were removed at each stop?

58. An oil well produces 4,690 gallons of oil in 7 days. It produces the same number of gallons each day. How many gallons of oil does this well produce in one day?

Averages

Sports and recreation have grown along with the growth of Carlton. Vivette is in a bowling league. These are her scores for 5 games.

80, 95, 85, 100, 90

● Find the **average**, or **mean**, of her scores.

Step 1
Find the sum of the scores.

$$80 + 95 + 85 + 100 + 90 = 450$$

Step 2
Divide the sum by the number of scores.

$$
\begin{array}{r}
90 \leftarrow \text{average} \\
\text{number of} \rightarrow 5\,)\overline{450} \leftarrow \text{sum of scores} \\
\text{scores}
\end{array}
$$

Vivette's average score is **90.**

● These are Althea's scores for 6 games.

75, 96, 98, 88, 100, 83

Find the average.

$$75 + 96 + 98 + 88 + 100 + 83 = 540 \qquad 6\,)\overline{540}^{\,90}$$

Althea's average score is **90.**

PRACTICE • Find the averages.

1. 55, 30, 80, 60, 75

2. 93, 70, 85, 80, 82

3. 95, 100, 164, 88, 123

4. 117, 92, 75, 100, 91

EXERCISES • Find the averages.

5. 83, 43, 63, 33, 53

6. 13, 27, 79, 85, 46

7. 91, 80, 34, 67, 13

8. 78, 97, 93, 84, 98

9. 82, 78, 62, 80, 71, 83

10. 79, 95, 80, 66, 77, 77

11. 93, 82, 100, 77, 100, 100

12. 86, 95, 59, 74, 58, 83, 70

13. 76, 93, 100, 84, 60, 57, 97

14. 80, 84, 76, 90, 94, 100, 99

15. 62, 74, 56, 47, 64, 82, 86, 73

16. 72, 64, 36, 57, 88, 97, 65, 57

17. 73, 100, 90, 98, 100, 80, 99, 96   **18.** 63, 56, 44, 17, 32, 50, 60, 76, 70

19. 93, 80, 92, 100, 74, 64, 86, 80, 87   **20.** 73, 72, 71, 40, 48, 64, 70, 80, 76

Another Method   Here is a shorter way to divide.

Divide. $6\overline{)1,582}$

Step 1
Divide the hundreds.

$$\begin{array}{r} 2 \\ 6\overline{)1,5^38\ 2} \end{array}$$

$6\overline{)15}$ is about 2.
$2 \times 6 = 12$
$15 - 12 = 3$

$1,582 \div 6 = $ **263 r4**

Step 2
Divide the tens.

$$\begin{array}{r} 2\ 6 \\ 6\overline{)1,5^38^22} \end{array}$$

$6\overline{)38}$ is about 6.
$6 \times 6 = 36$
$38 - 36 = 2$

Step 3
Divide the ones.

$$\begin{array}{r} 2\ 6\ 3\ r4 \\ 6\overline{)1,5^38^22} \end{array}$$

$6\overline{)22}$ is about 3.
$6 \times 3 = 18$
$22 - 18 = 4$

Divide. Use the shorter way.

21. $5\overline{)1,690}$ **22.** $8\overline{)2,508}$ **23.** $9\overline{)4,563}$ **24.** $4\overline{)6,029}$

PROBLEM SOLVING • APPLICATIONS

Find the average of each player's scores after 6 games. Use paper and pencil or a calculator.

25. Iola   **26.** Cora   **27.** Althea

★ **28.** Ann's average was 96 after six games. What was her score for the sixth game?

★ **29.** Ezell has an average of 104 after six games. What was his score for the first game?

Final Scores						
Games	1	2	3	4	5	6
Ezell	?	78	199	55	64	125
Althea	77	102	48	90	100	75
Ann	91	81	100	125	78	?
Iola	180	94	75	156	40	79
Cora	95	100	88	79	98	104

CALCULATOR • Finding Averages

Example • Find the average of the scores in Exercise 5.

83 ⊕ 43 ⊕ 63 ⊕ 33 ⊕ 53 ⊜ ÷ 5 ⊜ ⟨ 55 ⟩

Dividing by Multiples of Ten

A new shopping mall is opening in Carlton. When the mall opens, it will have 30 stores. These stores will hire 180 people.

● What is the average number of employees in each store?

 The sum is known, 180. Divide this sum by 30.

$$180 \div 30 = ?$$

You can use a basic fact to divide by tens.

$$3\overline{)18} \quad \frac{6}{} \qquad 30\overline{)180} \quad \frac{6}{}$$

There is an average of **6 employees** in each store.

● Divide: $165 \div 20$

Step 1
Think: $2\overline{)16}^{\,8}$

so $20\overline{)160}^{\,8}$.

$20\overline{)165}^{\,8}$ ◀ **Write 8 in the ones place.**

Step 2
Multiply.
$8 \times 20 = 160$

$$\begin{array}{r} 8 \\ 20\overline{)165} \\ 160 \end{array}$$

Step 3
Subtract.
Show the remainder.

$$\begin{array}{r} 8\ r5 \\ 20\overline{)165} \\ -160 \\ \hline 5 \end{array}$$

◀ **The remainder must be less than 20.**

Check:

Multiply the divisor ⟶ by the quotient.

Add the remainder. ⟶

$$\begin{array}{r} 20 \\ \times\ 8 \\ \hline 160 \\ +\quad 5 \\ \hline 165 \end{array}$$ ⟵ Should equal the dividend.

PRACTICE • Divide.

1. $30\overline{)60}$
2. $40\overline{)200}$
3. $20\overline{)80}$
4. $30\overline{)120}$
5. $90\overline{)270}$

6. $90\overline{)571}$
7. $80\overline{)321}$
8. $10\overline{)460}$
9. $50\overline{)161}$
10. $30\overline{)132}$

EXERCISES • Divide.

11. $60\overline{)420}$
12. $80\overline{)347}$
13. $80\overline{)240}$
14. $90\overline{)810}$
15. $90\overline{)104}$

16. $60 \overline{)376}$ **17.** $50 \overline{)200}$ **18.** $30 \overline{)168}$ **19.** $40 \overline{)295}$ **20.** $50 \overline{)250}$

21. $60 \overline{)280}$ **22.** $80 \overline{)493}$ **23.** $20 \overline{)40}$ **24.** $60 \overline{)191}$ **25.** $60 \overline{)540}$

26. $90 \overline{)754}$ **27.** $50 \overline{)378}$ **28.** $10 \overline{)80}$ **29.** $20 \overline{)199}$ **30.** $70 \overline{)639}$

31. $70 \overline{)350}$ **32.** $10 \overline{)650}$ **33.** $80 \overline{)745}$ **34.** $60 \overline{)483}$ **35.** $30 \overline{)90}$

36. $346 \div 40 = \underline{\quad?\quad}$ **37.** $168 \div 70 = \underline{\quad?\quad}$ **38.** $591 \div 60 = \underline{\quad?\quad}$

39. $95 \div 30 = \underline{\quad?\quad}$ **40.** $254 \div 30 = \underline{\quad?\quad}$ **41.** $258 \div 50 = \underline{\quad?\quad}$

★ **42.** $1,400 \div 70 = \underline{\quad?\quad}$ ★ **43.** $1,500 \div 30 = \underline{\quad?\quad}$ ★ **44.** $1,600 \div 20 = \underline{\quad?\quad}$

PROBLEM SOLVING • APPLICATIONS

45. The movie theater in the shopping mall has seating for 560 people. There are 80 seats in each section. How many sections are there?

46. In parking lot A there are spaces for 450 cars. There are 50 spaces in each row of the lot. How many rows are there?

47. The shopping mall receives a shipment of 210 banners. Each of the 30 stores will receive the same number of banners. How many banners does each store receive?

★ **48.** Each of the 30 stores receives at least one banner of each color. What color banner will not appear more than once in any store?

GRAND OPENING

OPENING DAY SALE

Number of Banners	Color
30	Orange
35	Green
50	Red
50	White
45	Blue

THINKER'S CORNER

A clothing store in the mall sells 4 times as many bright–colored ties as dark–colored ties. The store sold 35 ties in one week. How many dark–colored ties did the store sell?

PROBLEM SOLVING · STRATEGIES

Too Much or Not Enough Information

Sometimes a problem has more information than is needed to solve the problem.

Example 1 On opening day at the mall, Hal's Hat Shop sold 192 tie pins at $3 each, 47 ties at $9 each, and 82 hats at $19 each. How much money did they collect selling hats?

Step 1
Identify the question. ⟶ How much money did they collect selling hats?

Think (Number of hats) × (Cost per hat) = Amount collected

Step 2
Identify the infromation you need to answer the question. ⟶ Number of hats: 82
Cost per hat: $19

Step 3 Estimate the answer.   Find the actual answer.

$$
\begin{array}{r} 82 \\ \times\ 19 \\ \hline \end{array}
\longrightarrow
\begin{array}{r} 80 \\ \times\ 20 \\ \hline \$1{,}600 \end{array}
\blacktriangleleft \text{ Estimate}
\qquad
\begin{array}{r} 82 \\ \times\ 19 \\ \hline 738 \\ 82 \\ \hline 1{,}558 \end{array}
$$

82 ⊠ 19 ⊜ [1558]

Step 4
Compare the actual answer with the estimate to check whether it is sensible. Since 1,558 is close to 1,600, it is sensible. They collected **$1,558** selling hats.

The information about the tie pins and ties is not needed to solve the problem.

Sometimes there is not enough information to solve the problem.

Example 2 There were 375 customers at Sue's Shoppe on Thursday. They spent $4,025. On Friday, $4,250 was spent at the store. How many more people visited the store on Friday?

Step 1
Identify the question. ⟶ How many more people visited the store on Friday?

Think (Number on Friday) − (Number on Thursday) = Number of more people

Step 2
Identify the information you need to solve the problem. ⟶ Friday customers: Missing information
Thursday customers: 375

You need to know the number of customers on Friday.

PROBLEMS • Solve each problem when you have enough information. When there is not enough information, identify what else you need to know.

1. Hampton's Luggage Store sells suitcases for $79.95 and briefcases for $49.65. How much money will they collect if they sell 5 suitcases?

2. Roger's Flowers receives 36 mum arrangements and 42 daisy arrangements. They plan to display the mum arrangements on 6 shelves, placing the same number of arrangements on each shelf. How many mum arrangements will be displayed on each shelf?

3. Dino's Health Food store sold 16 oat bars and 22 rice patties on Tuesday. By Friday, the store sold an additional 48 oat bars. What is the total number of oat bars sold from Tuesday through Friday?

4. The Mall Toy Shoppe sold 24 tricycles from Monday through Saturday. They sold 14 scooters on Saturday. What is the average number of tricycles they sold each day?

Read the question. Think: Do I have all the information I need?

5. Comfort-Step Shoes is having a half-price sale. If you buy two pairs of shoes, the second pair is half-price. What is the cost of two pair of shoes?

Read all the facts carefully.

6. Landis Drug Store is selling school notebooks at a reduced price. In one day they sell 136 notebooks. One customer buys 11 notebooks. How much did the customer spend on notebooks.

7. Coughlin Pet Supply sells rawhide doggie chews for $1.39 each. They sell rubber mice for $2.75 each. A customer bought 4 doggie chews. How much money does the customer spend on doggie chews?

8. The Sounds Galore Record Store receives 54 record albums. Several of the albums will sell for $4.98. Sounds Galore paid a total of $162.00 for the shipment of albums. How much did they pay for each album?

Write Your Own Problem

Carlton Mall has 4 parking areas. Area A holds 450 cars, area B holds 365 cars, area C holds 175 cars, and area D holds 290 cars. The mall has enough space to build a 6-story parking garage which could hold 635 cars. Write a problem using this information.

MID-CHAPTER REVIEW

Divide. (Pages 74–75)

1. 5)42   **2.** 8)36   **3.** 9)75   **4.** 5)49   **5.** 9)83

Divide. (Pages 76–77)

6. 4)65   **7.** 6)282   **8.** 9)704   **9.** 5)136   **10.** 7)602

Divide. (Pages 78–79)

11. 3)954   **12.** 4)563   **13.** 7)5,501   **14.** 9)9,812   **15.** 6)23,650

16. $299 \div 4 = \underline{\ ?\ }$ **17.** $4,287 \div 5 = \underline{\ ?\ }$ **18.** $33,423 \div 8 = \underline{\ ?\ }$

Divide. (Pages 80–81)

19. 5)1,504   **20.** 3)1,320   **21.** 6)3,180   **22.** 9)84,780   **23.** 6)54,000

Find the averages. (Pages 82–83)

24. 21, 54, 38, 27   **25.** 85, 100, 79, 96, 75, 87

Divide. (Pages 84–85)

26. 30)48   **27.** 30)289   **28.** 70)639

29. Carlton State Park contains 43 acres of woods, a 26 acre lake, and 3 picnic areas. How many more acres of woods than water are there? (Pages 86–87)

30. The Carlton Soccer League has 10 boys teams and 12 girls teams. Each team has 21 members. How many girls played in the league? (Pages 86–87)

MAINTENANCE • MIXED PRACTICE

1. $33 \times 8 = \underline{\ ?\ }$ **2.** $46 \times 296 = \underline{\ ?\ }$ **3.** $61 \times 5,195 = \underline{\ ?\ }$

4. $27 \times 9 = \underline{\ ?\ }$ **5.** $316 \times 614 = \underline{\ ?\ }$ **6.** $797 \times 1,276 = \underline{\ ?\ }$

7. The Winslow High School band has 76 members. There are 16 more girls than boys in the band. How many girls are there in the band?

8. An airline wants to purchase the fastest airplane available which can carry at least 110 passengers, and weighs no more than 125,000 pounds. Which airplane should the airline buy? Refer to the table on page 14.

9. The Smithville Fire Department was called to 567 fires last year. Estimate the number of fire calls they received each month.

CAREER APPLICATIONS

Statistical Clerk

A statistical clerk collects data that is used to solve problems. The *mean, median,* and *mode* are used to interpret the data.

Recall that the term **mean** is another word for **average.** (See page 82.)

The **mode** is the measure that occurs most often in a set of data.

EXAMPLE 1: This table shows the traffic count at an intersection from 7 A.M. to noon.

    a. During which hour would a police officer be needed most?

    b. What hour is the mode?

Solutions: **a.** During the **8–9** hour because this is the busiest time.

    b. The mode is **8–9.**

Traffic at Charles and North

Time (A.M.)	Count
7-8	650
8-9	1350
9-10	550
10-11	510
11-12	405

When the highest count occurs more than once, there is more than one mode.

In a listing of data, the **median** is the middle measure or score.

EXAMPLE 2: This table shows the prices of five different used cars. What is the median?

Solution: [1] Arrange the prices in order. Start with the least.

$5,659 $5,719 $6,212 $6,365 $7,140

    [2] The median, or middle price, is **$6,212.**

Car	Price
A	$6,212
B	$5,659
C	$6,365
D	$5,719
E	$7,140

If there is an even number of items, the median is the average of the two middle numbers.

EXERCISES • Find the median and mode.

1.   **Renell School Enrollment**

Year	Number of Students
1976	1032
1977	1021
1978	1095
1979	1098
1980	1075

2.   **Survey of Favorite Sports**

Sport	Count
Bowling	17
Tennis	12
Swimming	25
Softball	27
Basketball	19
Football	15

Dividing by Two-Digit Numbers

The new "hi–tech" industries in Carlton have created a population "boom."

Liang packed 138 calculators in 23 cartons for shipment. Each carton holds the same number of calculators.

● How many calculators are in each carton?

Think To separate 138 into 23 equal parts you divide.

$$138 \div 23 = ?$$

$$23\overline{)138}$$

You can **estimate** to help you find the quotient. Round the divisor to the nearest ten.

Step 1
Think: $2\overline{)13}$ (6), so $20\overline{)130}$ (6).

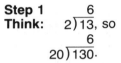

$$23\overline{)138}^{\,6}$$ ◀ Write the 6 over 8.

Step 2
Multiply: $6 \times 23 = 138$.

$$23\overline{)138}^{\,6}$$
$$138$$

Step 3
Subtract.

$$23\overline{)138}^{\,6}$$
$$\underline{-138}$$
$$0$$

There are **6 calculators** in each carton.

Another Estimation Method: Compatible Numbers

● You can use compatible numbers to help you estimate quotients. **Compatible numbers** are convenient numbers that are easy to use.

Problem	Estimate
$324 \div 8$	$320 \div 8 = \mathbf{40}$
$496 \div 7$	$490 \div 7 = \mathbf{70}$
$192 \div 38$	$200 \div 40 = \mathbf{5}$
$789 \div 21$	$800 \div 20 = \mathbf{4}$

◀ Compatible numbers

PRACTICE • Divide.

1. $83\overline{)332}$
2. $62\overline{)256}$
3. $71\overline{)440}$
4. $32\overline{)97}$
5. $53\overline{)283}$

6. $58\overline{)420}$
7. $67\overline{)386}$
8. $25\overline{)92}$
9. $38\overline{)175}$
10. $88\overline{)633}$

EXERCISES • Divide.

11. $53\overline{)384}$ **12.** $31\overline{)291}$ **13.** $64\overline{)273}$ **14.** $51\overline{)112}$ **15.** $43\overline{)301}$

16. $76\overline{)446}$ **17.** $46\overline{)350}$ **18.** $68\overline{)300}$ **19.** $48\overline{)221}$ **20.** $29\overline{)275}$

21. $39\overline{)170}$ **22.** $42\overline{)136}$ **23.** $50\overline{)487}$ **24.** $54\overline{)171}$ **25.** $36\overline{)168}$

26. $29\overline{)245}$ **27.** $52\overline{)277}$ **28.** $87\overline{)434}$ **29.** $74\overline{)450}$ **30.** $58\overline{)367}$

31. $77\overline{)500}$ **32.** $60\overline{)444}$ **33.** $38\overline{)173}$ **34.** $54\overline{)270}$ **35.** $90\overline{)312}$

36. $94\overline{)395}$ **37.** $56\overline{)213}$ **38.** $21\overline{)136}$ **39.** $93\overline{)237}$ **40.** $52\overline{)233}$

41. $124 \div 35 =$ ___?___   **42.** $449 \div 70 =$ ___?___   **43.** $295 \div 41 =$ ___?___

44. $171 \div 32 =$ ___?___   **45.** $163 \div 29 =$ ___?___   **46.** $467 \div 92 =$ ___?___

47. $285 \div 91 =$ ___?___   **48.** $185 \div 23 =$ ___?___   **49.** $237 \div 33 =$ ___?___

PROBLEM SOLVING • APPLICATIONS

50. There are 178 radios. 21 fit on each shelf. How many shelves can be filled? How many radios are left over?

51. Eila has 120 old tapes and 348 new tapes. He wants to display them on racks. 52 fit on each rack. How many racks does he need?

52. Complete the table. Find the number of cartons delivered to Radio Hut.

Radio Hut Order			
Item	Number of Cartons	Number of Items	Number in Each Carton
Pocket calculator	?	144	24
Headsets	?	84	12
Radios	?	432	48
Computer tennis	?	36	36
Tape recorders	?	144	18

THINKER'S CORNER

Use the digits 5, 6, 7, 8, and 9.

a. Arrange the digits to get the greatest quotient possible. Use each digit only once.

b. Arrange the digits to get the least quotient possible. Use each digit only once.   □□$\overline{)}$□□□

Correcting Estimates

Carlton is a good place to live because it is concerned with conservation. Mr. Reddy has prepared 148 seedlings for planting. They will be planted in rows with 24 trees in each row.

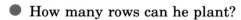

● How many rows can he plant?

● How many trees will be left over?

Think To separate 148 into 24 equal parts, divide.

$$148 \div 24 = ?$$

Sometimes your first **estimate** for the quotient is too large.

Step 1	Step 2	Step 3
Round 24 to 20.	Try 7. Then compare the remainder with 24.	Try 6. Then compare the remainder with 24.

Think: $2\overline{)14}^{\;7}$, so $20\overline{)140}^{\;7}$.

$$24\overline{)148}$$

$$\begin{array}{r} 7 \\ 24\overline{)148} \\ -168 \end{array}$$ ◀ **7 is too large.**

$$\begin{array}{r} 6\text{ r}4 \\ 24\overline{)148} \\ -144 \\ \hline 4 \end{array}$$

He can plant **6 rows** with **4 trees** left over.

● Divide: $192 \div 38$

Sometimes your first **estimate** is too small.

Step 1	Step 2	Step 3
Round 38 to 40.	Try 4. Then compare the remainder with 38.	Try 5. Then compare the remainder with 38.

Think: $4\overline{)19}^{\;4}$, so $40\overline{)190}^{\;4}$.

$$38\overline{)192}$$

$$\begin{array}{r} 4 \\ 38\overline{)192} \\ -152 \\ \hline 40 \end{array}$$ ◀ **Since 40 > 38, 4 is too small.**

$$\begin{array}{r} 5\text{ r}2 \\ 38\overline{)192} \\ -190 \\ \hline 2 \end{array}$$

The quotient is **5 r2.**

PRACTICE • Divide.

1. $22\overline{)183}$ **2.** $12\overline{)78}$ **3.** $53\overline{)401}$ **4.** $91\overline{)541}$ **5.** $42\overline{)205}$

6. $48\overline{)243}$ **7.** $94\overline{)729}$ **8.** $18\overline{)115}$ **9.** $47\overline{)282}$ **10.** $28\overline{)58}$

EXERCISES • Divide.

11. $93\overline{)361}$ **12.** $28\overline{)196}$ **13.** $61\overline{)226}$ **14.** $85\overline{)446}$ **15.** $24\overline{)99}$

16. $94\overline{)279}$ **17.** $25\overline{)224}$ **18.** $14\overline{)112}$ **19.** $69\overline{)403}$ **20.** $72\overline{)565}$

21. $62\overline{)492}$ **22.** $77\overline{)702}$ **23.** $64\overline{)597}$ **24.** $36\overline{)161}$ **25.** $11\overline{)108}$

26. $44\overline{)214}$ **27.** $16\overline{)105}$ **28.** $21\overline{)96}$ **29.** $46\overline{)322}$ **30.** $41\overline{)365}$

31. $19\overline{)100}$ **32.** $51\overline{)441}$ **33.** $23\overline{)181}$ **34.** $57\overline{)478}$ **35.** $32\overline{)235}$

36. $27\overline{)262}$ **37.** $84\overline{)403}$ **38.** $22\overline{)178}$ **39.** $39\overline{)355}$ **40.** $63\overline{)482}$

41. $68\overline{)553}$ **42.** $23\overline{)160}$ **43.** $39\overline{)238}$ **44.** $35\overline{)296}$ **45.** $71\overline{)565}$

46. $431 \div 74 = \underline{\ ?\ }$ **47.** $369 \div 46 = \underline{\ ?\ }$ **48.** $161 \div 34 = \underline{\ ?\ }$

49. $358 \div 86 = \underline{\ ?\ }$ **50.** $145 \div 21 = \underline{\ ?\ }$ **51.** $528 \div 75 = \underline{\ ?\ }$

52. $356 \div 59 = \underline{\ ?\ }$ **53.** $564 \div 72 = \underline{\ ?\ }$ **54.** $456 \div 57 = \underline{\ ?\ }$

★ **55.** $542 \div \underline{\ ?\ } = 67 \text{ r} \underline{\ ?\ }$ ★ **56.** $806 \div \underline{\ ?\ } = 89 \text{ r} \underline{\ ?\ }$ ★ **57.** $487 \div \underline{\ ?\ } = 81 \text{ r} \underline{\ ?\ }$

★ **58.** $397 \div \underline{\ ?\ } = 79 \text{ r} \underline{\ ?\ }$ ★ **59.** $672 \div \underline{\ ?\ } = 96 \text{ r} \underline{\ ?\ }$ ★ **60.** $203 \div \underline{\ ?\ } = 33 \text{ r} \underline{\ ?\ }$

★ **61.** $579 \div \underline{\ ?\ } = 72 \text{ r} \underline{\ ?\ }$ ★ **62.** $783 \div \underline{\ ?\ } = 97 \text{ r} \underline{\ ?\ }$ ★ **63.** $508 \div \underline{\ ?\ } = 84 \text{ r} \underline{\ ?\ }$

PROBLEM SOLVING • APPLICATIONS

64. Alecca Samuels runs a tree farm. She has 148 pine seedlings to plant. 24 fit in one row. How many rows can she fill? How many seedlings are left over?

65. It takes 18 workers to plant 162 small maple trees in one day. What is the average number of trees each worker plants in one day?

★ **66.** There are 276 spruce trees to plant. Workers plant 6 rows with 32 trees in each row. The remaining trees are planted with 28 trees in each row. How many rows of 28 can be made?

★ **67.** Alecca orders 315 hemlocks. She usually plants 45 in each row. How many more rows will she fill if she plants 35 in each row?

More Two-Digit Quotients

Carlton was first settled in 1820.
Wagon trains brought the first settlers.
The wagon train averaged 21
kilometers a day.

● How long did it take to go 1,155 kilometers?

Think   21 kilometers × number of days = 1,155 kilometers
or 21 × _?_ = 1,155

To find the missing factor, you divide.

1,155 ÷ 21 = ?

Step 1
Decide where to place the first digit.
There are 2 digits in the divisor.
Draw a line after the second digit in 1,155.

$21\overline{)1,1|55}$ ◀ Since 21 > 11, draw a new line. $2\overline{)1,15|5}$ ◀ Since 21 < 115, the first digit goes over the 5.

Step 2
Divide the tens.

$$\begin{array}{r}5\\2\overline{)11}\end{array}, \text{ so } \begin{array}{r}5\\20\overline{)110}\end{array}.$$

Think:

$$\begin{array}{r}5\\21\overline{)1,155}\\-1\ 05\\\hline 10\end{array}$$
←— 5 × 21

Step 3
Divide the ones.

$$\begin{array}{r}5\\2\overline{)10}\end{array}, \text{ so } \begin{array}{r}5\\20\overline{)100}\end{array}.$$

Think: ◀ **Compatible numbers**

$$\begin{array}{r}55\\21\overline{)1,155}\\-1\ 05\!\downarrow\\\hline 105\\-105\\\hline 0\end{array}$$
←— 5 × 21

It took **55 days** to go
1,155 kilometers.

More Examples:

$$\begin{array}{r}75\\24\overline{)1,800}\\-1\ 68\\\hline 120\\-120\\\hline 0\end{array}\qquad \begin{array}{r}18\ r14\\37\overline{)680}\\-37\\\hline 310\\-296\\\hline 14\end{array}\qquad \begin{array}{r}40\\56\overline{)2,240}\\-2\ 24\\\hline 00\\-\ 0\\\hline 0\end{array}$$

PRACTICE • Divide.

1. $32\overline{)544}$ 2. $21\overline{)882}$ 3. $70\overline{)5,809}$ 4. $48\overline{)2,688}$

5. $27\overline{)2,615}$ 6. $62\overline{)4,922}$ 7. $29\overline{)2,630}$ 8. $75\overline{)4,688}$

EXERCISES • Divide.

9. $83\overline{)1,771}$ 10. $39\overline{)2,450}$ 11. $67\overline{)2,909}$ 12. $32\overline{)2,616}$

13. $21\overline{)455}$ 14. $67\overline{)914}$ 15. $48\overline{)3,120}$ 16. $38\overline{)1,978}$

17. $42\overline{)3{,}321}$ **18.** $86\overline{)5{,}493}$ **19.** $74\overline{)5{,}000}$ **20.** $12\overline{)115}$

21. $12\overline{)756}$ **22.** $48\overline{)2{,}496}$ **23.** $58\overline{)1{,}914}$ **24.** $64\overline{)5{,}561}$

25. $16\overline{)99}$ **26.** $37\overline{)162}$ **27.** $25\overline{)1{,}775}$ **28.** $83\overline{)2{,}454}$

29. $25\overline{)1{,}500}$ **30.** $90\overline{)3{,}460}$ **31.** $54\overline{)4{,}032}$ **32.** $93\overline{)4{,}185}$

33. $654 \div 87 =$ ___?___   **34.** $2{,}443 \div 62 =$ ___?___

35. $6{,}300 \div 84 =$ ___?___   **36.** $1{,}530 \div 50 =$ ___?___

37. $7{,}660 \div 92 =$ ___?___   **38.** $3{,}689 \div 46 =$ ___?___

PROBLEM SOLVING • APPLICATIONS

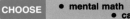

CHOOSE   • mental math   • pencil and paper   • calculator   SOLVE

39. A wagon train traveled 25 kilometers a day. At this rate, how many days did it take to go 1,650 kilometers?

40. One pony–express route was 432 kilometers long. The rider changed horses every 18 kilometers. How many horses did he use?

41. A wagon train traveled 44 miles in two days. It traveled 6 more miles the first day than it did the second day. How many miles did it travel the:
   a. first day?
   b. second day?

★ **42.** A pioneer family moved west. The first trail they followed was 779 kilometers long. The second trail was 985 kilometers long. They traveled 18 kilometers a day. At this rate, how many days did the trip take?

THINKER'S CORNER

Each letter in the exercises below represents a digit. Each time a letter is used, it represents the same digit. Find the missing digits.

a.
```
      C7
 8B)C39A
  − 8B
  ─────
   57A
  −57A
  ─────
     0
```

b.
```
      5F
 E7)DE91
  −DF5
  ─────
   1E1
  −1E1
  ─────
     0
```

c.
```
      9K r3
 G3)K9 8G
  −K7 7
  ─────
   HLG
  −HLH
  ─────
     3
```

More Dividing of Greater Numbers

Because of Carlton's growth the local newspaper now prints 25,210 papers each day. Forty–eight small vans are used to deliver these papers. Each van carries the same number of papers.

● How many newspapers are carried by each van?
● How many newspapers are left over?

 To separate 25,210 into 48 equal parts, divide.
25,210 ÷ 48 = ?

Step 1 Decide where to place the first digit.

$$48\overline{)25,210}$$ ◀ Since 48 > 25, draw a new line.

$$48\overline{)25,210}^{\quad X}$$ ◀ Since 48 < 252, the first digit goes over the 2.

Step 1 Divide the hundreds.	**Step 2** Divide the tens.	**Step 3** Divide the ones.
Think: $5\overline{)25}$, so $50\overline{)250}$.	**Think:** $5\overline{)12}$, so $50\overline{)120}$.	**Think:** $5\overline{)25}$, so $50\overline{)250}$.

Step 1:
$$
\begin{array}{r}
5 \\
48\overline{)25,210} \\
-24\,0 \quad \leftarrow 5 \times 48 \\
\hline
1\,2
\end{array}
$$

Step 2:
$$
\begin{array}{r}
52 \\
48\overline{)25,210} \\
-24\,0\downarrow \\
\hline
1\,21 \\
-96 \quad \leftarrow 2 \times 48 \\
\hline
25
\end{array}
$$

Step 3:
$$
\begin{array}{r}
525\ r10 \\
48\overline{)25,210} \\
-24\,0\downarrow \\
\hline
1\,21 \\
-96\downarrow \\
\hline
250 \\
-240 \quad \leftarrow 5 \times 48 \\
\hline
10
\end{array}
$$

Each van carries **525 newspapers.**
There are **10 newspapers** left over.

● Divide: 96,434 ÷ 26.

Sometimes there are thousands in the quotient.

$$
\begin{array}{r}
3,709 \\
26\overline{)96,434} \\
-78\downarrow \\
\hline
18\,4 \\
-18\,2\downarrow \\
\hline
23 \\
-0\downarrow \\
\hline
234 \\
-234 \\
\hline
0
\end{array}
$$

PRACTICE • Divide.

1. $75\overline{)23,550}$ 2. $43\overline{)7,654}$ 3. $24\overline{)7,865}$ 4. $42\overline{)54,364}$

5. $62\overline{)60,202}$ 6. $67\overline{)32,688}$ 7. $89\overline{)95,720}$ 8. $55\overline{)64,450}$

EXERCISES • Divide.

9. $92\overline{)77,777}$ 10. $94\overline{)27,434}$ 11. $47\overline{)81,688}$ 12. $40\overline{)7,516}$

13. $67\overline{)7,683}$ 14. $25\overline{)7,849}$ 15. $46\overline{)7,278}$ 16. $62\overline{)8,866}$

17. $18\overline{)6,250}$ 18. $28\overline{)14,448}$ 19. $42\overline{)8,728}$ 20. $82\overline{)47,810}$

21. $68\overline{)7,915}$ 22. $58\overline{)6,500}$ 23. $59\overline{)10,830}$ 24. $68\overline{)21,394}$

25. $82\overline{)16,762}$ 26. $85\overline{)15,603}$ 27. $57\overline{)5,249}$ 28. $89\overline{)82,173}$

29. $39\overline{)67,612}$ 30. $30\overline{)5,252}$ 31. $63\overline{)70,052}$ 32. $62\overline{)89,907}$

33. $38\overline{)43,300}$ 34. $23\overline{)2,254}$ ★ 35. $76\overline{)965,564}$ ★ 36. $72\overline{)848,840}$

PROBLEM SOLVING • APPLICATIONS

37. A local newspaper reporter travels 20,712 kilometers in one year. What is the average distance she travels each month?

38. In one hour 17,100 meters of paper can pass through an offset press. At this rate, how many meters of paper can pass through the press in one minute?

39. Two years ago, an average of 21,048 newpapers were sold each day. This year the average is 25,210. Estimate how many more are sold each day this year to the nearest thousand.

40. Each day 46,475 copies of the *Sundown News* are printed. Then 9,485 are mailed. The workers put the remaining papers into bundles of 50 each. How many bundles do they make? How many papers are left over?

Dividing by Three-Digit Numbers

Plays, musicals, concerts, and other cultural activities have helped to make Carlton a good place to live. Last month, 52,038 people saw a concert at the Crown Theater. All 388 seats were sold out for each performance.

● How many performances were there?

Think   To separate 52,038 into 388 equal parts, divide.

$$52,038 \div 388 = ?$$

Step 1   Decide where to place the first digit in the quotient. The division has 3 digits. Draw a line after the 0.

$$388\overline{)5\,2,0\,3\,8}\overset{\text{X}}{}$$

◀ Since 388 < 520, place the first digit over the 0.

Step 2 Round the divisor.

Think: $4\overline{)5}$, so

$$400\overline{)500}.$$
(1)

Step 3

Think: $4\overline{)13}$, so

$$400\overline{)1300}.$$
(3)

Step 4

Think: $4\overline{)19}$, so

$$400\overline{)1900}.$$
(4)
4 is too small. Try 5.

```
        1
388)52,380
   -38 8   ←1 × 388
    13 5
```

```
       13
388)52,380
  -38 8↓
   13 58
  -11 64   ←3 × 388
    1 94
```

```
      135
388)52,380
  -38 8↓|
   13 58|
  -11 64↓
    1 940   ←5 × 388
   -1 940
        0
```

There were **135 performances.**

More Examples:

```
          15 r504
564)8,964
   -5 64
    3 324
   -2 820
      504
```

```
         607 r13
926)562,095
   -555 6
     6 49
   -   0
     6 495
    -6 482
        13
```

```
           2,247
439)986,433
   -878
    108 4
   - 87 8
     20 63
    -17 56
     3 073
    -3 073
        0
```

PRACTICE • Divide.

1. $426\overline{)3,966}$
2. $236\overline{)3,317}$
3. $453\overline{)18,326}$
4. $341\overline{)79,560}$

5. $506\overline{)435,160}$
6. $768\overline{)321,024}$
7. $650\overline{)196,997}$
8. $246\overline{)123,000}$

EXERCISES • Divide.

9. $515\overline{)3,671}$
10. $302\overline{)19,552}$
11. $913\overline{)13,865}$
12. $800\overline{)81,600}$

13. $863\overline{)63,043}$
14. $738\overline{)94,208}$
15. $456\overline{)28,282}$
16. $898\overline{)5,688}$

17. $643\overline{)8,949}$
18. $523\overline{)10,992}$
19. $904\overline{)75,000}$
20. $259\overline{)98,841}$

21. $613\overline{)954,629}$
22. $636\overline{)294,516}$
23. $308\overline{)460,097}$
24. $214\overline{)145,167}$

25. $197\overline{)128,151}$
26. $216\overline{)712,536}$
27. $375\overline{)200,695}$
28. $363\overline{)854,216}$

29. $572\overline{)419,370}$
30. $400\overline{)497,256}$
31. $258\overline{)396,987}$
32. $142\overline{)997,097}$

PROBLEM SOLVING • APPLICATIONS

33. In one year (365 days) the Crown Theater sold a total of 359,890 tickets. What is the average number of tickets sold in one day?

34. The cashier collected a total of $2,541.50 after selling 598 adult tickets. What is the price of each ticket?

35. Concession workers collected $897.95 for selling 862 small containers of popcorn and 527 cups of apple juice. Each cup of juice costs $0.15. What was the price of each small container of popcorn?

36. The Crown sold 254 adult tickets for a total of $1,079.50. They sold 167 children's tickets for a total of $459.25. How much more does an adult ticket cost?

CALCULATOR • Quotients and Remainders

Use a calculator to find the quotient and remainder.

$562,095 \div 926 = ?$

Press: 5 6 2 0 9 5 $\boxed{\div}$ 9 2 6 $\boxed{=}$ $\boxed{607.0140389}$ **Quotient: 607**

This is the formula for finding the remainder.

Remainder = Dividend − (Quotient × Divisor)
Remainder = 562,095 − (607 × 926)

Press: 6 0 7 $\boxed{\times}$ 9 2 6 $\boxed{=}$ $\boxed{562082}$

Remainder = 562,095 − 562,082 = 13   **Answer: 607 r13**

EXERCISES • Use a calculator for Exercises 1–32.

PROBLEM SOLVING · STRATEGIES

Choosing the Operation

The words in a problem are the clues that tell you whether to add, subtract, multiply or divide. In some problems, you need to identify more than one clue in order to choose the operation.

Word Clues	Operation
How many **in all?** What is the **total?** How many are there **altogether?**	Add or Multiply Add or Multiply Add or Multiply
How many are **left?** How much **remains?** How many **more than** Sue does Bill have? How **many less** are there? What is the **difference?**	Subtract
What is the **product?** A number **times** a number is how many? How much is **double** the number? How many is **twice** the number? How much is **triple** the number?	Multiply
How many are in **each** can? How much is in **one** case? How much **per** day?	Divide

Example

The sixth grade class sold popcorn to raise money for the Native American exhibit at the museum. They sold 84 packages for $1.25.

● How much did they collect in all?

Think   First clue: How much in all?
        Operation: Add or multiply.
        Second clue: 84 packages
              for $1.25 each
        Operation: Multiply.

        $84 \times \$1.25 = \textbf{\$105.00}$

PROBLEMS • Which of **a–d** would you use to solve each problem?

1. In 5 school days, 360 students work on computers in the computer lab. How many students use the computers each day?
   a. 360 × 5   **b.** 360 ÷ 5
   c. 360 + 5   **d.** 360 − 5

Read the question carefully.
Find the key words.

---

2. A goal of the Conservation Club is to plant 210 seedlings in two years. This year they planted 86 seedlings. How many will they plant next year?
   a. 210 + 86   **b.** 210 ÷ 86
   c. 210 − 86   **d.** 210 × 86

3. On Tuesday, 150 crates of oranges were shipped. Each crate holds 60 oranges. How many oranges were shipped?
   a. 150 + 60   **b.** 150 − 60
   c. 150 ÷ 60   **d.** 150 × 60

4. At the Carlton Honey Festival, honey bars are sold by the box. There are 24 honey bars in a box. How many honey bars are there in 6 boxes?
   a. 24 × 6   **b.** 24 ÷ 6
   c. 24 − 6   **d.** 24 + 6

Solve. First write the number sentence.

5. Saunders Brothers Trucking Co. hauled 665 logs in 5 days to the Crosswaite Sawmill. What was the average number of logs they hauled each day?

6. The Carlton Oil Refinery employs 346 workers. Last year they employed 279 workers. How many more workers do they employ this year?

7. In 1820, a wagon train brought the first 27 settlers to Carlton. A year later, 36 more people settled in Carlton. How many settlers were there altogether in 1821?

Sometimes there are no clues.

---

8. On Monday through Friday, Roger delivers 230 copies of the Carlton Daily Mail. He delivers the same number of newspapers each day. How many papers does he deliver daily?

★ 9. Last year, the Carlton High School football team scored an average of 28 points in 9 games. How many points did they score in all?

─── Write Your Own Problem ───

Use the following information to write a word problem.

Crown Theater

Number of performances: 12
Average attendance: 178
Number of seats: 388
Sold out performances: 2

CHAPTER REVIEW

Part 1 • VOCABULARY

For Exercises 1–7, choose from the box at the right the word that completes the sentence.

1. The answer in a division problem is called the ?. (Page 74)

2. In the problem $3\overline{)12}$, 3 is call the ?. (Page 74)

3. In the problem $5\overline{)16}$ (with $3\,r1$ above), 1 is called the ?. (Page 74)

4. You can check an answer in a division problem by using multiplication because they are ? operations. (Page 75)

5. When you add a series of numbers and divide the sum by the number of addends, you can find the ?. (Page 82)

6. To separate a group into smaller groups of equal size, you can use the operation called ?. (Page 74)

7. In the problem $4\overline{)20}$, 20 is call the ?. (Page 74)

average
dividend
division
divisor
inverse
quotient
remainder

Part 2 • SKILLS

Divide. (Pages 74-75)

8. $5\overline{)37}$ 9. $7\overline{)50}$ 10. $9\overline{)85}$ 11. $6\overline{)29}$ 12. $7\overline{)54}$

13. $66 \div 8 = \underline{?}$ 14. $75 \div 9 = \underline{?}$ 15. $58 \div 8 = \underline{?}$

Divide. (Pages 76-77)

16. $5\overline{)92}$ 17. $7\overline{)149}$ 18. $9\overline{)702}$ 19. $6\overline{)295}$ 20. $4\overline{)358}$

21. $420 \div 9 = \underline{?}$ 22. $683 \div 8 = \underline{?}$ 23. $395 \div 6 = \underline{?}$

Divide. (Pages 78-81)

24. $4\overline{)896}$ 25. $5\overline{)726}$ 26. $8\overline{)9,376}$ 27. $7\overline{)3,017}$ 28. $9\overline{)46,876}$

29. $399 \div 5 = \underline{?}$ 30. $4,523 \div 3 = \underline{?}$ 31. $28,791 \div 7 = \underline{?}$

32. $425 \div 4 = \underline{?}$ 33. $6,208 \div 8 = \underline{?}$ 34. $30,243 \div 9 = \underline{?}$

Find the average. (Pages 82–83)

35. 60, 42, 18

36. 41, 50, 6, 103

37. 22, 37, 4, 97, 40

38. 3, 15, 30

39. 50, 16, 42, 52

40. 16, 6, 42, 17, 114

Divide. (Pages 84–85)

41. $50\overline{)370}$

42. $80\overline{)495}$

43. $70\overline{)631}$

44. $80\overline{)746}$

45. $40\overline{)1,300}$

46. $60\overline{)397}$

47. $30\overline{)256}$

48. $40\overline{)1,751}$

49. $50\overline{)4,782}$

50. $70\overline{)6,591}$

Divide. (Pages 90–93)

51. $25\overline{)640}$

52. $56\overline{)467}$

53. $38\overline{)274}$

54. $73\overline{)825}$

55. $85\overline{)906}$

56. $61\overline{)798}$

57. $42\overline{)597}$

58. $16\overline{)294}$

59. $29\overline{)385}$

60. $92\overline{)855}$

Divide. (Pages 94–95)

61. $38\overline{)3,245}$

62. $71\overline{)9,550}$

63. $50\overline{)4,185}$

64. $26\overline{)3,962}$

65. $85\overline{)9,337}$

66. $62\overline{)7,027}$

Divide. (Pages 96–97)

67. $18\overline{)26,145}$

68. $40\overline{)38,704}$

69. $82\overline{)56,234}$

70. $21\overline{)35,214}$

71. $37\overline{)41,006}$

72. $46\overline{)54,843}$

Divide. (Pages 98–99)

73. $425\overline{)3,819}$

74. $248\overline{)12,819}$

75. $642\overline{)145,253}$

76. $207\overline{)4,521}$

77. $332\overline{)16,285}$

78. $817\overline{)335,026}$

Part 3 • PROBLEM SOLVING • APPLICATIONS

79. Minneford's Hardware Store sells 12 golf balls for $9.65. How much would 3 dozen golf balls cost? (Pages 100–101)

81. The Rosewood Men's Club raised $1,450.00 for the Fourth of July picnic. How much more money do they need? (Pages 86–87)

83. Carlton motors sold 36 cars in January. They sold 27 cars and 18 trucks in February. How many more cars than trucks did they sell in February? (Pages 86–87)

80. The Carlton Civic Center has an 8-story parking garage which can hold 1,008 cars. Each level holds the same number of cars. How many cars can be parked on the third level? (Pages 100–101)

82. The Cidermill Restaurant places a basket of apples on each of their 36 tables. On Friday, they received 144 apples. How many apples could be equally placed in each basket? (Pages 100–101)

CHAPTER TEST

Divide.

1. $7\overline{)59}$

2. $6\overline{)357}$

3. $5\overline{)411}$

4. $8\overline{)3,659}$

5. $9\overline{)4,283}$

6. $7\overline{)3,562}$

7. $4\overline{)2,520}$

8. $20\overline{)178}$

9. $90\overline{)762}$

10. $26\overline{)92}$

11. $14\overline{)86}$

12. $51\overline{)3,264}$

13. $36\overline{)2,438}$

14. $46\overline{)3,851}$

15. $76\overline{)3,916}$

16. $27\overline{)3,893}$

17. $53\overline{)5,763}$

18. $61\overline{)7,389}$

19. $93\overline{)9,476}$

20. $125\overline{)85,636}$

21. $56,021 \div 402 = \underline{\quad ? \quad}$

22. This year there were 137 students who wrote books for the Carlton Library Young Authors program. The first year of the program, 76 students wrote books. How many more young authors were there this year?

23. The Carlton House Hotel employs 38 housekeepers and 12 office workers. The hotel has 266 guest rooms. Each housekeeper takes care of the same number of guest rooms. How many rooms are assigned to each housekeeper?

24. The Carlton Power Company replaces 11 poles each month. How many poles will be replaced in one year?

25. The Southland Telephone Company had 25,367 customers in January. They increased the number of customers in February. What additional information do you need to find the total number of customers at the end of February?

ENRICHMENT

Harry works at his parent's grocery store.
He makes $3.00 an hour.

● How much does he earn in 2 hours?   in 3 hours?   in 4 hours?

You can organize this data in a table.

Number of hours	1	2	3	4	5	6
Earnings	3	6	9	12	?	?

You can write an equation to show this.

Earnings = 3 × Number of hours

You can write this equation with letters.
Let e stand for earnings, and
let n stand for number of hours.

$$e = 3 \times n$$

To complete the table, replace n (number of hours) with 5.

$$e = 3 \times 5 = 15 \longleftarrow \text{He earned \$15.}$$

Now replace n with 6.

$$e = 3 \times 6 = 18 \longleftarrow \text{He earned \$18.}$$

Here is the
completed table.

n	1	2	3	4	5	6
e	3	6	9	12	15	18

Notice that all of the numbers in the e row are different. That is, no two numbers in the e row are the same. Because of this fact, the table describes a **function.** The equation is also a function.

EXERCISES • Use the equation to complete each table.

1. $r = 6 + s$

s	0	3	6	9	12
r	6	?	?	?	?

2. $g = 2 \times b$

b	2	4	6	8	10
g	4	?	?	?	?

3. $y = 10 - x$

x	2	4	6	8	10
y	8	?	?	?	?

ADDITIONAL PRACTICE

SKILLS

Divide.   (Pages 74–75)

1. $6\overline{)39}$ 2. $7\overline{)64}$ 3. $3\overline{)23}$ 4. $9\overline{)59}$ 5. $5\overline{)48}$

6. $5\overline{)29}$ 7. $8\overline{)51}$ 8. $6\overline{)41}$ 9. $5\overline{)33}$ 10. $9\overline{)88}$

Divide.   (Pages 76–77)

11. $8\overline{)92}$ 12. $4\overline{)57}$ 13. $7\overline{)65}$ 14. $3\overline{)19}$ 15. $6\overline{)97}$

16. $5\overline{)67}$ 17. $6\overline{)82}$ 18. $2\overline{)58}$ 19. $7\overline{)75}$ 20. $8\overline{)78}$

Divide.   (Pages 78–81)

21. $4\overline{)435}$ 22. $8\overline{)921}$ 23. $6\overline{)325}$ 24. $5\overline{)1,609}$ 25. $3\overline{)27,043}$

26. $7\overline{)659}$ 27. $4\overline{)175}$ 28. $5\overline{)3,405}$ 29. $3\overline{)2,960}$ 30. $8\overline{)35,722}$

Find the averages.   (Pages 82–83)

31. 16, 4, 45, 15   32. 32, 100, 18   33. 6, 8, 27, 43, 201

Divide.   (Pages 84–85)

34. $40\overline{)250}$ 35. $70\overline{)892}$ 36. $50\overline{)339}$ 37. $30\overline{)2,482}$ 38. $90\overline{)6,450}$

Divide.   (Pages 90–93)

39. $32\overline{)258}$ 40. $87\overline{)474}$ 41. $52\overline{)215}$ 42. $93\overline{)871}$ 43. $17\overline{)142}$

Divide.   (Pages 94–97)

44. $18\overline{)2,708}$ 45. $46\overline{)38,025}$ 46. $85\overline{)94,629}$

Divide.   (Pages 98–99)

47. $250\overline{)3,485}$ 48. $458\overline{)16,278}$ 49. $693\overline{)420,119}$

PROBLEM SOLVING • APPLICATIONS

50. Macklin Truck Sales receives 48 new pickup trucks and 57 new vans. They will display the trucks in 3 rows. Each row will have the same number of trucks. How many trucks will be in the first row?   (Pages 86–87)

51. The Carlton Bus Company carries an average of 2,076 passengers every day. At that rate, what is the total number of passengers they will carry in 7 days?   (Pages 100–101)

COMPUTER APPLICATIONS

Print Commands: * and /

The symbol for multiplication in BASIC is *.
On most computers, you must hold down the
SHIFT key and press the * key. On the
Commodore, you only have to press the * key.
Type this command.

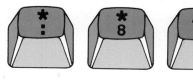

PRINT ⟋745*906 ⟍ Press the SPACE BAR to make this space.

Press **RETURN,** or **ENTER,** or ◄——⏋ to show the output, **674970.**

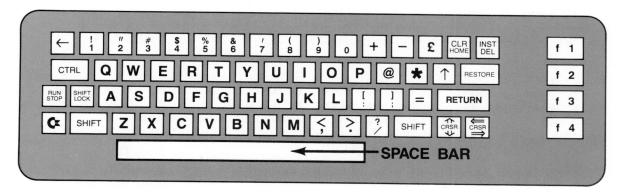

The symbol for division in BASIC is /. To type the /, you do
not have to hold down the **SHIFT** key. Simply press the / key.
Type this command.

PRINT 28116/198

Now press **RETURN,** or **ENTER,** or ◄——⏋to show the output, **142.**

EXERCISES • Find the output.

1. PRINT 2340/52

2. PRINT 748*287

3. PRINT 5297*462

4. PRINT 29106/198

5. PRINT 46601*938

6. PRINT 21353/163

Write a PRINT command that you would use to solve each problem.
Then solve the problem.

7. In one year (365 days), the Crown
Theater sold 359,890 tickets. What is
the average number of tickets sold in
one day?

8. The sixth-grade class collected 298
bags of aluminum cans. Each box
holds 54 cans. How many cans did
they collect in all?

MAINTENANCE

Chapters 1 through 4

Mixed Practice • Choose the correct answer.

1. 40 ⬤ 35

   A. >   **B.** =
   C. <   **D.** not here

2. 80 ⬤ 105

   A. =   **B.** >
   C. <   **D.** not here

3. 70 ⬤ 69

   A. <   **B.** >
   C. =   **D.** not here

4. Which number is the greatest?

   A. 440   **B.** 370
   C. 280   **D.** 410

5. Which number is the greatest?

   A. 815   **B.** 850
   C. 805   **D.** 855

6. Which number is the least?

   A. 600   **B.** 580
   C. 590   **D.** 630

7. Which number is the least?

   A. 345   **B.** 354
   C. 364   **D.** 435

8. Round 381 to the nearest ten

   A. 390   **B.** 380
   C. 400   **D.** not here

9. Estimate.
$228 + 785 = \underline{\quad?\quad}$

   A. 900   **B.** 800
   C. 1,000   **D.** not here

10. Subtract

$$\begin{array}{r} 100 \\ -\ 60 \\ \hline \end{array}$$

   A. 40
   B. 50
   C. 30
   D. not here

11. Subtract

$$\begin{array}{r} 49 \\ -18 \\ \hline \end{array}$$

   A. 33
   B. 21
   C. 31
   D. not here

12. Write in order from the least to the greatest.
486, 468, 586

   A. 586, 486, 468
   B. 468, 486, 586
   C. 486, 468, 586
   D. not here

13. $9 \times 10 = \underline{\quad?\quad}$

   A. 900   **B.** 90
   C. 9,000   **D.** not here

14. $8 \times 8 = \underline{\quad?\quad}$

   A. 64   **B.** 72
   C. 63   **D.** not here

15. What is the number indicated by the arrow?

   A. 7   **B.** 9
   C. 8   **D.** not here

16. Gail works in a photography studio. On Monday, she took 56 pictures. On Tuesday, she took 65 pictures, on Wednesday, she took 89 pictures. Which day did she take the fewest pictures?

   A. Monday   **B.** Thursday
   C. Tuesday   **D.** not here

17. The Glen County Zoo had about 12,000 visitors in June and about 17,000 visitors in July. About how many more visitors were there in July?

   A. 6,000   **B.** 5,000
   C. 4,000   **D.** not here

Graphing

Time	Temperature	Ordered Pair
6 A.M.	36°C	(6 A.M., 36°C)
10 A.M.	39°C	(10 A.M., 39°C)
2 P.M.	40°C	(2 P.M., 40°C)
6 P.M.	38°C	(6 P.M., 38°C)
10 P.M.	36°C	(10 P.M., 36°C)
2 A.M.	34°C	(2 A.M., 34°C)

The body temperatures of camels change to adjust to changes in temperature in the desert.

● Refer to the table to find how much a camel's body temperature changed from 6 A.M. to 10 A.M.

The red line in the graph shows the number of times each hour the male blue jay takes food to its young. The blue line shows the number of times each hour the female takes food to the young.

● During what period do the young receive food the same number of times from both parents?

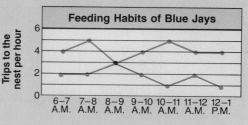

Feeding Habits of Blue Jays

Trips to the nest per hour

6–7 A.M. 7–8 A.M. 8–9 A.M. 9–10 A.M. 10–11 A.M. 11–12 A.M. 12–1 P.M.

Pictographs

A city zoo uses this **pictograph** as part of their mammal display.

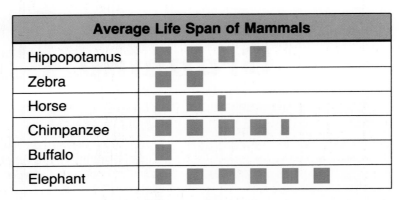

Each ■ stands for 10 years

● What is the average life span of a horse?

Think Each ■ stands for 10 years. Thus, two ■ equal 20 years.

Each ▌ stands for half of 10, or 5 years.

The average life span of a horse is **25 years.**

PRACTICE • Use the graph above to answer exercises 1 through 7.

1. Which mammal has the longest average life span?

2. Which mammal has the shortest average life span?

3. Compare the life spans of the hippopotamus and the chimpanzee. Which is longer?

What is the average life span of a

4. buffalo?　　　5. zebra?　　　6. hippopotamus?　　　7. chimpanzee?

EXERCISES • Use the graph below to answer exercises 8 through 13.

Life Span of Fish Each ■ stands for 6 years							
Perch	■	■					
Halibut	■	■	■	■	■	■	▌
Sole	■	■	▌				

8. Which fish has the longest life span?

9. Which fish has the shortest life span?

What is the life span of a

10. perch?   11. halibut?   12. sole?

13. About how much longer can a halibut expect to live than a sole?

Use the graph below to answer exercises 14–19.

Life Span of Birds	
Blue Jay	◖
Canada Goose	● ● ● ●
Condor	● ● ● ● ● ◖
Snowy Owl	● ● ●
Raven	● ● ● ● ● ● ● ◖

Each ● stands for 8 years

14. Which bird has the longest life span?

15. Which bird has the shortest life span?

What is the life span of a

16. Canada goose?   17. blue jay?   18. condor?

★ 19. The life span of an ostrich is 18 years less than the raven. What is the life span of an ostrich?

PROBLEM SOLVING • APPLICATIONS

20. Round each number in the table to the nearest ten.

★ 21. Use the rounded numbers to make a pictograph. Use △ to stand for 10 years.

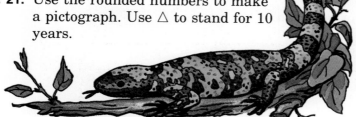

Life Span of Reptiles	
Kind	**Years**
Alligator	56
Gila Monster	20
Boa Constrictor	25
Box Turtle	123
Rattlesnake	18
Crocodile	13

Bar Graphs

There are 75 different kinds of whales. The table at the right shows the average lengths of some kinds of whales.

Whale	Average Length in Feet
Sei	55
Killer	30
Fin	80
Beluga	15
Bowhead	60
Blue	100

● The data from the table can be used to make a **bar graph.**

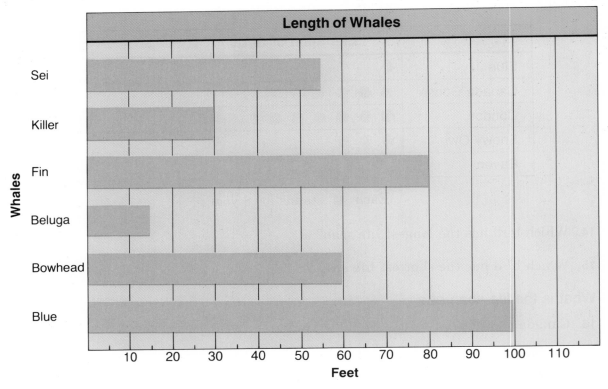

● Which whale has the longest average length?

Think   The longest bar is for the blue whale.

The **blue whale** is the longest whale.

PRACTICE • Use the bar graph above to answer Exercises 1 through 4.

1. Which whale is longer, beluga or bowhead?

2. Which whales are longer than sei whales?

3. Which whales are shorter than bowhead whales?

4. How long is a sei whale?

EXERCISES • Use the bar graph to answer Exercises 5 through 11.

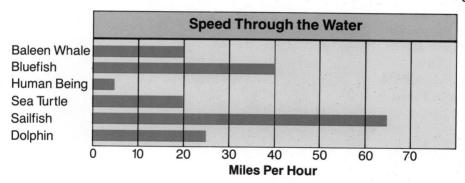

Speed Through the Water

Baleen Whale
Bluefish
Human Being
Sea Turtle
Sailfish
Dolphin

Miles Per Hour

Which can travel faster?

5. baleen whale or bluefish

6. sailfish or sea turtle

Which can travel

7. the fastest?

8. the slowest?

9. Which two can travel at the same speed?

10. A dolphin is a toothed whale. How much faster can a dolphin travel than a baleen whale?

★ **11.** How much longer than the dolphin would it take the baleen whale to travel a distance of 50 miles?

PROBLEM SOLVING • APPLICATIONS

Use the graph below to answer Exercises 12 through 15.

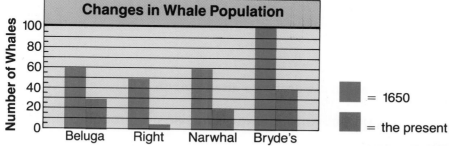

Changes in Whale Population

Number of Whales

Beluga   Right   Narwhal   Bryde's

= 1650

= the present

12. Which was the largest group of whales in 1650?

13. Which is presently the smallest group of whales?

14. Which group decreased by 40,000?

★ **15.** Which group had a decrease greater than the decrease in the number of right whales?

Graphs • 113

Line Graphs

In order to study the migration habits of birds, *mist nets* are used to capture them. This **line graph** shows the change in the number of species of birds captured daily for a 12–day period.

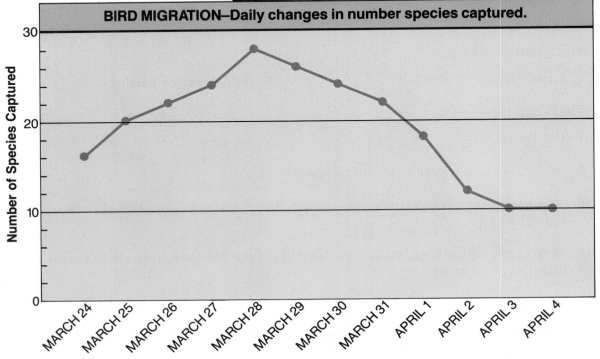

BIRD MIGRATION—Daily changes in number species captured.

(Number of Species Captured vs. MARCH 24, MARCH 25, MARCH 26, MARCH 27, MARCH 28, MARCH 29, MARCH 30, MARCH 31, APRIL 1, APRIL 2, APRIL 3, APRIL 4)

● After which day does the number of species captured begin to decrease?

Think The line **goes down** to show a decrease.

The number of species captured begins to decrease after **March 28.**

PRACTICE • Use the line graph above to answer Exercises 1 through 5.

1. On which day was the most species of birds captured?

2. On which days were the fewest species of birds captured?

3. On which days were more than 20 species captured?

4. On which days were fewer than 16 species captured?

5. On which days were the same number of species captured?

EXERCISES • Use the line graph below to answer Exercises 6 through 12.

The line graph below shows the number of blackcaps captured weekly in mist nets during spring migration.

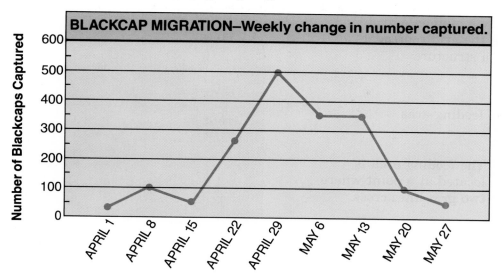

6. Which weeks did the number of captured blackcaps increase?

7. Which weeks were the greatest number of blackcaps captured?

8. Which weeks were more than 200 blackcaps captured?

9. Estimate the total number of blackcaps captured between April 1 and May 27.

PROBLEM SOLVING • APPLICATIONS

The red line shows the number of times each hour the male takes food to the young. The blue line shows the number of times each hour the female takes food to the young.

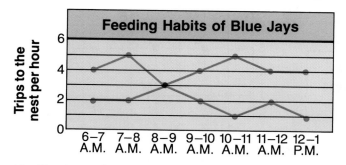

10. During what time period do the male and female blue jay take food to their young the same number of times?

11. During what time periods do the male blue jay's trips to the nest decrease?

★ 12. How many more trips than the female does the male blue jay make to the nest between 8 A.M. and 1 P.M.?

Graphing Ordered Pairs

A zoo plans to keep zebras, elands, and kudus in one section of the zoo. The zoo director drew a map on a grid. Each picture on the grid represents a tree, a pond, or a structure.

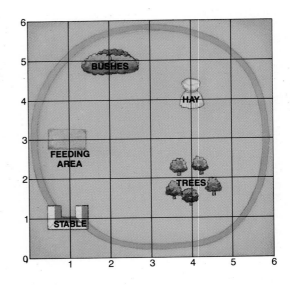

● Where is the feeding area located?

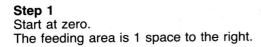

The feeding area is located at a point where two grid lines cross.

Step 1
Start at zero.
The feeding area is 1 space to the right.

Step 2
The feeding area is 3 spaces up.

The feeding area is located at the point where lines 1 and 3 intersect. This is point **(1,3)**.

The point (1,3) is an **ordered pair.**

● What letter is located at (6,5)?

Step 1
Count 6 spaces to the right.

Step 2
Count 5 spaces up.

The ordered pair (6,5) locates **point L.**

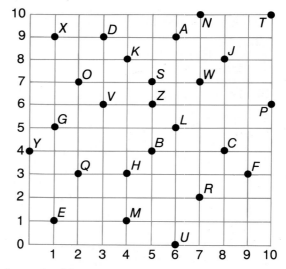

> *When using ordered pairs to locate a point:*
> *a. The first number means count to the right.*
> *b. The second number means count up.*

PRACTICE • Use the above grid for Exercises 1–40.
What letter is at each point?

1. (4, 1)   **2.** (7, 10)   **3.** (3, 9)   **4.** (4, 3)   **5.** (6, 9)

6. (9, 3)   **7.** (4, 8)   **8.** (2, 3)   **9.** (2, 7)   **10.** (10, 6)

11. (5, 4)   **12.** (7, 2)   **13.** (7, 7)   **14.** (8, 4)   **15.** (8, 8)

16. (5, 6)   **17.** (1, 1)   **18.** (3, 6)   **19.** (1, 5)   **20.** (10, 10)

What ordered pair tells the location of each point?

21. E   **22.** D   **23.** B   **24.** J   **25.** G

26. Q   **27.** A   **28.** M   **29.** H   **30.** R

31. X   **32.** C   **33.** K   **34.** U   **35.** T

36. Y   **37.** F   **38.** W   **39.** S   **40.** N

EXERCISES • Use the grid to answer Exercises 41 through 52.
What letter is at each point?

41. (1, 4)   **42.** (4, 0)   **43.** (4, 6)

44. (6, 3)   **45.** (3, 4)   **46.** (0, 1)

What ordered pair tells the location of each point?

47. F   **48.** Q   **49.** R

50. S   **51.** T   **52.** U

PROBLEM SOLVING • APPLICATIONS

Which ordered pair gives the location of the

53. stable?

54. trees?

55. feeding area?

56. hay pile?

57. bushes?

Use a sheet of graph paper. Locate the ordered pairs.
Draw a dot at each point. Label the points.

58.

POINT	ORDERED PAIR
A	(4, 8)
B	(7, 2)
C	(3, 3)
D	(1, 10)
E	(5, 0)

59.

POINT	ORDERED PAIR
S	(2, 3)
T	(3, 9)
U	(8, 7)
V	(6, 4)
W	(5, 9)

PROBLEM SOLVING • STRATEGIES

Using Line Graphs

Line graphs can help you solve problems.

Example

Camels are suited to desert life.
Their body temperature changes to
adjust to changes in the desert
temperature.

● How much does the camel's temperature change
between 6 A.M. and 6 P.M.?

Think   You need to find the temperature changes
which occur between 6 A.M. and 6 P.M.

You can make a line graph to answer the question.

Step 1: Use the information on the table as ordered pairs.
Step 2: Graph the ordered pairs. Connect the points
in order.

Time	Temperature	Ordered Pair
6 A.M.	36°C	(6 A.M., 36°C)
10 A.M.	39°C	(10 A.M., 39°C)
2 P.M.	40°C	(2 P.M., 40°C)
6 P.M.	38°C	(6 P.M., 38°C)
10 P.M.	36°C	(10 P.M., 36°C)
2 A.M.	34°C	(2 A.M., 34°C)

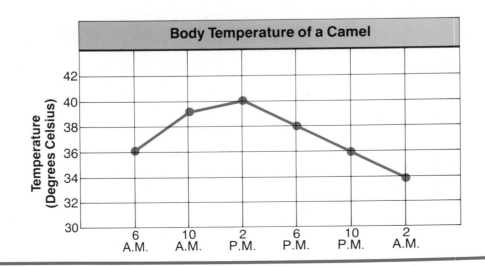

Body Temperature of a Camel

PROBLEMS

The table shows the changes in temperature on the Sahara Desert. The temperatures are shown in **degrees Fahrenheit** (°F). Use the table to make a line graph.

Time	Temperature
6 A.M.	50°F
10 A.M.	77°F
2 P.M.	104°F
6 P.M.	77°F
10 P.M.	59°F
2 A.M.	54°F

1. At what hour was the lowest temperature recorded?

2. At what hour was the highest temperature recorded?

3. During what time period does the temperature change the least?

4. What temperature changes take place between 10 A.M. and 2 P.M.?

When camels do not drink water, their body temperature changes greatly during one day.

5. At what time does the camel's body temperature show a decrease?

6. What is the difference between the camel's body temperature at midnight and at 3 A.M.?

7. Name two times when the camel's temperature is the same.

Time	Temperature	Time	Temperature
3 A.M.	93°F	3 P.M.	106°F
6 A.M.	99°F	6 P.M.	99°F
9 A.M.	102°F	9 P.M.	97°F
Noon	104°F	Midnight	95°F

The **range** in this table shows the lowest and highest temperature for 6 months of the year in Carlton.
The **median** (see page 89) is the middle reading when the temperatures are listed in order from lowest to highest.

8. Find the median temperature for each month.

9. During which month is the range:

   a. the greatest   b. the smallest.

10. Use graph paper and graph:

    a. the low temperatures
    b. the high temperatures
    c. the median temperatures

Month	Range	Median
Jan	47°F—55°F	51°F
Mar	52°F—66°F	?
May	59°F—75°F	?
July	63°F—83°F	?
Sept	57°F—69°F	?
Nov	51°F—61°F	?

CHAPTER REVIEW

Part 1 • VOCABULARY

For Exercises 1–4, choose from the box at the right the word(s) that complete the sentence.

1. A graph that uses pictures to show information is called a __?__. (Page 110)

2. A graph that uses points connected by lines to show information is called a __?__. (Page 114)

3. You can locate a point on a grid by using two numbers called an __?__. (Page 116)

4. A graph that uses shaded bars to show information is called a __?__. (Page 112)

bar graph
line graph
ordered pair
pictograph

Part 2 • SKILLS

Use the graph to answer the questions. (Pages 110–111)

5. Which reptile has the longest life span?

6. Which reptile has the shortest life span?

What is the life span of the

7. giant salamander?

8. toad?

9. alligator?

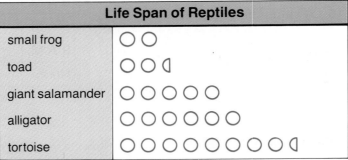

Life Span of Reptiles

Each ○ stands for 10 years.

Use the graph to answer the questions. (Pages 112–113)

10. How many more days does a peeper stay in the tadpole stage than a cricket frog?

How many days does each live as a tadpole?

11. American toad

12. pickerel frog

13. cricket frog

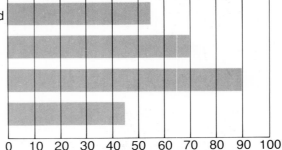

Length of Tadpole Stage (days)

14. Which frog lives as a tadpole the least number of days?

Use the graph for Exercises 15–19. (Pages 114–115)

How many paramecia are there on:

15. Monday?

16. Wednesday?

17. Friday?

18. During which days are there more than two paramecium?

19. How many more paramecia are there on Friday than on Tuesday?

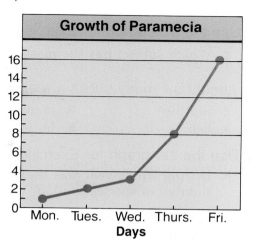

Use the grid at the right for Exercises 20–25. What letter is at each point? (Pages 116–117)

20. (1,5) **21.** (4,3) **22.** (5,0)

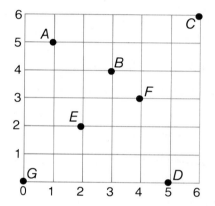

What ordered pair tells the location of each point? (Pages 116–117)

23. B **24.** C **25.** G

Part 3 • PROBLEM SOLVING • APPLICATIONS

26. Use the table. Make a pictograph. Use ▲ to stand for 2 inches.
(Pages 110–111)

Wing Span of Butterflies	
Monarch	4 inches
Giant Swallowtail	6 inches
Morning Cloak	3 inches
Roadside Skipper	1 inch

27. Use the table. Make a line graph. (Pages 114–115)

Date	Number of Bees Hatching
Jan. 1	3,000
Feb. 1	2,500
Mar. 1	3,500
Apr. 1	2,000

CHAPTER TEST

Use the pictograph for Exercises 1–5.

1. Which subject has the most books?

About how many books are about

2. reptiles?   3. mammals?
4. fish?   5. birds?

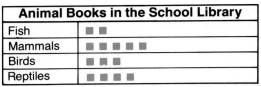

Animal Books in the School Library	
Fish	■ ■
Mammals	■ ■ ■ ■ ■
Birds	■ ■ ■
Reptiles	■ ■ ■ ■

Each ■ = 40 books

Use the bar graph for Exercises 7–11.

6. During which year was the largest number of species spotted?

7. During which year was the smallest number of species spotted?

8. During which year were there more than 30 species spotted?

9. During which year were there fewer than 20 species spotted?

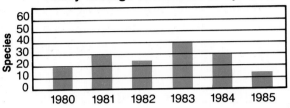

Bird Migration—
Yearly Change in Number of Species

10. In what years were the same number of species sighted?

Use the line graph for Exercises 12–17.

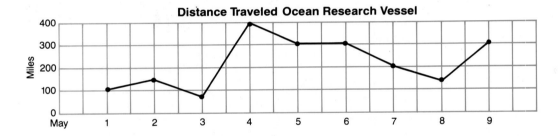

Distance Traveled Ocean Research Vessel

11. On what days did the ship travel the same number of miles?

12. On what days did the ship travel more than 200 miles a day?

13. On what days did the ship travel less than 200 miles a day?

14. On what day did the ship travel the greatest number of miles?

15. On what day did the ship travel the least number of miles?

16. Estimate the total number of miles traveled by the ship.

Use the grid for Exercises 18–25.
What letter is at each point?

17. (4, 2)   18. (3, 6)   19. (5, 3)   20. (1, 5)

What ordered pair tells the location of each point?

21. C   22. B   23. F

Day	Distance Traveled
1	20 miles
2	25 miles
3	15 miles
4	30 miles
5	18 miles

24. Use the table to make a line graph.

ENRICHMENT

The Histogram

A **histogram** is a special kind of bar graph.
To draw a histogram:

1. List the data by intervals.

2. Draw a rectangle to represent the count for each interval.

EXAMPLE: During Ecology Week, each student in Mrs. Gomez's class kept a record of the number of pounds of trash thrown away by his or her family.

Trash Thrown Away in One Week

Pounds of Trash	Number of Families
130–134	5
135–139	11
140–144	13
145–149	5
150–154	4
155–159	2

The data is shown in this histogram.

The **median** (see page 89) of each interval is at the center of the base of each bar in the graph. Each bar has the same width because each interval is the same "size".

EXERCISES • Make a nistogram to show the data.

1. **Diameters of 50 Trees**

Centimeters	Count
17–23	9
24–30	23
31–37	14
38–44	4

2. **Bowling Scores for One Week**

Scores	Count
121–140	2
141–160	14
161–180	10
181–200	1

ADDITIONAL PRACTICE

SKILLS

Use the graph for Exercises 1–5.
(Pages 110–111)

1. Which lizard is the shortest?

2. Which lizards are the same length?

What is the length of the

3. iguana?   4. reef gecko?   5. skink?

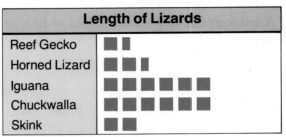

Length of Lizards

Reef Gecko	▪▪
Horned Lizard	▪▪▪
Iguana	▪▪▪▪▪
Chuckwalla	▪▪▪▪▪
Skink	▪▪

Each ▪ stands for 2 inches.

Use the graph for Exercises 6–9.
(Pages 112–113)

How fast does each insect fly?

6. housefly   7. wasp   8. dragonfly

9. How much slower does the housefly fly than the dragonfly?

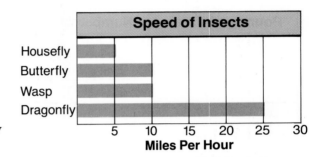

Speed of Insects

Miles Per Hour

Use the graph for Exercises 10–11.
The solid line stands for hares. The dotted line stands for lynxes. (Pages 114–115)

10. During which year did the number of hares decrease?

11. During which years did the number of lynxes increase?

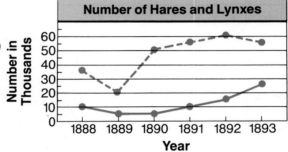

Number of Hares and Lynxes

Number in Thousands

Year

PROBLEM SOLVING • APPLICATIONS

12. Use the table. Make a pictograph. Use ○ to stand for 5 years. (Pages 110–111)

Life Span of Fish	
Guppy	5
Carp	50
Halibut	70
Sturgeon	100

13. Use the table. Make a line graph. (Pages 114–115)

Day	Bee's Trips to Gather Pollen
Mon.	20
Tues.	15
Wed.	35
Thurs.	10
Fri.	40

COMMON ERRORS

Each of these problems contains a common error.
a. Find the correct answer.
b. Find the error.

1. Write 4,302 in the expanded form.

$4,000 + 30 + 2$

2. Rounded 45,623 to the nearest thousand.

40,000

3. Write the number for 7^2.

$7^2 = 7 \times 2 = 14$

4. Add the numbers.

425, 57, 2354 and 210.

```
   425
    57
  2354
+  210
-------
12,514
```

5. Subtract

$800 - 329 = \underline{\ ?\ }$

```
 7  10 10
 8  0  0
-3  2  9
---------
 3  8  1
```

6. Write >, <, or =.

$73 + 34 \bullet 68 + 14$

<

7. Multiply.

$315 \times 7 = \underline{\ ?\ }$

```
    3
  315
×   7
------
2,475
```

8. Multiply.

$4,327 \times 6 = \underline{\ ?\ }$

```
 4,327
×    6
------
25962
```

9. Multiply.

$56 \times 27 = \underline{\ ?\ }$

```
   56
 ×27
-----
  392
  112
-----
  504
```

10. Divide.

$43 \div 6 = \underline{\ ?\ }$

```
    6 r7
6)43
  36
---
   7
```

11. Divide.

$3256 \div 8 = \underline{\ ?\ }$

```
     47
8)3256
  32
----
  056
   56
----
    0
```

12. Divide.

$3772 \div 6 = \underline{\ ?\ }$

```
   668 r4
6)3772
  36
----
  41
  36
----
  52
  48
----
   4
```

13. Divide.

$245 \div 31 = \underline{\ ?\ }$

```
    8 r5
31)245
   240
----
     5
```

14. Divide.

$197 \div 28 = \underline{\ ?\ }$

```
    6 r17
28)197
   180
----
    17
```

15. Divide.

$3528 \div 87 = \underline{\ ?\ }$

```
    4 r48
87)3528
   348
----
    48
```

CUMULATIVE REVIEW
Chapters 1 through 5

Choose the correct answers.

1. What number does the underlined digit name?

2<u>8</u>6,475

A. 8,000 **B.** 80,000
C. 800,000 **D.** not here

2. Write the number.

6,000 + 30 + 8

A. 6,308 **B.** 6,038
C. 638   **D.** not here

3. What digits are in the billions period?

476,239,851,902

A. 476 **B.** 851
C. 239 **D.** not here

4. Order the numbers from the least to the greatest.

2,385; 2,853; 2,583

A. 2,853 2,385 2,583
B. 2,583 2,385 2,853
C. 2,385 2,583 2,853
D. not here

5. Write the number.

3×10^4

A. 3,000
B. 300,000
C. 300
D. not here

6. Round 6,264,042 to the nearest hundred thousand.

A. 6,300,000
B. 6,260,000
C. 6,200,000
D. not here

7. Add.

4,687
+3,207

A. 7,884 **B.** 6,894
C. 7,894 **D.** not here

8. Subtract.

4,000
−3,291

A. 709   **B.** 1,709
C. 710   **D.** not here

9. Subtract.

7,268
−3,579

A. 3,679 **B.** 3,689
C. 3,789 **D.** not here

10. Add.

58,609
5,215
+364,364

A. 328,178 **B.** 428,188
C. 417,188 **D.** not here

11. Compare.

364 − 123 ● 231

A. >   **B.** =
C. <   **D.** not here

12. Subtract.

463,500
−31,826

A. 432,776 **B.** 432,684
C. 431,674 **D.** not here

13. Clarkstown has a population of 348,532. What is the population to the nearest ten thousand?

A. 350,000   **B.** 349,000
C. 340,000   **D.** not here

14. Lauren buys a pair of tennis shoes for $25.89. She gives the clerk $30.00. How much change does she get?

A. $5.21   **B.** $4.11
C. $14.11   **D.** not here

15. Multiply.

$$5{,}234 \times 5$$

- **A.** 26,050
- **B.** 26,170
- **C.** 25,070
- **D.** not here

16. Multiply.

$$486 \times 54$$

- **A.** 26,244
- **B.** 4,374
- **C.** 26,524
- **D.** not here

17. Multiply.

$$607 \times 234$$

- **A.** 131,038
- **B.** 142,078
- **C.** 142,038
- **D.** not here

18. Divide.

$$6\overline{)598}$$

- **A.** 90 r 1
- **B.** 98 r 1
- **C.** 98
- **D.** not here

19. Divide.

$$27\overline{)2{,}353}$$

- **A.** 80 r 3
- **B.** 87 r 4
- **C.** 87 r 6
- **D.** not here

20. Divide.

$$217\overline{)74{,}775}$$

- **A.** 349 r 89
- **B.** 349 r 81
- **C.** 339 r 79
- **D.** not here

21. Multiply.

$$96 \times 42 = \underline{\quad?\quad}$$

- **A.** 3,022　**B.** 2,732
- **C.** 4,032　**D.** not here

22. Divide.

$$136 \div 21 = \underline{\quad?\quad}$$

- **A.** 6 r 10　**B.** 7 r 1
- **C.** 6　　　**D.** not here

23. Divide.

$$4{,}329 \div 36 = \underline{\quad?\quad}$$

- **A.** 102 r 9　**B.** 120 r 9
- **C.** 120　　**D.** not here

24. How many candy bars did Sue sell?

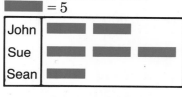

- **A.** 5　　**B.** 15
- **C.** 20　　**D.** not here

25. Find the average.

27, 65, 124, 84

- **A.** 150
- **B.** 100
- **C.** 75
- **D.** not here

26. How many votes did Mary receive?

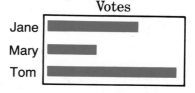

- **A.** 6　　**B.** 5
- **C.** 3　　**D.** not here

27. Tom unpacks 29 cartons of cereal boxes on Monday and 42 cartons on Tuesday. Estimate how many cartons he unpacked in all.

- **A.** 80
- **C.** 70
- **B.** 60
- **D.** not here

28. Mrs. Jones' car used 42 liters of gasoline on a 882 kilometer trip. How many kilometers did her car travel for each liter of gasoline?

- **A.** 21
- **C.** 31
- **B.** 20
- **D.** not here

MAINTENANCE

Mixed Practice • Choose the correct answers.

1. Which number is in the tens place?

6,341

A. 6   **B.** 3
C. 4   **D.** not here

2. Which number is in the hundreds place?

90,864

A. 9   **B.** 6
C. 0   **D.** not here

3. Which number is in the thousands place?

432,179

A. 1   **B.** 3
C. 2   **D.** not here

4. Which number is the greatest?

A. 61,311   **B.** 61,111
C. 61,131   **D.** 61,133

5. Which number is the least?

A. 4,681   **B.** 4,816
C. 4,618   **D.** 4,861

6. Round $18.33 to the nearest dollar.

A. $18   **B.** $19
C. $20   **D.** not here

7.
$$9,581 + 7,468$$

A. 16,949   **B.** 17,049
C. 16,059   **D.** not here

8.
$$36,118 + 65,403$$

A. 92,522   **B.** 91,521
C. 101,521   **D.** not here

9. $298 + 3,544 = \underline{\ ?\ }$

A. 3,842   **B.** 5,542
C. 5,524   **D.** not here

10.
$$6,534 - 1,718$$

A. 4,726   **B.** 4,816
C. 5,224   **D.** not here

11.
$$9,310 - 2,806$$

A. 6,516   **B.** 7,504
C. 6,504   **D.** not here

12.
$$6,000 - 4,386$$

A. 1,614   **B.** 1,724
C. 2,386   **D.** not here

13. The quarterback of the football team threw passes of 43 yards, 34 yards, and 38 yards in the game. What was the total yardage for the 3 passes?

A. 105   **B.** 115
C. 116   **D.** not here

14. Anthony threw the javelin 151 feet. Carl threw it 119 feet. How much farther did Anthony throw the javelin?

A. 270   **B.** 48
C. 32   **D.** not here

Decimals: Addition and Subtraction

Marathon runners prepare for a race by increasing the distance they run each week. The table shows a possible training schedule.

● How many miles will be run during the 5th, 6th, and 7th weeks?

Week	1	2	3	4	5	6	7
Miles Run	21	27	34	42	?	?	?

The total weight of a bobsled used for racing must be 350 pounds. The sled has a body and runners. The runners weigh 159 pounds.

● Write an equation you could use to find the weight of the body of the sled. Solve the equation.

Tenths and Hundredths

A swimming meet is held in a pool which is divided into 10 equal lanes. One lane is **one tenth** of the pool.

The shaded part may be named by a fraction or by a decimal.

fraction: $\frac{1}{10}$
decimal: 0.1
one tenth

fraction: $\frac{4}{10}$
decimal: 0.4
four tenths

You can use place value to show tenths.

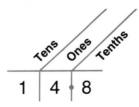

Read → fourteen **and** eight **tenths**
Read the decimal point as **and.**
Write → 14.8

There are bleachers on one side of the pool. There are a total of 100 seats. One seat is **one hundredth** of the total seats.

The shaded part may be named by a fraction or by a decimal.

fraction: $\frac{1}{100}$
decimal: 0.01
one hundredth

fraction: $\frac{27}{100}$
decimal: 0.27
twenty-seven hundredths

You can use place value to show hundredths.

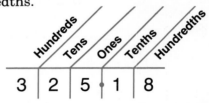

Read → three hundred twenty-five **and** eighteen **hundredths**
Write → 325.18

PRACTICE • Mental Math   Name the decimals that tell how much is blue.

1.

2.

3.

4.

Write a decimal for each fraction.

5. $\frac{3}{10}$ **6.** $14\frac{8}{10}$ **7.** $\frac{15}{100}$ **8.** $89\frac{67}{100}$ **9.** $9\frac{6}{100}$ **10.** $5\frac{4}{100}$

11. nine tenths **12.** fourteen hundredths **13.** six and one tenth

EXERCISES • Mental Math Name a decimal for each fraction.

14. $\frac{5}{10}$ **15.** $\frac{8}{10}$ **16.** $\frac{4}{100}$ **17.** $17\frac{38}{100}$ **18.** $4\frac{2}{10}$ **19.** $6\frac{9}{100}$

20. $6\frac{5}{100}$ **21.** $\frac{4}{10}$ **22.** $87\frac{7}{10}$ **23.** $98\frac{1}{100}$ **24.** $10\frac{49}{100}$ **25.** $42\frac{7}{10}$

26. nine hundredths **27.** fifty-six and four tenths

28. five thousand and fifty-four hundredths **29.** three hundred seven and eighty-two hundredths

30. seven tenths **31.** eight hundred forty and twelve hundredths

Write the decimals in words.

32. 146.1 **33.** 49.72

34. 7.03 **35.** 34.8

36. 14.01 **37.** 374.75

38. 9,010.6 **39.** 3,552.07

Complete the patterns.

40. 0.1 0.2 0.3 0.4 0.5 _?_ _?_ _?_ _?_ _?_ _?_

41. 0.91 0.92 0.93 _?_ _?_ _?_ _?_ _?_ _?_ _?_ _?_

⋆ **42.** 1.0 1.3 1.6 1.9 2.2 _?_ _?_ _?_ _?_ _?_ _?_

⋆ **43.** 10.7 10.3 9.9 9.5 9.1 _?_ _?_ _?_ _?_ _?_ _?_

⋆ **44.** 14.98 14.83 14.68 _?_ _?_ _?_ _?_ _?_ _?_ _?_ _?_

PROBLEM SOLVING • APPLICATIONS

45. The pool record for the 100–meter freestyle is forty-nine and three hundred thirty-five thousandths of a second. Write the word as a decimal.

46. During a diving competition, the judges gave one diver scores of 9.6, 9.5, and 9.2 for a back dive. Write the scores as words.

Thousandths

A marathon race has 1,000 runners competing for the first place trophy. *One* runner drops out of the race 10 minutes after the start. That runner is **1 thousandth** of the total number of runners competing in the race.

One thousandth can be written as a fraction or a decimal.

$\dfrac{1}{1,000}$ 0.001

ones	tenths	hundredths	thousandths
0	0	0	1

● You can use place value to show thousandths.

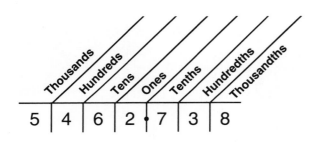

5	4	6	2	7	3	8

Read: five thousand, four hundred sixty-two **and** seven hundred thirty-eight **thousandths**

Write: 5,462.738

PRACTICE • **Mental Math**   Name the decimals.

1. $\dfrac{895}{1,000}$ 2. $3\dfrac{48}{1,000}$ 3. $16\dfrac{7}{1,000}$ 4. $107\dfrac{136}{1,000}$ 5. $2,325\dfrac{95}{1,000}$ 6. $445\dfrac{20}{1,000}$

7. twenty-seven thousandths

8. twelve and nineteen thousandths

9. nine thousandths

10. five hundred and sixteen thousandths

EXERCISES • **Mental Math**   Name the decimals.

11. $\dfrac{328}{1,000}$ 12. $7\dfrac{17}{1,000}$ 13. $438\dfrac{4}{1,000}$ 14. $8,421\dfrac{39}{1,000}$ 15. $\dfrac{92}{1,000}$

16. $200\dfrac{7}{1,000}$ 17. $3\dfrac{26}{1,000}$ 18. $205\dfrac{60}{1,000}$ 19. $7,234\dfrac{14}{1,000}$ 20. $\dfrac{3}{1,000}$

21. $8\dfrac{98}{100}$ 22. $15\dfrac{20}{100}$ 23. $560\dfrac{1}{10}$ 24. $8,516\dfrac{23}{100}$ 25. $\dfrac{565}{1,000}$

26. $2\dfrac{9}{1,000}$ 27. $3,535\dfrac{432}{1,000}$ 28. $96\dfrac{40}{1,000}$ 29. $379\dfrac{36}{1,000}$ 30. $\dfrac{738}{1,000}$

31. five thousandths

32. forty-three thousandths

33. six thousand, thirty-eight and ten thousandths

34. seven hundred ninety-six and fifty-two hundredths

35. twenty thousand, four hundred and three hundred seven thousandths

Complete the patterns.

★ **36.** 3.988 3.993 3.998 __?__ __?__ __?__ __?__ __?__

★ **37.** 2.064 2.056 2.048 __?__ __?__ __?__ __?__ __?__

Use the three digits and a decimal point to write 18 different numbers.

★ **38.** 6 4 8   ★ **39.** 1 2 4   ★ **40.** 7 3 5   ★ **41.** 9 6 1

PROBLEM SOLVING • APPLICATIONS

42. Write the Marathon Finish times in decimal form.

Fiesta Marathon Score Board

Place	Hours	Time/Minutes	Seconds
1	2	32	$28\frac{613}{1,000}$
2	2	32	$32\frac{186}{1,000}$
3	2	33	$46\frac{555}{1,000}$
4	2	33	$59\frac{999}{1,000}$
5	2	35	$12\frac{323}{1,000}$
6	2	36	$2\frac{793}{1,000}$

43. Rewrite the newspaper article so that the numbers are in decimal form.

Marathon races are becoming very competitive. In one recent race the winner was twelve and three hundred thirty–six thousandths seconds ahead of the third place finisher. Second place was six and five hundred sixteen thousandths seconds behind the winner. The tenth person to finish was only forty–nine and three hundred seventy–six thousandths seconds off the pace. Only five hundred fifty thousandths of a second separated the fourth and fifth place finishers.

Decimals and Place Value

The world's first automobile races were
held in France in 1894 and 1895. The
winning cars averaged about 24
kilometers per hour (**kph**). In 1983, a
rocket-propelled automobile set a
record of 1,019.440 kph.

● What is the value of each 4 in 1,019.440?

Think Use the place value chart to identify the place name.
Use the digit and the place name to give the value.

Millions	Hundred Thousands	Ten Thousands	Thousands	Hundreds	Tens	Ones	Tenths	Hundredths	Thousandths	Ten thousandths	Hundred thousandths	Millionths
			1	0	1	9.	4	4	0			

1019.440   Place name: **tenths**   Value: **0.4** ←— **four tenths**
1019.440   Place name: **hundredths**   Value: **0.04** ←— **four hundredths**

● Our system of naming numbers is called the **decimal system.**
Each place in a decimal has a value

   a. 10 times the value of the place at its right.
   b. 0.1 of the value of the place at its left.

● Decimals that name the same number are **equivalent decimals.**

   0.5 = 0.50 = 0.500   1.7 = 1.70 = 1.700

PRACTICE • In what place is each underlined digit?

   1. 25.613   **2.** 37.946   **3.** 54.258   **4.** 246.088   **5.** 63.472

What number does each underlined digit name?

   6. 92.851   **7.** 30.789   **8.** 26.735   **9.** 343.004   **10.** 582.341

EXERCISES • In which place is each underlined digit?

   11. 1.936   **12.** 21.483   **13.** 498.325   **14.** 6,432.363   **15.** 9.548

16. 5.042   **17.** 54.971   **18.** 135.006   **19.** 3,535.198   **20.** 3,384.212

What number does each underlined digit name?

21. 2.672   **22.** 85.304   **23.** 548.652   **24.** 3,005.235   **25.** 54.208

26. 9.585   **27.** 27.216   **28.** 415.806   **29.** 7,723.008   **30.** 621.742

31. 4.684   **32.** 43.301   **33.** 540.016   **34.** 4,716.695   **35.** 6,584.271

In which number does the digit 5 have the greatest value?

36. 26.5   **37.** 16.526   **38.** 432.153   **39.** 8,451.77   **40.** 3,764.051
      265   15.626   432.5   8,541.77   3,764.005

Write decimals that name the same number.

41. 0.6 = 0.60 = ___?___   **42.** 1.5 = 1.50 = ___?___   **43.** 41.3 = 41.30 = ___?___

44. 3.7 = ___?___ = 3.700   **45.** ___?___ = 2.80 = 2.800   **46.** ___?___ = 95.20 = 95.200

47. 9.1 = ___?___ = ___?___   **48.** ___?___ = ___?___ = 5.100   **49.** 67.5 = ___?___ = ___?___

★ **50.** 8.45 = ___?___ = ___?___   ★ **51.** ___?___ = 2.640 = ___?___   ★ **52.** 95.29 = ___?___ = ___?___

★ **53.** ___?___ = 5.360 = ___?___   ★ **54.** 3.76 = ___?___ = ___?___   ★ **55.** ___?___ = 32.890 = ___?___

PROBLEM SOLVING • APPLICATIONS

56. The fastest speed by an automobile around a track is 250.958 mph. Write the place value for each of the digits.

57. Two race drivers finish a race in first and second place. The winner averages 132.763 mph. The second place finisher averages 132.673 mph. What is the place value of each of the digits which are different for the two drivers?

58. In 1984, Rick Mears won the Indianapolis 500 race. His speed in miles per hour has a 1 in the hundreds place, a 6 in the tens place, a 3 in the ones place, a 6 in the tenths place, and a 1 in the hundredths place. What was the speed?

59. The world speed record in miles per hour for rocket powered cars has a 6 in the hundreds place, a 3 in the tens place and in the ones place, a 4 in the tenths place, a 6 in the hundredths place, and an 8 in the thousandths place. What was the speed?

Comparing and Ordering Decimals

A speed skater raced 500 meters in 39.44 seconds. Another skater raced 500 meters in 39.17 seconds.

 Which one was faster?

Think   You must **compare** the decimals.

39.44 39.17

Step 1
Compare the tens.

Think: $3 = 3$

Step 2
Compare the ones.

Think: $9 = 9$

Step 3
Compare the tenths

Think: $4 > 1$

39.44 > 39.17

The skater with the **39.17 seconds time was faster.**

 Compare 0.41 and 0.415.

Step 1
Compare the tenths.

Think: $4 = 4$

Step 2
Compare the hundredths.

Think: $1 = 1$

Step 3
Compare the thousandths.

Think: $0 < 5$

0.41 < 0.415

 Write these speed-skating times in order from least to greatest.

43.4   40.2   43.1

Think $40.2 < 43.1$
$43.1 < 43.4$

So **40.2 < 43.1 < 43.4.**

PRACTICE • Write $>$, $<$, or $=$ to make a true sentence.

1. 0.22 0.37

2. 8.01 8.1

3. 92.6 92.56

4. 0.273 2.73

5. 6.75 6.7

6. 46.41 4.64

7. 0.964 0.97

8. 9.98 9.980

9. 72.03 72.3

EXERCISES • Write >, <, or = to make a true sentence.

10. 19.85 ⬤ 18.9   **11.** 4.035 ⬤ 4.3   **12.** 36.060 ⬤ 36.06

13. 84.64 ⬤ 86.46   **14.** 9.099 ⬤ 9.99   **15.** 45.7 ⬤ 45.57

16. 33.94 ⬤ 34.0   **17.** 6.6 ⬤ 6.066   **18.** 70.08 ⬤ 70.7

19. 7.700 ⬤ 7.70   **20.** 25.8 ⬤ 25.9   **21.** 88.124 ⬤ 88.421

22. 96.550 ⬤ 96.55   **23.** 8.889 ⬤ 8.888   **24.** 68.050 ⬤ 68.05

Which is greater?

25. 6.4 m or 6.0 m   **26.** 2.2 km or 3.1 km   **27.** 9.0 cm or 9.1 cm

28. 37.5 cm or 38.0 cm   **29.** 18.4 km or 14.8 km   **30.** 16.4 cm or 14.6 cm

Write in order from least to greatest.

31. 7.06, 7.059, 7.013   **32.** 18.047, 1.8450, 18.046

★ **33.** 26.073, 20.673, 25.898, 2.976, 2.959   ★ **34.** 8.063, 80.002, 8.603, 80.01, 80.009

PROBLEM SOLVING • APPLICATIONS

Compare the decimals. Use >, <, or = to write a true sentence.

35. Two brothers, Peter and Roger, competed in a 3,000-meter speed-skating event. At the end of the first 100-meters, Peter's time is 10.836 seconds, and Roger's time is 10.387 seconds.

36. At the end of an international speed skating competition, the winner had earned 121.386 points. Second place was won with 121.322 points.

CALCULATOR • Ordering Decimals

1. Use a calculator to complete the chart.
2. List the finishing order, from first to last.

Event ___500 Meters___ Lap Times/Total Time (Seconds)

Name	First	Second	Third	Fourth	Fifth	Total Time
Bonono	8.516	7.919	8.379	8.772	9.052	
Graham	8.217	8.446	8.046	8.296	9.909	
Sylvester	8.371	8.471	8.917	8.593	7.947	
Manfred	8.006	8.392	8.251	8.641	8.983	
Stumph	7.871	8.488	8.436	8.576	8.927	

Rounding Decimals · Mental Math

Dr. Allan V. Abbott set the speed record for a bicycle at
the Bonneville Salt Flats, Utah, on August 25, 1973. His
speed was 138.8 miles per hour.

● Round his speed to the nearest whole number.

Think: Use a number line.

His speed was about **139 miles per hour.**

Rounding Without A Number Line

To round decimals, look at the digit to the right
of the place to which you are rounding.

a. When the digit is 5 or more, round <u>up</u>.
b. When the digit is less than 5, round <u>down</u>.

Leon Vanderstuyft of Belgium rode 76.2864 miles
to set a record for the greatest distance traveled
on a bicycle in 1 hour.

● Round this distance to the nearest:

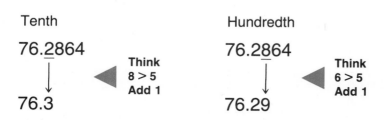

Tenth	Hundredth	Thousandth
76.2864	76.2864	76.2864
Think 8 > 5 Add 1	Think 6 > 5 Add 1	Think 4 < 5 No change
76.3	76.29	76.286

PRACTICE • Round to the nearest whole number.

1. 3.52   **2.** 6.20   **3.** 18.75   **4.** 326.14

Round to the nearest tenth.

5. 6.68   **6.** 9.24   **7.** 25.09   **8.** 459.83

Round to the nearest hundredth.

9. 8.065   **10.** 6.433   **11.** 72.011   **12.** 520.068

EXERCISES • Round to the nearest whole number.

13. 4.5 **14.** 9.06 **15.** 5.123 **16.** 6.4

17. 7.47 **18.** 8.674 **19.** 25.9 **20.** 35.12

Round to the nearest tenth.

21. 7.26 **22.** 2.60 **23.** 4.55 **24.** 6.41 **25.** 5.06

26. 56.35 **27.** 85.69 **28.** 592.55 ★ **29.** 355.96 ★ **30.** 731.98

Round to the nearest hundredth.

31. 2.648 **32.** 6.002 **33.** 8.407 **34.** 3.502 **35.** 9.364

36. 84.111 **37.** 63.863 **38.** 143.105 **39.** 161.989 ★ **40.** 400.999

Round to the nearest thousandth.

41. 0.001429 **42.** 0.00973 **43.** 0.24654

44. 39.0983 **45.** 74.9216 **46.** 58.9332

Round to the nearest ten thousandth.

★ **47.** 9.130475 ★ **48.** 14.261132 ★ **49.** 58.1967349

PROBLEM SOLVING • APPLICATIONS

50. About 100 years ago, a bicycle known as a "high wheeler" had a front wheel which had a diameter of 1.5 meters. A modern racing bike has a wheel which has a diameter of 0.686 meters. Estimate the difference between the two diameters to the nearest tenth.

51. One of the longest single-day bicycle races is from Bristol to Bradford, England. A racer completes 109.86 miles before stopping to have lunch. There are 136.24 miles left to race. Estimate the total length of the race to the nearest hundredth.

52. The most famous bicycle race in the world is the Tour de France. The course runs through the French countryside. The race lasts about 21 days. A racer drops out after 1,934.632 miles, or 1,040.368 miles short of the finish. Estimate the total distance of the race to the nearest hundredth.

53. In 1982, Lon Haldeman rode a bicycle from California to New York in 236.03 hours. In the same year, Susan Notorongelo made the same trip in 280.4 hours. Estimate the difference to the nearest hour.

PROBLEM SOLVING · STRATEGIES

Finding Patterns

Some problems can be solved by finding a pattern.

Example

Marathon runners prepare for a race by increasing the distance they run each week. The table shows a possible schedule for training.

Week	1	2	3	4	5	6	7
Miles Run	21	27	34	42	?	?	?

● How many miles will be run during weeks 5, 6, and 7?

Think Find the number pattern.

$$21 \quad 27 \quad 34 \quad 42$$
$$\quad +6 \quad +7 \quad +8$$

Rule: Start with 21 (Week 1).

Week 2 = Week 1 + **6**
Week 3 = Week 2 + **7**
Week 4 = Week 3 + **8**

This is the pattern of addends.

6, 7, 8, 9, 10, 11, 12, ···

This leads to the solution.

Week 5: 42 ⟵ **Week 4**
                + 9
            51 miles

Week 6: 51 ⟵ **Week 5**
                +10
            61 miles

Week 7: 61 ⟵ **Week 6**
                +11
            72 miles

PROBLEMS • Complete the pattern.

1. 3, 6, 9, 12, _?_ _?_ _?_ _?_

2. 2, 4, 6, 8, _?_ _?_ _?_ _?_

3. 15, 13, 11, 9, _?_ _?_ _?_ _?_ HINT: The numbers decrease. Subtract.

4. 2, 4, 8, 16, _?_ _?_ _?_ _?_ HINT: The numbers increase. Do you multiply or add?

Find the pattern. Solve each problem.

5. How many miles will the marathon runner plan to run for weeks 8, 9 and 10? Use the table in the example.

6. A beginning runner uses a computer to plan the training program. Find the miles run for week 6, 7, and 8.

Week	Miles Run
2	3
3	8
4	15
5	24

Compare the information. Is there a pattern?

7. A city recreation department plans to build running trails in the city parks. They prepare a 7-year plan. Find the pattern and complete the plan.

Year	1	2	3	4	5	6	7
Km of Trails	2	3	5	9	?	?	?

8. The athletic department of a high school builds a triangular obstacle course. Each year they add more obstacles as shown below. How many obstacles will they have added after four years?

First Year   Second Year   Third Year

9. A track club sponsors a 10,000–meter run. They accept entries for 6 weeks. The first week they receive 2 entries. The second week they receive 27 entries. The third week they receive 57 entries. The fourth week they receive 92 entries. At this rate, how many entries will they receive in weeks 5 and 6?

10. Two track clubs hold a track meet. The numbers 1, 4, 9, 16, and 25 are given to 5 Sandpipers. The Sandpipers need two more numbers. Which of the following numbers can they use? 48, 36, 49, 51, 55

MID-CHAPTER REVIEW

Write a decimal for each of the following. (Pages 130–133)

1. $5\frac{8}{10}$

2. $27\frac{4}{10}$

3. $89\frac{13}{100}$

4. $4{,}280\frac{27}{1{,}000}$

5. $629\frac{479}{1{,}000}$

6. five and nineteen hundredths

7. three hundred and thirteen thousandths

Write each decimal in words.
(Pages 130–133)

8. 45.3

9. 474.45

10. 28.07

11. 8.428

12. 465.023

In which place is each underlined digit? (Pages 134–135)

13. 1.8̲25

14. 452̲.71

15. 16.093̲

16. 0.82̲7

17. 2̲49.5

What number does each underlined digit name? (Pages 134–135)

18. 2.3̲5

19. 6.73̲

20. 14.92̲6

21. 48.995̲

22. 1̲,683.303

Write <, >, or = to make a true sentence. (Pages 136–137)

23. 13.05 ⬤ 13.50

24. 0.655 ⬤ 0.565

25. 142.3 ⬤ 142.30

Round 9.9607 to the nearest (Pages 138–139)

26. tenth

27. hundredth

28. thousandth

29. whole number

Complete the pattern. (Pages 140–141)

30. 15, 19, 23, 27, _?_, _?_, _?_, _?_

31. 2, 7, 13, 20, _?_, _?_, _?_, _?_

32. 3, 9, 27, 51, _?_, _?_, _?_, _?_

33. Jon practiced the hammer throw on May 2, 4, 7, and May 11. He practiced with the shot put on May 3, 4, 6, and 9. What is the next day he will practice the hammer throw? With the shot put?

MAINTENANCE • MIXED PRACTICE

Add, subtract, multiply, or divide.

1. $142 + 67 + 1{,}502 = $ _?_

2. $960 + 3 + 12{,}795 = $ _?_

3. $701 \times 12 = $ _?_

4. $3{,}621 - 738 = $ _?_

5. 645×206 _?_

6. $9{,}000 - 1{,}528 = $ _?_

7. Find the average: 100, 78, 91, 101, 125, 81

8. A theater sold 237 children's tickets for a total of $651.75. They sold 345 adult tickets for a total of $1,293.75. Estimate the total sales to the nearest dollar.

9. There are 20 people waiting to take a helicopter ride. How many trips must the helicopter make? What additional information do you need to solve the problem?

CONSUMER APPLICATIONS

Estimating a Bill

Ann Jefferson orders three books through her class book club. The class treasurer tells her she owes $15.96.

● Was the treasurer correct?

You can check the bill by using **front–end estimation.**

Readers Book Club		
Domingo	$4.19	☑
Sally's Song	$2.95	☑
The Book of Tricks	$3.65	☐
Tales of The Herndons	$2.75	☐
How To Live With Your Dog	$3.15	☑
Your Face, Your Future	$2.98	☐
Baseball's Greatest Hits	$3.69	☐

Step 1
Add the dollars.

$$\begin{array}{r} \$4.00 \\ 2.00 \\ +\ 3.00 \\ \hline \$9.00 \end{array}$$

Step 2
Round to the nearest ten cents.
Add the cents.

$\$0.19 \longrightarrow \$0.20$
$0.95 \longrightarrow 1.00$
$0.15 \longrightarrow 0.20$
$\hline \$1.40$

Step 3
Add the dollars and cents.

$$\begin{array}{r} \$9.00 \\ +\ 1.40 \\ \hline \$10.40 \end{array}$$ ◄ **Estimated total cost**

Since $\$10.40 < \$15.96$, the treasurer was **incorrect.**

ⓔ EXERCISES • Choose the best estimate. Choose a, b, or c.

1. $3.97 + $6.42   **a.** $10 + $1.40   **b.** $9 + $1.20   **c.** $9 + $1.40

2. $5.33 + $7.75   **a.** $12 + $1.20   **b.** $13 + $.90   **c.** $12 + $1.10

3. Ann Chen buys a two–book set for $7.85 and one book for $3.12. Estimate the total bill.

   a. $10.80   **b.** $11.00   **c.** $11.35

4. Leroy Dockery orders one sports book for $2.89 and an almanac for $5.65. Estimate the total bill.

   a. $8.40   **b.** $7.60   **c.** $8.60

5. Sandra Leopold orders a 3–book spy series for $9.36, an animal book for $2.75, and a magic book for $1.86. Estimate her total bill.

   a. $14.70   **b.** $14.80   **c.** $14.10

PROJECT   Collect six receipts from shopping trips. Estimate the total bill. Compare the estimate with the actual total.

Adding Decimals

A long distance swimmer practices twice a day. One morning he swims 4.36 kilometers. In the afternoon he swims 2.89 kilometers.

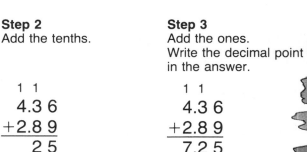

● How many kilometers does he swim in all?

Think **In all** means to add or multiply. Given the kilometers for the morning and afternoon, you must **add.**

$$4.36 + 2.89 = ?$$

Estimate first. 4 kilometers plus 3 kilometers equals 7 kilometers. The answer is about 7.

Step 1	Step 2	Step 3
Line up the decimal points. Add the hundredths.	Add the tenths.	Add the ones. Write the decimal point in the answer.

```
    1              1 1            1 1
   4.3 6          4.3 6          4.3 6
 + 2.8 9        + 2.8 9        + 2.8 9
  ------         ------         ------
       5            2 5          7.2 5
```

The estimate is 7 kilometers. Therefore, **7.25 kilometers** is reasonable.

● $8.59 + 4.928 = ?$

Step 1	Step 2	Step 3	Step 4
Line up the decimal points. **Think:** 8.59 = 8.590. Add the thousandths.	Add the hundredths.	Add the tenths.	Add the ones. Write the decimal point.

```
                      1              1 1            1 1
   8.5 9 0          8.5 9 0        8.5 9 0        8.5 9 0
 + 4.9 2 8        + 4.9 2 8      + 4.9 2 8      + 4.9 2 8
  --------         --------       --------       --------
         8              1 8          5 1 8       1 3.5 1 8
```

PRACTICE • Add.

1. 3.8 +5.5	**2.** 16.11 +25.92	**3.** 8.7 +6.51	**4.** 23.1 + 4.95	**5.** 98.07 +57.385

EXERCISES • Add.

6. 0.8 +0.5	**7.** 21.7 +67.9	**8.** 8.9 +6.7	**9.** 9.6 +8.0	**10.** 562.9 + 49.3

11. 2.37 +5.12	**12.** 8.31 +7.70	**13.** 54.57 +38.03	**14.** 816.018 + 13.55	**15.** 319.08 + 0.47

16. 6.682 2.316 +4.745	**17.** 8.756 6.297 +2.214	**18.** 3.049 5.106 +8.994	**19.** 1.357 2.876 +7.245	**20.** 8.995 4.760 +2.075

21. 12.95 17.3 8.246 + 6.9	**22.** 15.6 7.8 10.365 + 0.84	**23.** 43.67 812.55 8.1 + 5.67	**24.** 0.1 21.976 98.02 + 0.338	**25.** 198.1 45.06 713.948 + 0.799

26. 9.57 + 3.4 = ___?___

27. 29.9 + 391.0 = ___?___

28. 8.9 + 0.76 + 3.075 = ___?___

29. 1.568 + 8.870 + 16.4 = ___?___

Write >, <, or = to make a true sentence.

★ **30.** 5.321 + 6.007 ⬤ 11.328

★ **31.** 1.50 + 9.78 ⬤ 12.28

★ **32.** 12.873 + 6.445 ⬤ 18.318

★ **33.** 3.82 + 5.50 ⬤ 9.32

PROBLEM SOLVING • APPLICATIONS

CHOOSE • mental math • pencil and paper • calculator SOLVE

34. In 1961, Antonio Abertondo swam from England to France in 18.833 hours. After a 4 minute rest, he swam back to England in 24.267 hours. How many hours did he swim in all?

35. A swim relay sets a record for the 4 × 100 meter relay. The times for each leg were 49.89, 51.03, 50.48, and 48.92. What was the total time for the relay team?

36. In 1977, Cindy Nicholas swam from England to France and returned to England in a total of 19.83 hours. In 1875, the first person to swim one way from England to France took 1.92 hours longer. What was the person's time?

★ **37.** The route for a swim marathon has four parts. The last part is 2.9 kilometers long. The third part is 0.5 kilometers longer than the last part. The second part is 0.7 kilometers longer than the third part. The first part is 0.8 kilometers longer than the fourth part. What is the total distance of the race?

THINKER'S CORNER

In a European Men's 1,500–meter swimming race, Gary Wiatt finished 1.3 seconds ahead of Pierre de Bolle. De Bolle did not finish last. Lars Nordin finished 1.5 seconds ahead of Franz Schmidt and 1.2 seconds behind Wiatt. Nordin finished 1.4 seconds behind Ky Chung. In what order did they finish?

Subtracting Decimals

The elementary schools in Castleton hold a field day each year. This year the record for the pole vault was broken when the winner vaulted 4.05 meters. The first record, set 10 years ago, was 2.89 meters.

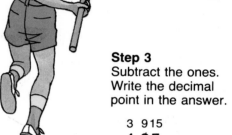

● What is the difference between the two records?

Think   **Difference** means to subtract.
4.05 − 2.89 = ?

Estimate first.

4 meters minus 3 meters equals 1 meter.

The answer is about 1.

Step 1
Line up the decimal points.
Subtract the hundredths.

$$
\begin{array}{r}
3\ 915 \\
4.0\cancel{5} \\
-2.89 \\
\hline
6
\end{array}
$$

Step 2
Subtract the tenths.

$$
\begin{array}{r}
3\ 915 \\
4.0\cancel{5} \\
-2.89 \\
\hline
16
\end{array}
$$

Step 3
Subtract the ones.
Write the decimal point in the answer.

$$
\begin{array}{r}
3\ 915 \\
4.0\cancel{5} \\
-2.89 \\
\hline
1.16
\end{array}
$$

The estimate is 1 meter. Therefore, **1.16 meters** is reasonable.

Sometimes it is necessary to annex zeros.

● 9.27 − 3.845 = ?

Step 1
Line up the decimal points.
Think: 9.27 = 9.270.
Subtract the thousandths.

$$
\begin{array}{r}
6\ 10 \\
9.2\cancel{7}\cancel{0} \\
-3.845 \\
\hline
5
\end{array}
$$

Step 2
Subtract the hundredths.

$$
\begin{array}{r}
6\ 10 \\
9.2\cancel{7}\cancel{0} \\
-3.845 \\
\hline
25
\end{array}
$$

Step 3
Subtract the tenths and ones.
Write the decimal point.

$$
\begin{array}{r}
8\ 126\ 10 \\
\cancel{9}.\cancel{2}\cancel{7}\cancel{0} \\
-3.845 \\
\hline
5.425
\end{array}
$$

PRACTICE • Subtract.

1. 8.7
−2.3

2. 9.35
−4.73

3. 19.15
− 6.50

4. 7.1
−3.459

5. 16
− 2.163

EXERCISES • Subtract.

6. 146.7
    − 82.8

7. 371.2
    − 45.6

8. 387.6
    −149.9

9. 16.5
    −11.6

10. 100.4
    − 97.9

11. 10.36
    − 5.38

12. 5.89
    −1.8

13. 19.15
    − 7.65

14. 86.12
    − 8.8

15. 6.78
    −5.07

16. 0.011
    −0.007

17. 0.975
    −0.460

18. 0.49
    −0.184

19. 3.047
    −1.829

20. 15
    − 3.644

21. 416.4
    − 11.468

22. 58.164
    − 2.09

23. 14.42
    − 5.247

24. 18.87
    − 4.5

25. 32.9
    −16.46

26. 9.8 − 2.4 = ___?___

27. 3.1 − 1.7 = ___?___

28. 91.43 − 77.68 = ___?___

29. 45 − 36.99 = ___?___

30. 567 − 36.982 = ___?___

31. 645.362 − 289.86 = ___?___

PROBLEM SOLVING • APPLICATIONS

32. In 1958, at age 35, Dana Zatopkya threw a javelin 182.83 feet to become the oldest woman to set a world record. In 1983, the women's record for the javelin throw was 245.25 feet. What is the difference between the two records?

33. In 1977, Duncan McLean, at age 92, ran a 100-meter race in 21.7 seconds to set a world record. In 1904, he had run a 100-yard race in 9.9 seconds. What is the difference between the two times?

34. A women's relay team sets a track meet record. The slowest runner on the team ran her lap in 11.01 seconds. Compared to the slowest runner, one team member ran 0.59 seconds faster. A second team member was 0.02 seconds faster. The third team member was 0.33 seconds faster. What was the total time for all four laps?

★ 35. At the end of a 1,500 meter run, the fourth place finisher was 15.8 meters behind the winner. The second place finisher was 9.7 meters behind the leader. The third place runner was 3.3 meters behind the second place runner. How far was the fourth place runner from the third place runner?

PROJECT Find the records for each summer Olympic games from 1896 to 1984 in an encyclopedia. Find the difference between the winning time in 1896 and 1984 for the following events (m is meters): Men's 100−m run, 400−m run, 400−m hurdles, 400−m relay. Women's 100−m run, 400−m run, 400−m relay, 100−m hurdles.

PROBLEM SOLVING · STRATEGIES

Using Equations: Addition and Subtraction

Example 1

A bobsled team is building a sled. The sled must be lightweight. They want to use front runners weighing 75 pounds and rear runners weighing 84 pounds.

● What is the total weight of both sets of runners?

Think Word Rule: Total weight = $\dfrac{\text{Weight of}}{\text{front runners}}$ + $\dfrac{\text{Weight of}}{\text{rear runners}}$

This can be written as a number sentence. A number sentence is an **equation.**

Step 1 Write an equation.

Let n = total weight ⟵ **The unknown**
$n = 75 + 84$

Step 2 Solve the equation.

n = 75 + 84
n = 159

Example 2

A sled consists of runners and a body. The total weight of the sled must be 350 pounds. The runners weigh 159 pounds.

● What must the body of the sled weigh?

Think Word Rule: $\dfrac{\text{Weight of}}{\text{the body}}$ = Total weight − $\dfrac{\text{Weight of}}{\text{the runners}}$

Step 1 Write an equation.

Let n = weight of the body
$n = 350 - 159$

Step 2 Solve the equation.

n = 350 − 159
n = 191

The body must weigh **191 pounds.**

PROBLEMS • Choose the equation you could use to solve the problem.

1. An English figure skater scores 96.3 points in the first event and 87.12 points in the second event. What is the total score after two events?
   a. $n = 96.3 - 87.12$ b. $n + 87.12 = 96.3$
   c. $n = 96.3 + 87.12$

2. A West German track team needs 346 points in order to win a meet. As the last event begins, they have 293 points. How many more points do they need to win the meet?
   a. $n = 346 - 293$ b. $346 + 293 = n$
   c. $n + 346 = 293$

Write an equation for each problem. Solve.

3. A downhill skier has collected 468 world championship points. A second place finish in the next competition will give him 538 points. How many points will be awarded for second place?

4. The first runner on a 400m relay team completes her run in 10.3 seconds. The second runner's time was 9.7 seconds. What was the total time after the first two runners finished their run?

8. In a speed-skating event, the winner completed the first half of the race in 21.6 seconds. The second half was skated in 19.7 seconds. What was the winner's total time for the event?

What is the word rule?

5. A discus event is won with a toss of 310.8 meters. The third place finisher threw it 308.9 meters. How much further did the first place finisher throw the discus?

6. After three members of an 800-meter relay team complete their runs, the total time is 31.6 seconds. The fourth team member ran the last lap in 10.7 seconds. What is the time at the finish for the team?

7. In the ski jumping event, the first skier jumped 179.6 meters. The second skier jumped 182.3 meters. How much further did the second skier jump?

Write the word rule as an equation.

9. In a springboard diving event, a diver completed four of five dives with a total of 736.73 points. The diver needs at least 813.53 points in order to win. How many points must the diver score on his fifth dive?

Write Your Own Problem

Use the information in this table to write a word problem.

Runner	Jane	Ruth	Peg	Mary
Time in Seconds	50.8	50.1	51.2	51.9

CHAPTER REVIEW

Part 1 • VOCABULARY

For Exercises 1-5, choose from the box at the right the word(s) that complete the sentence.

1. When a square is divided into 10 equal parts, each part is one __?__ of the square.   (Page 130)

2. When __?__ to the nearest thousandth, first look at the digit to the right of the thousandths place.   (Page 138)

3. When a square is divided into 100 equal parts, each part is one __?__ of the square.   (Page 130)

4. A digit can have many different __?__ depending on its place in a number.   (Page 134)

5. When adding or subtracting decimals, all of the __?__ must be in a line.   (Page 144)

decimal points
hundredth
rounding
tenth
values

Part 2 • SKILLS

Write the decimals.   (Pages 130–133)

6. $\frac{7}{10}$

7. $19\frac{1}{10}$

8. $\frac{9}{100}$

9. $2\frac{39}{100}$

10. $51\frac{5}{100}$

11. $\frac{483}{1,000}$

12. $\frac{62}{1,000}$

13. $9\frac{7}{1,000}$

14. $60\frac{840}{1,000}$

15. $326\frac{15}{1,000}$

16. seven tenths

17. forty-one hundredths

18. one and fifteen thousandths

19. two hundred nine thousandths

20. fifty-two and seven thousandths

What number does each underlined digit name?   (Pages 134–135)

21. 36.0<u>9</u>1

22. 0.<u>7</u>83

23. 4.62<u>8</u>

24. 0.4<u>79</u>

25. 1<u>7</u>.0426

Write <, >, or = to make a true sentence.   (Pages 136–137)

26. 0.065 ⬤ 0.65

27. 2.92 ⬤ 2.920

28. 0.813 ⬤ 0.810

29. 18.362 ⬤ 17.632

30. 5.2 ⬤ 5.098

31. 6.037 ⬤ 5.999

Round to the nearest whole number.   (Pages 138–139)

32. 6.7

33. 29.410

34. 15.55

35. 8.097

Round to the nearest tenth.   (Pages 138–139)

36. 2.69

37. 15.12

38. 26.08

39. 19.79

Round to the nearest hundredth.   (Pages 138–139)

40. 1.075

41. 86.312

42. 0.9062

43. 0.655

Round to the nearest thousandth.   (Pages 138–139)

44. 68.19752   **45.** 3.10849   **46.** 0.54972   **47.** 0.39175

Add.   (Pages 144–145)

48. $1.3 + 7.4 = \underline{\ ?\ }$ **49.** $23.6 + 6.8 = \underline{\ ?\ }$ **50.** $12.598 + 28.261 = \underline{\ ?\ }$

51. $76.1 + 1.7 = \underline{\ ?\ }$ **52.** $0.83 + 0.565 = \underline{\ ?\ }$ **53.** $9.386 + 0.49 = \underline{\ ?\ }$

54. $12.4 + 10.66 = \underline{\ ?\ }$ **55.** $23.328 + 19.72 = \underline{\ ?\ }$ **56.** $0.039 + 0.087 = \underline{\ ?\ }$

Subtract.   (Pages 146–147)

57. $54.9 - 20.1 = \underline{\ ?\ }$ **58.** $3.2 - 0.8 = \underline{\ ?\ }$ **59.** $94.04 - 12.66 = \underline{\ ?\ }$

60. $3.9 - 1.36 = \underline{\ ?\ }$ **61.** $46.37 - 29.814 = \underline{\ ?\ }$ **62.** $84.0 - 67.59 = \underline{\ ?\ }$

63. $8.67 - 0.412 = \underline{\ ?\ }$ **64.** $42.1 - 35.42 = \underline{\ ?\ }$ **65.** $35.2 - 0.68 = \underline{\ ?\ }$

Part 3 • *PROBLEM SOLVING* • *APPLICATIONS*

Write an equation for each of Problems 66–71. Solve.   (Pages 148–149)

66. Olga Korbut scored 9.90 points on the uneven parallel bars in the 1976 Olympics. Nadia Comaneci scored 10.0 and won. What is the difference in their scores?

67. Suppose a gymnast scores 9.96, 8.90, and 10.0 points in 3 events. What is the total score for the 3 events?

68. A woman's field hockey team won 27 games over a three–year period. During that time, they played a total of 36 games. How many did they lose?

69. A cross country skier managed to average 4.6 miles per hour for 6 hours. How far did she ski?

70. A ski shop receives a shipment of 36 pairs of ski boots. The manager has available 3 display shelves. How many pairs can he get on each shelve?

71. A rowboat used for racing is called a shell. A shell can weigh 285 pounds. The weight of the crew could be 5 times as heavy. How much would the crew weigh?

72.

Games Played	2	4	6	8	10	12
Penalties	3	7	11	15	?	?

The coach of a hockey team kept a record of the number of penalties his team was given. How many penalties would there be after the 10th game? 12th game? (Pages 140–141)

73.

Week	1	2	3	4	5	6
Miles per hour	2	6	12	20	?	?

A swimming coach makes a 6-week schedule for his long distance swimmers. Complete the schedule for weeks 5 and 6.   (Pages 140–141)

CHAPTER TEST

Write the decimals.

1. $\frac{9}{10}$ 2. $6\frac{3}{100}$ 3. $\frac{56}{100}$ 4. $8\frac{12}{1000}$

In what place is the 3?

5. 19.137456   6. 425.853126

Write the fraction.

7. 6.9   8. 3.04   9. 4.039

Write $>$, $<$, or $=$ to make a true sentence.

10. 18.362 ⬤ 17.632   11. 5.2 ⬤ 5.098

Round each number as indicated.

12. 0.75; to the nearest whole number.
13. 29.410; to the nearest tenth.
14. 53.548; to the nearest hundredth.
15. 2.07169; to the nearest thousandth.

Add or subtract.

16. $\begin{array}{r} 9.38 \\ +0.49 \\ \hline \end{array}$ 17. $\begin{array}{r} 3.2 \\ -0.8 \\ \hline \end{array}$ 18. $\begin{array}{r} 0.83 \\ +0.565 \\ \hline \end{array}$ 19. $\begin{array}{r} 56 \\ -38.278 \\ \hline \end{array}$

20. $\begin{array}{r} 23.6 \\ +\ 8.8 \\ \hline \end{array}$ 21. $\begin{array}{r} 54.9 \\ -20.1 \\ \hline \end{array}$ 22. $\begin{array}{r} 12.598 \\ +28.261 \\ \hline \end{array}$ 23. $\begin{array}{r} 84 \\ -67.59 \\ \hline \end{array}$

24. An American gymnast has earned 49.3 points in 5 of 6 events. He must have at least a total of 58.5 points to qualify for the Olympic team. How many points must he score on the sixth event? Write an equation and solve.

25. Each year the National Park Service plants sequoia trees in Sequoia National Park. A ranger makes a planting schedule. Find the pattern and complete the schedule.

Year	1	2	3	4	5	6
Trees Planted	10	20	40	80	?	?

ENRICHMENT

Magic Squares

In a magic square, the sum of the numbers in each row, column, and diagonal is the same. This sum is called the **magic sum**.

EXERCISES

1. Find the sum of each row, column, and diagonal for this magic square.

What is the magic sum?

4.85	4.91	5.3	5.24
5.06	5.27	4.88	5.09
5.21	5	5.15	4.94
5.18	5.12	4.97	5.03

For Exercises 2 and 3, use the magic square in Exercise 1 to make new squares.

2. Add 8.6 to each number.

4.85 + 8.6 = **13.45**

Is this a magic square?
If your answer is yes,
what is the magic sum?

13.45			

3. Subtract 1.08 from each number.

4.85 − 1.08 = **3.77**

Is this a magic square?
If your answer is yes,
what is the magic sum?

3.77			

ADDITIONAL PRACTICE

SKILLS

Write the decimals.   (Pages 130–133)

1. $\frac{5}{10}$ **2.** $\frac{3}{100}$ **3.** $\frac{76}{1000}$ **4.** $3\frac{9}{10}$ **5.** $56\frac{8}{1000}$

Write the place value of the underlined digit.   (Pages 134–135)

6. 0.5$\underline{6}$1   **7.** 14.7$\underline{6}$3   **8.** 465.03$\underline{1}$ **9.** 2.4$\underline{5}$0   **10.** $\underline{2}$9.387

Write <, >, or =.   (Pages 136–137)

11. 0.217 ● 0.271   **12.** 8.4 ● 8.398   **13.** 17.39 ● 17.390

Round to the nearest tenth and hundredth.   (Pages 138–139)

14. 3.891   **15.** 28.359   **16.** 462.231   **17.** 62.085

Round to the nearest thousandth.   (Pages 138–139)

18. 0.2482   **19.** 3.0635   **20.** 28.1345   **21.** 287.0091

Add.   (Pages 144–145)

22. $3.682 + 2.16 = \underline{\,?\,}$ **23.** $0.951 + 32.6 = \underline{\,?\,}$ **24.** $42.01 + 0.998 = \underline{\,?\,}$

Subtract.   (Pages 146–147)

25. $4.8 - 0.69 = \underline{\,?\,}$ **26.** $45.235 - 1.9 = \underline{\,?\,}$ **27.** $24.314 - 15.08 = \underline{\,?\,}$

PROBLEM SOLVING • APPLICATIONS

28. A zookeeper fed the snakes on July 1, 9, and 17. The tigers were fed on July 7, 9, and 11. What is the next day the snakes will be fed? What is the next day the tigers will be fed?   (Pages 140–141)

30. Al Oerter set a world record in 1960 by throwing the discus 58.18 meters. He broke his record in 1964 with a distance of 60.98 meters. How much farther did he throw the discus in 1964? Write an equation. Solve the equation. (Pages 148–149)

29. This table shows the temperature change in degrees Fahrenheit.

Time	9:00	10:00	11:00	12:00
°F	70	72	75	79

If this pattern continues, what will be the temperature at 1:00? (Pages 140–141)

31. In 1964, Henry Carr won the 200 meter dash with a time of 20.3 seconds. In 1968, Tommie Smith ran the 200 meter dash in 19.83 seconds. What is the difference in the two times? Write an equation. Solve the equation.   (Pages148–149)

PROBLEM SOLVING MAINTENANCE

Chapters 1 through 6

Use the table to solve Problems 1–2.
(Page 14)

Ocean	Average Depth
Arctic	3,407 ft
Atlantic	11,730 ft
Indian	12,598 ft
Pacific	12,925 ft

1. Write the average depth of the Indian Ocean to the nearest hundred.

2. Write the average depth of the Arctic Ocean to the nearest hundred.

3. Cindy travels from Croft (C-1 on a map) to Dairyton (C-6 on a map). In which direction does she travel?
(Page 30)

4. A scientific expedition collected three bags of volcanic rock. The bags weighed 35, 42, and 67 pounds. Estimate the total weight. (Page 58)

5. The sixth-grade class is planning a trip to the NASA mission control center in Texas. It costs $96.47 to fly one way per student. Estimate the cost for 51 students. (Page 58)

Vacation Spending

Use the graph for problems 4–6.
(Page 118)

6. On what two days did the Smith's spend the same amount of money?

7. On which day did they spend the most money?

8. How much more money did the Smith's spend on Tuesday than Monday?

Write an equation. Solve. (Page 148)

9. By Thursday the family had traveled 1,823 km. They planned to travel a total of 2,467 km. How much farther do they have to travel?

10. The Smith family spent $19.50 for gasoline on Thursday and $21.75 for gasoline on Friday. What was the total cost of gasoline for those two days?

11. Sara Feldman is preparing for a 6–day bicycle race. She made this 6–week training schedule. Complete the schedule. (Page 140)

Week	1	2	3	4	5	6
Miles Traveled	2	5	9	14	?	?

MAINTENANCE

Chapters 1 through 6

Mixed Practice • Choose the correct answers.

1. Round 14.83 to the nearest whole number.

   A. 15   **B.** 14.8
   C. 14   **D.** not here

2. Round 349.83 to the nearest whole number.

   A. 349   **B.** 349.8
   C. 350   **D.** not here

3. Estimate. $49 \times 9 = $ __?__

   A. 300   **B.** 500
   C. 360   **D.** not here

4. 243
    $\times\ 35$

    A. 8,505   **B.** 8,495
    C. 8,405   **D.** not here

5. 184
    $\times\ \ 6$

    A. 1,004   **B.** 684
    C. 1,104   **D.** not here

6. 905
    $\times\ 67$

    A. 59,935   **B.** 60,635
    C. 603,335   **D.** not here

7. $22\overline{)308}$

   A. 14 r 20   **B.** 18 r 12
   C. 14   **D.** not here

8. $35\overline{)8,525}$

   A. 243 r 20   **B.** 215
   C. 272 r 5   **D.** not here

9. $32\overline{)668}$

   A. 22 r 12   **B.** 20 r 28
   C. 21 r 16   **D.** not here

10. $462 \div 7 = $ __?__

    A. 66   **B.** 68
    C. 66 r 3   **D.** not here

11. $782 \div 8 = $ __?__

    A. 98 r 6   **B.** 100
    C. 96 r 8   **D.** not here

12. $879 \div 6 = $ __?__

    A. 143 r 6   **B.** 163 r 4
    C. 146 r 3   **D.** not here

13. $310\overline{)6510}$

    A. 21   **B.** 20 r 210
    C. 210   **D.** not here

14. Round 8.346 to the nearest tenth.

    A. 8   **B.** 8.3
    C. 8.4   **D.** not here

15. Round 0.878 to the nearest hundredth.

    A. 0.9   **B.** 0.88
    C. 0.8   **D.** not here

16. A ship averages about 28 miles per hour. About how many miles will the ship travel in 24 hours?

    A. 642 miles   **B.** 652 miles
    C. 672 miles   **D.** not here

17. Mr. Clay and his team participated in a charity drive-a-thon. They drove 2,496 in 48 hours. What was the average speed per hour?

    A. 52 mph   **B.** 59 mph
    C. 50 mph   **D.** not here

CHAPTER 7

Decimals: Multiplication and Division

The S.S. United States traveled 34.5 nautical miles in one hour. The Flying Cloud traveled 7.1 nautical miles in one hour.

● How much further could the S.S. United States travel in 24 hours?

The sea can be used for farming. Oysters planted in shallow water grow for 4 years and reach a length of 7.4 centimeters.

● Assume that the oysters grow the same amount each year. How many centimeters do they grow per year?

Estimating Products • Mental Math

The length of this Spanish ship is
1.8 times the length of this Viking
ship.

● What is the length of the Spanish ship?

The multiplication has been done for you.
Estimate the product to know where to
place the decimal point.

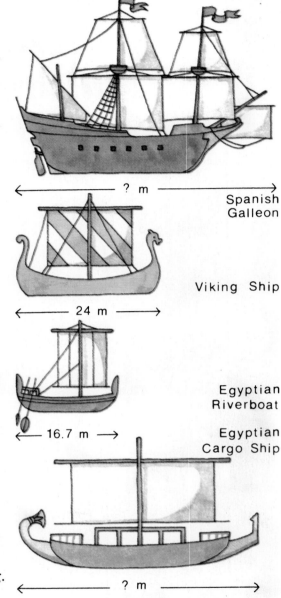

| Spanish Galleon |
| Viking Ship |
| Egyptian Riverboat |
| Egyptian Cargo Ship |

Think

Round 24 to 20.
Round 1.8 to 2.
2 × 20 = 40
The answer is about 40.
The answer must be 43.2.

$$\begin{array}{r} 2\,4 \\ \times 1.8 \\ \hline 1\,9\,2 \\ 2\,4 \\ \hline 4\,3\,2 \end{array}$$

The Spanish ship is **43.2 meters** long.

The length of this Egyptian cargo
ship is 2.4 times the length of this
riverboat.

● What is the length of the cargo ship?

The multiplication has been done for you.
Estimate the product to know where to
place the decimal point.

Think

Round 16.7 to 20.
Round 2.4 to 2.
2 × 20 = 40
The answer is about 40.
The answer must be 40.08.

$$\begin{array}{r} 1\,6.7 \\ \times\ \ 2.4 \\ \hline 6\,6\,8 \\ 3\,3\,4 \\ \hline 4\,0\,0\,8 \end{array}$$

The Egyptian cargo ship is **40.08 meters** long.

E **PRACTICE** • Estimate to place the decimal points in the answers.

1.	24	2.	5.6	3.	18.3	4.	14.8	5.	3.65
	×1.7		×4.2		×2.76		× 3.9		× 2.3
	408		2352		50508		5772		8395

E **EXERCISES** • Estimate to place the decimal point in the answers.

6.	83	7.	74	8.	126	9.	403	10.	19
	×1.6		×9.5		× 3.2		× 1.9		×8.7
	1328		7030		4032		7657		1653

11. 4.2
  ×6.3
  2646

12. 5.5
  ×3.3
  1815

13. 7.1
  ×1.4
  994

14. 10.2
  × 9.8
  9996

15. 8.9
  ×3.4
  3026

16. 19.7
  ×4.21
  82937

17. 87.6
  ×3.19
  279444

18. 54.6
  ×7.93
  432978

19. 98.3
  ×1.45
  142535

20. 46.3
  ×2.91
  134733

21. 9.46
  ×8.12
  768152

22. 7.98
  ×8.32
  663936

23. 4.83
  ×2.96
  142968

24. 6.42
  ×1.83
  117486

25. 6.62
  ×2.47
  163514

26. 5.31
  × 4.5
  23895

27. 6.24
  × 8.7
  54288

28. 8.99
  × 3.2
  28768

29. 3.48
  × 6.5
  22620

30. 5.62
  × 9.1
  51142

31. 3.7
  ×8.4
  3108

32. 198
  × 3.6
  7128

33. 9.5
  ×8.7
  8265

34. 11.4
  ×1.28
  14592

35. 9.37
  ×8.14
  762718

Estimate to place the decimal point in the underlined factors.

★ 36. $4.8 \times \underline{68} = 32.64$

★ 37. $\underline{134} \times 2.4 = 32.16$

★ 38. $8.76 \times \underline{345} = 30.222$

★ 39. $\underline{152} \times 3.8 = 57.76$

PROBLEM SOLVING • APPLICATIONS

Ⓔ Estimate to place the decimal point in the answers.

40. A modern steel sailing ship is 16 meters wide. The length is 8.25 times the width. How long is the ship?

16
×8.25
13200 meters

41. The length of the *United States* is 7.55 times the length of this Roman grain ship. How long is the *United States?*

40
×7.55
30200 meters

42. A Viking ship was 24 meters long. The *Queen Elizabeth 2* is 12.25 times as long. How long is the *Queen Elizabeth 2?*

24
×12.25
29400 meters

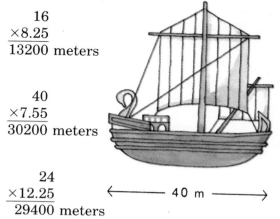

← 40 m →

★ 43. The width of a certain ship is 12 meters. It is 28.75 meters longer than 9.5 times the width. How long is the ship?

$(12 \times 9.5) + 28.75 = 14275$ meters

Multiplying Decimals

In 650 B.C., the Greeks invented a
warship called a "trireme"
(tri'rem). It had three rows of
oarsmen on each side. The trireme was
3.2 times as long as a Greek galley.
A galley was 17.6 meters long.

● How long was a trireme?

| Think | "Times" means multiply.

$$17.6 \times 3.2 = ?$$

Step 1
Multiply as if you were
multiplying whole numbers.

Step 2
Place the decimal point.
Think: Round each factor.
$3 \times 20 = 60$
The answer is about 60.

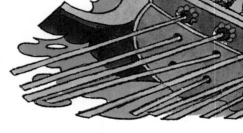

```
    1 7.6
  ×   3.2
    3 5 2
  5 2 8 0
  5 6 3 2
```

```
    1 7.6
  ×   3.2
    3 5 2
  5 2 8 0
  5 6.3 2
```

The trireme was **56.32 meters** long.

● Each place to the right of the decimal point is a decimal place.
Compare the number of decimal places in the product with the total
number of decimal places in the factors.

```
  42.6 ←——— 1
  ×   8 ←——— 0
  340.8 ←——— 1
```

```
  3.75 ←——— 2
  × 1.3 ←——— 1
  4.875 ←——— 3
```

```
  4.25 ←——— 2
  ×0.75 ←——— 2
  3.1875 ←——— 4
```

> *The number of decimal places in the product equals the*
> *sum of the number of decimal places in the factors.*

PRACTICE • Multiply.

1. 37.8	2. 38	3. 0.16	4. 156.1	5. 2.25
× 5	×0.9	× 0.7	× 8.7	×0.178

EXERCISES • Multiply.

6.   1.01
   × 99

7.   4.2
   × 8

8.   25
   ×1.1

9.   3.6
   ×0.9

10.   5.6
   × 9

11.   4.2
   ×3.7

12.   15.8
   × 1.1

13.   79.6
   ×0.54

14.   4.2
   ×0.06

15.   2.76
   × 1.3

16.   7.01
   × 0.9

17.   10.06
   ×0.302

18.   6.008
   × 0.9

19.   10.12
   × 0.22

20.   100.25
   × 0.15

21.   7.03
   ×21.4

22.   1.93
   ×0.65

23.   200.8
   × 3.45

24.   35.5
   × 8.8

25.   0.84
   ×0.303

26. $1.001 \times 246 =$ ___?___

27. $2.22 \times 200 =$ ___?___

28. $8.9 \times 1.5 =$ ___?___

29. $0.25 \times 0.83 =$ ___?___

30. $9.03 \times 5.78 =$ ___?___

31. $7.6 \times 0.9 =$ ___?___

32. $6.15 \times 0.23 =$ ___?___

33. $112 \times 0.387 =$ ___?___

34. $4.5 \times 8.3 =$ ___?___

Mental Math   Insert the missing decimal point in each underlined factor to make the sentence true.

★ **35.** $\underline{209} \times 5.32 = 11.1188$ ★ **36.** $\underline{134} \times 0.03 = 0.402$ ★ **37.** $\underline{5614} \times 3.8 = 21.3332$

PROBLEM SOLVING • APPLICATIONS

38. A trireme used three different lengths of oars. The shortest was about 8.6 meters. The longest was about 2.2 times as long. About how long was the longest oar?

39. The trireme carried a sail which was about 18.6 meters tall. The sail was about 2.3 times as wide. How wide was the sail?

40. The trireme's most important weapon was a ram. It was mounted underwater and was used to punch holes in enemy ships. The average trireme was 38.1 meters long including the ram. The ram was 0.2 times as long as the trireme. How long was the trireme without the ram?

41. A trireme could travel at 11.5 miles per hour for short periods of time. On a training mission, a trireme moved at 6.8 miles per hour for 0.25 hours. How far did it travel during that time?

Decimals: Multiplication and Division • **161**

Zeros in the Product

In the 1200's sailors began using crude maps. They were called *portolan sea charts*. One chart was 0.0029 inch thick.

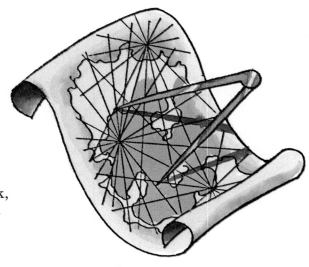

● How thick was a collection of 14 charts?

Think   If one chart is 0.0029 inches thick, 14 charts are 14 "times" as thick.

$$14 \times 0.0029 = ?$$

Sometimes you need to place zeros in the product to locate the decimal point.

Step 1
Multiply.

```
    0.0029
  ×     14
     116
     290
     406
```

Step 2
Write one zero to show four decimal places in the answer. Place the decimal point.

```
    0.0029 ←——— 4
  ×     14 ←——— 0
     116
     290
  0.0406 ←——— 4
```

The thickness of 14 charts is **0.0029 inch**.

● $0.036 \times 0.09 = ?$

```
     0.09 ←——— 2
  × 0.036 ←——— 3
      54
     270
  0.00324 ←——— 5   Write two zeros.
```

PRACTICE • Multiply.

1. 1.49 ×0.05	**2.** 0.37 ×0.04	**3.** 0.35 ×0.08	**4.** 16 ×0.006	**5.** 0.302 × 0.05
6. 0.012 × 0.82	**7.** 0.0037 × 15	**8.** 0.43 ×0.02	**9.** 8.03 ×0.006	**10.** 0.62 ×0.104

EXERCISES • Multiply.

11. 24 ×0.004	**12.** 0.085 × 0.07	**13.** 0.95 ×0.08	**14.** 0.076 × 1.3	**15.** 0.454 × 0.2
16. 0.506 × 0.12	**17.** 0.253 ×0.006	**18.** 0.25 ×0.15	**19.** 2.31 ×0.03	**20.** 0.027 × 1.5
21. 0.106 × 0.17	**22.** 0.793 × 0.5	**23.** 0.94 ×0.03	**24.** 0.008 × 4.5	**25.** 13.4 ×0.003
26. 8.6 ×0.004	**27.** 0.038 × 0.04	**28.** 1.89 × 0.3	**29.** 0.007 ×0.009	**30.** 0.005 × 3.57

31. $0.07 \times 0.082 =$ ___?___   **32.** $8.45 \times 0.009 =$ ___?___   **33.** $1.5 \times 0.23 =$ ___?___

34. $0.002 \times 6.3 =$ ___?___   **35.** $0.004 \times 0.016 =$ ___?___   **36.** $0.02 \times 0.483 =$ ___?___

★ **37.** $0.075 \times 53 \times 0.009 =$ ___?___   ★ **38.** $5.86 \times 0.14 \times 0.08 =$ ___?___

★ **39.** $0.125 \times 0.003 \times 0.045 =$ ___?___   ★ **40.** $0.004 \times 0.07 \times 0.008 =$ ___?___

PROBLEM SOLVING • APPLICATIONS

41. Today sailors can buy books of charts. A single chart is 0.0041 of an inch thick. A book contains 12 charts. How thick is the entire book of charts?

42. An English ship designer in 1650 used paper which was 0.0063 of an inch thick. One set of plans required 9 sheets of paper. How thick was the set of plans?

CALCULATOR • Estimation

Estimate the product. Use the calculator to find the exact answer. Compare.

$$\begin{array}{r} 3.316 \longrightarrow 3 \\ \times 2.973 \longrightarrow \times 3 \end{array}$$ ◀ **Round to the nearest whole number.** $3 \times 3 = 9$ ←

Press: 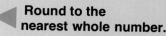 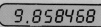 9.858468

Since 9 is close to 9.858468, the actual answer is reasonable.

E **EXERCISES • Estimate the product. Find the exact answer. Compare.**

1. $4.796 \times 8.351 =$ ___?___   **2.** $3.396 \times 7.239 =$ ___?___   **3.** $9.936 \times 7.327 =$ ___?___

4. $6.727 \times 2.612 =$ ___?___   **5.** $8.196 \times 5.903 =$ ___?___   **6.** $1.816 \times 9.457 =$ ___?___

Dividing by Whole Numbers

When drilling for oil on the ocean floor, large platforms are towed to the drilling site and anchored to the sea bottom. One platform was towed 22.47 kilometers from the shore. It took 7 days. It was towed an equal distance each day.

● How many kilometers a day did it travel?

Think   You know the distance towed in 7 days.
Divide to find the distance towed in 1 day.

$$22.47 \div 7 = \underline{\ \ ?\ \ }$$

Step 1 Place the decimal point in the quotient directly above the decimal point in the dividend.

$$7\overline{)22.47}$$

Step 2 Divide as if you were dividing whole numbers.

```
    3.21
7)22.47
  -21 ↓
    1 4
   -1 4↓
      07
     - 7
       0
```

The platform was towed **3.21 kilometers** each day.

More Examples:

```
   0.028
6)0.168
 - 0
   16
  -12
   48
  -48
    0
```

```
    0.96
38)36.48
  -34 2
    2 28
   -2 28
       0
```

```
    4.633
16)74.128
  -64
   10 1
  - 9 6
     52
    -48
     48
    -48
      0
```

PRACTICE • **Mental Math**   Place the decimal point in the quotient.

1. $\overset{5\ 3}{3\overline{)15.9}}$ 2. $\overset{1\ 44}{12\overline{)17.28}}$ 3. $\overset{6}{8\overline{)0.48}}$ 4. $\overset{89}{23\overline{)2.047}}$

Divide.

5. $6\overline{)3.54}$ 6. $8\overline{)27.2}$ 7. $6\overline{)404.4}$ 8. $4\overline{)0.1516}$

EXERCISES • Divide.

9. $5\overline{)21.5}$ 10. $8\overline{)23.28}$ 11. $2\overline{)74.4}$ 12. $4\overline{)2.5528}$

13. $9\overline{)3.825}$ 14. $3\overline{)27.3}$ 15. $4\overline{)12.24}$ 16. $7\overline{)66.7107}$

17. $6\overline{)24.36}$ 18. $7\overline{)0.2667}$ 19. $5\overline{)0.675}$ 20. $9\overline{)0.0585}$

21. $4\overline{)6.48}$ 22. $8\overline{)2.80}$ 23. $9\overline{)77.67}$ 24. $6\overline{)272.22}$

25. $23\overline{)20.47}$ 26. $15\overline{)0.45}$ 27. $27\overline{)5.481}$ 28. $39\overline{)16.8402}$

29. $25\overline{)103.75}$ 30. $63\overline{)2.646}$ 31. $33\overline{)35.97}$ 32. $74\overline{)8.0290}$

33. $54\overline{)127.98}$ 34. $73\overline{)4.745}$ 35. $49\overline{)287.63}$ 36. $86\overline{)68.198}$

37. $341.6 \div 56 =$ ___?___   38. $2.856 \div 34 =$ ___?___   39. $1.508 \div 58 =$ ___?___

40. $169.67 \div 47 =$ ___?___   41. $15.25 \div 61 =$ ___?___   42. $241.02 \div 39 =$ ___?___

43. $263.63 \div 643 =$ ___?___   44. $276.42 \div 542 =$ ___?___   45. $1{,}000.5 \div 345 =$ ___?___

PROBLEM SOLVING • APPLICATIONS

46. When the drilling platform reaches its destination, the legs are lowered to the ocean floor. In one case, it took 9 hours to lower the legs 26.1 meters. How far could the legs be lowered in 1 hour?

47. The drilling tower on a platform is 36.8 meters tall. It is constructed by attaching 12 identical sections together. How tall is each section? Round the answer to the nearest tenth.

48. A supply boat requires 6 trips to deliver 2541.6 pounds of drilling supplies to one platform. What is the average number of pounds carried each trip?

★ 49. Each platform has a boat landing attached to one of the legs. The crew climbs to the platform on rungs welded to the leg. The distance from the landing to the first rung is 1.1 meters. The distance from the last rung to the platform is 1 meter. There are 11 rungs, each 0.75 meters apart. How far is it from the landing to the platform?

THINKER'S CORNER

The crew of an oil rig has to prepare a solution for cleaning equipment. The solution requires 7 liters of water. They have one 4-liter and one 9-liter bucket. Neither bucket has any volume markings. Using both buckets, how do they get the required 7 liters of water?

PROBLEM SOLVING · STRATEGIES

Multistep Problems

Record Breaking Ocean Voyages

Date	Ship	From	To	Days	Knots
1838	Great Western (steam)	U.S.	England	14.9	9.2
1854	Flying Cloud (sail)	N.Y.	San Francisco	89.3	7.1
1935	Normandie (steam)	England	U.S.	4.2	29.9
1938	Queen Mary (steam)	England	U.S.	3.9	31.7
1952	S.S. United States (steam)	U.S.	England	3.4	34.5
1960	U.S.S. Triton (nuclear)	U.S.	U.S.	83.9	20.6
1973	Sea Land Exchange (diesel)	England	U.S.	3.5	34.9

One knot = One nautical mile per hour

The Normandie and the S.S. United States were among the
fastest ships to cross the Atlantic Ocean in their time.

● How much further than the Normandie would the S.S.
United States travel in a 24–hour period?

Think To solve this problem, you first
have to answer this question:

**How far did each ship travel in
24 hours?**

This is the **hidden question**.

Step 1 Find the distance each travels in 24 hours.
Think: You know the distance traveled
in one hour. You multiply.

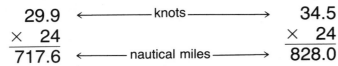

Normandie		S.S. United States
29.9	← knots →	34.5
× 24		× 24
717.6	← nautical miles →	828.0

Step 2
Think: You must compare. So subtract.

$$\begin{array}{r} 828.0 \\ -717.6 \\ \hline 110.4 \end{array}$$

The S.S. United States travels **110.4 nautical miles** further.

PROBLEMS • Answer the hidden question. Then solve the problem.

1. The submarine, U.S.S. Triton, made an unusual trip around the world. It was underwater the entire time. How many nautical miles did it travel in one week?

   Hidden question: How many nautical miles did the U.S.S. Triton travel in one 24-hour day?

2. The crew of the Flying Cloud worked 12-hour shifts called *watches*. How far would the ship travel in 6 watches?

   Hidden question: How far did the Flying Cloud travel in one 12-hour shift?

Solve. Look for the hidden questions.

3. The Sea Land Exchange is a record-setting cargo ship. A record speed for helicopters is 7.15 times faster than the Sea Land. How much further would the helicopter travel in one hour?

4. In 1838, the Great Western set a record for trans-Atlantic crossings. One hundred years later, the Queen Mary made the same trip. How much further would the Queen Mary have traveled in a 24–hour period?

5. The fastest airplane flight from England to the United States took almost six hours. The speed of the plane was 26.6 times as fast as the speed of the S.S. United States. How much further would the plane have traveled in a 6-hour period?

6. The Normandie's fastest trip in 1935 took 4.2 days. How many nautical miles did she travel?

What is the hidden question?

---

7. The S.S. United States and the Sea Land Exchange each set a speed record. Which one traveled the furthest?

Write Your Own Problem

Use the table on page 166 to write a word problem that has a hidden question.

Decimals: Multiplication and Division • 167

MID-CHAPTER REVIEW

Estimate to place the decimal point in the answers.   (Pages 158–159)

1. 3.2 ×5.1 ‾‾‾‾ 1632	**2.** 14.5 × 8.3 ‾‾‾‾ 12035	**3.** 6.34 × 3.68 ‾‾‾‾ 233312	**4.** 4.25 × 7.9 ‾‾‾‾ 33575	**5.** 13.7 ×4.33 ‾‾‾‾ 59321

Multiply.   (Pages 160–161)

6. 16.2 × 5	**7.** 45.8 × 1.3	**8.** 20.03 × 0.96	**9.** 0.84 ×30.5	**10.** 600.07 × 36.2

Multiply.   (Pages 162–163)

11. 0.07 ×0.08	**12.** 8 ×0.004	**13.** 0.023 × 0.05	**14.** 0.009 × 5.1	**15.** 0.052 × 0.08

16. $0.036 \times 0.14 = \underline{\ ?\ }$ **17.** $0.005 \times 32 = \underline{\ ?\ }$ **18.** $0.068 \times 46.8 = \underline{\ ?\ }$

Divide.   (Pages 164–165)

19. $4\overline{)33.6}$ **20.** $22\overline{)25.476}$ **21.** $49\overline{)332.22}$ **22.** $63\overline{)8.568}$ **23.** $73\overline{)684.959}$

24. A fishing boat travels at 4.5 miles per hour for 2.8 hours. Then it travels at 5.2 miles per hour for 2.5 hours. How many miles did the fishing boat travel altogether? (Pages 166–167)

25. In 15 trips, a fishing boat averaged 4,884.3 pounds of fish per trip. To the nearest 10 pounds, what is the total "catch" for 45 trips? (Pages 166–167)

MAINTENANCE • MIXED PRACTICE

Subtract.

1. 32.06 − 4.82	**2.** 168.90 − 2.95	**3.** 400.03 −199.7	**4.** 25.06 − 9.482	**5.** 365.7 − 2.914

Multiply.

6. $10 \times 456 = \underline{\ ?\ }$ **7.** $100 \times 3,942 = \underline{\ ?\ }$ **8.** $1,000 \times 232 = \underline{\ ?\ }$

Divide.

9. $50\overline{)1,600}$ **10.** $80\overline{)6,800}$ **11.** $35\overline{)7,000}$ **12.** $24\overline{)72,000}$ **13.** $38\overline{)19,000}$

14. There are 317 guests at Outdoor Lodge. Each table in the dining room seats 8. How many tables are needed?

15. A ticket to a football game costs $12.75. A ticket to a hockey game costs $8.95. How much more does the football ticket cost than the hockey ticket?

CONSUMER APPLICATIONS

Heating Costs

Off-shore oil wells have helped to improve our supply of energy. Conservation methods have also helped a great deal. By following this rule, every consumer can help to conserve fuel and save money at the same time.

> **HEATING COSTS:** For every degree Fahrenheit (F°) that the thermostat setting is lowered, you can lower heating costs by a factor of 0.03.

EXAMPLE: Last year, the Ortega family spent $1275.00 to heat their home with the thermostat set at 70°F. How much could they save by setting the thermostat at 65°F?

Solution:

1 Find the change in setting.

$70° - 65° = $ **5° lower**

2 Find the factor.

> **Think** Since 1° lower reduces the cost by 0.03, 5° lower reduces the cost by
>
> 5×0.03 or **0.15.**

3 Find the amount saved.

$$\boxed{1}\ \boxed{2}\ \boxed{7}\ \boxed{5}\ \boxed{\times}\ \boxed{\cdot}\ \boxed{1}\ \boxed{5}\ \boxed{=}\ \boxed{191.25}$$

The Ortega family will save **$191.25.**

EXERCISES • How much can each family save on last year's heating costs?

	Yearly Heating Costs	Last Year's Thermostat Setting	This Year's Thermostat Setting		Yearly Heating Costs	Last Year's Thermostat Setting	This Year's Thermostat Setting
1.	$800	68°F	64°F	5.	$1020	66°F	61°F
2.	$1100	69°F	63°F	6.	$1285	67°F	64°F
3.	$720	66°F	64°F	7.	$1305	66°F	62°F
4.	$570	70°F	65°F	8.	$1095	70°F	65°F

Zeros in Division

The sea is used for farming. For example, oysters are planted in shallow water. Some grow for 4 years and reach a length of 7.4 centimeters. These oysters grow the same amount each year.

● How many centimeters do they grow each year?

Think   You know the growth for 4 years. They grow the same amount each year. You divide.

$7.4 \div 4 = ?$

Step 1
Divide.
There is a remainder of 2.

```
    1.8
4)7.4
  −4 ↓
    3 4
   −3 2
      2
```

Step 2
Think: 7.4 = 7.40. Write a zero in the dividend. Divide.

```
    1.85
4)7.40
  −4 ↓|
    3 4|
   −3 2↓
      20
     −20
       0
```

They grow **1.85 centimeters** each year.

More Examples:

```
     5.375
4)21.500
 −20
   1 5
  −1 2
     30
    −28
      20
     −20
       0
```

```
      3.68
55)202.40
 −165
   37 4
  −33 0
     4 40
    −4 40
        0
```

```
     0.675
12)8.100
  −7 2
     90
    −84
      60
     −60
       0
```

PRACTICE • Divide until the remainder is zero.

1. $6)\overline{8.7}$ 2. $5)\overline{7.1}$ 3. $6)\overline{0.57}$ 4. $2)\overline{7.5}$ 5. $4)\overline{8.2}$

6. $8)\overline{19.6}$ 7. $4)\overline{12.6}$ 8. $8)\overline{7.4}$ 9. $15)\overline{34.8}$ 10. $28)\overline{60.9}$

EXERCISES • Divide until the remainder is zero.

11. $2\overline{)3.5}$ **12.** $6\overline{)9.3}$ **13.** $5\overline{)4.8}$ **14.** $8\overline{)8.4}$ **15.** $4\overline{)7.8}$

16. $8\overline{)17.2}$ **17.** $4\overline{)30.7}$ **18.** $4\overline{)0.46}$ **19.** $6\overline{)57.3}$ **20.** $2\overline{)38.7}$

21. $4\overline{)0.87}$ **22.** $6\overline{)90.3}$ **23.** $5\overline{)6.35}$ **24.** $8\overline{)25.4}$ **25.** $4\overline{)0.85}$

26. $18\overline{)4.5}$ **27.** $24\overline{)29.4}$ **28.** $16\overline{)43.6}$ **29.** $52\overline{)98.8}$ **30.** $65\overline{)0.104}$

31. $42\overline{)8.19}$ **32.** $38\overline{)87.4}$ **33.** $25\overline{)65.3}$ **34.** $70\overline{)89.6}$ **35.** $85\overline{)87.04}$

36. $0.27 \div 6 =$ ___?___ **37.** $13.9 \div 4 =$ ___?___ **38.** $5.1 \div 15 =$ ___?___

39. $26.6 \div 95 =$ ___?___ **40.** $140.4 \div 80 =$ ___?___ **41.** $0.56 \div 32 =$ ___?___

★ **42.** $95.4 \div 48 =$ ___?___ ★ **43.** $47.1 \div 16 =$ ___?___ ★ **44.** $245.6 \div 125 =$ ___?___

★ **45.** $25 \div$ ___?___ $= 2.5$ ★ **46.** $1.8 \div$ ___?___ $= 0.2$ ★ **47.** $15 \div$ ___?___ $= 0.75$

★ **48.** $3.5 \div$ ___?___ $= 0.5$ ★ **49.** $0.42 \div$ ___?___ $= 0.07$ ★ **50.** $56 \div$ ___?___ $= 0.7$

PROBLEM SOLVING • APPLICATIONS

51. It takes an oyster farmer on the Chesapeake Bay 5 days to plant the oyster beds. The farm has a total of 14.7 acres. How many acres are planted in one day?

52. Clams are harvested from the bottom of shallow bays. A clammer collects 26.1 pounds of clams in a 6-hour period. At this rate, how many clams does he collect in one hour?

53. In Japan, seaweed is raised for food. One seaweed farmer operates two farms. One farm is 5 acres. One year the farmer grew 957.2 pounds of seaweed on both farms. What additional information do you need to find the average yield per acre?

★ **54.** A chemist is testing the quality of the water before an oyster bed is planted. She has 5 kilograms of a powder. She used 0.7 kilograms for an experiment. She stored the rest of the powder equally in 4 containers. How much does she put into each container?

Multiplying or Dividing by 10, 100, or 1,000

Lobsters are caught in traps called *pots*. Because lobsters fight with each other, the pot holds only one lobster. An average lobster weighs about 4.546 kilograms.

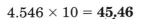

● About how many kilograms of lobster could be caught in 10 pots? 100 pots? 1,000 pots?

Think: You know the average weight in one pot. You multiply.

$$4.546 \times 10 = \mathbf{45.46} \qquad 4.546 \times 100 = \mathbf{454.6} \qquad 4.546 \times 1,000 = \mathbf{4546.}$$

The example suggests the following rule for multiplying by 10, 100, 1,000, and so on:

> *To multiply a decimal   by 10,   by 100,   or by 1,000:*
>
> *move the decimal point   one,   two,   or   three places to the right.*

A record black marlin weighed 709.1 kilograms. It weighed 10 times more than the record amberjack, 100 times more than the record sea trout, and 1,000 times more than a sea bass.

● What was the weight of the marlin, the amberjack, and the sea bass?

Think: You know the weight of the Marlin. You divide to find the weight of the smaller fish.

$$709.1 \div 10 = \mathbf{70.91} \qquad 709.1 \div 100 = \mathbf{7.091} \qquad 709.1 \div 1,000 = \mathbf{0.7091}$$

The example suggests the following rule for dividing by 10, 100, 1,000 and so on:

> *To divide a decimal   by 10,   by 100,   or by 1,000:*
>
> *move the decimal point   one,   two,   or   three   places to the left.*

PRACTICE • Multiply.

1. $10 \times 8.37 =$ ___?___

2. $100 \times 9.365 =$ ___?___

3. $1,000 \times 3.842 =$ ___?___

Divide.

4. $69.3 \div 10 =$ ___?___

5. $4.82 \div 100 =$ ___?___

6. $71.04 \div 1,000 =$ ___?___

EXERCISES • Multiply.

7. $10 \times 6.4 =$ ___?___

8. $100 \times 9.04 =$ ___?___

9. $1,000 \times 0.2354 =$ ___?___

10. $100 \times 0.6 =$ ___?___

11. $1,000 \times 4.86 =$ ___?___

12. $100 \times 4.602 =$ ___?___

13. $10 \times 5.132 =$ ___?___

14. $100 \times 95.673 =$ ___?___

15. $10 \times 0.007 =$ ___?___

16. $1,000 \times 0.018 =$ ___?___

17. $10 \times 29.46 =$ ___?___

18. $100 \times 0.0143 =$ ___?___

Divide.

19. $53.29 \div 10 =$ ___?___

20. $1.666 \div 100 =$ ___?___

21. $0.437 \div 1,000 =$ ___?___

22. $7.924 \div 1,000 =$ ___?___

23. $84.5 \div 10 =$ ___?___

24. $372.4 \div 1,000 =$ ___?___

25. $20.106 \div 1,000 =$ ___?___

26. $54.8 \div 1,000 =$ ___?___

27. $0.494 \div 10 =$ ___?___

28. $750.2 \div 1,000 =$ ___?___

29. $6.832 \div 100 =$ ___?___

30. $117.6 \div 1,000 =$ ___?___

PROBLEM SOLVING • APPLICATIONS

31. A *purse seine* (sān) is a net used to catch many of the fish used for food. Some seines are about 200.8 meters long. The largest nets are 10 times that length. About how long are the largest nets?

32. Bait fishing and trolling are two methods used to catch fish by commercial fleets. Bait fishing is done with a pole and about 4.3 meters of line. Trollers use a line 100 times as long. The longest trolling line is 10 times as long as this. What is the length of the longest trolling line?

PROJECT A chef in a seafood restaurant has to prepare 6 different kinds of fish. Find the weight per serving of 6 kinds of fish. Compute the number of pounds of each fish you would need if you planned to serve 10, 100, and 1,000 diners.

Dividing Decimals

Multiply the dividend and the divisor by the same number.
The quotient does not change.

	Multiply both by 10.	Multiply both by 100.

$$6\overline{)42}^{7}$$

$$60\overline{)420}^{7}$$

$$600\overline{)4,200}^{7}$$

When dividing with decimals, you need to divide by a whole number.
Sometimes, therefore, you must multiply the dividend and the
divisor by 10, 100, or 1,000.

A shrimp boat harvests shrimp by
dragging nets over the bottom of the
ocean. One fleet of shrimpers caught
6.12 tons of shrimp in 1.8 days at
sea.

● At that rate, how many tons
would they harvest each day?

Think   You know the total tons and the total number of days.
You divide to find how many tons are harvested in one day.

$$6.12 \div 1.8. = ?$$

Step 1
There is one decimal place
in the divisor. Multiply the
dividend and the divisor by 10.
Move the decimal point
one place to the right.

$$1.8.\overline{)6.1.2}$$

Step 2
Place the decimal point
in the quotient directly above
the decimal point that you
wrote in the dividend.

$$1.8.\overline{)6.1.2}^{\,\cdot}$$

Step 3
Divide as if you were
dividing whole numbers.

$$
\begin{array}{r}
3.4 \\
1.8.\overline{)6.1.2} \\
-5\,4\downarrow \\
\hline
7\,2 \\
-7\,2 \\
\hline
0
\end{array}
$$

There were **3.4 tons** harvested in one day.

PRACTICE • **Mental Math**   Place the decimal point in the quotient.

1. $2.3\overline{)10.58}^{\,46}$

2. $0.4\overline{)0.76}^{\,19}$

3. $0.12\overline{)0.0516}^{\,43}$

4. $0.36\overline{)0.288}^{\,8}$

Divide.

5. $0.4\overline{)0.212}$

6. $0.7\overline{)2.59}$

7. $0.65\overline{)0.780}$

8. $0.003\overline{)0.0027}$

EXERCISES • Mental Math Place the decimal point in the quotient.

9. $0.8\overline{)1.44}$ → 18

10. $0.9\overline{)0.099}$ → 11

11. $2.9\overline{)98.6}$ → 34

12. $9.5\overline{)45.505}$ → 479

Divide.

13. $1.2\overline{)49.2}$

14. $0.4\overline{)13.36}$

15. $4.1\overline{)0.3321}$

16. $1.6\overline{)64.32}$

17. $0.82\overline{)5.166}$

18. $0.23\overline{)10.35}$

19. $0.06\overline{)6.624}$

20. $0.36\overline{)339.48}$

21. $0.16\overline{)2.56}$

22. $5.8\overline{)3.48}$

23. $0.005\overline{)0.0185}$

24. $0.021\overline{)0.504}$

25. $0.83\overline{)42.33}$

26. $6.8\overline{)0.2312}$

27. $61.8\overline{)5.562}$

28. $0.551\overline{)23.142}$

29. $2.024 \div 0.08 = $ __?__

30. $1.28 \div 3.2 = $ __?__

31. $26.52 \div 0.39 = $ __?__

32. $0.0522 \div 0.006 = $ __?__

33. $1.8032 \div 0.046 = $ __?__

34. $0.9204 \div 0.354 = $ __?__

PROBLEM SOLVING • APPLICATIONS

35. A modern fishing ship caught 39.1 tons of fish in 9.2 hours. What was the average catch per hour?

36. A dory fisherman in Nova Scotia carries his fishing line in tubs. One tub holds 130.2 meters of fishing line. He attaches a hook every 0.62 meters. How many hooks will he need for the line in one tub?

37. Complete the following chart.

Ship: Maru Toschica

Type: Trawler

Production Log Dates 9/12–9/15

Date	Total Catch (lbs)	Keep (lbs)	Throwback (lbs)	Hours Worked	Average Catch Per Hour (lbs)
9/12		1,489.3	266.3	16.5	
9/13			194.6	17.4	102.5
9/14	1,732.5	1,567.1			112.5
9/15		1,352	379.6	14.8	

Zeros in the Dividend

The *Sea Star* returned to shore with a cargo of 18.2 kilograms of sea sponges. The average weight of each sponge was 0.07 kilograms.

● About how many sponges were on the *Sea Star*?

Think   You know the total weight of the cargo and the average weight of each sponge. So you divide.

$$18.2 \div 0.07 = ?$$

Step 1
Multiply the divisor and dividend by 100. To move the decimal point two places to the right, you must write a zero in the dividend.

$$0.07.\overline{)18.20.}$$

Step 2
Place the decimal point in the quotient.

$$0.07.\overline{)18.20.}^{\,\cdot}$$

Step 3
Divide.

```
           2 60.
0.07.)18.20.
      -14 ↓|
        4 2|
       -4 2↓
          00
         - 0
           0
```

There were about **260 sponges** on the *Sea Star*.

When you divide by decimals, you may need to write more zeros in the dividend in order to divide until there is a zero remainder.

● Divide: $3.055 \div 2.5$

Step 1
Multiply the divisor and dividend by 10. Place the decimal point in the quotient.

$$2.5.\overline{)3.0.55}^{\,\cdot}$$

Step 2
Divide. There is a remainder of 5.

```
          1.22
2.5.)3.0.55
    -2 5 ↓|
      5 5|
     -5 0↓
        55
       -50
         5
```

Step 3
Think: 3.055 = 3.0550.
Write a zero in the dividend. Divide.

```
          1.222
2.5.)3.0.550
    -2 5 ↓||
      5 5|
     -5 0↓
        55
       -50↓
         50
        -50
          0
```

PRACTICE • Divide.

1. $0.7\overline{)42}$ **2.** $7.2\overline{)216}$ **3.** $0.22\overline{)31.9}$ **4.** $0.03\overline{)82.8}$

5. $0.4\overline{)2.9}$ **6.** $0.45\overline{)1.107}$ **7.** $0.06\overline{)1.41}$ **8.** $2.4\overline{)300}$

EXERCISES • Divide.

9. $0.05\overline{)470}$ **10.** $0.29\overline{)153.7}$ **11.** $0.04\overline{)146.8}$ **12.** $2.5\overline{)60}$

13. $0.38\overline{)87.4}$ **14.** $0.2\overline{)16.7}$ **15.** $0.8\overline{)1.8}$ **16.** $4.4\overline{)37.4}$

17. $0.004\overline{)16}$ **18.** $1.6\overline{)0.84}$ **19.** $3.1\overline{)27.59}$ **20.** $0.5\overline{)7.5}$

21. $1.5\overline{)8.79}$ **22.** $0.006\overline{)0.504}$ **23.** $0.16\overline{)32}$ **24.** $0.08\overline{)0.576}$

25. $3.6\overline{)14.85}$ **26.** $0.48\overline{)40.8}$ **27.** $3.6\overline{)5.94}$ **28.** $8.4\overline{)31.5}$

29. $4.79 \div 0.5 =$ __?__ **30.** $35.07 \div 4.2 =$ __?__ **31.** $0.416 \div 0.08 =$ __?__

32. $1.206 \div 0.268 =$ __?__ **33.** $6.72 \div 0.064 =$ __?__ **34.** $3.61 \div 0.8 =$ __?__

★ **35.** $0.01 \div 0.125 =$ __?__ ★ **36.** $4.95 \div 0.004 =$ __?__ ★ **37.** $3.98 \div 0.016 =$ __?__

PROBLEM SOLVING • APPLICATIONS

38. Alex strings 1.54 kilograms of sponges. The average weight of each sponge is 0.055 kilogram. About how many sponges does he string?

39. John's string of sponges measures 3.4 meters long. The average length of each sponge is 0.025 meter. About how many sponges are on the string?

★ **40.** The *Sea Star* often brings back shells. One kind of snail shell is so tiny that 30 of them in a row measure 2.34 centimeters long.
   a. What is the average length of each shell?
   b. How long would a row of 40 snail shells be?

★ **41.** One bucket of shells weighs 4.13 kilograms. Another weighs 5.9 kilograms. The average weight of each shell is 0.295 kilogram. About how many shells are in both buckets?

THINKER'S CORNER

The Captain of the sponge boat *Inez* stacks his navigation charts on a shelf in the wheelhouse. There are 5 charts in each stack. He tried stacking them with 2, 3, and 4 charts in a stack, but there was always just one left over. What is the minimum number of charts he has in the wheelhouse?

Decimals and Fractions • Rounding Quotients

> To round a decimal quotient to a given *place:*
> Divide to one place beyond the given place.
> Round the quotient to the given place.

On the Rance River at St. Malo, France, the movement of the tide turns turbines which make electricity. The tide causes the water to drop 13 meters in 6 hours.

● To the nearest tenth, how many meters does the river drop in 1 hour?

Think   You know the *total* distance the river dropped in 6 hours. You divide to find the distance the river dropped in 1 hour.

$13 \div 6 = ?$

Step 1
Think: You must have hundredths in order to round to the nearest tenth. Divide to the hundredths place.

```
     2.16
 6)13.00
  -12 ↓
    1 0
  -  6↓
     40
   -36
      4
```

Step 2
Round to the nearest tenth.

2.16 rounded to the nearest tenth is **2.2.**

The river drops **2.2 meters** in 1 hour.

● Find a decimal for $\frac{2}{3}$. Find the answer to the nearest hundredth.

(Find the quotient to three decimal places.)

Step 1

```
   0.6
3)2.0
 -1 8
    2
```

Step 2

```
   0.66
3)2.00
 -1 8↓
    20
  -18
    2
```

Step 3

```
   0.666
3)2.000
 -1 8
    20
  -18↓
    20
  -18
    2
```

The decimal 0.666 is between 0.66 and 0.67. It is nearer to 0.67.
The decimal to the nearest hundredth for $\frac{2}{3}$ is **0.67.**

PRACTICE • Find the decimals. Divide until the remainder is 0.

1. $\frac{1}{4}$ 2. $\frac{3}{8}$ 3. $\frac{4}{5}$ 4. $\frac{3}{10}$ 5. $\frac{5}{8}$ 6. $\frac{1}{8}$

Find the decimals to the nearest hundredth.

7. $\frac{1}{3}$ 8. $\frac{2}{6}$ 9. $\frac{4}{9}$ 10. $\frac{9}{11}$ 11. $\frac{5}{7}$ 12. $\frac{3}{9}$

EXERCISES • Find the decimals. Divide until the remainder is 0.

13. $\frac{3}{5}$ 14. $\frac{4}{25}$ 15. $\frac{2}{5}$ 16. $\frac{9}{10}$ 17. $\frac{7}{8}$ 18. $\frac{3}{50}$

19. $\frac{7}{20}$ 20. $\frac{21}{25}$ 21. $\frac{3}{16}$ 22. $\frac{5}{16}$ 23. $\frac{9}{4}$ 24. $\frac{15}{8}$

Find the decimals to the nearest hundredth.

25. $\frac{3}{11}$ 26. $\frac{7}{12}$ 27. $\frac{2}{7}$ 28. $\frac{7}{33}$ 29. $\frac{1}{9}$ 30. $\frac{5}{6}$

31. $\frac{2}{9}$ 32. $\frac{3}{22}$ 33. $\frac{5}{12}$ 34. $\frac{8}{6}$ 35. $\frac{26}{14}$ 36. $\frac{38}{17}$

PROBLEM SOLVING • APPLICATIONS

37. Tides help keep coastal waters clean. They carry waste out to deeper water where it settles to the bottom. One day, the tide carried waste 46.3 kilometers out to sea in 6 hours. How far, to the nearest hundredth, is the waste carried in one hour?

38. A ship waits for high tide in order to enter a harbor. It must have an additional 2.73 feet of water. The tide raised the water level 18.6 feet in 6.2 hours. Will the ship have to wait more than one hour?

39. The Bay of Fundy in Nova Scotia has tides which drop the water level 50 feet in 6 hours. To the nearest tenth, how many feet does the water drop in 3 hours?

40. In a New England harbor, the water level at high tide is 36.8 feet. At low tide, the water level is 24.3 feet. It takes the tide 6 hours to go out. To the nearest tenth, how far does the water drop in 2 hours?

Decimals: Multiplication and Division • **179**

NON-ROUTINE PROBLEM SOLVING

The William Crealock Elementary School holds a social studies fair each year. Each fifth– and sixth–grade student can display a project. Students may not spend more than $80 on their projects.

Debbie Monroe decides to make a display showing different kinds of ships. She knows that there are 5 different model kits available at the Moran Hobby Shop. Each kit costs $22.50.

Each model will require several colors of paint. A jar of paint costs $0.79.

Model	Jars of Paint Required
Moran Tug	4
S.S. United States	3
Supertanker	3
Container Ship	2
Savannah	4

Debbie knows that she has 3 weeks to complete the project, so she listed these 4 possible choices.

CHOICE 1

Build the Moran tug, the supertanker, and the container ship.

CHOICE 2

Build the Moran tug, the container ship, and the Savannah.

CHOICE 3

Build the supertanker, the Savannah, and the container ship.

CHOICE 4

Build the S.S. United States and the Savannah.

FINDING THE COST

Suppose Debbie decides to paint all the models.

1. Which choice is the most expensive?

2. Which choice is the least expensive?

Suppose Debbie decides not to paint the models.

3. Which choice is the least expensive?

4. Which choices will cost the same amount?

MAKING A CHOICE

5. Debbie would like to make a background for her display. She estimates it will cost at least $8. Which choice does she have if she decides to paint the models? If she decides not to paint the models?

6. Suppose Debbie decides to have 3 models in her display and to paint the models. She also decides not to spend more than $75. Which choices does she have?

7. Debbie thought about having unpainted and painted ships in her display. What is the least expensive way for her to do this for Choices 1, 2, and 3?

PROJECT Visit a hobby shop that has model ships. List the names of several models and their costs. Plan a display of 2 or 3 model ships that would cost less than $80. Compare the cost of your plan with that of at least two friends.

CHAPTER REVIEW

Part 1 • VOCABULARY

For Exercises 1–7, choose from the box at the right the word that completes the sentence.

1. The answer in a division problem is called the _?_
(Page 164)

2. You use a _?_ to separate whole numbers from tenths.
(Page 160)

3. The number of decimal places in the product will equal the sum of the number of _?_ in the factors.
(Page 160)

4. In the division problem $42\overline{)328}$, the number 328 is called the _?_. (Page 164)

5. In the division problem $12\overline{)249}$, the number 12 is called the _?_. (Page 174)

6. An _?_ can tell you if your answer is reasonable.
(Page 158)

7. If you _?_ 16.85 to the nearest tenth, the answer is 16.9. (Page 158)

decimal places
decimal point
dividend
divisor
estimate
quotient
round

Part 2 • SKILLS

Place the decimal point in the product. (Pages 158–159)

8.	9.	10.	11.	12.
8.2	32.6	4.06	6.39	55.8
×3.5	× 4.3	× 7.33	× 8.4	× 3.27
2870	14018	297598	53676	182466

Multiply. (Pages 160–161)

13.	14.	15.	16.	17.
18.7	63.5	40.06	0.97	400.28
× 3	× 2.4	× 0.82	×47.5	× 29.8

18.	19.	20.	21.	22.
56.3	4.8	7.26	23.4	252.13
× 0.7	×0.9	× 5.3	×0.62	× 0.822

Multiply. (Pages 162–163)

23. $0.025 \times 0.9 =$ _?_

24. $0.007 \times 48 =$ _?_

25. $0.046 \times 33.9 =$ _?_

26.	27.	28.	29.	30.
0.04	6	0.215	0.006	0.42
×0.09	×0.007	× 0.89	× 0.75	×0.04

Divide until the remainder is zero. (Pages 164–165)

31. $6 \overline{)37.2}$ **32.** $4 \overline{)2.5528}$ **33.** $27 \overline{)5.481}$ **34.** $39 \overline{)16.8402}$ **35.** $33 \overline{)1187.67}$

Divide until the remainder is zero. (Pages 170–171)

36. $6 \overline{)21.03}$ **37.** $4 \overline{)52.2}$ **38.** $5 \overline{)18.2}$ **39.** $15 \overline{)45.6}$ **40.** $6 \overline{)35.1}$

Multiply. (Pages 172–173)

41. $10 \times 7.5 = \underline{\ ?\ }$ **42.** $100 \times 4.309 = \underline{\ ?\ }$ **43.** $1,000 \times 0.023 = \underline{\ ?\ }$

Divide. (Pages 172–173)

44. $64.22 \div 10 = \underline{\ ?\ }$ **45.** $2.407 \div 100 = \underline{\ ?\ }$ **46.** $5.903 \div 1,000 = \underline{\ ?\ }$

47. $624.7 \div 10 = \underline{\ ?\ }$ **48.** $324.5 \div 100 = \underline{\ ?\ }$ **49.** $98.01 \div 1,000 = \underline{\ ?\ }$

Divide. (Pages 174–177)

50. $2.1 \overline{)85.05}$ **51.** $61.8 \overline{)5.562}$ **52.** $0.39 \overline{)81.9}$ **53.** $0.23 \overline{)0.1035}$

54. $0.3 \overline{)279}$ **55.** $0.08 \overline{)448}$ **56.** $4.2 \overline{)1.554}$ **57.** $0.007 \overline{)2.5347}$

Find the decimals to the nearest hundredth. (Pages 178–179)

58. $\frac{3}{4}$ **59.** $\frac{5}{9}$ **60.** $\frac{11}{3}$ **61.** $\frac{7}{16}$ **62.** $\frac{15}{8}$ **63.** $\frac{3}{7}$

Part 3 • *PROBLEM SOLVING* • *APPLICATIONS*

Use the table for Exercises 64–66.

Fish and Shellfish	Amount Caught in 1 Year Worldwide (metric tons)
Mackerel	3,623,000
Tuna	1,713,000
Shrimp	1,526,000
Squid	1,094,000
Oyster	873,000
Salmon	625,000

64. What was the average amount of shellfish caught worldwide in one month? Round the answer to the nearest tenth. (Pages 166–167)

65. Shrimp and oysters are the only shellfish listed on the chart. What is the difference between the number of tons of fish and shellfish caught in 1 year? (Pages 166–167)

66. There were 3,271,000 tons of cod caught in 1 year. How many more tons of cod were caught than shellfish in 1 year? (Pages 166–167)

67. A Japanese fishing boat caught 3,423.6 pounds of fish in 12 days. A Greek fishing boat caught 2,632.5 pounds of fish in 9 days. Which boat caught more fish per day? How many more pounds of fish does this boat bring back per day? (Pages 166–167)

CHAPTER TEST

Multiply.

1.	56.3	2.	4.8	3.	7.26	4.	23.4
	× 7		×0.9		× 5.3		× 0.62

5.	0.07	6.	10	7.	0.023	8.	0.006
	×0.08		×0.004		× 0.05		× 100

Divide until the remainder is zero.

9. $6\overline{)21.24}$ **10.** $9\overline{)4.932}$ **11.** $12\overline{)987.6}$

12. $41\overline{)133.414}$ **13.** $12\overline{)6.06}$ **14.** $8\overline{)2.7}$

15. $12\overline{)507.72}$ **16.** $32\overline{)53.76}$ **17.** $0.8\overline{)2.74}$

18. $0.4\overline{)3}$ **19.** $0.06\overline{)4.2}$ **20.** $1.2\overline{)174}$

Find the decimals to the nearest hundredth.

21. $\frac{4}{11}$ **22.** $\frac{7}{12}$ **23.** $\frac{6}{7}$

Solve.

24. A bluefish swims 40.3 miles per hour, while a sailfish swims 65.8 miles per hour. How much further will the sailfish swim in a 24 hours?

25. The navigator of a supertanker estimates the ship will travel 248 miles in 24 hours. The ship travels at an average speed of 11.5 miles per hour. What is the difference between the actual distance traveled and the estimated difference?

ENRICHMENT

Scientific Notation

The decimal numeration system is based on powers of ten.

Look for a pattern.

$$10 = 10^1 \qquad 100 = 10^2 \qquad 1{,}000 = 10^3 \qquad 10{,}000 = 10^4$$

Compare the number of zeros in the number with the exponent in the exponent form.

Scientists often work with very large numbers. For example, the number 900,000 is a large number. This number can be renamed by using **scientific notation.**

Step 1
Move the decimal point to the left to name a number less than 10 but not less than 1.

9.00000.

Step 2
You moved the decimal point 5 places to the left. Thus, you divided by 10^5. So multiply by 10^5.

9×10^5

The scientific notation for 900,000 is **9×10^5.**

● Name 87,600 using scientific notation.

Step 1
Move the decimal point to the left to name a number less than 10 but not less than 1.

8.7600.

Step 2
You have divided by 10^4. So multiply by 10^4.

8.76×10^4

The scientific notation for 87,600 is **8.76×10^4.**

EXERCISES • Write the exponent forms of the numbers.

1. 100
2. 10,000
3. 100,000
4. 1,000,000
5. 10,000,000
6. 100,000,000

Write the numbers.

7. 6×10^5
8. 4×10^2
9. 7×10^7
10. 2×10^6
11. 6.25×10^3
12. 5.2×10^4

Write in scientific notation.

13. 7,000
14. 400
15. 80,000
16. 400,000
17. 432,000
18. 625

ADDITIONAL PRACTICE

SKILLS

Place the decimal point in the product.   (Pages 158–159)

1. 4.5	**2.** 62.3	**3.** 4.53	**4.** 2.38	**5.** 70.9
×6.2	× 3.7	× 9.22	× 7.5	×6.24
2790	23051	417666	17850	442416

Multiply.   (Pages 160–163)

6. 32.6	**7.** 0.04	**8.** 50.08	**9.** 0.25	**10.** 300.87
× 5	×0.03	× 0.96	×0.386	× 45.5

Divide until the remainder is zero.   (Pages 170–171)

11. 6)8.7   **12.** 15)34.8   **13.** 16)49.6   **14.** 25)0.4905   **15.** 42)8.484

Multiply.   (Pages 172–173)

16. $10 \times 3.8 = \underline{?}$ **17.** $100 \times 6.809 = \underline{?}$ **18.** $1,000 \times 0.485 = \underline{?}$

Divide.   (Pages 172–173)

19. $45.92 \div 10 = \underline{?}$ **20.** $0.173 \div 100 = \underline{?}$ **21.** $3,240.7 \div 1,000 = \underline{?}$

Divide.   (Pages 174–177)

22. 1.3)4.498   **23.** 0.24)4944   **24.** 0.251)5.0451   **25.** 0.006)0.03846

26. 0.25)157.5   **27.** 3.14)16.3908   **28.** 0.39)0.17862   **29.** 0.003)0.1956

Divide. Round to the nearest tenth.   (Pages 178–179)

30. 7)4   **31.** 24)1,904   **32.** 36)5,248   **33.** 3.5)2.509

Find the decimals to the nearest hundredth.   (Pages 178–179)

34. $\frac{2}{25}$ **35.** $\frac{4}{9}$ **36.** $\frac{13}{8}$ **37.** $\frac{11}{16}$ **38.** $\frac{19}{6}$ **39.** $\frac{6}{7}$

PROBLEM SOLVING • APPLICATIONS

40. The water level in a harbor is 42.5 feet at high tide and 17.3 feet at low tide. It takes the tide 5 hours to go out. How far does the water level drop in 3 hours?
(Pages 166–167)

41. An oyster farmer harvested 1,039.4 pounds of oysters Monday and 1,687.8 pounds on Tuesday. The farmer used 28 containers to hold the oysters. What is the average number of pounds each container will hold?   (Pages 166–167)

COMPUTER APPLICATIONS

Programs: LIST and RUN

The computer will display whatever is between quotation marks in PRINT statements. On most computers, you must hold down a **SHIFT** key and press the " key.
Type this command.

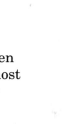

PRINT "2.5347/.007=" ◄ Then press **RETURN, or ENTER, or** ⏎.

Output: 2.5347/.007= ◄ The quotation marks are not displayed.

Now type the same command but <u>without</u> quotation marks or the =.

PRINT 2.5347/.007 ◄ Then press **RETURN, or ENTER, or** ⏎.

Output: 362.1

You can now use a *program* to instruct the computer to display the problem <u>and</u> the answer. A **program** is a set of instructions given in a step–by–step form. The steps in a program are numbered in order. The last step is **END.**

Type: 10 PRINT ".5472/.012=" ⟵ Then press RETURN, or ENTER, or ⏎.
Type: 20 PRINT .5472/.012 ⟵ Then press RETURN, or ENTER, or ⏎.
Type: 30 END ⟵ Then press RETURN, or ENTER, or ⏎.

To see this program, type **LIST.** To see the output, type **RUN.**
Then press **RETURN, or ENTER, or** ⏎

EXERCISES • Find the output when each program is RUN.

1. 10 PRINT 507.72/12
   20 END

2. 10 PRINT 78/16
   20 PRINT

3. 10 PRINT 5.4/.003
   20 END

4. 10 PRINT "14.4/.32="
   20 PRINT 14.4/.32
   30 END

5. 10 PRINT "5.6/.08="
   20 PRINT 5.6/.08
   30 END

6. 10 PRINT "3.98/.016="
   20 PRINT 3.98/.016
   30 END

MAINTENANCE

Mixed Practice • Choose the correct answers.

1. $0.47 \times 1{,}000 = $ ___?___

   A. 470   **B.** 47,000
   C. 47   **D.** not here

2. $7.46 \times 100 = $ ___?___

   A. 74.6   **B.** 74,600
   C. 746   **D.** not here

3. $8{,}596 \div 100 = $ ___?___

   A. 8.596   **B.** 85.96
   C. 859,600 **D.** not here

4. $56 + 38.5 + 54 = $ ___?___

   A. 138.5 **B.** 1,485
   C. 148.5 **D.** not here

5. $3.14 \times 30 = $ ___?___

   A. 94.2   **B.** 942
   C. 9.42   **D.** not here

6. $3.14 \times 15.8 = $ ___?___

   A. 49,612 **B.** 496.12
   C. 49.612 **D.** not here

7. $9.6 \times 141 = $ ___?___

   A. 1,353.6 **B.** 135.36
   C. 1,343.6 **D.** not here

8. $7.6 + 3.4 + 9.5 = $ ___?___

   A. 2.05   **B.** 19.5
   C. 20.5   **D.** not here

9. $4.3 \times 7.2 = $ ___?___

   A. 24.768 **B.** 247.68
   C. 2,476.8 **D.** not here

10. Round 9.405 to the nearest tenth.

    A. 9.41   **B.** 9.42
    C. 9.4   **D.** not here

11. $10 \times 36.5 \times 10 = $ ___?___

    A. 3,650 **B.** 365
    C. 36,500 **D.** not here

12. $5.3 \times 8 \times 3 = $ ___?___

    A. 120   **B.** 127.2
    C. 16.3   **D.** not here

13. $(3 \times 2) + (6 \times 8) = $ ___?___

    A. 56   **B.** 49
    C. 54   **D.** not here

14. $60\overline{)145}$

    A. 2 r 25 **B.** 2 r 6
    C. 1 r 70 **D.** not here

15. $2.7 \times 6.5 = $ ___?___

    A. 1.755 **B.** 17.55
    C. 175.5 **D.** not here

16. A ship returned to shore carrying 25.2 kilograms of sponges. The average weight of each sponge was 0.07 kilograms. How many sponges was the boat carrying?

    A. 25   **B.** 175
    C. 176.4   **D.** not here

17. The temperature was 48° on Monday and 50° on Wednesday. What is the average temperature for those two days?

    A. 49°   **B.** 51°
    C. 50°   **D.** not here

Measurement

The largest sequoia tree in Sequoia National Park has a diameter of 8.05 meters.

● What is the circumference of the tree?

A ranger in Bryce Canyon National Park travels 43.6 kilometers in the morning and 79.3 kilometers in the afternoon.

● Estimate the total distance traveled.

Metric Units of Length

The **kilometer, meter, decimeter, centimeter,** and **millimeter** are metric units of length.

Despite the heat, the desert is home for many animals, both large and small. Most desert animals keep out of the sun during the day. They come out only in the cool of the night.

A large desert animal is the coyote. It is about **1 meter (m)** long.

A smaller animal is the pocket mouse. It is about **1 decimeter (dm)** long.

10 dm	= 1 m
10 cm	= 1 dm
100 cm	= 1 m
10 mm	= 1 cm
100 mm	= 1 dm
1,000 mm	= 1 m
1,000 m	= 1 km

Ants are found on the desert. They are about **1 centimeter (cm)** in length.

The leg of an ant is about **1 millimeter (mm)** thick.

A **kilometer (km)** equals 1,000 meters.

E **PRACTICE** • Estimate the lengths. Then measure each to the nearest unit.

1.
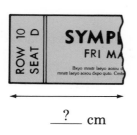

_____ cm

2.
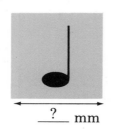

_____ mm

3.
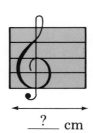

_____ cm

4.

____?____ mm

5.
____?____ cm

6.
____?____ cm

Use a ruler. Draw a picture of

7. a pencil that is 14 cm long.

8. a pen that is 122 mm long.

9. a piece of chalk that is 6 cm long.

10. a comb that is 180 mm long.

Which unit of measure would you use for each?
Write MILLIMETER, CENTIMETER, METER, or KILOMETER.

11. the thickness of a violin string

12. the distance from your house to school

13. the width of a stage

14. the length of a straw

Add the measures.

15.	**16.**	**17.**	**18.**	**19.**
23 cm	48 cm	123 mm	295.5 m	132.6 m
36 cm	32 cm	146 mm	48.4 m	34.2 m
+98 cm	+65 cm	+238 mm	+ 76.6 m	+396.9 m

PROBLEM SOLVING • **APPLICATIONS**

A wild animal consultant visits wild animal parks in several cities. Find each distance.

20. from New York to Atlanta to Houston

21. from Houston to Los Angeles to Chicago

22. from New York to Chicago to San Francisco

23. from New York to Chicago to Los Angeles

★ **24.** Which is the longer trip, from San Francisco to Chicago to New York to Atlanta or from San Francisco to Chicago to Los Angeles?

Changing Metric Units

The Grand Canyon is about 183 meters wide at its narrowest point, and about 1.6 kilometers deep. A group of hikers follow a 4–kilometer trail to the bottom. The narrowest part of the trail is about 37 centimeters wide.

● How many meters do they walk?

● How many meters wide is the narrowest part of the trail?

Think The metric system is based on the number 10. Each unit is 10 times the next smaller unit.

thousands	hundreds	tens	unit	tenths	hundredths	thousandths
kilometer km 1 km = 1,000 m 0.001 km = 1 m	hectometer hm 1 hm = 100 m 0.01 hm = 1 m	dekameter dam 1 dam = 10 m 0.1 dam = 1 m	meter m	decimeter dm 1 dm = 0.1 m 10 dm = 1 m	centimeter cm 1 cm = 0.01 m 100 cm = 1 m	millimeter mm 1 mm = 0.001 m 1,000 mm = 1 m

4 km = __?__ m

Step 1 Think: 1 km = 1,000 m

Step 2 4 km = 4 × 1,000 m
4 km = 4,000 m

They walk **4,000 m.**

$$4 \text{ km} = 4,000. \text{ m}$$

37 cm = __?__ m

Step 1 Think: 1 cm = 0.01 m

Step 2 37 cm = 3.7 × 0.01 m
37 cm = 0.37 m

The trail is **0.37 m** wide at the narrowest point.

$$37 \text{ cm} = 0.37 \text{ m}$$

PRACTICE • Complete.

1. 6 m = __?__ km

2. 3 km = __?__ m

3. 5 m = __?__ cm

4. 11 mm = __?__ m

5. __?__ mm = 14 m

6. __?__ mm = 9 m

7. __?__ m = 2.4 cm

8. 8.6 km = __?__ m

9. 0.63 km = __?__ m

EXERCISES • Complete.

10. 1 m = __?__ km

11. 4 km = __?__ m

12. __?__ m = 800 cm

13. _?_ cm = 0.08 m

14. 16 m = _?_ cm

15. 9 km = _?_ m

16. 4 mm = _?_ m

17. _?_ m = 3,000 mm

18. 6 m = _?_ cm

19. 30.2 m = _?_ km

20. _?_ m = 190 cm

21. 0.06 m = _?_ cm

22. 7.4 cm = _?_ m

23. 0.027 m = _?_ mm

24. _?_ m = 7 mm

★ **25.** _?_ cm = 5.28 dm

★ **26.** 4.6 dm = _?_ mm

★ **27.** 52.4 km = _?_ cm

★ **28.** 73.2 km = _?_ dam

★ **29.** _?_ dam = 10.3 dm

★ **30.** 48.5 hm = _?_ cm

Complete.

	Kilometer	Hectometer	Dekameter	Meter	Decimeter	Centimeter	Millimeter
	0.006 km	0.06 hm	0.6 dam	6 m	60 dm	600 cm	6,000 mm
31.	0.037	0.37	3.7 dam	37 m	370	3700	37,000
32.	0.024	0.24 hm	2.4	24	240	2400	24,000
33.	0.004	0.04	0.4	4.0	40 dm	400	4,000
34.	0.00085	0.0085	0.085	0.85	8.5	85 cm	850
35.	0.0098	0.098	0.98	9.8 m	98.	980	9800
★ **36.**							8×10^9 mm

Mental Math Compare. Use >, <, or =.

★ **37.** 6.8 m **>** 69.2 cm

★ **38.** 15.32 m **>** 1,500 cm

★ **39.** 230 cm ⬤ 2.3 m

★ **40.** 2.18 m ⬤ 2,184 cm

★ **41.** 30 cm ⬤ 0.003 m

★ **42.** 61.4 cm ⬤ 0.6 m

PROBLEM SOLVING • APPLICATIONS

43. The north rim of the Grand Canyon is about 2,512 meters above sea level. How many kilometers is this?

44. The south rim of the Grand Canyon is about 2.103 kilometers above sea level. How many meters is this?

45. The north rim of the Grand Canyon gets about 356 centimeters of snow each year. Its trails are open from May to October. The South Rim gets about 1.55 meters of snow and is open all year. How many more centimeters of snow fall on the North Rim?

46. Tanner Trail was originally called Horsethief Trail because it was used to move stolen horses from Utah to New Mexico and Texas. The trail is 27.5 kilometers long. How long would it take to travel this distance if it took a half–hour to cover 3,212.5 meters?

Perimeter

Not far from the Grand Canyon is Monument Valley National Park. Like giant building blocks, unusual rock formations rise 300 meters straight up from the desert floor. A tourist wishes to hike around a formation. The trail forms a rectangle. Two sides are each 40 meters long. The remaining two sides are each 21 meters long.

● How many meters will the visitor walk?

Think You need to find the distance around all four sides. This distance is called the **perimeter.**

> *The perimeter of a figure is the sum of the lengths of the sides.*

Find the perimeter.

Step 1 Find the measure of each side.

Step 2 Find the sum of the measures.

$$40 + 21 + 40 + 21 = 122$$ A visitor will walk **122 meters.**

PRACTICE • Find the perimeter of each figure.

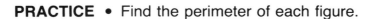

1.

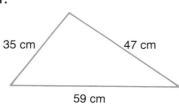

35 cm 47 cm 59 cm

2.

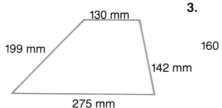

130 mm 199 mm 142 mm 275 mm

3.

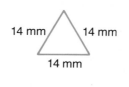

88 m 160 m 160 m 88 m

4.

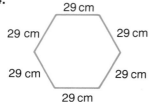

29 cm 29 cm 29 cm 29 cm 29 cm 29 cm

5.

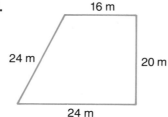

16 m 24 m 20 m 24 m

6.

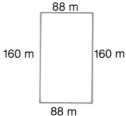

14 mm 14 mm 14 mm

EXERCISES • Find the perimeter of each figure.

7.
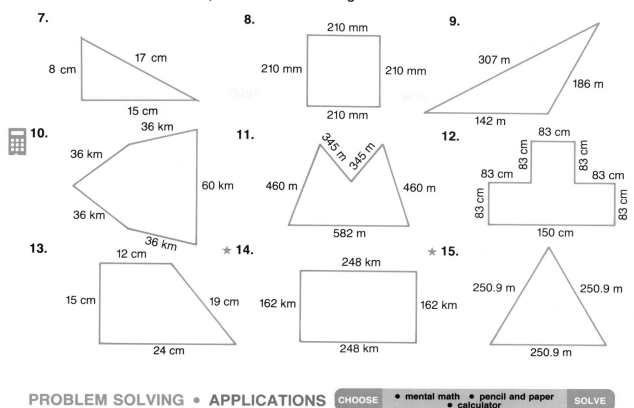
8 cm, 17 cm, 15 cm

8.
210 mm, 210 mm, 210 mm, 210 mm

9.
307 m, 186 m, 142 m

10.
36 km, 36 km, 60 km, 36 km, 36 km

11.
345 m, 345 m, 460 m, 460 m, 582 m

12.
83 cm, 83 cm, 83 cm, 83 cm, 83 cm, 83 cm, 83 cm, 83 cm, 150 cm

13.
12 cm, 15 cm, 19 cm, 24 cm

★ 14.
248 km, 162 km, 162 km, 248 km

★ 15.
250.9 m, 250.9 m, 250.9 m

PROBLEM SOLVING • APPLICATIONS

CHOOSE • mental math • pencil and paper • calculator SOLVE

16. What is the perimeter of the Visitor's Center?

17. What is the perimeter of the deck?

18. Sarah buys a large photograph of the highest formation in Monument Valley. She wants to frame it. The four sides of the photograph are 160 millimeters, 22 centimeters, 160 millimeters, and 22 centimeters long. How many centimeters of framing will she need?

★ 19. A back-packing group follows a triangular route around a group of formations in Monument Valley. The longest side is 8.5 meters long. The next longest side is 0.5 of a meter shorter than the longest side. The third side is 11 meters less than the sum of the lengths of the other. What is the perimeter?

Park Visitor's Center

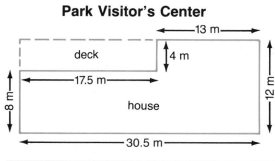

deck — 13 m, 4 m, 17.5 m, 8 m, house, 12 m, 30.5 m

Circumference of a Circle

The distance around a circle is its **circumference**.

The largest Giant Sequoia tree in the Sequoia National Park has a diameter of 8.05 meters.

● What is the circumference of the tree?

| **Think** | How are the diameter and circumference of the tree related? |

> The circumference, C, of any circle divided by the length of its diameter, d, is always the same number. It is about 3.14. The number is named by the Greek letter π (pi, pronounced pie).
>
> $$\frac{C}{d} = \pi$$
>
> The formula for finding the circumference is C = π × d.

Step 1
Think: $C = \pi \times d$

$d = 8.05$
Let $\pi = 3.14$.

Step 2

$C = 8.05 \times 3.14$
$C = 25.277$

The circumference of the tree is about **25.277 m.**

PRACTICE • Find the circumference of each. Let $\pi = 3.14$.

1.	2.	3.	4.
9 cm	10 mm	14 mm	68 mm

5. $d = 40$ mm   **6.** $d = 21$ cm   **7.** $d = 35$ cm   **8.** $d = 5.3$ m

---

EXERCISES • Find the circumference of each. Let $\pi = 3.14$.

9.	10.	11.	12.
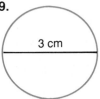 3 cm	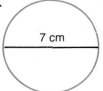 7 cm	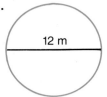 12 m	 46 km

13. $d = 4$ mm	**14.** $d = 11$ mm	**15.** $d = 18$ cm	**16.** $d = 27$ cm
17. $d = 62$ m	**18.** $d = 93$ m	**19.** $d = 325$ km	**20.** $d = 126$ km
21. $d = 8.6$ m	**22.** $d = 36.4$ m	**23.** $d = 17.9$ km	**24.** $d = 86.06$ km

Find the perimeter of each figure. Let $\pi = 3.14$.

25.

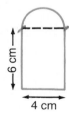

★ **26.**

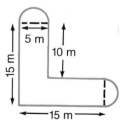

PROBLEM SOLVING • APPLICATIONS

The "pygmy forest" of the Grand Canyon is so named because the pinon pines and Utah junipers found there are smaller than normal pines. For Exercises 27–30, let $\pi = 3.14$.

27. Pinon pines in the Grand Canyon have a diameter of about 0.38 of a meter. Find the circumference of a pinon tree.

28. Utah junipers in the Canyon are about 7.6 meters tall and have a diameter of about 61 centimeters. What is the circumference of a juniper?

29. Normally, a ponderosa pine is between 18.3 and 39.6 meters tall and has a diameter of 1 meter. The Grand Champion ponderosa pine is 68 meters tall. What is the normal circumference of a ponderosa pine?

30. The Galberry Holly is a tree with a circumference of 12.7 meters. What is its diameter? Round the answer to the nearest tenth.

CALCULATOR • You can use a calculator to find circumference.

The largest Sequoia tree has a diameter of 11.4 meters. What is it's circumference? Let $\pi = 3.14$.

Think: $C = \pi \times d$

③ ⊙ ① ④ ⊗ ① ① ⊙ ④ ⊜ 〔 *35.796* 〕

EXERCISES. Find the circumference for each diameter.

1. 38.6 m	**2.** 2.146 cm	**3.** 10.392 mm	**4.** 36.32 dm	**5.** 15.22 km

Area of Rectangles

Metric units of area are the **square millimeter (mm²)**, **square centimeter (cm²)**, **square meter (m²)**, and **square kilometer (km²)**.

About 550 A.D., the Anasizi Indians built pit homes in what is now Mesa Verde National Park, Colorado. Ruins of these homes can still be seen. The ruins show that the houses were about 5 meters long and 3 meters wide.

● What was the area of a house?

Think You know the length and width.
You can use the information to find the area.

The number of square units that cover a surface is the **area** of the surface.

You can count the number of squares to find the area. You can also multiply to find the area.

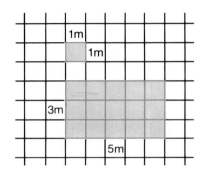

$$\text{Area} = \text{length} \times \text{width}$$
$$A = l \times w$$

Step 1
Write a number sentence.

$L = 5$
$W = 3$
$A = 5 \times 3$

Step 2
Multiply.

$A = 5 \times 3$
$A = 15$
$A = 15 \text{ m}^2$ The area is **15 square meters.**

PRACTICE • Count to find the area of each figure in square centimeters.

1.
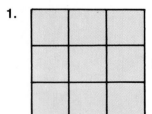
3 cm
3 cm

2.
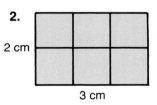
2 cm
3 cm

3.
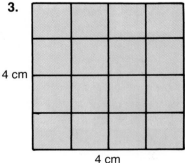
4 cm
4 cm

The length and the width are given. Find the area of each.

4. $l = 6$ cm, $w = 5$ cm

5. $l = 12$ mm, $w = 7$ mm

EXERCISES • Find the area of each figure.

6.

3 mm

6 mm

7.

4 cm

7 cm

8.

5 m

5 m

The length and the width are given. Find the area of each rectangle.

9. $l = 9$ mm, $w = 5$ mm

10. $l = 6$ mm, $w = 4$ mm

11. $l = 10$ cm, $w = 7$ cm

12. $l = 12$ cm, $w = 12$ cm

13. $l = 14$ cm, $w = 8$ cm

14. $l = 13$ cm, $w = 6$ cm

15. $l = 2.2$ km, $w = 7$ km

16. $l = 3.6$ km, $w = 10$ km

17. $l = 41.6$ m, $w = 15.2$ m

18. $l = 73.9$ m, $w = 73.9$ m

★ **19.** $l = 55$ mm, $w = 28$ cm

★ **20.** $l = 93$ m, $w = 0.8$ km

★ **21.** $l = 8.7$ m, $w = 129$ cm

★ **22.** $l = 134$ mm, $w = 185$ cm

PROBLEM SOLVING • APPLICATIONS

23. Pueblo Bonito was nearly 213.4 meters long and over 91.4 meters wide. What was the area of this ancient pueblo?

24. A modern 3-bedroom house is about 9.1 meters wide and 18.3 meters long. How much area does it cover?

25. Use your answers to Exercises 1 and 2 to find about how many modern houses would fit in Pueblo Bonito.

26. Pueblo Bonito is shaped like the letter D. About 800 rooms formed the outside. The inside was a courtyard. If each room was 3.7 meters long by 2.5 meters wide, what was the total indoor living area for the 1,000 people who lived in this ancient "apartment house?"

Area of Parallelograms

It is illegal to build fires in Utah's Bryce Canyon National Park. This allows fallen trees to rot and return nourishment to the soil. Suppose that rangers from Ranger Station I patrol the area shown by figure ABCD.

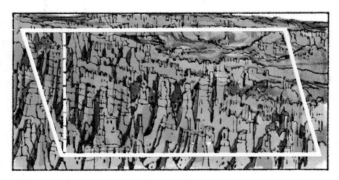

● How much area does this station protect?

Think You know the length of the base and the height of the parallelogram. You can use these numbers to find the area.

Use what you know about the area of a rectangle to find the area of a parallelogram.

a.	**b.**	**c.**
Cut off one end of the parallelogram.	Slide it around to the other end.	It now forms a rectangle.

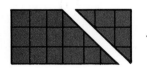

The area of the parallelogram is equal to the area of the rectangle. To find the area of a parallelogram, multiply the base times the height.

$$\text{Area} = \text{base} \times \text{height}$$
$$A = b \times h$$

Step 1
Think: $A = b \times h$
$b = 40$ km
$h = 20$ km

Step 2
$A = 40 \times 20$
$A = 800$
$A = 800$ km^2

The station protects an area of **800 km^2**.

PRACTICE • Find the area of each figure.

1.

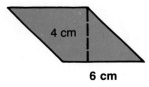

4 cm

6 cm

2.

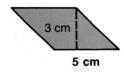

3 cm

5 cm

3.

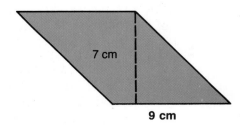

7 cm

9 cm

EXERCISES • Find the area of each figure.

4.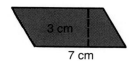
3 cm
7 cm

5.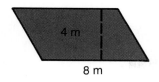
4 m
8 m

6.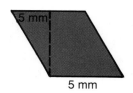
5 mm
5 mm

The base and the height are given. Find the area of each parallelogram.

7. $b = 8$ mm, $h = 7$ mm

8. $b = 8$ m, $h = 3$ m

9. $b = 10$ dm, $h = 3$ dm

10. $b = 12$ cm, $h = 9$ cm

11. $b = 24$ cm, $h = 6$ cm

12. $b = 36$ mm, $h = 10$ mm

★ **13.** $b = 42$ cm, $h = 150$ mm

★ **14.** $b = 0.78$ km, $h = 28$ m

★ **15.** $b = 550$ mm, $h = 36$ cm

★ **16.** $b = 0.93$ m, $h = 4.4$ cm

How much paper is needed to make each shape?

★ **17.**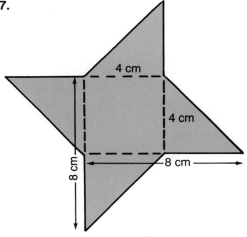
4 cm
4 cm
8 cm
8 cm

★ **18.**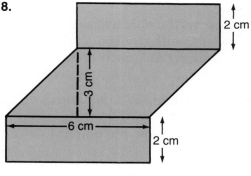
2 cm
3 cm
6 cm
2 cm

PROBLEM SOLVING • APPLICATIONS

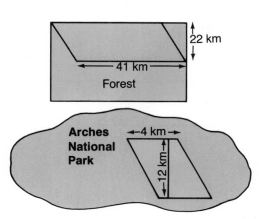

22 km
41 km
Forest

Arches National Park
4 km
12 km

19. A fire caused by lightning burned the forest area shown. How much of the forest was destroyed?

20. In Arches National Park, overgrazing destroyed grasslands leaving only weeds behind. The area shown has been reseeded. How much area has been reseeded?

Area of Triangles

You can use what you know about the area of a parallelogram to find the area of a triangle.

a.
Draw a diagonal of the parallelogram as shown below.

b.
You now have two triangles with the same area.

c.
The area of each triangle is $\frac{1}{2}$ the area of the parallelogram.

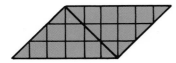
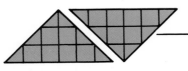
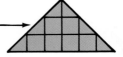
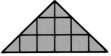

> To find the area of a triangle, multiply $\frac{1}{2}$ times the base times the height.
>
> $$\text{Area} = \frac{1}{2} \times \text{base} \times \text{height}$$
> $$A = \frac{1}{2} \times b \times h$$

Being lost in the wilderness can be frightening. Experts advise that when lost, a person should "hug a tree" until found. Suppose a search is conducted over this triangular area.

● How many square kilometers will this be?

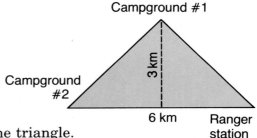

Think You know the height and the base of the triangle.

Step 1
$A = \frac{1}{2} \times b \times h$
$b = 6$
$h = 3$

Step 2
$A = \frac{1}{2} \times 6 \times 3$
$A = 9$
$A = 9 \text{ km}^2$

The area is **9 km²**.

PRACTICE • Find the area of each figure.

1.
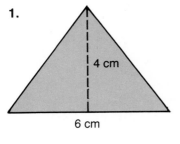
4 cm
6 cm

2.
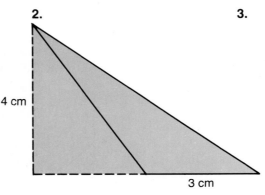
4 cm
3 cm

3.
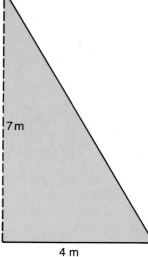
7 m
4 m

EXERCISES • Find the area of each figure.

4.

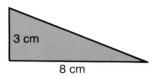

3 cm

8 cm

5.

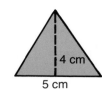

4 cm

5 cm

6.

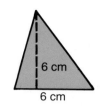

6 cm

6 cm

7.

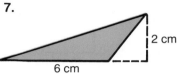

2 cm

6 cm

8.

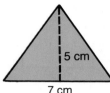

5 cm

7 cm

9.

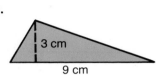

3 cm

9 cm

The base and the height are given. Find the area for each.

10. $b = 8$ cm, $h = 7$ cm

11. $b = 6$ cm, $h = 4$ cm

12. $b = 10$ m, $h = 3$ m

13. $b = 12$ cm, $h = 9$ cm

14. $b = 14$ cm, $h = 7$ cm

15. $b = 13$ m, $h = 8$ m

16. $b = 24$ m, $h = 6$ m

17. $b = 36$ cm, $h = 10$ cm

★ **18.** $b = 420$ mm, $h = 15$ cm

★ **19.** $b = 0.73$ m, $h = 28$ cm

★ **20.** $b = 5.5$ dm, $h = 0.36$ m

★ **21.** $b = 930$ mm, $h = 44$ cm

PROBLEM SOLVING • APPLICATIONS

22. A group of backpackers leaves a trip plan at the Ranger Station. If they do not return on time, how much area must be searched?

Ranger station

30 km

Red Canyon   50 km   Deer Mesa

23. A team of National Park rangers had to conduct a search based on this trip plan. What was the area they had to cover?

Fire Tower

12 km

Ravine Bridge   40 km   Visitor Center

★ **24.** Estimate the total area of the land shown on the map. Round each length to the nearest 10 meters.

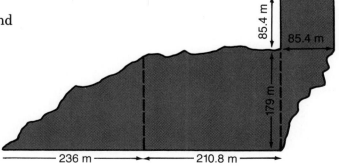

85.4 m

85.4 m

179 m

236 m   210.8 m

MID-CHAPTER REVIEW

Complete.   (Pages 192–193)

1. 5k = _?_ m

2. 40.5 cm = _?_ m

3. _?_ m = 6.8 cm

Find the perimeter.   (Pages 194–195)

4.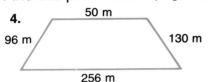

5.

6.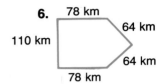

Find the circumference. Let π = 3.14.   (Pages 196–197)

7.
14 cm

8.
452 km

9.
18.12 m

Find the area of each figure.   (Pages 198–203)

10.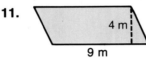
5 cm
11 cm

11.
4 m
9 m

12.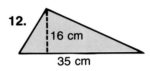
16 cm
35 cm

13. A Giant Sequoia tree has a diameter of 7.3 meters. What is the circumference of the tree? Let π = 3.14.   (Pages 196–197)

14. The north rim of the Grand Canyon is 2.512 kilometers above sea level and the south rim is 2,103 meters above sea level. How much higher is the north rim? (Pages 192–193)

MAINTENANCE • MIXED PRACTICE

Multiply.

1. $(3 \times 2) \times 5 = $ _?_

2. $(6 \times 8) \times 3 = $ _?_

3. $7 \times (2 \times 4) = $ _?_

4. $6 \times (7 \times 7) = $ _?_

5. $(3 \times 7) \times 9 = $ _?_

6. $3 \times (8 \times 5) = $ _?_

Add.

7. $35.6 + 48.2 = $ _?_

8. $59.6 + 82.7 = $ _?_

9. $125.3 + 45.6 + 27.2 = $ _?_

Subtract.

10. $48.3 - 16.7 = $ _?_

11. $82.5 - 78.9 = $ _?_

12. $206.7 - 99.8 = $ _?_

13. Find the pattern. How many trees will there be after 6 years?

Year	1	2	3	4	5	6
Number of Trees	2	6	12	20	30	?

14. A Giant Sequoia tree produces 345 cones each year. How many cones will the tree produce in 15 years?

CAREER APPLICATIONS

Travel Agent

Travel agents use maps to plan trips. A travel agent used this map to plan a vacation trip throughout the Southwestern United States.

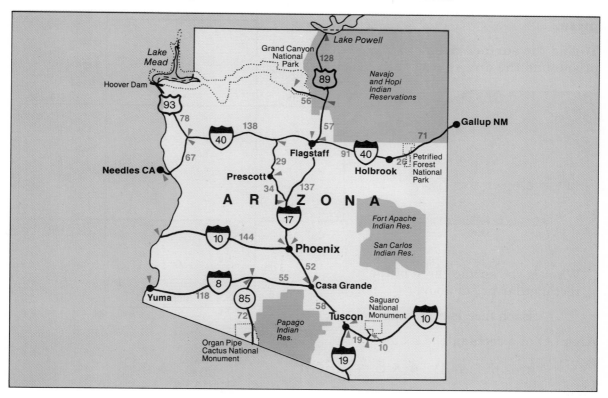

EXERCISES • For Exercises 1–6, use the road distances shown on the map.

1. How far is it from Flagstaff to the Grand Canyon?

2. How far is it from Tuscon to Lake Powell?

3. Which city, Flagstaff or Yuma, is closer by highway to the Saguro National Monument?

4. Which city, Yuma or Tucson, is closer by highway to Organ Pipe National Monument?

5. What is the distance between Flagstaff and the Petrified Forest?

6. Which is the shorter route: Yuma to Casa Grande to Tucson; or Flagstaff to Phoenix to Tuscon?

PROJECT Find a highway map of a state you would like to visit. Plan a five–day trip. Decide the distance you would like to travel each day. Locate where you would stop each evening. Select places you would like to visit.

Surface Area

The dimensions of this box are 4 centimeters by 5 centimeters by 3 centimeters.

Look at the box opened up.
The six **faces** are rectangles.
This box is a **rectangular prism.**

To find the **surface area** of a rectangular prism, find the area of each face. Then add.

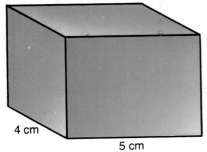

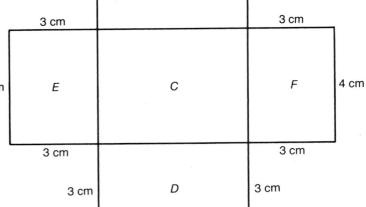

● What is the surface area of the rectangular prism above?

Think Each face is a rectangle.

Area (A) of a rectangle = $l \times w$.

Area of face A: $4 \times 5 = 20$ cm^2
Area of face B: $3 \times 5 = 15$ cm^2
Area of face C: $4 \times 5 = 20$ cm^2
Area of face D: $3 \times 5 = 15$ cm^2
Area of face E: $3 \times 4 = 12$ cm^2
Area of face F: $3 \times 4 = \underline{12}$ cm^2
Surface area: **94 cm^2**

PRACTICE • Find the surface area of each figure.

1.

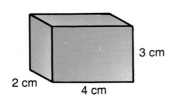

3 cm
2 cm
4 cm

2.

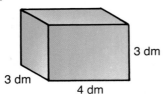

3 dm
3 dm
4 dm

3.

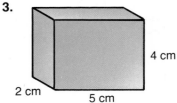

4 cm
2 cm
5 cm

EXERCISES • Find the surface area of each figure.

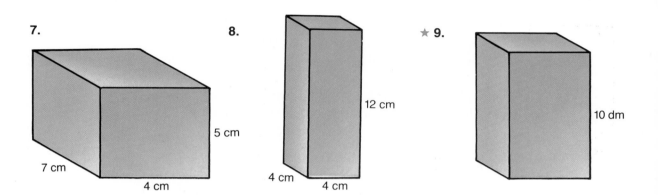

4. 4 cm, 5 cm, 6 cm

5. 4 cm, 7 cm, 8 cm

6. 6 cm, 6 cm, 6 cm

7. 5 cm, 7 cm, 4 cm

8. 12 cm, 4 cm, 4 cm

★ **9.** 10 dm

PROBLEM SOLVING • APPLICATIONS

10. The four sides of the tent shown are to be waterproofed. The bottom does not need to be waterproofed. How much area will have to be treated?

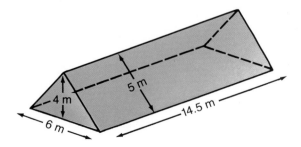

4 m, 5 m, 6 m, 14.5 m

11. Some ancient ruins have figures painted on the inside walls of the rooms. If a room is 3.6 meters long, 2.7 meters wide, and 2.1 meters high, how much space was available on walls, ceiling and floor for paintings?

12. The Iroquois Indians of the eastern United States built rectangular "long huts" where several families lived together. Some huts were 30 meters long, 15 meters wide, and 17 meters high. Find the surface area of the long hut. Do not include the area of the floor.

Volume and Rectangular Prisms

Some metric units of volume are the **cubic meter (m³)**, **cubic centimeter (cm³)**, and **cubic millimeter (mm³)**.

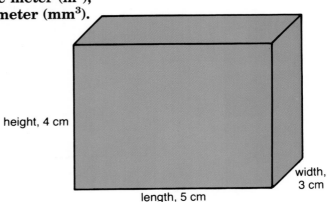

Officials at Utah's Zion National Park are asked to send soil samples to a museum in Boston. The museum requests 60 cubic centimeters of soil. The Park Service has available a box which is 5 centimeters long, 3 centimeters wide, and 4 centimeters high.

height, 4 cm

width, 3 cm

length, 5 cm

● How much soil will the box hold?

Think You know the length, width, and height of the box. You can use this information to find how much soil the box will hold.

The number of cubic units that will fit in this box is called the **volume** of the box.

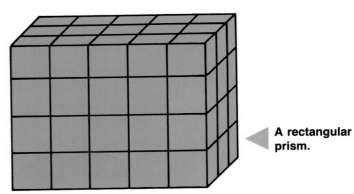

A rectangular prism.

> *To find the volume of a rectangular prism, you multiply length times width times height.*
>
> **Volume = length × width × height**
> **V = l × w × h**

Step 1
$V = l \times w \times h$
$l = 5$
$w = 4$
$h = 3$

Step 2
$V = 5 \times 4 \times 3$
$V = 60$
$V = 60 \text{ cm}^3$

The box will hold **60 cm³** of soil.

PRACTICE • Find the volume of each figure.

1.
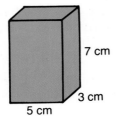
7 cm
3 cm
5 cm

2.
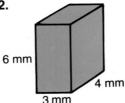
6 mm
4 mm
3 mm

3.
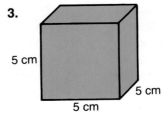
5 cm
5 cm
5 cm

EXERCISES • Find the volume of each figure.

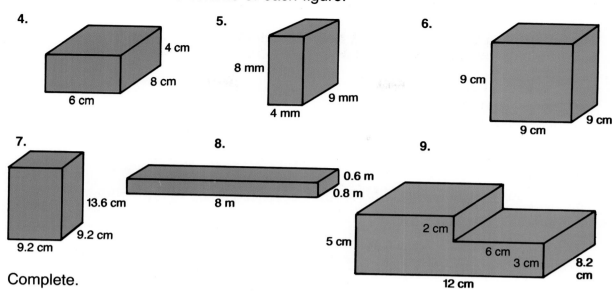

4.
4 cm
8 cm
6 cm

5.
8 mm
9 mm
4 mm

6.
9 cm
9 cm
9 cm

7.
13.6 cm
9.2 cm
9.2 cm

8.
0.6 m
0.8 m
8 m

9.
2 cm
5 cm
6 cm
3 cm
8.2 cm
12 cm

Complete.

	Length	Width	Height	Volume
10.	5 m	2 m	2 m	? m³
11.	10 cm	12.5 cm	10 cm	? cm³
12.	32 cm	20.6 cm	18 cm	? cm³
★ **13.**	8 m	5 m	? m	120 m³
★ **14.**	? m	9.8 m	4.3 m	505.68 m³
★ **15.**	70 cm	0.5 m	640 mm	? cm³

PROBLEM SOLVING • APPLICATIONS

16. Pioneers packed their possessions and supplies in wooden crates and trunks before they started West. How much room was there in a trunk 78 centimeters long, 45 centimeters wide, and 50 centimeters deep?

17. A folded quilt is about 60 centimeters long, 48 centimeters wide, and 5 centimeters thick. How much room did a pioneer woman need to allow for 1 folded quilt?

18. Big Bend National Park in Texas has more than 100 kinds of grasshoppers, 21 kinds of lizards and 30 kinds of snakes. A display uses clear, plastic boxes 15 centimeters by 7 centimeters by 4 centimeters to show each grasshopper. What is the volume of each box?

19. How much space would you have to allow in a crate for 21 lizard cages, if each cage is a box that is 20 centimeters long, 9 centimeters wide, and 5 centimeters high?

Metric Units of Liquid Capacity

The **milliliter (mL)**, **metric cup (c)**, **liter (L)**, and **kiloliter (kL)** are metric units used to measure liquid capacity.

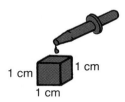

It takes 1 **milliliter** of water to fill 1 cubic centimeter.

The volume of a **metric cup** is 250 cubic centimeters. It takes 250 milliliters of water to fill a metric cup.

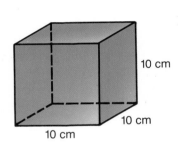

The volume of the cube is 1,000 cubic centimeters. It takes 4 metric cups of water to fill the cube. It takes 1,000 milliliters to fill the cube. The cube holds 1 **liter.**

$$1,000 \text{ mL} = 1 \text{ L}$$
$$1 \text{ mL} = 0.001 \text{ L}$$

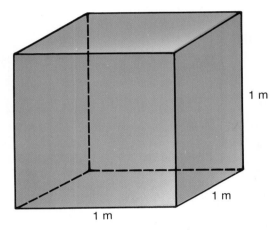

The volume of the cube is 1 cubic meter. It takes 1,000 liters to fill the cube. The cube holds 1 **kiloliter.**

$$1,000 \text{ L} = 1 \text{ kL}$$
$$1 \text{ L} = 0.001 \text{ kL}$$

PRACTICE • Choose the correct measure for each.

1.

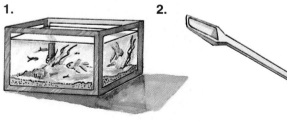

20 kL   20 L

2.

5 L   5 mL

3.

250 L   250 mL

4.

1 L   1 mL

EXERCISES • Choose the correct measure for each.

5. **6.** **7.** **8.**

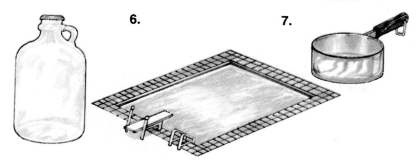

4 L   4 mL   80 kL   80 L   2 L   2 mL   250 L   250 mL

Mental Math   Complete. Write only the answers.

9. 34 L = __?__ mL   **10.** 0.5 kL = __?__ L   **11.** 3.2 L = __?__ mL

12. 2.86 L = __?__ mL   **13.** __?__ kL = 1,845 L   **14.** __?__ L = 482 mL

15. 9.41 L = __?__ mL   **16.** __?__ kL = 4,600 L   **17.** __?__ L = 5,000 mL

18. 0.25 kL = __?__ L   ★ **19.** 9 kL = __?__ mL   ★ **20.** 2.5 kL = __?__ mL

Add the measures.

21.	**22.**	**23.**	**24.**	**25.**
76 L	36 mL	562 kL	165.8 L	314.9 mL
76 L	19 mL	89 kL	209.6 L	85.2 mL
+98 L	+87 mL	+497 kL	+597.5 L	+268.7 mL

PROBLEM SOLVING • APPLICATIONS

26. In Bryce Canyon, a hiker should carry 4 liters of water for each day. A hiker carries 4,464 milliliters of water. How many liters of water is this?

27. In the desert 5 liters of water per person is recommended for each day's hiking. Four hikers are carrying 89,760 cubic centimeters of water in all. How many more liters of water should they carry for a 5–day hike?

Metric Units of Mass

The **milligram (mg), gram (g),** and **kilogram (kg)** are metric units
used to measure mass.

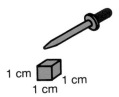

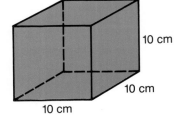

The cube is 1 cubic centimeter. It holds
1 milliliter of water. 1 milliliter of water
has a mass of **1 gram.**

$$1,000 \text{ mg} = 1 \text{ g}$$
$$1 \text{ mg} = 0.001 \text{ g}$$

The cube is 1,000 cubic centimeters. It
holds 1 liter of water. 1 liter of water
has a mass of **1 kilogram.**

$$1,000 \text{ g} = 1 \text{ kg}$$
$$1 \text{ g} = 0.001 \text{ kg}$$

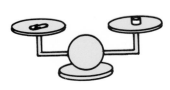

A paper clip has a mass of about
1 gram.

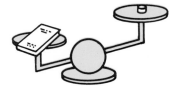

Your math book has a mass of about
1 kilogram.

PRACTICE • Which unit of measure would you use? Write GRAM or KILOGRAM.

1.   **2.**   **3.**   **4.**

EXERCISES • Choose the correct measure for each.

5.

5 g   5 kg

6.

500 mg   500 g

7.

3 g   3 kg

8.

6 g   6 kg

9.

7 g   7 kg

10.

315 g   315 kg

11.

1 g   1 kg

12.

150 g   150 kg

Mental Math   Complete.

13. 8 kg = __?__ g

14. 9 g = __?__ mg

15. __?__ g = 7 mg

16. 7.3 kg = __?__ g

17. __?__ kg = 88 g

18. __?__ g = 95 mg

19. __?__ kg = 348 g

20. 12.6 kg = __?__ g

21. 55.8 kg = __?__ g

22. __?__ kg = 500 g

★ **23.** 1.85 kg = __?__ mg

★ **24.** 53.9 kg = __?__ mg

PROBLEM SOLVING • APPLICATIONS

25. Camels are almost the only source of transportation, food, and clothing in some desert places. A camel has a mass of 450 to 726 kilograms. How many grams is this?

26. Camels can carry heavy loads for long distances. A camel can carry a load of up to 445,000 grams. How many kilograms is this?

27. In summer, a camel may drink about 19 liters of water per day. How many kilograms of water is this?

28. A fennec is a small desert fox with unusually large ears. The mass of a fennec is about 1,600 grams. How many times as large as a fennec is a camel with a mass of 640 kilograms?

Degrees Celsius

During the summer, temperatures in the southwestern deserts can reach 45 degrees Celsius. You can write this temperature as 45°C.

There are also deserts near the North and South poles. In winter, temperatures in these deserts are about 34 degrees below zero (⁻34°C).

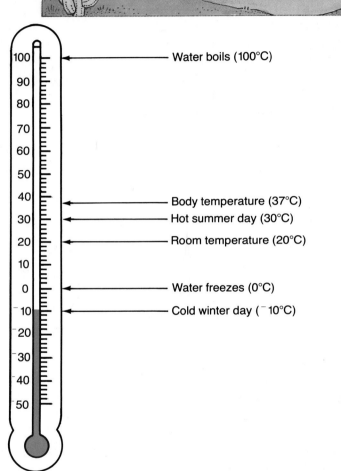

Water boils (100°C)

Body temperature (37°C)
Hot summer day (30°C)
Room temperature (20°C)

Water freezes (0°C)
Cold winter day (⁻10°C)

PRACTICE • Choose the correct temperature for each.

1.

30°C   3°C

2.

80°C   ⁻8°C

3.

90°C   9°C

EXERCISES • Give the temperature in degrees Celsius for each.

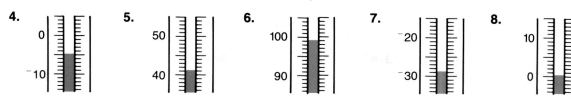

4. 0 / ‾10   5. 50 / 40   6. 100 / 90   7. ‾20 / ‾30   8. 10 / 0

PROBLEM SOLVING • APPLICATIONS

The **mean temperature** for a month is the average of the high and low temperatures for that month. Yuma Arizona is located on the edge of a desert. Find the mean Celsuis temperature in Yuma for each month.

	Month	High C	Low C	Mean
9.	January	19	6	?
10.	March	26	11	?
11.	May	35	18	?
12.	July	42	28	?
13.	September	39	24	?
14.	November	25	11	?

★ **15.** The mean temperature for February was 20°C. If the high temperature was 25°C what was the low temperature?

★ **16.** In June, the low temperature was 23°C. If the mean was 31°C, what was the high temperature?

THINKER'S CORNER

A Southwestern frontier town holds an arm wrestling tournament as part of the Fourth of July celebration. There are 30 contestants. Any contestant who loses a match must drop out of the competition. How many matches must be held in order to find a champion?

Time: Addition and Subtraction

<table>
<tr>
<td>

CLOCKS `8:00`

60 seconds (sec) = 1 minute (min)
60 minutes (min) = 1 hour (h)
24 hours (h) = 1 day (d)
From midnight to noon is A.M.
From noon to midnight is P.M.

</td>
<td>

CALENDAR

7 days (d) = 1 week (wk)
52 weeks (wk) = 1 year (yr)
12 months (mo) = 1 year (yr)
100 years (yr) = 1 century (cen)

</td>
</tr>
</table>

The Grand Canyon's Bright Angel Trail winds 21 miles from the rim to the Colorado River at the bottom. A group of hikers reach the halfway point in 135 minutes.

● Write 135 minutes as hours and minutes.

Think   60 min = 1 h

To change smaller units to larger units, divide.

$$135 \div 60 = 2 \text{ r}15$$ **They hike for 2 h 15 min.**

● 3 weeks 4 days = ___?___ days

Think   1 w = 7 d

To change larger units to smaller units, multiply.

$$3 \text{ w} = 3 \times 7 \text{ d}$$
$$= 21 \text{ d}$$
$$21 \text{ d} + 4 \text{ d} = 25 \text{ d}$$ 3 weeks 4 days = **25 days**

● 5 h 25 min + 9 h 55 min = ___?___

Think   Add the minutes and add the hours.

Step 1
Add.

  5 h 25 min
+9 h   5 min
14 hr 80 min

Step 2
If necessary, change
min to h.

80m = 1 h 20 min

Step 3
Add.

  14 h
+ 1 h 20 min
15 h 20 min

PRACTICE • Copy and complete.

1. 260 w = __?__ d

2. 55,000 yr = __?__ cen

3. 10 yr = __?__ mo

4. 12 d = __?__ h

5. 36,000 sec = __?__ min

6. 45 h = __?__ min

Add.

7. 1 h 20 min
     +3 h 10 min

8. 12 h 2 min
     + 1 h 50 min

9. 7 h 18 min
     +9 h 45 min

EXERCISES • Copy and complete.

10. 1 h 45 min = __?__ min

11. 4 wk = __?__ d

12. 7 yr = __?__ mo

13. 2 d 12 h = __?__ hr

14. 240 s = __?__ min

15. 72 h = __?__ d

16. 1 h 24 min = __?__ min

17. 360 s = __?__ min

18. 96 h = __?__ d

19. 7 wk = __?__ d

20. 180 min = __?__ h

21. 48 mo = __?__ yr

Add or subtract.

22. 2 h 30 min
     +6 h 40 min

23. 7 d 18 h
     −5 d 20 h

24. 11 h 46 min
     − 9 h 51 min

25. 7 h 25 min
     +3 h 54 min

26. 15 h 55 min
     − 7 h 58 min

27. 10 h 15 min
     − 3 h 33 min

28. 5 h 40 min
     −2 h 37 min

29. 5 h 17 min
     +11 h 29 min

30. 21 h 26 min
     + 1 h 32 min

31. 15 h 35 min
     + 8 h 28 min

32. 2 d 15 h
     +3 d 12 h

33. 5 d 20 h
     +1 d 6 h

PROBLEM SOLVING • APPLICATIONS

Solve.

34. A sunset at the Grand Canyon lasted 2,100 seconds. How many minutes is this?

35. Some rocks in the deepest part of the Grand Canyon date back 2 billion years. How many centuries old are these rocks?

36. The Colorado River began to form the Grand Canyon about 6 million years ago. Various Indian tribes have lived in the Grand Canyon for the last 4,000 years. How many centuries after the Colorado River began to form the Grand Canyon did Indian tribes began to live there?

PROBLEM SOLVING · STRATEGIES

Estimation

You can use estimation to determine whether an answer is reasonable.
You use rounding to estimate.

Example

Estimate the sum: $1.6 + 6.8$

Think Round each number. Then add.

Step 1
Round to the nearest whole number.

$$1.6 \longrightarrow 2$$
$$+6.8 \longrightarrow 7$$

Step 2
Add.

$$\begin{array}{r} 2 \\ +7 \\ \hline 9 \end{array}$$ ◀ **Estimated answer**

More Examples

Round to the nearest ten.

$$28.3 \longrightarrow 30$$
$$-11.6 \longrightarrow -10$$
$$\overline{20}$$

Round to the nearest hundred.

$$106.3 \longrightarrow 100$$
$$\times 217.6 \longrightarrow \times 200$$
$$\overline{20{,}000}$$

Round to the nearest ten.

$$236.5 \div 32.6$$
$$\downarrow \qquad \downarrow$$
$$240 \div 30 = 8$$

PRACTICE

E Choose the best estimate.

1. $3.6 + 7.2$ **a.** $4 + 8$ **b.** $3 + 7$ **c.** $4 + 7$

2. 93.7×28.1 **a.** 100×30 **b.** 90×30 **c.** 90×20

3. $436.3 - 192.6$ **a.** $400 - 100$ **b.** $500 - 100$ **c.** $400 - 200$

4. $319.7 \div 81.2$ **a.** $320 \div 90$ **b.** $310 \div 80$ **c.** $320 \div 80$

5. $5.2 + 8.6$ **a.** 14 **b.** 13 **c.** 15

6. 56.3×45.1 **a.** $2{,}400$ **b.** $2{,}000$ **c.** $3{,}000$

7. $936.7 - 397.3$ **a.** 600 **b.** 500 **c.** 700

8. $317.6 \div 44.4$ **a.** 8 **b.** 6 **c.** 10

PROBLEMS

9. An observation area at the edge of the Grand Canyon is 1.2 meters wide. It is 3.8 times as long. Estimate the length.

   a. 2 m × 3 m   **b.** 2 m × 5 m
   c. 1 m × 4 m

10. A ranger in Bryce Canyon National Park travels 43.6 kilometers in the morning and 79.3 kilometers in the afternoon. Estimate the total distance traveled.

    a. 40 km + 80 km
    b. 50 km + 80 km
    c. 40 km + 70 km

11. A hiking party in Canyonlands National Park carries 299.25 kilograms of supplies. The supplies are divided equally among 19 hikers. Estimate the number of kilograms carried by each hiker.

    a. 300 ÷ 10   **b.** 300 ÷ 20
    c. 200 ÷ 20

12. A four–wheel drive truck crosses a desert in 19.6 hours. The truck averages 58.6 kilometers per hour. Estimate the total distance traveled.

    a. 20 × 50 km   **b.** 10 × 50 km
    c. 20 × 60 km

13. A group of backpackers begin a trip across Arches National Park with 68.6 liters of water. At the end of the first day, they have 40.8 liters of water. Estimate how much water they used that first day.

    a. 80 L − 40 L   **b.** 60 L − 40 L
    c. 70 L − 40 L

14. Desert temperatures at night are lower than daytime temperatures. One night, the temperature is 27.8°C. The daytime temperature is 22.6° C higher. Estimate the daytime temperature.

    a. 40°C   **b.** 50°C   **c.** 60°C

Did you round correctly?

---

15. A ranger on horseback patrols an area of 675.5 square kilometers in one week. A ranger in a helicopter can patrol 20.2 times as much area. Estimate the area the helicopter can patrol.

    a. 13,600 km^2 **b.** 13,400 km^2
    c. 13,800 km^2

Write Your Own Problem

This table lists 3 kinds of bears and information about each kind.

Use some or all of this data to write two problems similar to Exercise 15. Have a classmate solve the problems.

	Length	Mass
Black bear	1.5 m	140.8 kg
Grizzly bear	2.4 m	278.9 kg
Polar bear	2.67 m	451.8 kg

CHAPTER REVIEW

Part 1 • VOCABULARY

For Exercises 1–9, choose from the box at the right the word that best completes each sentence.

1. Meters, liters, and grams are ___?___ units of measure. (Page 190)

2. One kilometer equals 1,000 ___?___. (Page 192)

3. Water freezes at 0° ___?___. (Page 214)

4. One kilogram equals 1,000 ___?___. (Page 212)

5. The distance around a circle is its ___?___. (Page 196)

6. Add the lengths of the sides of a figure to find its ___?___. (Page 194)

7. Multiply the length and width of a figure to find its ___?___. (Page 198)

8. Multiply the length, width, and height to find its ___?___. (Page 208)

9. 1,000 milliliters equals one ___?___. (Page 210)

area
Celsius
circumference
grams
liter
meters
metric
perimeter
volume

Part 2 • SKILLS

Complete. (Pages 192–193)

10. 8 k = ___?___ m

11. 38.9 mm = ___?___ cm

12. ___?___ k = 858.6 m

Find the perimeter of each figure. (Pages 194–195)

13.
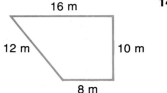

14.
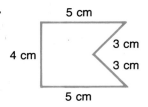

15.
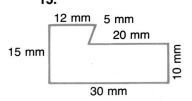

Find the area of each figure. (Pages 198–203)

16.
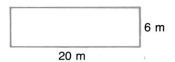

17.
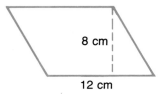

18.

Find the circumference of each. Let $\pi = 3.14$. (Pages 196–197)

19. d = 5 mm　　　**20.** d = 36 km　　　**21.** d = 282 cm　　　**22.** d = 47.4 m

Find the surface area of each figure. (Pages 206–207)

23.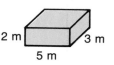

24.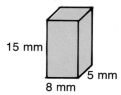

25.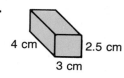

Find the volume of each figure. (Pages 208–209)

26.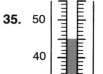

27.

28.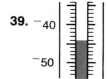

Complete. (Pages 210–211)

29. 12 L = __?__ mL　　　**30.** __?__ kL = 3,800L　　　**31.** __?__ L = 972 mL

Complete. (Pages 212–213)

32. 28 kg = __?__ g　　　**33.** __?__ kg = 658 g　　　**34.** __?__ kg = 451 g

Write the temperature in degrees Celsius for each. (Pages 214–215)

35. 50　40

36. 20　0

37. ⁻10　⁻20

38. 80　70

39. ⁻40　⁻50

Add or subtract. (Pages 216–217)

40.　3 h 30 min
　　　+5 h 50 min

41.　10 h 22 min
　　　− 7 h 39 min

42.　3 d 42 h
　　　+4 d 36 h

43.　26 h 15 min
　　　−19 h 46 min

Part 3 • PROBLEM SOLVING • APPLICATIONS

44. A national park lays out a campground nature study reserve. Estimate the perimeter of the reserve. (Pages 218–219)

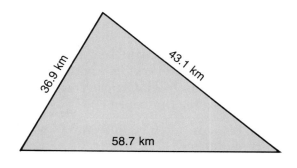

45. A construction company is pouring concrete parking slabs in a camping area. Estimate how many cubic meters of concrete will be needed. (Pages 218–219)

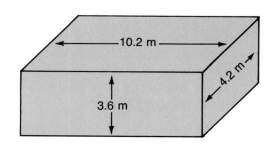

CHAPTER TEST

Which unit of measure would you use for each? Write millimeter, centimeter, meter, or kilometer.

1. The thickness of a guitar string

2. The distance a bird can fly in a day

3. The width of a classroom

4. The length of a harmonica

Complete.

5. 12 cm = ___ m

6. 17,000 m = ___ km

7. 30 cm = ___ mm

8. 18,000 mL = ___ L

9. 0.8 kg = ___ g

10. 0.6 kL = ___ L

11. 7 cm = ___ m

12. ___ g = 7 mg

13. ___ kg = 1 g

Complete.

14.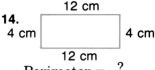
12 cm
4 cm   4 cm
12 cm
Perimeter = _?_

15.
8mm
Circumference = _?_

16.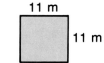
11 m
11 m
Area = _?_

17.
14 m
4 m
Area = _?_

18.
5 cm
20 cm
Area = _?_

19.
5 m
4 m
8 m
Surface area = _?_

20.
13 cm
13 cm
Perimeter = _?_

21.
6 m
11 m
Area = _?_

22.
6 cm
Circumference = _?_

23.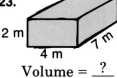
2 m
4 m
7 m
Volume = _?_

24. Two hikers travel for 3.5 days through Yosemite National Park. They hike 12.4 kilometers each day. Choose the best estimate for the total distance.

a. 48 km   **b.** 52 km   **c.** 36 km

25. A box is 40.3 centimeters long, 19.7 centimeters wide, and 4.2 centimeters high. Choose the best estimate for the volume.

a. 800 cm³   **b.** 3,200 cm³
c. 4,000 cm³

ENRICHMENT

Area of a Circle

This circle has a radius of 3 centimeters. Each quarter of the large blue square has an area of 3 × 3, or 3^2. The area of the large square is 4 times 3^2.

The area of the circle is more than 3^2 but less than 4 times 3^2. The area of the circle is more than 9 but less than 36.

Ancient mathematicians found that π times the radius squared could be used to find the area of a circle. π is a decimal number between 3 and 4. We use 3.14 for π.

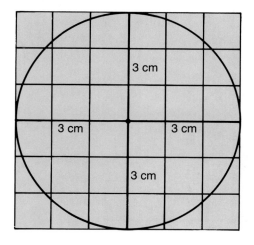

Find the area of a circle when the radius is 3 cm. Use 3.14 for π.

≈ means "is about".

$$A = \pi \times r^2$$
$$A \approx 3.14 \times 3 \times 3$$
$$A \approx 28.26$$

The area of the circle is **28.26 square centimeters** or **28.26 cm²**.

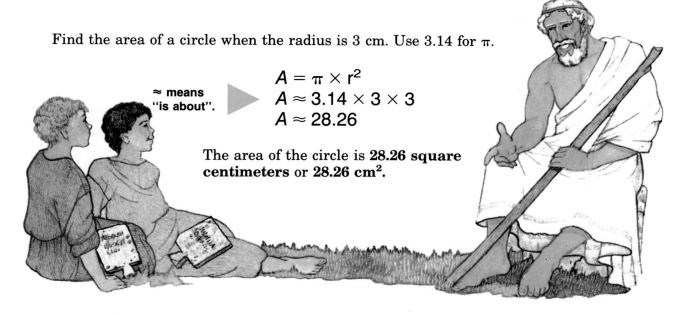

EXERCISES • The length of a radius is given. Find the area of each circle.

1. 6 cm	**2.** 2 cm	**3.** 8 cm	**4.** 10 m
5. 7 m	**6.** 3 m	**7.** 5 m	**8.** 9 m
9. 12 m	**10.** 15 m	**11.** 8.1 cm	**12.** 3.3 cm

ADDITIONAL PRACTICE

SKILLS

Complete. (Pages 192–193)

1. 7 km = __?__ m

2. 3.5 cm = __?__ m

3. __?__ k = 348.2 m

Find the perimeter of each figure. (Pages 194–195)

4.
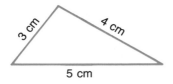

5.
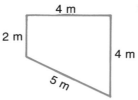

6.
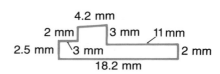

Find the area of each figure. (Pages 198–203)

7.
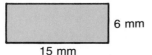

8.

9.
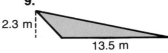

Find the surface area and the volume of each figure. (Pages 206–209)

10.
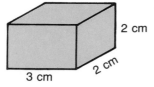

11.
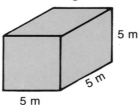

12.
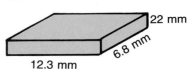

Complete. (Pages 210–213)

13. 17L = __?__ mL

14. __?__ kg = 4,583 g

15. 34.8 kg = __?__ g

Add or subtract. (Pages 216–217)

16.   4 h 16 min
     +7 h 58 min

17.   9 d 13 h
     −3 d 21 h

18.   34 h 12 min
     −17 h 59 min

PROBLEM SOLVING • APPLICATIONS

19. Pine seedlings are to be planted in a national forest. The dimensions and shape of the area are shown below. Estimate the number of square kilometers to be planted. (Pages 218–219)

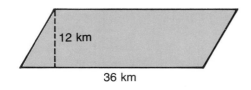

20. A circular garden in front of a mountain lodge has a diameter of 4.8 meters. Estimate the circumference of the garden. (Pages 218–219)

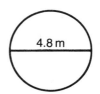

COMMON ERRORS

Each of these problems contains a common error.
a. Find the correct answer.
b. Find the error.

1. Write 77.1, 0.771, 7.71 and 0.077 in order from least to greatest.

0.771, 0.077, 7.71, 77.1

2. Round 83.65 to nearest tenth.

$83.65 \rightarrow$ **80.65**

3. Add.

$36.74 + 2.56 =$ _?_

$$\begin{array}{r} 36.74 \\ +\ 2.56 \\ \hline \mathbf{38.130} \end{array}$$

4. Subtract.

$75.6 - 0.93 =$ _?_

$$\begin{array}{r} {\scriptstyle 4\ 16} \\ 7\ 5.6 \\ -\ \ 0.9\ 3 \\ \hline \mathbf{7\ 4.7\ 3} \end{array}$$

5. Subtract.

$35.5 - 2.67 =$ _?_

$$\begin{array}{r} 39.5 \\ -2.67 \\ \hline \mathbf{12.8} \end{array}$$

6. Multiply

$27.3 \times 0.48 =$ _?_

$$\begin{array}{r} 27.3 \\ \times 0.48 \\ \hline 2184 \\ 10920 \\ \hline \mathbf{1310.4} \end{array}$$

7. Multiply.

$0.38 \times 0.03 =$ _?_

$$\begin{array}{r} 0.38 \\ \times 0.03 \\ \hline \mathbf{001.14} \end{array}$$

8. Divide.

$1.632 \div 32 =$ _?_

$$\begin{array}{r} .51 \\ 32\overline{)1.632} \\ \underline{1\ 60} \\ 32 \\ \underline{32} \\ 0 \end{array}$$

9. Divide until the remainder is zero.

$9.6 \div 15 =$ _?_

$$\begin{array}{r} \mathbf{0.6} \\ 15\overline{)9.6} \\ \underline{9\ 0} \\ 6 \end{array}$$

10. Divide.

$5.06 \div 1.1 =$ _?_

$$\begin{array}{r} \mathbf{46.} \\ 1.1.\overline{)5.06.} \\ \underline{4\ 4} \\ 66 \\ \underline{66} \\ 0 \end{array}$$

11. 860 mm = _?_ m

$860 \div 10 =$ _?_ m
$860\ mm =$ **86 mm**

12. Find the perimeter.

```
      6 m
    ┌──────┐
4 m │      │ 4 m
    └──────┘
      6 m
```

$P = 4 \times 6 \times 4 \times 6$
$P =$ **576 m**

CUMULATIVE REVIEW

Chapters 1 through 8

Choose the correct answer.

1. Subtract.

$$560,076$$
$$- 24,342$$

A. 546,734
B. 536,334
C. 535, 734
D. not here

2. Round to the nearest thousand.

378,475

A. 370,000
B. 380,000
C. 378,000
D. not here

3. Multiply.

$$679$$
$$\times 35$$

A. 23,765
B. 5,432
C. 23,425
D. not here

4. Divide.

$$35\overline{)7,250}$$

A. 27 r5
B. 207 r5
C. 207 r15
D. not here

5. In what place is the underlined digit?

23.7<u>4</u>5

A. tenths
B. thousands
C. hundredths
D. not here

6. Compare.

7.6 ⬤ 7.064

A. =
B. <
C. >
D. not here

7. Round to the nearest hundredth.

24.369

A. 24.000   **B.** 24.37
C. 24.36   **D.** not here

8. Add.

$8.62 + 24.3 = \underline{?}$

A. 32.92   **B.** 11.05
C. 3.292   **D.** not here

9. Subtract.

$$19.24$$
$$- 5.72$$

A. 14.34   **B.** .1474
C. 13.74   **D.** not here

10. Add.

$93.85 + 16.7 = \underline{?}$

A. 110.55   **B.** 11.055
C. 109.55   **D.** not here

11. Subtract.

$167.4 - 26.13 = \underline{?}$

A. 149.33   **B.** 139.27
C. 139.33   **D.** not here

12. Add.

$16.437 + 26.32 = \underline{?}$

A. 190.69   **B.** 32.757
C. 42.757   **D.** not here

13. Karen traveled 853 kilometers on Monday and 714 kilometers on Tuesday. Which equation could be used to find how much further she traveled on Monday?

A. $853 + 714 = n$ **B.** $714 - 853 = n$
C. $853 - 714 = n$ **D.** not here

14. Barney jogs 5.2 miles on Monday, 3.43 miles on Tuesday, and 4.6 miles on Wednesday. How far did he jog in all?

A. 4.41 miles   **B.** 13.23 miles
C. 1.323 miles   **D.** not here

15. Multiply.

$10 \times 42.367 =$ ___?___

A. 4.2367
B. 423.67
C. 42.0367
D. not here

16. Multiply.

$9.3 \times 8.5 =$ ___?___

A. 79.05
B. 7.905
C. 7,895
D. not here

17. Multiply.

$12.36 \times 3.43 =$ ___?___

A. 412.948
B. 423.948
C. 42.3948
D. not here

18. Multiply.

$$\begin{array}{r} 0.005 \\ \times\ 0.13 \\ \hline \end{array}$$

A. 0.00065
B. 0.00095
C. 0.0050
D. not here

19. Divide until the remainder is zero.

$25\overline{)78.9}$

A. 3.116
B. 315.6
C. 3.156
D. not here

20. Divide.

$49.36 \div 1000 =$ ___?___

A. 0.04936
B. 0.4936
C. 0.49360
D. not here

21. Divide.

$0.62\overline{)16.74}$

A. 0.27
C. 27
B. 0.027
D. not here

22. Circumference = ___?___

9 m

A. 18 m
C. 28.26 m
B. 27 m
D. not here

23. Area = ___?___

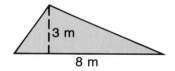
3 m
8 m

A. 12 m²
C. 11 m²
B. 24 m²
D. not here

24. Perimeter = ___?___

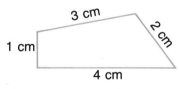
3 cm
2 cm
1 cm
4 cm

A. 10 cm
C. 24 cm
B. 7 cm
D. not here

25. Volume = ___?___

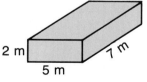
2 m
7 m
5 m

A. 14 m³
C. 70 m³
B. 45 m³
D. not here

26. Surface Area = ___?___

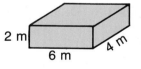
2 m
4 m
6 m

A. 44 m²
C. 64 m²
B. 88 m²
D. not here

27. If Ben runs 25.2 km in one week, how far will he run in 9 days?

A. 3.6 km
C. 32.4 km
B. 28 km
D. not here

28. Sara made 84.2 grams of strawberry jam. She has 10 jars of equal size. Estimate how many grams of jam she can put in each jar?

A. 8 g
C. 9 g
B. 10 g
D. not here

Mixed Practice • Choose the correct answers.

1. $3\overline{)27}$

The remainder = ___?___

A. 0   B. 11
C. 5   D. not here

2. $5\overline{)29}$

The remainder = ___?___

A. 0   B. 2
C. 4   D. not here

3. $56 = $ ___?___ $\times 8$

A. 6   B. 7
C. 3   D. not here

4. $25 = 5 \times$ ___?___

A. 6   B. 4
C. 5   D. not here

5. $30 = $ ___?___

A. 5×6 B. 4×5
C. 4×8 D. not here

6. $36 = $ ___?___

A. 6×7 B. 7×4
C. 6×6 D. not here

7. Which number will go into both 36 and 48 evenly?

A. 8   B. 12
C. 9   D. not here

8. Which number will go into both 12 and 25 evenly?

A. 4   B. 1
C. 5   D. not here

9. How many parts of the circle are blue?

A. 2   B. 3
C. 4   D. not here

10. Which are factors of 8?

A. 3×2 B. 4×2
C. 4×3 D. not here

11. Which are factors of 21?

A. 7×3 B. 7×2
C. 7×4 D. not here

12. 12 ● 11

A. <   B. =
C. >   D. not here

13. Which number is *not* a multiple of 6?

A. 15   B. 12
C. 18   D. not here

14. Which number is *not* a multiple of 9?

A. 18   B. 21
C. 27   D. not here

15. Divide.

$4\overline{)13}$

A. 3 r 1   B. 3
C. 2 r 5   D. not here

16. If 3 candy bars weigh 504 grams, how many grams does 1 candy bar weigh?

A. 158   B. 1,512
C. 101   D. not here

17. Saul had 18 fish in several bowls. Each bowl contained 3 fish. How many bowls did he have?

A. 6   B. 3
C. 4   D. not here

Number Theory and Fractions

Growers of plum trees plant the trees about 20 feet apart. Cherry trees are planted about 24 feet apart.

● Find the common factors of 20 and 24.

A farm is divided into five equal parcels (parts).

● How many acres could there have been in all?

   a. 911 **b.** 940 **c.** 356

229

Divisibility · Mental Math

Divide one number by another.
● If the remainder is 0, then the first number **is divisible** by the second.

16 **is divisible** by 2.

$$\begin{array}{r} 8 \\ 2)\overline{16} \\ -16 \\ \hline 0 \end{array}$$

◀ The remainder is 0.

17 is **not divisible** by 2.

$$\begin{array}{r} 8 \\ 2)\overline{17} \\ -16 \\ \hline 1 \end{array}$$

◀ The remainder is not 0.

Here are rules for finding if a number is divisible by 2, 5, or 10.

Even numbers are divisible by 2.
Here are six even numbers. ⟶ 2, 4, 6, 8, 10, 12
Divide each by 2. There is no remainder.

Odd numbers are not divisible by 2.
Here are six odd numbers. ⟶ 3, 5, 7, 9, 11, 13
Divide each by 2. There is a remainder.

If there is a 0 or a 5 in the ones place, then the number is divisible by 5.

These numbers are divisible by 5. ⟶ 0, 5, 10, 15, 20, 25, 30

If there is a 0 in the ones place, the number is divisible by 10.

These numbers are divisible by 10. ⟶ 10, 20, 30, 40, 50

PRACTICE · Mental Math   Is the first number divisible by the second?
Answer YES or NO.

1. 26, 4	**2.** 65, 5	**3.** 32, 8	**4.** 74, 10	**5.** 96, 12
6. 87, 3	**7.** 34, 17	**8.** 93, 8	**9.** 146, 5	**10.** 278, 2

EXERCISES · Is the first number of each divisible by the second?
Answer YES or NO.

11. 57, 8	**12.** 15, 3	**13.** 27, 9	**14.** 26, 6	**15.** 37, 6
16. 147, 7	**17.** 85, 10	**18.** 101, 3	**19.** 104, 4	**20.** 250, 25

Is each number divisible by 2? Answer YES or NO.

21. 20	**22.** 14	**23.** 23	**24.** 75	**25.** 180
26. 220	**27.** 233	**28.** 400	**29.** 450	**30.** 316

Is each number divisible by 5?

31. 20 **32.** 25 **33.** 36 **34.** 74 **35.** 180

36. 220 **37.** 225 **38.** 400 **39.** 450 **40.** 555

Is each number divisible by 10?

41. 20 **42.** 25 **43.** 90 **44.** 105 **45.** 180

46. 220 **47.** 250 **48.** 400 **49.** 450 **50.** 585

> *A number is divisible by 3 if the sum of its digits is divisible by 3.*

$$15 \qquad 1 + 5 = 6$$

6 is divisible by 3,
so 15 is divisible by 3.

Is each number divisible by 3?

★ **51.** 25 ★ **52.** 36 ★ **53.** 738 ★ **54.** 571 ★ **55.** 3,996

> *A number is divisible by 9 if the sum of its digits is divisible by 9.*

$$108 \qquad 1 + 0 + 8 = 9$$

9 is divisible by 9,
so 108 is divisible by 9.

Is each number divisible by 9?

★ **56.** 24 ★ **57.** 72 ★ **58.** 651 ★ **59.** 333 ★ **60.** 5,283

PROBLEM SOLVING • APPLICATIONS

61. A farm is divided into five equal parcels (parts). How many acres could there have been in all?

a. 911   **b.** 440   **c.** 356

62. Cattle ranching is the chief type of farming in the western grasslands of the United States. The number of acres in the largest ranches is a number that is divisible by 2, 5, and 10. How many acres could this be?

a. 39,605   **b.** 34,388   **c.** 40,000

Factors, Primes, and Composites

Farmers use machines called *drills* to plant their crops. Drills cut furrows in the soil, drop seeds into the furrows, and cover the seeds with soil. The largest drills can plant 12 or more rows at the same time.

● Two **factors** of 12 are 4 and 3.

$$3 \times 4 = 12$$ ◀ **3 and 4 are factors.**

● A number **is divisible** by its factors.

$$
\begin{array}{r}
4 \\
3{\overline{)12}} \\
12 \\
\hline
0
\end{array}
\qquad
\begin{array}{r}
3 \\
4{\overline{)12}} \\
12 \\
\hline
0
\end{array}
$$

● Find all the factors of 12. List them in order.

Think Write 12 as the product of two whole numbers.

Factors of 12: **1, 2, 3, 4, 5, 12** ◀ **List each factor only once.**

● A **prime number** has exactly two factors: itself and 1. The number 1 is not a prime number. It has only one factor, itself.

Factors of 5: **1, 5**

● A **composite number** is greater than 1 and has more than two different factors.

Factors of 8: **1, 2, 4, 8**

PRACTICE • Find all the factors for each. List them in order.

1. 9 **2.** 14 **3.** 18 **4.** 30 **5.** 28 **6.** 36

Mental Math Identify each number as PRIME or COMPOSITE.

7. 31 **8.** 22 **9.** 48 **10.** 53 **11.** 64 **12.** 71

EXERCISES • Find all the factors for each. List them in order.

13. 10 **14.** 25 **15.** 56 **16.** 63 **17.** 64 **18.** 144

19. 27 **20.** 42 **21.** 48 **22.** 81 **23.** 58 **24.** 225

25. 32 **26.** 40 **27.** 77 **28.** 39 **29.** 35 **30.** 100

31. 54   **32.** 72   **33.** 24   **34.** 96   **35.** 90   **36.** 150

Mental Math   Identify each number PRIME or COMPOSITE.

37. 59   **38.** 43   **39.** 51   **40.** 21   **41.** 72   **42.** 35

43. 23   **44.** 96   **45.** 26   **46.** 17   **47.** 34   **48.** 54

49. 13   **50.** 46   **51.** 57   **52.** 25   **53.** 83   **54.** 100

55. 12   **56.** 67   **57.** 93   **58.** 76   **59.** 87   **60.** 117

PROBLEM SOLVING • APPLICATIONS

The **prime-number sieve** is a method for finding all the prime numbers that are less than a given number.

61. Copy the table at the right below. Use it to find all the prime numbers less than 50.

   a. Cross out 1, since it is not a prime number.

   b. Circle 2, since it is a prime number. Then cross out all the numbers in the table that are divisible by 2.

   c. Circle 3, the next prime number. Cross out all the numbers in the table that are divisible by 3.

1̶	②	③	4	⑤	6	7	8	9	10
11	12	13	14	15	16	17	18	19	20
21	22	23	24	25	26	27	28	29	30
31	32	33	34	35	36	37	38	39	40
41	42	43	44	45	46	47	48	49	50

   d. Repeat steps **b.** and **c.** for the numbers 5, 7, and 11. Since there are no numbers remaining that are divisible by 11, you are finished.

62. The circled numbers in the table are the prime numbers less than 50. Complete: Prime numbers less than 50: ___?___

63. Are the numbers crossed out in Exercise 60 prime or composite? Explain your answer.

64. Make a table for the numbers between 51 and 100. Use the table to find all the prime numbers between 51 and 100.

★ **65.** Two prime numbers that have a difference of 2 are called **twin primes.** Find all the twin primes less than 50.

★ **66.** Find all the twin primes greater than 50 and less than 100.

Prime Factors

Livestock farms include beef cattle, hog, sheep, dairy, and poultry farms. Most livestock farms use large amounts of prepared feed. For example, a herd of 40 dairy cows can eat as much as 2 tons of hay and other feed each day.

● What are the prime factors of 40?

Think Find the factors of 40 that are also prime numbers.

Step 1 Find a pair of factors for 40. Use a **factor tree.**

Step 2 If both factors are not prime, continue until all are prime.

$40 = 2 \times 2 \times 2 \times 5$ ◀ **Prime factorization**

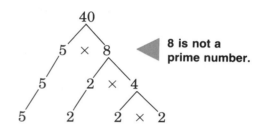

◀ 8 is not a prime number.

● A composite number can be written as the product of prime factors. This is called the **prime factorization** of the number.

● The prime factors of a number are always the same. Only the order may be different. Always write the prime factors of a number in order from least to greatest.

More Examples

```
        30                      110                          400
       / \                     /  \                         /    \
      5 × 6                  11 ×  10                      100  ×   4
         / \                      /  \                     /  \    / \
   5 × 3 × 2               11 ×  5  × 2              10 × 10  2 × 2
                                                      / \    / \
                                                   5× 2   5 × 2
```

PRACTICE • Complete the factor trees.

1.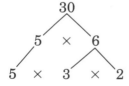
    18
    2×9
    $2 \times \underline{\ ?\ } \times \underline{\ ?\ }$

2.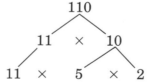
    42
    $6 \times \underline{\ ?\ }$
    $\underline{\ ?\ } \times \underline{\ ?\ } \times \underline{\ ?\ }$

3.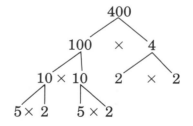
    36
    $9 \times \underline{\ ?\ }$
    $\underline{\ ?\ } \times \underline{\ ?\ } \times \underline{\ ?\ } \times \underline{\ ?\ }$

Write the prime factorization of each number. Use a factor tree.
Write the prime factors in order from least to greatest.

4. 20   **5.** 63   **6.** 44   **7.** 95   **8.** 56   **9.** 38

EXERCISES • Complete the factor trees.

10.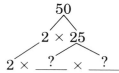
```
        50
       /  \
     2 × 25
    /    \
2 × __?__ × __?__
```

11.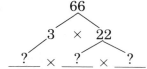
```
         66
        /  \
      3  ×  22
     /   \
__?__ × __?__ × __?__
```

12.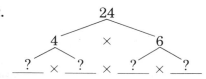
```
              24
           /      \
        4    ×    6
       / \       / \
__?__ × __?__ × __?__ × __?__
```

Write the prime factorization of each number. Use a factor tree.
Write the prime factors in order from least to greatest.

13. 12	**14.** 40	**15.** 28	**16.** 32	**17.** 35	**18.** 65
19. 16	**20.** 27	**21.** 88	**22.** 54	**23.** 48	**24.** 78
25. 72	**26.** 81	**27.** 64	**28.** 75	**29.** 99	**30.** 84
31. 80	**32.** 25	**33.** 33	**34.** 45	**35.** 52	**36.** 90

PROBLEM SOLVING • APPLICATIONS

37. In many parts of the western United States, ranchers need as many as 125 acres of land to provide enough grass for one animal. How many factors of 5 are there in the prime factorization of 125?

38. The average cost of running a farm in the United States was 300 times as great in 1975 as in 1970. How many factors of 2 are there in the prime factorization of 300?

THINKER'S CORNER

Find the prime factors of each number in this sequence: 4, 6, 10, 14 . . .
What is the pattern in the sequence?
What are the next four numbers in the sequence?

Greatest Common Factor

Growers of plum trees plant the trees about 20 feet apart. Plum trees flower from one to five years after planting.

Cherry trees are planted about 24 feet apart. Some cherry trees can produce fruit only after bees transfer pollen from another cherry tree.

● Find the common factors of 20 and 24.

Think   The **common factors** will be factors of both 20 and 24.

Factors of 20:   **1, 2, 4,** 5, 10, 20

Factors of 24:   **1, 2,** 3, **4,** 6, 8, 12, 24

Common factors: **1, 2, 4**

The **greatest common factor (GCF)** of 20 and 24 is **4.**

● Find the greatest common factor of 12 and 30.

Think   Find all the factors of 12 and all the factors of 30.

Find the greatest common factor for each pair.

Step 1 List the factors of 12 in order. ⟶ 1, 2, 3, 4, 6, 12

Step 2 List the factors of 30 in order. ⟶ 1, 2, 3, 5, 6, 10, 15, 30

Step 3 List the common factors. ⟶ 1, 2, 3, 6

Step 4 Write the greatest common factor. ⟶ 6

PRACTICE • **Mental Math**   List all the factors in order for each.

1. 21   **2.** 15   **3.** 18   **4.** 20   **5.** 32

List the common factors in order for each pair.

6. 21, 15   **7.** 15, 18   **8.** 18, 20   **9.** 20, 32   **10.** 15, 32

Find the greatest common factor for each pair.

11. 21, 15   **12.** 15, 18   **13.** 18, 20   **14.** 20, 32   **15.** 15, 32

EXERCISES • Mental Math   List all the factors in order for each.

16. 8   **17.** 16   **18.** 36   **19.** 40   **20.** 25

21. 30   **22.** 48   **23.** 14   **24.** 27   **25.** 54

List the common factors in order for each.

26. 8, 16   **27.** 36, 27   **28.** 14, 40   **29.** 25, 30   **30.** 16, 48

31. 54, 27   **32.** 25, 40   **33.** 36, 16   **34.** 14, 30   **35.** 48, 54

Find the greatest common factor for each pair.

36. 8, 16   **37.** 36, 27   **38.** 14, 40   **39.** 25, 30   **40.** 16, 48

41. 54, 27   **42.** 25, 40   **43.** 36, 16   **44.** 14, 30   **45.** 48, 54

Another Method: Find the greatest common factor of 12 and 30.

Step 1 Write 12 and 30. Divide each by a common factor. $\longrightarrow$ $2 \dfrac{\underline{|12 \qquad 30}}{6 \qquad 15}$

Step 2 Write the quotients from Step 1. Divide each by a common factor. $\longrightarrow$ $3 \dfrac{\underline{|\ 6 \qquad 15}}{2 \qquad 5}$

Step 3 Divide the quotients until there are no more common factors. $\longrightarrow$ | *There is no common factor for 2 and 5.* |

Step 4 Multiply the divisors. The product is the greatest common factor. $\longrightarrow$ $2 \times 3 = 6$

The **greatest common factor is 6.**

Use this method to find the greatest common factor for each pair.

46. 24, 28   **47.** 18, 36   **48.** 32, 48   **49.** 15, 40   **50.** 20, 30

PROBLEM SOLVING • APPLICATIONS

51. Apple growers plant their trees 30 feet apart. Growers of peach trees plant the trees 18 feet apart. What is the greatest common factor of 30 and 18?

52. One peach tree may produce 220 kilograms of peaches per year. Estimate how many kilograms of peaches one tree could produce over its productive life of about 18 years.

THINKER'S CORNER

The product of three whole numbers is 3,861. The three numbers have no common factors. What are the numbers.

Least Common Multiple

- When you multiply a number by 0, 1, 2, 3, and so on, the product is a **multiple** of that number.

Multiples of 4:   0, 4, 8, **12**, 16, 20, **24**, 28, 32, **36**, . . .

Multiples of 6:   0, 6, **12**, 18, **24**, 30, **36**, 42, 48, . . .

◀ **The 3 dots mean that the numbers continue.**

- Multiples that are the same for two or more numbers are called **common multiples.**

Common multiples of 4 and 6:   **0, 12, 24, 36,** . . .

- The **least common multiple (LCM)** of two or more numbers is the smallest common multiple that is not zero.
Least common multiple of 4 and 6:   **12**

Farmers use plows to turn over the soil to prepare it for planting. One kind of plow has 15 blades. Farmers use cultivators to turn over the soil between rows to control the growth of weeds. A four-row cultivator has 20 blades.

- Find the least common multiple of 15 and 20.

Think   List the multiples of 15 and 20.

Step 1 List multiples of 15.   ⟶   **0**, 15, 30, 45, **60**, 75, 90, 105, **120**, . . .

Step 2 List multiples of 20.   ⟶   **0**, 20, 40, **60**, 80, 100, **120**, . . .

Step 3 List the common multiples.   ⟶   **0, 60, 120,** . . .

Step 4 Write the least common multiple.   ⟶   **60**

Here is another way to find the least common multiple.

- Find the least common multiple of 6 and 8.

	0	8	16	24	32
Step 1 List the multiples of the greater number. **Step 2** Check whether each multiple is also a multiple of the smaller number.	Yes	No	No	Yes	Stop!

Least common multiple of 6 and 8: **24**

PRACTICE • **Mental Math**   Name the first six multiples. Start with 0.

1. 8   **2.** 10   **3.** 7   **4.** 9   **5.** 12

Find the least common multiple for each pair.

6. 4, 8   **7.** 6, 10   **8.** 7, 8   **9.** 6, 9   **10.** 9, 12

Name the first six multiples in order for each. Start with zero.

11. 2   **12.** 3   **13.** 5   **14.** 11   **15.** 13

16. 15   **17.** 20   **18.** 25   **19.** 50   **20.** 100

EXERCISES • Find the least common multiple for each pair.

21. 2, 3   **22.** 10, 15   **23.** 5, 25   **24.** 6, 15   **25.** 3, 5

26. 2, 5   **27.** 15, 20   **28.** 4, 5   **29.** 25, 50   **30.** 20, 100

★ **31.** 2, 3, 4   ★ **32.** 3, 6, 9   ★ **33.** 4, 5, 10   ★ **34.** 5, 6, 10   ★ **35.** 3, 9, 12

PROBLEM SOLVING • APPLICATIONS

36. Clare earns $10 an hour working at the Farmer's Market and Joe earns $8 an hour. On Friday, both worked a whole number of hours and both earned the same amount. What is the smallest amount each could have earned?

37. A Farmer's Market receives deliveries 6 days a week (Monday through Saturday). Vegetables are delivered every fourth day, eggs are delivered every third day, and fruit is delivered every other day. All three items are delivered on Tuesday. How many delivery days will pass before all three will again be delivered on the same day?

CALCULATOR
Least Common Multiple and Greatest Common Factor

You can use this word rule to find the LCM of two numbers.

$$LCM = \frac{\text{first number} \times \text{second number}}{GCF}$$

Find the LCM of 120 and 160.
Think: GCF of 120 and 160: 40   Use the word rule and a calculator.

(1)(2)(0)(×)(1)(6)(0)(÷)(4)(0)(=) [480.]

EXERCISES Use the word rule above and a calculator to find the LCM of each pair of numbers.

1. 56 and 48   **2.** 95 and 100   **3.** 61 and 62

4. 17 and 68   **5.** 15 and 25   **6.** 144 and 168

PROBLEM SOLVING · STRATEGIES

Using Equations: Multiplication/Division

Heather's parents own an apple orchard. Heather is making applesauce for a school potluck dinner. She knows that there are about 80 calories in one medium-sized apple.

● How many calories are there in 6 of these apples?

Think   Word rule: $$\text{Total number of calories} = \text{Calories per apple} \times \text{Number of apples}$$

The rule can be written as a number sentence. A number sentence is an **equation.**

Step 1 Write the equation.

Let n = total calories.
$$n = 80 \times 6$$

Step 2 Solve the equation.

$$n = 80 \times 6$$
$$n = \mathbf{480}$$
◀ **There are 480 calories.**

Heather made 12 quarts of applesauce. She wants to divide it into four equal portions, one for each table.

● How many quarts will there be in each portion?

Think   Word rule: $$\text{Number of quarts per portion} = \text{Quarts of applesauce} \div \text{Number of portions}$$

Step 1 Write the equation.

Let n = the number of quarts per portion.
$$n = 12 \div 4$$

Step 2 Solve the equation.

$$n = 12 \div 4$$
$$n = 3$$

There will be **3 quarts** in each portion.

PROBLEMS • Choose the equation you could use to solve each problem.

1. A recipe for molasses cookies calls for 8 tablespoons of molasses. One tablespoon contains 55 calories. How many calories does the molasses add to the recipe?

   a. $55 \times n = 8$ **b.** $n = 55 \times 8$
           c. $8 \times n = 55$

2. Brian prepares a salad to serve 6 people. The salad contains 456 calories. Brian divides the salad equally. How many calories are there in each serving?

   a. $n \div 456 = 6$ **b.** $6 \div n = 456$
           c. $n = 456 \div 6$

Write an equation for each problem.
Then solve the equation.

3. Dick prepared 9 pieces of chicken. Each piece contained 64 calories. How many calories were in the 9 pieces?

4. A bowl of cottage cheese contains 500 calories. The cheese is divided into five equal portions. How many calories are there in each portion?

What is the word rule?

---

5. Ernie eats 3 slices of chicken. Each slice contains 166 calories. How many calories is this in all?

6. A casserole calls for 2.5 cups of skim milk. One cup contains 88 calories. How many calories does this add to the casserole?

7. Sue had two servings of fish for dinner. Each serving contained 84 calories. How many calories was this in all?

8. Ralph prepared 4 servings of mushrooms. The mushrooms contained 312 calories. How many calories per serving is this?

9. Anita prepared enough peas for 5 servings. The peas contained 280 calories. What is the average number of calories per serving?

10. One medium-sized raw carrot contains 24 calories. Janet slices the carrot equally into 3 salad bowls. How many calories are added to each salad?

11. One cup of fresh milk contains 166 calories. How many calories are there in 4 cups of milk?

★ 12. Twelve slices of cucumber contain 10 calories. How many calories would 36 slices of cucumber add to a salad?

MID-CHAPTER REVIEW

Is each number divisible by 2?   Answer YES or NO.   (Pages 230–231)

1. 36   **2.** 54   **3.** 124   **4.** 296   **5.** 89

Write PRIME or COMPOSITE.   (Pages 232–233)

6. 7   **7.** 15   **8.** 19   **9.** 21   **10.** 64

Write the prime factorization. Use a factor tree. Write the factors in order from least to greatest.   (Pages 234–235)

11. 8   **12.** 24   **13.** 50   **14.** 36   **15.** 63

Find the greatest common factor for each pair.   (Pages 236–237)

16. 6, 20   **17.** 8, 36   **18.** 14, 63   **19.** 40, 60   **20.** 72, 36

21. 18, 30   **22.** 6, 7   **23.** 20, 50   **24.** 15, 45   **25.** 45, 72

Find the least common multiple for each pair.   (Pages 238–239)

26. 3, 4   **27.** 5, 8   **28.** 10, 15   **29.** 6, 8   **30.** 15, 20

31. 5, 6   **32.** 9, 3   **33.** 9, 8   **34.** 20, 3   **35.** 10, 8

For Exercises 36–37, write an equation. Then solve the equation.   (Pages 240–241)

36. A broccoli casserole contains 186 calories. The casserole makes 6 servings. How many calories per serving is this?

37. One cup of blueberries contains 80 calories. How many calories are there in 7 cups?

MAINTENANCE • MIXED PRACTICE

Multiply.

1. $42.3 \times 6.8 = $ __?__   **2.** $59.1 \times 9.37 = $ __?__   **3.** $0.208 \times 0.47 = $ __?__

Divide.

4. $8\overline{)32.16}$ **5.** $8\overline{)6.446}$ **6.** $1.9\overline{)188.3698}$ **7.** $0.72\overline{)2.5632}$ **8.** $0.005\overline{)0.0341}$

Solve.

9. $(3 \times 5) + 7 = $ __?__   **10.** $(8 \times 4) + 5 = $ __?__   **11.** $(11 \times 8) + 9 = $ __?__

12. There are 52 people at a picnic lunch. Each picnic table seats 13. How many picnic tables are needed?

13. A worker can harvest 40 pounds of tea leaves in a day. At this rate, how many pounds will the worker harvest in 45 days?

CAREER APPLICATIONS

Cashier

A cashier collects money and makes change. The best way to make change is to use as few bills and coins as possible.

EXERCISES • Choose the best way of making change. Choose *a, b,* or *c.*

1.

Amount of Sale	Money Received	Change Due
$3.20	$5–bill	$1.80

  a. A $1–bill, 3 quarters, one nickel
  b. A $1–bill and 8 dimes
  c. A $1–bill, 2 quarters, 3 dimes

2.

Amount of Sale	Money Received	Change Due
$4.12	$5–bill	$0.88

  a. Two quarters, 7 nickels, 3 pennies
  b. Two quarters, 3 dimes, 8 pennies
  c. Three quarters, 1 dime, 3 pennies

3.

Amount of Sale	Money Received	Change Due
$7.65	$10–bill	$2.35

  a. Two $1–bills, 1 quarter, 1 dime
  b. Two $1–bills, 1 quarter, 2 nickels
  c. Two $1–bills, 3 dimes, one nickel

4.

Amount of Sale	Money Received	Change Due
$36.85	Two $20–bills	$3.15

  a. Three $1–bills and 15 pennies
  b. Twelve quarters and 15 pennies
  c. Three $1–dollar bills, a dime, one nickel.

Make a chart like the one shown below. Write the number of bills and coins in the boxes to show the best way to make change. The first one is done for you.

	Amount of Sale	Money Received	Change Due	Change: Number of						
				$10–bills	$5–bills	$1–bills	Quarters	Dimes	Nickels	Pennies
5.	$ 6.19	$10	$ 3.81	None	None	3	3	None	1	1
6.	$ 8.55	$10	$ 1.45	?	?	?	?	?	?	?
7.	$ 3.89	$20	$16.11	?	?	?	?	?	?	?
8.	$12.60	$20	$ 7.40	?	?	?	?	?	?	?

> **PROJECT** Collect ten cash register receipts. Find how much change was due. Write the best way to make change.

Fractions

Since adult sheep can withstand most cold weather, ranchers do not have to provide shelter for them. In some areas, however, sheep do need protection against their natural enemy, the bear.

A wild animal park is divided into 4 equal parts. Animals occupy 3 parts.

● A **fraction** tells what part of the park is occupied by animals.

parts with animals ⟶ $\dfrac{3}{4}$ ⟵ numerator
parts in all ⟶ ⟵ denominator

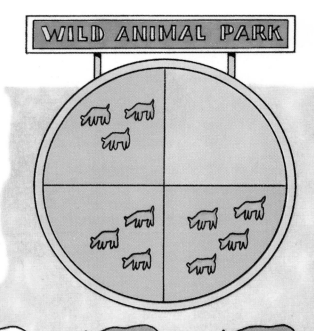

There are 6 bears
in a group.
Five are brown.

● What fraction are brown?

Think	number of brown bears ⟶	$\dfrac{4}{6}$
	number in all ⟶	

So $\dfrac{4}{6}$ of the bears are brown.

There are 3 feeding stations for bears.
Two are used by brown bears.
● What fraction are used by brown bears?

Think	feeding stations used by brown bears ⟶	$\dfrac{2}{3}$
	feeding stations in all ⟶	

Fraction used by brown bears: $\dfrac{2}{3}$

PRACTICE • Write the fraction that tells what part is blue for each.

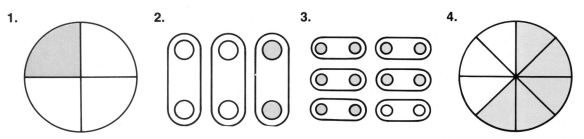

1. 2. 3. 4.

EXERCISES • Write the fraction that tells what part is blue for each.

5. 6. 7. 8.

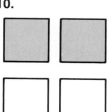

9. 10. 11. 12.

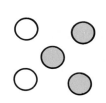

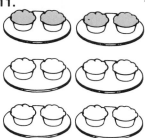

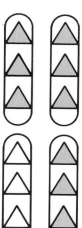

The number line between 0 and 1 is divided into 6 equal parts.

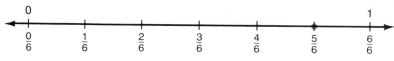

0   1
$\frac{0}{6}$ $\frac{1}{6}$ $\frac{2}{6}$ $\frac{3}{6}$ $\frac{4}{6}$ $\frac{5}{6}$ $\frac{6}{6}$

The point $\frac{5}{6}$ is located five-sixths of the way from 0 to 1.

Use a fraction to name the point for each.

13. 0   1
$\frac{0}{4}$ $\frac{1}{4}$ $\frac{2}{4}$? $\frac{4}{4}$

14. 0   1
$\frac{0}{3}$? $\frac{2}{3}$ $\frac{3}{3}$

15. 0   1
$\frac{0}{8}$ $\frac{1}{8}$ $\frac{2}{8}$ $\frac{3}{8}$ $\frac{4}{8}$? $\frac{6}{8}$ $\frac{7}{8}$ $\frac{8}{8}$

★ 16. 0   1
?

★ 17. 0   1
?

★ 18. 0   1
?

PROBLEM SOLVING • APPLICATIONS

Write a fraction to answer each question.

19. There are 7 apes. Four of them are chimps. What part of the apes are chimps?

20. Fifteen animals in the park belong to the cat family. Two of them are lions. What part of the cats are lions?

21. Twelve workers care for the animals. Three of them feed the animals. What part of the workers do not feed the animals?

22. There are nine reptiles. Two of them are snakes. What part of the reptiles are not snakes?

Equivalent Fractions

Equivalent fractions name the same number.
There are two ways to find equivalent fractions.

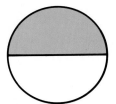 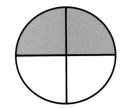 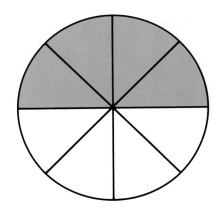

Multiply the numerator and the denominator by the same number.	Divide the numerator and the denominator by the same number.
	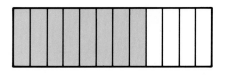
$\dfrac{1}{3}$	$\dfrac{8}{12}$
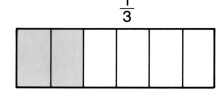	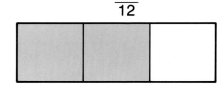
$\dfrac{1}{3} = \dfrac{2 \times 1}{2 \times 3} = \dfrac{\mathbf{2}}{\mathbf{6}}$	$\dfrac{8}{12} = \dfrac{8 \div 4}{12 \div 4} = \dfrac{\mathbf{2}}{\mathbf{3}}$

$\dfrac{1}{3}$ and $\dfrac{2}{6}$ are equivalent fractions.
● Make the fractions equivalent.

$$\frac{7}{8} = \frac{?}{16}$$

Think What number times 8 is 16?

$$\frac{7}{8} = \frac{2 \times 7}{2 \times 8} = \frac{\mathbf{14}}{\mathbf{16}}$$

$\dfrac{8}{12}$ and $\dfrac{2}{3}$ are equivalent fractions.
● Make the fractions equivalent.

$$\frac{24}{32} = \frac{?}{4}$$

Think 32 divided by what number is 4?

$$\frac{24}{32} = \frac{24 \div 8}{32 \div 8} = \frac{\mathbf{3}}{\mathbf{4}}$$

PRACTICE • **Mental Math** Complete.

1. $\dfrac{2}{3} = \dfrac{?}{6}$ 2. $\dfrac{6}{15} = \dfrac{?}{5}$ 3. $\dfrac{3}{7} = \dfrac{?}{28}$ 4. $\dfrac{6}{24} = \dfrac{?}{4}$

5. $\dfrac{3}{4} = \dfrac{6}{?}$ 6. $\dfrac{10}{16} = \dfrac{?}{8}$ 7. $\dfrac{4}{7} = \dfrac{40}{?}$ 8. $\dfrac{3}{36} = \dfrac{?}{12}$

EXERCISES • Complete.

9. $\frac{3}{5} = \frac{?}{10}$

10. $\frac{5}{9} = \frac{?}{27}$

11. $\frac{8}{9} = \frac{64}{?}$

12. $\frac{1}{9} = \frac{?}{36}$

13. $\frac{4}{5} = \frac{?}{10}$

14. $\frac{3}{4} = \frac{?}{32}$

15. $\frac{4}{5} = \frac{?}{25}$

16. $\frac{9}{10} = \frac{?}{50}$

17. $\frac{14}{16} = \frac{7}{?}$

18. $\frac{10}{15} = \frac{?}{3}$

19. $\frac{8}{22} = \frac{16}{?}$

20. $\frac{21}{24} = \frac{?}{8}$

21. $\frac{4}{12} = \frac{?}{3}$

22. $\frac{6}{48} = \frac{?}{8}$

23. $\frac{18}{24} = \frac{?}{4}$

24. $\frac{18}{27} = \frac{?}{3}$

25. $\frac{2}{3} = \frac{4}{?}$

26. $\frac{12}{16} = \frac{?}{4}$

27. $\frac{2}{4} = \frac{6}{?}$

28. $\frac{?}{40} = \frac{3}{8}$

29. $\frac{?}{4} = \frac{10}{20}$

30. $\frac{?}{15} = \frac{2}{5}$

31. $\frac{?}{30} = \frac{4}{5}$

32. $\frac{12}{?} = \frac{3}{5}$

You can test fractions to find out if they are equivalent.

> *The cross products of equivalent fractions are equal.*

Cross multiply.

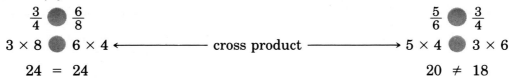

$$\frac{3}{4} \quad \bullet \quad \frac{6}{8}$$

$3 \times 8 \quad \bullet \quad 6 \times 4 \longleftarrow$ cross product $\longrightarrow$ $5 \times 4 \quad \bullet \quad 3 \times 6$

$$\frac{5}{6} \quad \bullet \quad \frac{3}{4}$$

$24 = 24$

$20 \neq 18$

($\neq$ means "is not equal to.")

The fractions are equal.

The fractions are not equal.

Write = or $\neq$.

33. $\frac{4}{5} \quad \bullet \quad \frac{7}{8}$

★ 34. $\frac{3}{16} \quad \bullet \quad \frac{18}{96}$

★ 35. $\frac{3}{10} \quad \bullet \quad \frac{25}{100}$

★ 36. $\frac{1}{3} \quad \bullet \quad \frac{3}{8}$

★ 37. $\frac{5}{25} \quad \bullet \quad \frac{3}{15}$

PROBLEM SOLVING • APPLICATIONS

38. Three out of every 4 cows on Sunnydale Farm give milk. There are 60 cows on the farm. How many give milk?

$$\frac{3}{4} = \frac{?}{60}$$

★ 39. A rancher has 2,000 sheep. Of these, 1,800 graze on the south range. The rancher buys 1,000 more sheep. The fraction kept on the south range will be the same. How many sheep will there be on the south range?

Lowest Terms

The early Roman farmers practiced crop rotation by leaving half of every field *fallow* (unplanted).

In the 1700's, English farmers used a four-crop rotation plan. They rotated (changed) the crops grown in each field each year.

Planted	Fallow
$\frac{1}{2}$	$\frac{1}{2}$

Wheat	Corn	Clover	Turnips
$\frac{1}{4}$	$\frac{1}{4}$	$\frac{1}{4}$	$\frac{1}{4}$

$$\underbrace{\phantom{\frac{1}{4}\qquad\frac{1}{4}}}_{\frac{2}{4}}$$

The fractions $\frac{1}{2}$ and $\frac{2}{4}$ are equivalent.

$$\frac{2}{4} = \frac{1}{2} \quad \blacktriangleleft \quad \textbf{Lowest terms}$$

> *A fraction is in lowest terms when the numerator and the denominator have no common factor greater than 1.*

● Write $\frac{8}{12}$ in lowest terms.

Think   What is the greatest common factor of 8 and 12?

Step 1   Find the greatest common factor.

List the factors ▶
$$8 \longrightarrow 1, 2, 4, 8$$
$$12 \longrightarrow 1, 2, 3, 4, 6, 12$$

Greatest Common Factor: 4

Step 2 Divide the numerator and the denominator by the greatest common factor, 4.

$$\frac{8}{12} = \frac{8 \div 4}{12 \div 4} = \frac{2}{3} \quad \blacktriangleleft \quad \textbf{Lowest terms}$$

PRACTICE • List the factors in order. Find the greatest common factor for each pair.

1. 12 and 16   **2.** 4 and 14   **3.** 8 and 10

4. 12 and 20   **5.** 8 and 32   **6.** 18 and 27

Write each fraction in lowest terms.

7. $\frac{12}{16}$ **8.** $\frac{4}{14}$ **9.** $\frac{8}{10}$ **10.** $\frac{12}{20}$ **11.** $\frac{8}{32}$ **12.** $\frac{18}{27}$

EXERCISES • List the factors in order. Find the greatest common factor for each pair.

13. 28 and 42

14. 30 and 32

15. 6 and 9

16. 10 and 15

17. 4 and 32

18. 50 and 60

Mental Math Name each fraction in lowest terms.

19. $\frac{28}{42}$ **20.** $\frac{30}{32}$ **21.** $\frac{6}{9}$ **22.** $\frac{10}{15}$ **23.** $\frac{4}{32}$ **24.** $\frac{50}{60}$

25. $\frac{8}{16}$ **26.** $\frac{12}{18}$ **27.** $\frac{8}{20}$ **28.** $\frac{12}{36}$ **29.** $\frac{20}{25}$ **30.** $\frac{6}{10}$

31. $\frac{12}{15}$ **32.** $\frac{9}{24}$ **33.** $\frac{10}{40}$ **34.** $\frac{24}{36}$ **35.** $\frac{25}{30}$ **36.** $\frac{40}{56}$

37. $\frac{36}{48}$ **38.** $\frac{24}{60}$ **39.** $\frac{25}{75}$ **40.** $\frac{24}{100}$ **41.** $\frac{400}{600}$ **42.** $\frac{100}{300}$

Another Method You can use prime factors to write a fraction in lowest terms.

● Write $\frac{18}{24}$ in lowest terms.

Step 1
Write the prime factors.

$$\frac{18}{24} = \frac{2 \times 3 \times 3}{2 \times 2 \times 2 \times 3} = ?$$

Step 2
Divide the numerator and the denominator by the common factors.

$$\frac{\overset{1}{2} \times \overset{1}{3} \times 3}{\underset{1}{2} \times 2 \times 2 \times \underset{1}{3}} = ?$$

Step 3
Multiply the remaining factors.

$$\frac{3}{2 \times 2} = \frac{3}{4}$$

Write each fraction in lowest terms. Use the prime factors.

★ **43.** $\frac{26}{36}$ ★ **44.** $\frac{12}{27}$ ★ **45.** $\frac{20}{44}$ ★ **46.** $\frac{27}{48}$ ★ **47.** $\frac{14}{35}$ ★ **48.** $\frac{39}{48}$

PROBLEM SOLVING • **APPLICATIONS**

Write each fraction in lowest terms.

49. The world's peanut farmers produce about 22 million tons of peanuts each year. About 2 million tons are harvested in the United States. What fraction of the total is this?

50. Twenty-five out of every 100 tons of oranges harvested in the world come from the United States. What fraction do not come from the United States?

51. The worldwide fish harvest per year is 80 million tons. About 6 million tons come from fish farms. What fraction of the total harvest is this?

52. Fish farms produce 6 million tons of fish yearly. China's fish farms produce 3 million tons. What fraction of the total is this?

Comparing Fractions

Wheat growers in North Dakota harvest $\frac{5}{8}$ as much wheat as farmers in Kansas. Wheat growers in the state of Washington harvest $\frac{3}{8}$ as much wheat as growers in Kansas.

● Which is greater, $\frac{5}{8}$ or $\frac{3}{8}$?

Think The denominators are the same.
Compare the numerators.

Since $5 > 3$, $\frac{5}{8} > \frac{3}{8}$.

To compare fractions when both have the same denominator, compare the numerators.

When the denominators of two or more fractions are not the same, you can use equivalent fractions with the same denominators to compare.

● Compare $\frac{3}{4}$ and $\frac{2}{5}$.

Think Use the **least common denominator** for $\frac{3}{4}$ and $\frac{2}{5}$.

Step 1 Find the least common multiple (LCM) of the denominators.
This multiple, 20, is the least common denominator.

$$4 \longrightarrow 4,\ 8,\ 12,\ 16,\ 20$$
$$5 \longrightarrow 5,\ 10,\ 15,\ 20$$

Step 2 Write equivalent fractions. Use 20 as the denominator.

$$\frac{3}{4} = \frac{5 \times 3}{5 \times 4} = \frac{15}{20} \qquad\qquad \frac{2}{5} = \frac{4 \times 2}{4 \times 5} = \frac{8}{20}$$

Since $\frac{15}{20} > \frac{8}{20}$, then $\frac{3}{4} > \frac{2}{5}$.

PRACTICE • **Mental Math** Find the Least Common Multiple (LCM) for each pair.

1. 4, 6   **2.** 7, 8   **3.** 6, 10   **4.** 6, 9

Find the least common denominator for each pair. Write equivalent fractions.

5. $\frac{3}{4}, \frac{5}{6}$ **6.** $\frac{4}{7}, \frac{3}{8}$ **7.** $\frac{1}{6}, \frac{3}{10}$ **8.** $\frac{5}{6}, \frac{5}{9}$

Write >, <, or =.

9. $\frac{1}{4}$ $\frac{1}{5}$ 10. $\frac{7}{8}$ ⬤ $\frac{5}{6}$ 11. $\frac{6}{15}$ ⬤ $\frac{4}{10}$ 12. $\frac{3}{4}$ ⬤ $\frac{7}{12}$

EXERCISES • ⬛ Mental Math Find the Least Common Multiple (LCM).

13. 8, 6   **14.** 9, 7   **15.** 3, 7   **16.** 8, 16

Find the least common denominator for each pair. Write equivalent fractions.

17. $\frac{3}{8}, \frac{5}{6}$ **18.** $\frac{1}{9}, \frac{1}{7}$ **19.** $\frac{2}{3}, \frac{3}{7}$ **20.** $\frac{5}{8}, \frac{9}{16}$

21. $\frac{2}{3}, \frac{1}{2}$ **22.** $\frac{1}{3}, \frac{2}{5}$ **23.** $\frac{1}{9}, \frac{5}{8}$ **24.** $\frac{3}{4}, \frac{5}{8}$

Write >, <, or =.

25. $\frac{4}{12}$ ⬤ $\frac{7}{12}$ **26.** $\frac{3}{4}$ ⬤ $\frac{7}{9}$ **27.** $\frac{5}{6}$ ⬤ $\frac{4}{5}$ **28.** $\frac{5}{8}$ ⬤ $\frac{11}{12}$

29. $\frac{5}{8}$ ⬤ $\frac{2}{3}$ **30.** $\frac{8}{14}$ ⬤ $\frac{12}{21}$ **31.** $\frac{3}{10}$ ⬤ $\frac{5}{16}$ **32.** $\frac{7}{12}$ ⬤ $\frac{2}{9}$

Write fractions in order from least to greatest.
Hint: Find an equivalent fraction for each.

33. $\frac{3}{4}, \frac{1}{2}, \frac{8}{9}$ **34.** $\frac{5}{8}, \frac{2}{3}, \frac{1}{2}$ **35.** $\frac{4}{5}, \frac{2}{5}, \frac{1}{2}$

★**36.** $\frac{7}{8}, \frac{2}{3}, \frac{1}{4}, \frac{29}{36}$ ★**37.** $\frac{3}{4}, \frac{4}{5}, \frac{1}{2}, \frac{3}{10}$ ★**38.** $\frac{2}{3}, \frac{5}{6}, \frac{4}{5}, \frac{1}{2}$

PROBLEM SOLVING • APPLICATIONS

39. Canada produces $\frac{3}{5}$ as much grain as the United States. India produces $\frac{2}{3}$ as much grain as the United States. Which country produces more, Canada or India?

40. A *grain elevator* is a tall building with machinery for loading, unloading, cleaning, mixing, and storing grain. One elevator can hold $\frac{5}{6}$ as much as a second elevator. A third elevator holds $\frac{7}{8}$ as much as the second. Which elevator holds more, the first or the third?

Whole Numbers, Mixed Numbers, and Fractions

A fraction names a whole number when the numerator is a multiple of the denominator.

$$1 = \frac{3}{3}$$

$$4 = \frac{12}{3}$$

You can change a whole number to a fraction by writing it over a denominator of 1 and finding an equivalent fraction.

$$1 = \frac{1}{1} = \frac{3 \times 1}{3 \times 1} = \frac{3}{3}$$

$$4 = \frac{4}{1} = \frac{3 \times 4}{3 \times 1} = \frac{12}{3}$$

Bread is made from wheat flour or grain meal mixed with water or milk. Bread is usually sold in units called loaves.

● How many half-loaves are there in $3\frac{1}{2}$ loaves?

Think $3\frac{1}{2}$ means $3 + \frac{1}{2}$.

The number $3\frac{1}{2}$ is called a **mixed number**.

$$3\frac{1}{2} = 3 + \frac{1}{2}$$
$$= \frac{3}{1} + \frac{1}{2}$$
$$= \frac{6}{2} + \frac{1}{2}$$
$$= \frac{7}{2}$$

Because the numerator in $\frac{7}{2}$ is larger than the denominator, $\frac{7}{2}$ is sometimes called an **improper fraction.**

Here is another way to write $3\frac{1}{2}$ as a fraction.

$$3\frac{1}{2} = \frac{7}{2} \quad \blacktriangleleft \quad \frac{2 \times 3 + 1}{2}$$

PRACTICE • Mental Math   Name the whole number or the mixed number.

1.

2.

3.

4.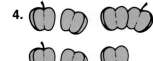

Complete.

5. $1 = \frac{?}{5}$

6. $9 = \frac{?}{2}$

7. $5 = \frac{?}{7}$

8. $3 = \frac{?}{9}$

Write as fractions.

9. $6\frac{1}{2}$

10. $3\frac{2}{3}$

11. $2\frac{3}{8}$

12. $1\frac{4}{9}$

EXERCISES • Complete.

13. $6 = \frac{?}{4}$ **14.** $3 = \frac{?}{5}$ **15.** $4 = \frac{?}{8}$ **16.** $1 = \frac{?}{12}$

Write as fractions.

17. $3\frac{4}{7}$ **18.** $5\frac{1}{3}$ **19.** $9\frac{1}{5}$ **20.** $7\frac{3}{4}$ **21.** $6\frac{3}{5}$ **22.** $3\frac{1}{4}$

23. $7\frac{2}{4}$ **24.** $4\frac{3}{4}$ **25.** $10\frac{5}{12}$ **26.** $5\frac{5}{9}$ **27.** $4\frac{1}{3}$ **28.** $6\frac{1}{2}$

29. $6\frac{5}{8}$ **30.** $1\frac{2}{5}$ **31.** $7\frac{2}{9}$ **32.** $1\frac{1}{8}$ **33.** $5\frac{3}{4}$ **34.** $9\frac{3}{10}$

35. $4\frac{3}{8}$ **36.** $5\frac{3}{7}$ **37.** $8\frac{2}{3}$ **38.** $9\frac{4}{5}$ **39.** $6\frac{1}{5}$ **40.** $7\frac{8}{9}$

● To compare mixed numbers,
1. compare the whole numbers and
2. compare the fractions.

$$6\frac{3}{8} \,\bullet\, 6\frac{5}{8}$$

$$6 = 6$$

$$\frac{3}{8} < \frac{5}{8}$$

So $6\frac{3}{8} < 6\frac{5}{8}$.

● If the fractions have different denominators, find equivalent fractions then compare.

$$4\frac{2}{3} \,\bullet\, 4\frac{3}{5}$$

$$4 = 4$$

$$\frac{2}{3} = \frac{10}{15} \qquad \frac{3}{5} = \frac{9}{15}$$

$$\frac{10}{15} > \frac{9}{15}$$

So $4\frac{2}{3} > 4\frac{3}{5}$.

Write >, <, or =.

★ **41.** $6\frac{7}{8} \,\bullet\, 6\frac{3}{8}$ ★ **42.** $2\frac{4}{5} \,\bullet\, 5\frac{4}{5}$ ★ **43.** $1\frac{2}{8} \,\bullet\, 1\frac{3}{12}$

★ **44.** $7\frac{2}{3} \,\bullet\, 7\frac{10}{15}$ ★ **45.** $10\frac{5}{9} \,\bullet\, 10\frac{7}{12}$ ★ **46.** $14\frac{5}{6} \,\bullet\, 14\frac{17}{24}$

PROBLEM SOLVING • APPLICATIONS

47. A cook uses $5\frac{1}{4}$ loaves of bread to make sandwiches. How many fourths of a loaf is this?

48. There are $6\frac{2}{3}$ baskets of apples to be divided. How many thirds of a basket will there be?

49. Some students share a pizza. There are $3\frac{1}{3}$ pizzas. Each student receives $\frac{1}{3}$ of a pizza. How many students can share?

50. There are $2\frac{3}{8}$ pounds of spaghetti. One serving takes $\frac{1}{8}$ of a pound. How many servings are there?

Dividing to Find Mixed Numbers

To encourage pioneers to move to the Great Plains of the American West, Congress passed the Homestead Act in 1862. This act gave 160 acres of land to anyone who lived on it and farmed it for 5 years.

● How could a farmer divide 11 acres into 4 equal parts?

Think   "Divide" suggests $11 \div 4$, or $\frac{11}{4}$.

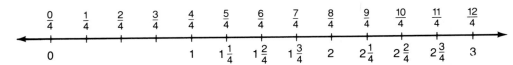

$$\frac{11}{4} \longrightarrow \frac{8}{4} + \frac{3}{4} \longrightarrow 2 + \frac{3}{4} = 2\frac{3}{4}$$

Each part will contain $2\frac{3}{4}$ **acres.**

● You can also divide to find the mixed number for $\frac{11}{4}$.

Step 1
Divide the numerator by the denominator.

$$\begin{array}{r} 2 \\ 4\overline{)11} \\ -8 \\ \hline 3 \end{array}$$

Step 2
Show the remainder as a fraction. The remainder is the numerator. The divisor is the denominator.

$$\begin{array}{r} 2\frac{3}{4} \\ 4\overline{)11} \\ -8 \\ \hline 3 \end{array}$$

A mixed number for $\frac{11}{4}$ is $2\frac{3}{4}$.

PRACTICE • Divide. Show the remainders as fractions.

1. $4\overline{)9}$
2. $20 \div 6$
3. $5\overline{)17}$
4. $6\overline{)41}$
5. $52 \div 9$
6. $8\overline{)75}$

Divide to find the mixed numbers.

7. $\frac{13}{4}$
8. $\frac{29}{5}$
9. $\frac{38}{7}$
10. $\frac{22}{3}$
11. $\frac{34}{7}$
12. $\frac{19}{2}$

EXERCISES • Divide. Show the remainders as fractions.

13. $7\overline{)17}$
14. $23 \div 4$
15. $33 \div 5$
16. $7\overline{)48}$
17. $9\overline{)65}$
18. $3\overline{)29}$

Divide to find the mixed numbers. Write the answers in lowest terms.

19. $\frac{9}{2}$ **20.** $\frac{12}{5}$ **21.** $\frac{5}{4}$ **22.** $\frac{7}{4}$ **23.** $\frac{5}{2}$ **24.** $\frac{8}{6}$

25. $\frac{16}{3}$ **26.** $\frac{7}{6}$ **27.** $\frac{11}{2}$ **28.** $\frac{17}{4}$ **29.** $\frac{7}{2}$ **30.** $\frac{9}{5}$

31. $\frac{21}{4}$ **32.** $\frac{25}{2}$ **33.** $\frac{7}{3}$ **34.** $\frac{9}{7}$ **35.** $\frac{15}{4}$ **36.** $\frac{19}{4}$

37. $\frac{15}{2}$ **38.** $\frac{21}{10}$ **39.** $\frac{53}{6}$ **40.** $\frac{52}{8}$ **41.** $\frac{27}{5}$ **42.** $\frac{39}{8}$

43. $\frac{48}{5}$ **44.** $\frac{22}{7}$ **45.** $\frac{76}{9}$ **46.** $\frac{85}{10}$ **47.** $\frac{35}{4}$ **48.** $\frac{46}{6}$

Write the fraction and mixed number for the indicated point.

★ **49.** $\frac{24}{4}$ A $\frac{28}{4}$
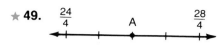

★ **50.** $\frac{12}{6}$ B $\frac{19}{6}$
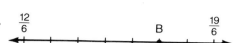

★ **51.** $\frac{25}{5}$ C $\frac{30}{5}$

★ **52.** $\frac{8}{8}$ D $\frac{16}{8}$

PROBLEM SOLVING • APPLICATIONS

53. In the early 1920's, a farmer could produce 1,700 bushels of corn on 60 acres of land. How many bushels per acre was this?

54. In the 1970's, a farmer could produce 5,840 bushels of corn on 60 acres of land. How many bushels per acre was this?

55. About 11 billion acres of land, or one-third of the earth's land area, are used for farming. The world's farmers grow crops on a third of this land.

a. How many billion acres of the earth's land area are used for farming?

b. What information did you not need to solve the problem?

PROBLEM SOLVING · STRATEGIES

Make A Drawing

Sometimes drawing a picture can help you to solve problems.

EXAMPLE

There are 5 contestants in the 50–yard dash at the County Fair. Laura came in first. Tom finished last. Luke finished ahead of Janet. Sally finished after Janet.

● Who came in second?

| Think | You must know the order of the finish.

Step 1
Draw a picture of the finish.

Finish Line

Step 2
Think: You know who finished first and last.
Locate them on the drawing.

Tom ▲   Laura ▲

Tom is last.   Laura is first.

Step 3
Locate the other runners on the drawing.

Tom   Sally ▲   Janet   Luke ▲   Laura

Luke came in second.

Sally is behind Janet.   Luke is ahead of Janet.

Solve. Use the drawing to help you.

1. Six 4–H Club members enter a calf in the County Fair competition. Adam's entry won second place. Sue's entry placed next to last. Jane's entry placed just ahead of Sue's. Chen's entry placed right after Adam's. Flora's entry did not place sixth. In what place was Nona's entry?

Sue

2. Each year a baking contest is held at the County Fair. This year, there were 7 finalists. Entry A won fifth place. Entry C placed ahead of A and behind F. Entry F won third prize. Entry D won first prize and entry E placed seventh. Entry G placed after A. In what place was Entry B?

A

3. The town of Maxwell runs special buses for the convenience of its citizens who wish to go to the Fair. The bus makes four stops. The railroad stop comes before the stop at Zeke's Grocery. The stop at Zeke's comes before the stop at Nellie's News. The courthouse stop is between the railraod station and Zeke's Grocery. Which is the second stop?

Draw a picture to help you see the solution.

4. The County Fair games follow this schedule. The javelin throw comes after the pole-climbing contest. The 50–yard dash comes before the pole-climbing contest. The relay races come between the 50–yard dash and the pole-climbing event. Which event comes first?

5. The County Fair Album Shop keeps a record of its sales. More Murky Mills albums are sold then Breezy Blues. The Thunder Tots sell one fewer album than the Breezy Blues. More Cloud Trio albums are sold than Murky Mills albums. Which album had the highest sales?

6. Four neighboring towns have a softball league. The two teams with the best record hold a play-off at the County Fair. The Reapers won more games than the Plows. The Harvesters won more games than the Balers and 2 fewer games than the Plows. Which teams were in the play-off?

7. There are 6 contestants in the carry-the-egg race at the County Fair. Corey finished second, and Luis finished next to last. Mai finished just before Luis, and Ben finished right behind Corey. Yoki did not finish last. In what place did Alix finish?

Write Your Own Problem

Felicia, George, Sol, and Wesley are finalists in the archery competition at the County Fair.

Use these facts to write a problem similar to Problem 7 above. Exchange problems with a classmate. Solve each other's problem.

CHAPTER REVIEW

Part 1 • VOCABULARY

For Exercises 1–8, choose from the box at the right the word that completes the sentence.

1. A number is __?__ by another number if the remainder is zero. (Page 230)

2. Since 7 has only two factors, 7 and 1, 7 is called a __?__ number. (Page 232)

3. If a number has more than two factors, it is called a __?__ number. (Page 232)

4. The largest factor common to two numbers is called the __?__. (Page 236)

5. You can multiply one number by different factors. The answers are called __?__ of that number. (Page 238)

6. You can use a __?__ to name part of a whole group. (Page 244)

7. If you write $\frac{3}{6}$ in __?__, the answer is $\frac{1}{2}$. (Page 248)

8. A number which is made up of a whole number and a fraction is called a __?__. (Page 252)

> composite
> divisible
> fraction
> greatest common
>   factor
> lowest terms
> mixed number
> multiples
> prime

Part 2 • SKILLS

Is each number divisible by 5? Answer YES or NO. (Pages 230–231)

9. 125   **10.** 94   **11.** 110   **12.** 345   **13.** 57

Write PRIME or COMPOSITE. (Pages 232–233)

14. 11   **15.** 59   **16.** 65   **17.** 98   **18.** 113

Write the prime factorization. Use a factor tree. Write the factors in order from least to greatest. (Pages 234–235)

19. 16   **20.** 45   **21.** 48   **22.** 85   **23.**

Find the greatest common factor for each pair. (Pages 236–237)

24. 8, 24   **25.** 14, 35   **26.** 15, 45   **27.** 60, 12   **28.** 54, 36

Find the least common multiple for each pair. (Pages 238–239)

29. 4, 6   **30.** 5, 7   **31.** 6, 8   **32.** 25, 50   **33.** 15, 20

Write the fraction that tells what part is blue. (Pages 244–245)

34.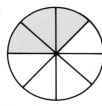

35.

36.

Complete. (Pages 246–247)

37. $\frac{2}{3} = \frac{?}{9}$ **38.** $\frac{6}{8} = \frac{?}{24}$ **39.** $\frac{9}{10} = \frac{45}{?}$ **40.** $\frac{?}{7} = \frac{12}{14}$ **41.** $\frac{6}{?} = \frac{36}{54}$

Write each fraction in lowest terms. (Pages 248–249)

42. $\frac{12}{15}$ **43.** $\frac{20}{30}$ **44.** $\frac{48}{72}$ **45.** $\frac{25}{100}$ **46.** $\frac{200}{400}$

Find the least common denominator for each pair. Write equivalent fractions.
(Pages 250–251)

47. $\frac{3}{4}, \frac{2}{8}$ **48.** $\frac{2}{5}, \frac{6}{10}$ **49.** $\frac{2}{3}, \frac{3}{5}$ **50.** $\frac{1}{3}, \frac{5}{7}$ **51.** $\frac{2}{8}, \frac{6}{12}$

Write <, >, or =. (Pages 250–251)

52. $\frac{2}{3} \bullet \frac{6}{12}$ **53.** $\frac{4}{5} \bullet \frac{7}{8}$ **54.** $\frac{9}{10} \bullet \frac{3}{4}$ **55.** $\frac{15}{24} \bullet \frac{10}{16}$ **56.** $\frac{16}{32} \bullet \frac{25}{50}$

Write as fractions. (Pages 252–253)

57. $2\frac{2}{3}$ **58.** $3\frac{1}{8}$ **59.** $7\frac{5}{9}$ **60.** $8\frac{3}{5}$ **61.** $9\frac{9}{10}$

Divide to find the mixed numbers. Write the answers in lowest terms. (Pages 254–255)

62. $\frac{7}{3}$ **63.** $\frac{8}{5}$ **64.** $\frac{24}{7}$ **65.** $\frac{38}{6}$ **66.** $\frac{95}{10}$

Part 3 • *PROBLEM SOLVING* • *APPLICATIONS*

For Exercises 67–68, write an equation. Solve the equation.

67. A recipe for onion-spinach soup contains 900 calories. The recipe makes 6 servings. How many calories per serving is this?
(Pages 240–241)

68. One slice of roast lamb contains 103 calories. How many calories are there in 3 slices?
(Pages 240–241)

69. At a 4–H Club party, Alma arrived first. Joe arrived after Alma and before Pete. Pete arrived before Lynn who was last. Who was the second to arrive?
(Pages 256–257)

70. In a horseshoe tournament, A made fewer points than B, and C made fewer points than A. D made more points than A but fewer points than B. Who had the lowest score? (Pages 256–257)

CHAPTER TEST

Find all the prime factors for each number. List them in order.

1. 32

2. 53

Find the greatest common factor for each pair.

3. 9, 15

4. 12, 40

Find the least common multiple for each pair.

5. 18, 24

6. 6, 10

Complete.

7. $\frac{3}{5} = \frac{?}{15}$

8. $\frac{1}{8} = \frac{4}{?}$

Write each fraction in its lowest terms.

9. $\frac{18}{27}$

10. $\frac{20}{25}$

11. $\frac{7}{21}$

Find the least common denominator. Write the equivalent fractions.

12. $\frac{2}{3}, \frac{3}{8}$

13. $\frac{4}{5}, \frac{1}{9}$

14. $\frac{5}{7}, \frac{1}{2}$

Write >, <, or =.

15. $\frac{3}{8}$ ⬤ $\frac{2}{3}$

16. $\frac{5}{12}$ ⬤ $\frac{1}{9}$

17. $\frac{8}{14}$ ⬤ $\frac{12}{21}$

Write as fractions.

18. $3\frac{1}{4}$

19. $6\frac{3}{8}$

20. $12\frac{3}{5}$

Divide to find mixed numbers. Write in lowest terms.

21. $\frac{7}{2}$

22. $\frac{18}{5}$

23. $\frac{9}{4}$

24. Gina plans to have a 380-calorie breakfast each day for 7 days.

   a. Write the equation you could use to find the total number of calories for the 7 days.

   b. Solve the equation.

25. In the 10-mile walk at the County Fair, Ann finished last. Tracy finished before Ann and after Meg. Kara finished 2 minutes before Meg. Who finished second?

ENRICHMENT

Patterns

Choose the correct response.

A is to **V** as **T** is to ?

T	⊢	⊣	⊥
a	b	c	d

Think   **V** is the same as **A** except that it is upside down. Look for the upside-down letter **T**. It is **⊥**. Look for the box that shows this. It is box **d**. The correct choice is **d**.

Now try this one.

○ is to ◯ as □ is to ?

◯	□	▫	○
a	b	c	d

Think   ◯ is the same as ○ except that it is larger. Look for the same shape as □ but larger. It is ▢. The correct choice is **b**.

Choose the correct responses.

E	ョ	Ǝ	ᴲ
a	b	c	d

1. P is to **P** as **E** is to ___?___

△	▲	○	⬤
a	b	c	d

2. △ is to ▲ as ○ is to ___?___

D	◖	○	◑
a	b	c	d

3. ○ is to ◖ as ⬤ is to ___?___

□	□	△	▵
a	b	c	d

4. ▲ is to △ as ◼ is to ___?___

⌂	⌔	□	⌔
a	b	c	d

5. □ is to ⌂ as ⬤ is to ___?___

ADDITIONAL PRACTICE

SKILLS

Write the prime factorization. Use a factor tree. Write the factors in order from least to greatest. (Pages 234–235)

1. 12   **2.** 20   **3.** 36   **4.** 49   **5.** 100

Find the greatest common factor for each pair. (Pages 236–237)

6. 10, 25   **7.** 18, 36   **8.** 20, 50   **9.** 30, 15   **10.** 81, 18

Find the least common multiple for each pair. (Pages 238–239)

11. 3, 5   **12.** 7, 8   **13.** 4, 6   **14.** 20, 15   **15.** 9, 10

Write the fraction that tells what part is blue for each. (Pages 244–245)

16.   **17.**   **18.**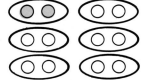

Write each fraction in lowest terms. (Pages 248–249)

19. $\frac{10}{12}$ **20.** $\frac{14}{21}$ **21.** $\frac{20}{35}$ **22.** $\frac{54}{72}$ **23.** $\frac{300}{600}$

Write <, >, or =. (Pages 250–251)

24. $\frac{8}{11}$ ⬤ $\frac{9}{11}$ **25.** $\frac{10}{30}$ ⬤ $\frac{25}{50}$ **26.** $\frac{5}{8}$ ⬤ $\frac{20}{32}$

Write as improper fractions. (Pages 252–253)

27. $2\frac{3}{4}$ **28.** $5\frac{1}{3}$ **29.** $6\frac{2}{8}$ **30.** $9\frac{8}{9}$ **31.** $4\frac{3}{11}$

Divide to find the mixed numbers. Write the answers in lowest terms. (Pages 254–255)

32. $\frac{5}{2}$ **33.** $\frac{9}{7}$ **34.** $\frac{38}{5}$ **35.** $\frac{4}{8}$ **36.** $\frac{84}{9}$

PROBLEM SOLVING • APPLICATIONS

37. Wayne has 2 corn muffins for breakfast. Each muffin contains 125 calories. Write an equation to determine how many calories this is in all. Then solve the equation. (Pages 240–241)

38. A wild animal park has fewer bears than lions. The number of tigers is 2 more than the number of lions. There are fewer leopards than lions but more leopards than bears. Are there more tigers or leopards? (Pages 256–257)

PROBLEM SOLVING MAINTENANCE

Chapters 1 through 9

Use the chart to answer Problems 1–3.

Distance Run in One Week

Ben	25.2 km
Jane	41.3 km
Lois	19.6 km

Write the hidden question.
Solve the problem.

1. The students on the track team practice every day. The chart shows how far each student ran in one week. How far did Jane run in 3 days?   (Page 166)

2. How much farther does Ben run than Lois in one day?   (Page 166)

3. Estimate the total distance run by the three students in one week. (Page 218)

   a. 70 km   **b.** 80 km   **c.** 90 km

For Problems 4–5, first write an equation. Then solve.   (Page 240)

4. Sam saves $18.00 to buy presents for his 3 sisters. He wants to spend the same amount on each sister. How much can he spend on one sister?

5. Mrs. Rivera is baking oatmeal cookies. She will bake 6 dozen cookies and use about 4 cups of oatmeal for each dozen cookies. About how many cups of oatmeal will she need?

For Problems 6–7, draw a picture to help you.   (Page 256)

6. Jason feeds his pets in the following order. The dog is fed before the parrot. The snake is fed last. The turtle is fed first, and the cat is fed before the dog. Which pet is fed before the snake?

7. The teacher asks 5 students to stand in order of their heights from the smallest to the tallest. Sue is first. Megan stands in the middle. Bill is last. Joe stands between Sue and Megan. Evan stands between Megan and Bill. Who is taller, Joe or Megan?

Write an equation. Solve.   (Page 148)

8. Brent earned $15.00 on Saturday and $27.00 on Sunday doing yard work for his neighbors. How much did he make altogether?

9. The Timberjack baseball club played 24 ball games during the month of July. They won 17 games. How many did they lose?

MAINTENANCE

Chapters 1 through 9

Mixed Practice • Choose the correct answers.

1. Write $\frac{6}{18}$ in lowest terms.

    A. $\frac{6}{18}$ **B.** $\frac{1}{3}$

    C. $\frac{2}{6}$ **D.** not here

2. Write $\frac{15}{20}$ in lowest terms.

    A. $\frac{2}{3}$ **B.** $\frac{3}{5}$

    C. $\frac{3}{4}$ **D.** not here

3. Write $\frac{10}{21}$ in lowest terms.

    A. $\frac{10}{21}$ **B.** $\frac{3}{7}$

    C. $\frac{1}{2}$ **D.** not here

4. Write $\frac{13}{5}$ as a mixed number.

    A. $2\frac{3}{5}$ **B.** $5\,3.5$

    C. $3\frac{2}{5}$ **D.** not here

5. Write $\frac{46}{30}$ as a mixed number.

    A. $1\frac{1}{2}$ **B.** $1\frac{8}{15}$

    C. $1\frac{4}{7}$ **D.** not here

6. $1 = \frac{?}{8}$

    A. 1   **B.** 9

    C. 8   **D.** not here

7. $\frac{3}{4} = \frac{?}{16}$

    A. 3   **B.** 12
    C. 7   **D.** not here

8. $\frac{5}{8} = \frac{?}{24}$

    A. 15   **B.** 5
    C. 8   **D.** not here

9. $\frac{7}{12} = \frac{?}{60}$

    A. 7   **B.** 12
    C. 45   **D.** not here

10. What is the least common multiple of 4 and 6?

    A. 2   **B.** 12

    C. 24   **D.** not here

11. What is the least common multiple of 3 and 10?

    A. 20   **B.** 60

    C. 30   **D.** not here

12. $17 \div 4 = \underline{\quad ? \quad}$

    A. $4\frac{1}{17}$ **B.** $4\frac{4}{17}$

    C. $3\frac{2}{17}$ **D.** not here

13. The class had 20 projects to do. The boys did 8 of the projects and the girls did 9 projects. Three projects were not completed. What fraction of the projects did the girls complete?

    A. $\frac{8}{20}$ **B.** $\frac{9}{20}$

    C. $\frac{3}{20}$ **D.** not here

14. Jenny had $3\frac{3}{5}$ yards of fabric. Angie had $3\frac{4}{5}$ yards of fabric. Which sentence is correct?

    A. Jenny had more fabric.
    B. Angie had more fabric.
    C. They had the same amount.
    D. not here

CHAPTER 10

Fractions: Addition and Subtraction

In order to reach underground steam, a well is drilled to a depth of 238 feet. The well pipe comes in 6-foot lengths.

● How many lengths of pipe will be needed?

The manager of a solar-powered factory plans to increase the present number of solar panels to 100. The manager first adds 10 to the present system, then doubles the number of panels to use to reach the goal of 100 panels.

● How many panels were there originally?

Addition with Like Denominators

East of Los Angeles, California, a solar energy electric plant heats water to 1,500°F. In a two–day period, sunlight was available $\frac{3}{8}$ of one day and $\frac{1}{8}$ of the second day.

● What part of the two days was sunlight available?

Think   You add to find the sunlight available for both days.

$$\frac{3}{8} + \frac{1}{8} = \ ?$$

Step 1
The denominators are the same. $\quad \frac{3}{8} + \frac{1}{8} = \frac{4}{8}$
Add the numerators.

Step 2
Write the answer in lowest terms. $\quad \frac{3}{8} + \frac{1}{8} = \frac{4}{8} = \frac{1}{2}$

Sunlight was available $\frac{1}{2}$ **of the time.**

● Add: $4\frac{1}{6} + 2\frac{2}{6}$.

Step 1	**Step 2**	**Step 3**
Add: $\frac{1}{6} + \frac{2}{6}$.	Add: $4 + 2$.	Write the answer in lowest terms.

$$\begin{array}{r} 4\frac{1}{6} \\ +2\frac{2}{6} \\ \hline \frac{3}{6} \end{array} \qquad \begin{array}{r} 4\frac{1}{6} \\ +2\frac{2}{6} \\ \hline 6\frac{3}{6} \end{array} \qquad \begin{array}{r} 4\frac{1}{6} \\ +2\frac{2}{6} \\ \hline 6\frac{3}{6} = 6\frac{1}{2} \end{array}$$

PRACTICE • Add. Write the answers in lowest terms.

1. $\frac{5}{8} + \frac{1}{8} = \underline{\quad?\quad}$ 2. $\frac{3}{10} + \frac{4}{10} = \underline{\quad?\quad}$ 3. $\frac{3}{7} + \frac{1}{7} = \underline{\quad?\quad}$

4. $\begin{array}{r} 3\frac{1}{5} \\ +4\frac{3}{5} \\ \hline \end{array}$ 5. $\begin{array}{r} 2\frac{2}{7} \\ +3\frac{3}{7} \\ \hline \end{array}$ 6. $\begin{array}{r} 1\frac{3}{8} \\ +5\frac{3}{8} \\ \hline \end{array}$ 7. $\begin{array}{r} 4\frac{3}{10} \\ +6\frac{5}{10} \\ \hline \end{array}$ 8. $\begin{array}{r} 10\frac{4}{12} \\ + \ 3\frac{6}{12} \\ \hline \end{array}$

EXERCISES • Add. Write the answers in lowest terms.

9. $\frac{4}{10} + \frac{2}{10} = $ _____   10. $\frac{1}{9} + \frac{2}{9} = $ _____   11. $\frac{3}{8} + \frac{2}{8} = $ _____

12. $\frac{9}{12} + \frac{2}{12} = $ _____   13. $\frac{5}{11} + \frac{4}{11} = $ _____   14. $\frac{3}{15} + \frac{2}{15} = $ _____

15. $3\frac{4}{10}$ 16. $6\frac{1}{4}$ 17. $3\frac{5}{13}$ 18. $4\frac{2}{8}$ 19. $12\frac{2}{6}$
    $+1\frac{1}{10}$ $+2\frac{2}{4}$ $+6\frac{5}{13}$ $+7\frac{2}{8}$ $+3\frac{2}{6}$

20. $3\frac{5}{12}$ 21. $6\frac{6}{16}$ 22. $8\frac{9}{21}$ 23. $6\frac{5}{18}$ 24. $15\frac{4}{24}$
    $+4\frac{4}{12}$ $+5\frac{6}{16}$ $+3\frac{5}{21}$ $+7\frac{3}{18}$ $+8\frac{6}{24}$

25. $\frac{4}{12}$ 26. $\frac{6}{15}$ 27. $1\frac{2}{9}$ 28. $3\frac{5}{20}$ 29. $14\frac{6}{35}$
    $\frac{2}{12}$ $\frac{3}{15}$ $2\frac{1}{9}$ $8\frac{6}{20}$ $8\frac{3}{35}$
    $+\frac{3}{12}$ $+\frac{4}{15}$ $+4\frac{4}{9}$ $+9\frac{3}{20}$ $+5\frac{5}{35}$

Both denominators are the same for each. Write the missing denominators.

★ 30. $\frac{1}{?} + \frac{3}{?} = \frac{1}{2}$ ★ 31. $\frac{3}{?} + \frac{5}{?} = \frac{4}{5}$ ★ 32. $\frac{1}{?} + \frac{2}{?} = \frac{1}{5}$

PROBLEM SOLVING • APPLICATIONS [CHOOSE • mental math • pencil and paper • calculator SOLVE]

33. In 212 B.C. the Greek mathematician Archimedes used solar energy reflected from mirrors to set fire to attacking Roman ships. An ancient writer reported that $\frac{1}{5}$ of the fleet was burning by noon and $\frac{2}{5}$ was burning by sundown. What part of the fleet is this in all?

34. Satellites used for world–wide communications use solar energy for power. Each satellite services $\frac{1}{3}$ of the earth's surface. One satellite is located over the Atlantic Ocean. Another is located over the Indian Ocean. How much of the earth's surface do they service?

35. Space absorbs about $\frac{2}{5}$ of the sun's energy and about $\frac{1}{5}$ disappears into the earth's atmosphere. The earth's surface receives $\frac{2}{5}$ of the sun's energy. About how much solar energy never reaches the earth's surface?

★ 36. A possible source of electricity is the sun's heat reflected from mirrors. Mirrors are placed in lines 500 feet long. There is a mirror at the start of each line and the mirrors are 2 feet apart. There are 22 lines of mirrors in each section. How many mirrors are there in a section?

Addition with Unlike Denominators

Two thirds of the coal mined in the United States is used to produce electricity. An electric power plant uses $\frac{3}{4}$ of the coal in a railroad car in 15 minutes, and $\frac{5}{8}$ of a railroad car in the next 15 minutes.

● How many carloads were used?

Think You *add* to find the total number of carloads.

$$\frac{3}{4} + \frac{5}{8} = ?$$

The denominators are not the same. You can use equivalent fractions with the same denominator. Use the least common denominator.

Step 1
Find the least common denominator. Write equivalent fractions.

$$\begin{array}{r} \frac{3}{4} = \frac{6}{8} \\ + \frac{5}{8} = \frac{5}{8} \\ \hline \end{array}$$

Step 2
Add.

$$\begin{array}{r} \frac{3}{4} = \frac{6}{8} \\ + \frac{5}{8} = \frac{5}{8} \\ \hline \frac{11}{8} \end{array}$$

Step 3
Write the answer using a mixed number.

$$\begin{array}{r} \frac{3}{4} = \frac{6}{8} \\ + \frac{5}{8} = \frac{5}{8} \\ \hline \frac{11}{8} = 1\frac{3}{8} \end{array}$$

They used $1\frac{3}{8}$ **carloads** of coal.

● Add: $3\frac{1}{4} + 2\frac{3}{5}$.

Step 1
Write equivalent fractions.

$$\begin{array}{r} 3\frac{1}{4} = 3\frac{5}{20} \\ +2\frac{3}{5} = 2\frac{12}{20} \\ \hline \end{array}$$

Step 2
Add: $\frac{5}{20} + \frac{12}{20}$.

$$\begin{array}{r} 3\frac{1}{4} = 3\frac{5}{20} \\ +2\frac{3}{5} = 2\frac{12}{20} \\ \hline \frac{17}{20} \end{array}$$

Step 3
Add the whole numbers.

$$\begin{array}{r} 3\frac{1}{4} = 3\frac{5}{20} \\ +2\frac{3}{5} = 2\frac{12}{20} \\ \hline 5\frac{17}{20} \end{array}$$

PRACTICE ● Add. Write the answers in lowest terms.

1. $\begin{array}{r} \frac{1}{2} \\ + \frac{3}{8} \\ \hline \end{array}$

2. $\begin{array}{r} \frac{2}{3} \\ + \frac{1}{4} \\ \hline \end{array}$

3. $\begin{array}{r} \frac{2}{3} \\ + \frac{7}{12} \\ \hline \end{array}$

4. $\begin{array}{r} \frac{1}{8} \\ + \frac{3}{4} \\ \hline \end{array}$

5. $\begin{array}{r} \frac{3}{4} \\ + \frac{2}{3} \\ \hline \end{array}$

6. $1\frac{2}{5}$
$+2\frac{3}{10}$

7. $2\frac{1}{6}$
$+1\frac{5}{12}$

8. $3\frac{1}{5}$
$+4\frac{2}{3}$

9. $4\frac{1}{6}$
$+2\frac{2}{9}$

10. $5\frac{3}{7}$
$+6\frac{1}{2}$

EXERCISES • Add. Write the answers in lowest terms.

11. $\frac{5}{6}$
$+\frac{2}{3}$

12. $\frac{3}{4}$
$+\frac{1}{6}$

13. $\frac{3}{8}$
$+\frac{1}{6}$

14. $\frac{4}{12}$
$+\frac{5}{6}$

15. $\frac{2}{5}$
$+\frac{1}{10}$

16. $\frac{3}{8}$
$+\frac{2}{3}$

17. $\frac{5}{6}$
$+\frac{3}{4}$

18. $\frac{1}{2}$
$+\frac{2}{9}$

19. $\frac{3}{15}$
$+\frac{2}{5}$

20. $\frac{3}{8}$
$+\frac{1}{4}$

21. $4\frac{1}{4}$
$+5\frac{1}{4}$

22. $6\frac{2}{4}$
$+3\frac{2}{7}$

23. $4\frac{2}{6}$
$+5\frac{3}{5}$

24. $6\frac{4}{9}$
$+2\frac{2}{9}$

25. $7\frac{3}{10}$
$+4\frac{1}{2}$

★ **26.** $\frac{1}{2} + \frac{1}{6} + \frac{1}{4} = $ _____?_____

★ **27.** $\frac{2}{6} + \frac{1}{3} + \frac{1}{9} = $ _____?_____

★ **28.** $5\frac{3}{7} + 5\frac{2}{35} + 6\frac{1}{5} = $ _____?_____

★ **29.** $4\frac{2}{4} + 3\frac{2}{12} + 1\frac{1}{6} = $ _____?_____

PROBLEM SOLVING • APPLICATIONS   CHOOSE   • mental math • pencil and paper • calculator   SOLVE

30. A "unit train" carries coal from the mine to the power plant. The train travels nonstop from its loading point to its unloading point. The trip from a power plant to a mine takes $5\frac{1}{4}$ hours. The return trip takes $4\frac{3}{8}$ hours. What is the total time for the round trip?

31. Slurry is coal mixed with water. In Ohio, slurry was pumped from a mine to a power plant through a pipeline 108 miles long. The top of the pipe is $3\frac{1}{2}$ feet underground. The pipe is $1\frac{3}{8}$ feet in diameter. How deep is the trench for the pipe?

For Exercises 32–33, use this table.

32. Which three appliances require a total of $\frac{2}{3}$ of a ton of coal yearly?

33. Which requires more coal yearly, the water heater or the range, dishwasher, T.V., and dryer combined?

Coal to Electricity	
Appliance	**Approximate tons of coal needed yearly**
Water Heater	$2\frac{1}{2}$
Range	$\frac{1}{3}$
Dishwasher	$\frac{1}{6}$
T.V.	$\frac{1}{6}$
Dryer	$\frac{1}{2}$

More Addition with Mixed Numbers

Water falling from dams provides about $\frac{1}{8}$ of our electric power. Often moving over 100 mph, the water drives generators which produce electricity. A generator operates for $4\frac{4}{5}$ hours one day and $2\frac{5}{8}$ hours the next day.

● What are the total number of hours of operation for the generator?

Think　You add to find the total number of hours.

$$4\frac{4}{5} + 2\frac{5}{8} = ?$$

Step 1
Write equivalent fractions.

Step 2
Add: $\frac{32}{40} + \frac{25}{40}$

Step 3
Add: $4 + 2$.
$\frac{57}{40} > 1$. Regroup. Write the answer in lowest terms.
$6\frac{57}{40} = 6\frac{40}{40} + \frac{17}{40}$
Add: $6 + 1$.

$$
\begin{aligned}
4\frac{4}{5} &= 4\frac{32}{40}\\
+2\frac{5}{8} &= 2\frac{25}{40}\\
\hline
\end{aligned}
$$

$$
\begin{aligned}
4\frac{4}{5} &= 4\frac{32}{40}\\
+2\frac{5}{8} &= 2\frac{25}{40}\\
\hline
&\quad\ \frac{57}{40}
\end{aligned}
$$

$$
\begin{aligned}
4\frac{4}{5} &= 4\frac{32}{40}\\
+2\frac{5}{8} &= 2\frac{25}{40}\\
\hline
6\frac{57}{40} &= 7\frac{17}{40}
\end{aligned}
$$

The generator operates for $7\frac{17}{40}$ **hours.**

More Examples:

$$
\begin{aligned}
8\frac{7}{10} &= 8\frac{21}{30}\\
+3\frac{5}{6} &= 3\frac{25}{30}\\
\hline
11\frac{46}{30} &= 12\frac{16}{30} = \mathbf{12\frac{8}{15}}
\end{aligned}
$$

$$
\begin{aligned}
4\frac{7}{12}&\\
+5\frac{5}{12}&\\
\hline
9\frac{12}{12} &= 9 + \frac{12}{12}\\
&= 9 + 1 = \mathbf{10}
\end{aligned}
$$

PRACTICE • Add. Write the answers in lowest terms.

1. $5\frac{2}{3}$
   $+1\frac{3}{6}$

2. $1\frac{1}{2}$
   $+2\frac{3}{5}$

3. $3\frac{3}{8}$
   $+5\frac{3}{4}$

4. $3\frac{2}{3}$
   $+4\frac{1}{2}$

5. $2\frac{3}{5}$
   $+4\frac{5}{8}$

6. $1\frac{3}{8}$
$+1\frac{2}{3}$

7. $4\frac{5}{7}$
$+3\frac{2}{3}$

8. $6\frac{4}{7}$
$+8\frac{2}{4}$

9. $4\frac{3}{5}$
$+4\frac{7}{10}$

10. $2\frac{4}{5}$
$+4\frac{6}{15}$

EXERCISES • Add. Write the answers in lowest terms.

11. $6\frac{2}{3}$
$+2\frac{3}{4}$

12. $5\frac{3}{4}$
$+2\frac{7}{10}$

13. $10\frac{9}{10}$
$+\ \ \frac{3}{5}$

14. $9\frac{5}{6}$
$+2\frac{7}{9}$

15. $5\frac{5}{8}$
$+5\frac{3}{4}$

16. $3\frac{4}{9}$
$+4\frac{5}{6}$

17. $8\frac{7}{10}$
$+4\frac{9}{15}$

18. $4\frac{3}{5}$
$+4\frac{5}{8}$

19. $5\frac{5}{6}$
$+2\frac{2}{4}$

20. $9\frac{3}{4}$
$+8\frac{3}{7}$

21. $\frac{7}{10}$
$+\frac{8}{15}$

22. $3\frac{3}{4}$
$+4\frac{5}{16}$

23. $5\frac{1}{8}$
$+3\frac{3}{4}$

24. $11\frac{7}{12}$
$+\ 5\frac{3}{4}$

25. $9\frac{2}{3}$
$+8\frac{4}{7}$

26. $2\frac{3}{4} + 6\frac{7}{8} = $ _____?_____

27. $5\frac{2}{5} + 6\frac{7}{10} = $ _____?_____

28. $3\frac{2}{3} + 9\frac{2}{4} = $ _____?_____

29. $7\frac{4}{5} + 4\frac{2}{3} = $ _____?_____

30. $5\frac{5}{12} + 6\frac{1}{12} = $ _____?_____

31. $5\frac{9}{12} + 3\frac{2}{8} = $ _____?_____

32. $\frac{3}{4} + \frac{5}{8} = $ _____?_____

★ **33.** $4\frac{2}{3} + 2\frac{5}{6} + 5\frac{2}{3} = $ _____?_____

★ **34.** $9\frac{4}{6} + 4\frac{3}{5} + 5\frac{8}{10} = $ _____?_____

PROBLEM SOLVING • APPLICATIONS

35. The Grand Coulee Dam generates $\frac{1}{3}$ of all the hydroelectric power in the United States. Suppose one of it's nine generators runs for $7\frac{3}{4}$ hours in the morning and $5\frac{9}{10}$ hours in the afternoon. How many hours does it run that day?

36. A hydroelectric plant uses water from a storage lake and pumps it back into the lake again. Suppose a lake is $1\frac{1}{5}$ miles long. When the plant releases water into it, the lake is lengthened by $\frac{9}{10}$ of a mile. How long will the lake be then?

37. A New England family uses a dam to generate their own electricity. A generator breaks down. It takes $3\frac{4}{5}$ hours to find parts and $1\frac{3}{10}$ hours to make repairs. How long will the family be without electricity?

★ **38.** An employee of a hydroelectric plant worked for $5\frac{2}{5}$ hours on Monday, $7\frac{1}{2}$ hours on Tuesday, and $6\frac{1}{10}$ hours on Wednesday. How many hours was this in all?

Subtraction with Like Denominators

At The Geysers in northern California, steam found deep in the earth is used to produce electricity. The Geysers provides a California ranch with $\frac{5}{8}$ of its electricity in March and $\frac{3}{8}$ of its electricity in April.

● How much more of the ranch's electricity was supplied in March?

Think "How much more" suggests subtraction.

$$\frac{5}{8} - \frac{3}{8} = \,?$$

Step 1
The denominators are the same. Subtract the numerators.

$$\frac{5}{8} - \frac{3}{8} = \frac{2}{8}$$

Step 2
Write the answer in lowest terms.

$$\frac{5}{8} - \frac{3}{8} = \frac{2}{8} = \frac{1}{4}$$

The rancher received $\frac{1}{4}$ **more** electricity in March.

● Subtract: $5\frac{7}{9} - 2\frac{1}{9}$

Step 1
Subtract:
$\frac{7}{9} - \frac{1}{9}$

$$\begin{array}{r} 5\frac{7}{9} \\ -2\frac{1}{9} \\ \hline \frac{6}{9} \end{array}$$

Step 2
Subtract: $5 - 2$.

$$\begin{array}{r} 5\frac{7}{9} \\ -2\frac{1}{9} \\ \hline 3\frac{6}{9} \end{array}$$

Step 3
Write the answer in lowest terms.

$$\begin{array}{r} 5\frac{7}{9} \\ -2\frac{1}{9} \\ \hline 3\frac{6}{9} = \mathbf{3\frac{2}{3}} \end{array}$$

PRACTICE • Subtract. Write the answers in lowest terms.

1. $\frac{5}{6} - \frac{1}{6} = \underline{\quad ? \quad}$

2. $\frac{7}{8} - \frac{2}{8} = \underline{\quad ? \quad}$

3. $\frac{5}{7} - \frac{2}{7} = \underline{\quad ? \quad}$

4. $\begin{array}{r} 8\frac{7}{8} \\ -2\frac{1}{8} \\ \hline \end{array}$

5. $\begin{array}{r} 7\frac{9}{10} \\ -1\frac{6}{10} \\ \hline \end{array}$

6. $\begin{array}{r} 3\frac{4}{5} \\ -1\frac{2}{5} \\ \hline \end{array}$

7. $\begin{array}{r} 8\frac{6}{7} \\ -5\frac{4}{7} \\ \hline \end{array}$

8. $\begin{array}{r} 15\frac{2}{9} \\ -\ 3\frac{1}{9} \\ \hline \end{array}$

EXERCISES • Subtract. Write the answers in lowest terms.

9. $\dfrac{7}{8} - \dfrac{5}{8} =$ _____?_____

10. $\dfrac{5}{7} - \dfrac{3}{7} =$ _____?_____

11. $\dfrac{7}{9} - \dfrac{6}{9} =$ _____?_____

12. $\dfrac{7}{10} - \dfrac{3}{10} =$ _____?_____

13. $\dfrac{13}{15} - \dfrac{7}{15} =$ _____?_____

14. $\dfrac{5}{12} - \dfrac{1}{12} =$ _____?_____

15. $3\dfrac{5}{8}$
$-2\dfrac{1}{8}$
_____

16. $5\dfrac{2}{3}$
$-1\dfrac{1}{3}$
_____

17. $7\dfrac{11}{20}$
$-3\dfrac{6}{20}$
_____

18. $4\dfrac{6}{9}$
$-1\dfrac{1}{9}$
_____

19. $10\dfrac{9}{11}$
$-\ 4\dfrac{7}{11}$
_____

20. $9\dfrac{19}{20}$
$-2\dfrac{7}{20}$
_____

21. $16\dfrac{6}{7}$
$-\ 3\dfrac{1}{7}$
_____

22. $5\dfrac{7}{8}$
$-2\dfrac{3}{8}$
_____

23. $8\dfrac{7}{12}$
$-3\dfrac{5}{12}$
_____

24. $18\dfrac{9}{10}$
$-\ 9\dfrac{3}{10}$
_____

25. $9\dfrac{9}{12}$
$-3\dfrac{3}{12}$
_____

26. $12\dfrac{7}{8}$
$-\ 4\dfrac{3}{8}$
_____

27. $13\dfrac{13}{16}$
$-\ 2\dfrac{9}{16}$
_____

★ 28. $768\dfrac{19}{20}$
$-321\dfrac{15}{20}$
_____

★ 29. $419\dfrac{15}{36}$
$-212\dfrac{12}{36}$
_____

PROBLEM SOLVING • APPLICATIONS

30. In Reykjavik, Iceland, water pipes carry water from nearby hot springs to heat most of the city's houses. A pipe $58\dfrac{1}{3}$ kilometers long is extended $62\dfrac{2}{3}$ kilometers. How long is the pipe now?

31. A water main is $21\dfrac{7}{8}$ feet long. It is made from three shorter pipes. One pipe is $5\dfrac{1}{8}$ feet long and another is $8\dfrac{5}{8}$ feet long. How long is the third pipe?

CALCULATOR • Fractions and Decimals

To enter a fraction into a calculator, you must change it to a decimal. You change a fraction to a decimal by dividing the numerator by the denominator.

Change $\dfrac{5}{8}$ to a decimal.

Press: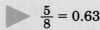

If necessary, round to the nearest hundredth. ▶ $\dfrac{5}{8} = 0.63$

Change the following fractions to decimals.

1. $\dfrac{2}{5}$ 2. $\dfrac{1}{9}$ 3. $\dfrac{11}{20}$ 4. $\dfrac{3}{25}$ 5. $\dfrac{2}{11}$ 6. $\dfrac{17}{20}$ 7. $\dfrac{5}{6}$

PROBLEM SOLVING · STRATEGIES

Working Backwards

> Sometimes you can solve problems by working backwards.
> To work backwards, you use **opposite,** or **inverse,** operations.

- Addition and subtraction are opposite operations.

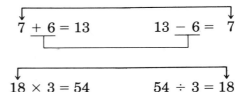

$$7 + 6 = 13 \qquad 13 - 6 = 7$$

- Multiplication and division are opposite operations.

$$18 \times 3 = 54 \qquad 54 \div 3 = 18$$

Example

The manager of a solar powered factory plans to increase the present number of solar panels to 100. First, she adds 10 panels to the present system. Then she doubles the number of panels in use to reach the goal of 100 panels.

- How many panels were there originally?

Think   A **flow chart** will show the order of the operations.

Step 1
Draw a flow chart.

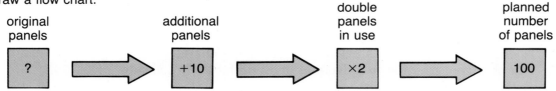

original panels		additional panels		double panels in use		planned number of panels
?	⇒	+10	⇒	×2	⇒	100

Step 2
Work backwards. Use the opposite operations.

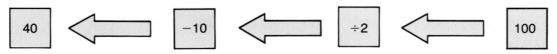

40	⇐	−10	⇐	÷2	⇐	100

There were **40 panels** originally.

PROBLEMS

Solve. Use opposite operations.

1. A coal train drops 50 cars at an
   electric power plant. It then goes to
   a switching yard where it is
   separated into 3 separate trains.
   Each train is 46 cars long. How
   many cars were in the original train?

| ? | → | −50 cars | → | ÷3 | → | 46 cars |

Draw a flow chart. Use opposite operations to solve.

2. An electric company records wind
   speeds at a possible site for
   windmills. From 7 A.M. to 9 A.M., the
   speed increased 3 mph. At 2:00 P.M.
   the increase in wind speed was 4
   times the increase from 7:00 A.M. to
   9 A.M. The wind speed was now
   22 mph. What was wind speed at
   7:00 A.M.?

3. The water flow at a hydroelectric
   plant is increased by 3,000 gallons
   per second at 8 A.M. At 11 A.M., the
   water flow is doubled. It is now
   8,000 gallons per second. What was
   the water flow per second before 8
   A.M.?

Addition and subtraction are opposite
operations.

4. A communications satellite lost 11
   power cells when it was placed in
   orbit. After 36 hours, another 138
   cells were not working. The satellite
   now had only 46 cells working. How
   many power cells were there
   originally?

5. A geothermal power plant now has
   18 turbines in use. A year after it
   was built, three turbines were
   added. Five years later the number
   of turbines was tripled. How many
   turbines were originally in
   operation?

6. A central California farmer uses
   windmills to produce electricity for
   irrigation pumps. One windmill can
   power 6 pumps. There are now 36
   pumps. A year ago the farmer
   tripled the number of pumps. Two
   years ago six more pumps were
   added. How many windmills were
   built originally?

MID-CHAPTER REVIEW

Add. Write the answers in lowest terms.   (Pages 266–267)

1. $\frac{6}{9} + \frac{2}{9} =$ ___?___

2. $3\frac{2}{7} + 2\frac{3}{7} =$ ___?___

3. $6\frac{4}{6} + 9\frac{1}{6} =$ ___?___

4. $\begin{array}{r} \frac{2}{12} \\ \frac{3}{12} \\ +\frac{5}{12} \\ \hline \end{array}$

5. $\begin{array}{r} \frac{3}{21} \\ \frac{5}{21} \\ +\frac{6}{21} \\ \hline \end{array}$

6. $\begin{array}{r} 1\frac{2}{16} \\ 2\frac{4}{16} \\ +5\frac{2}{16} \\ \hline \end{array}$

7. $\begin{array}{r} 8\frac{4}{32} \\ 3\frac{3}{32} \\ +4\frac{1}{32} \\ \hline \end{array}$

8. $\begin{array}{r} 14\frac{5}{20} \\ 16\frac{3}{20} \\ +\ 4\frac{2}{20} \\ \hline \end{array}$

Add. Write the answers in lowest terms.   (Pages 268–269)

9. $\begin{array}{r} \frac{2}{3} \\ +\frac{2}{9} \\ \hline \end{array}$

10. $\begin{array}{r} \frac{3}{4} \\ +\frac{2}{3} \\ \hline \end{array}$

11. $\begin{array}{r} 7\frac{1}{4} \\ +2\frac{1}{6} \\ \hline \end{array}$

12. $\begin{array}{r} 8\frac{1}{3} \\ +7\frac{2}{7} \\ \hline \end{array}$

13. $\begin{array}{r} 61\frac{1}{2} \\ +91\frac{1}{8} \\ \hline \end{array}$

Add. Write the answers in lowest terms.   (Pages 270–271)

14. $\begin{array}{r} 3\frac{6}{8} \\ +2\frac{2}{4} \\ \hline \end{array}$

15. $\begin{array}{r} 5\frac{5}{8} \\ +6\frac{7}{10} \\ \hline \end{array}$

16. $\begin{array}{r} 8\frac{8}{9} \\ +8\frac{19}{36} \\ \hline \end{array}$

17. $\begin{array}{r} 6\frac{3}{5} \\ +2\frac{7}{10} \\ \hline \end{array}$

18. $\begin{array}{r} 3\frac{5}{8} \\ +7\frac{15}{24} \\ \hline \end{array}$

Subtract. Write the answers in lowest terms.   (Pages 272–273)

19. $\begin{array}{r} \frac{7}{10} \\ -\frac{4}{10} \\ \hline \end{array}$

20. $\begin{array}{r} \frac{8}{12} \\ -\frac{4}{12} \\ \hline \end{array}$

21. $\begin{array}{r} 8\frac{6}{8} \\ -2\frac{2}{8} \\ \hline \end{array}$

22. $\begin{array}{r} 42\frac{6}{20} \\ -18\frac{1}{20} \\ \hline \end{array}$

23. $\begin{array}{r} 309\frac{9}{16} \\ -145\frac{7}{16} \\ \hline \end{array}$

Solve each problem.   (Pages 274–275)

24. A windmill power system has 50 windmills. Three years ago, the original number of windmills was doubled. One year ago, 22 more windmills were added. How many windmills were there originally?

25. A space shuttle is now operating with 86 fuel cells. After lift off, half of the fuel cells failed to operate. The crew managed to repair 12 of the cells. How many fuel cells were on the shuttle before the launch?

MAINTENANCE • MIXED PRACTICE

Multiply.

1. $20.3 \times 1.68 =$ ___?___

2. $4.506 \times 0.399 =$ ___?___

3. $26.507 \times 1.9 =$ ___?___

Divide.

4. $1.5\overline{)55.35}$

5. $0.08\overline{)0.4808}$

6. $0.057\overline{)5.073}$

7. $32.6\overline{)49.878}$

CONSUMER APPLICATIONS

Cost of Electricity

Electricity is measured in **kilowatts.** You use one **kilowatt–hour** of electricity when you use one kilowatt for one hour. The tables below show the average number of kilowatt–hours used per week by some household appliances.

Appliance	Kilowatt–hours per week
Radio	3
Refrigerator	43
Television (color)	10
Washing Machine	2

You can find the cost of operating an appliance if you know the cost of 1 kilowatt–hour of electricity.

EXAMPLE: Suppose electricity costs $0.10 per killowatt–hour.

● Find the cost of operating a radio for 1 week.

Think You know the number of kilowatt–hours used and the cost for 1 kilowatt–hour. Multiply.

$3 \times \$0.10 = \$0.30$ ◀ **Cost per week to operate a radio**

EXERCISES • Suppose electricity costs $0.08 per kilowatt–hour. Find the cost per week for each appliance.

1. Washing machine   **2.** Refrigerator   **3.** Television

4. Suppose electricity costs $0.13 per kilowatt–hour. What is the cost of operating a color television for 4 weeks?

5. Suppose electricity costs $0.12 per kilowatt–hour. What is the cost of operating a radio and a color television for one week?

6. Suppose electricity for an electric clock costs $0.23 per month. Find the cost of electricity for the clock for one year.

PROJECT Contact your local power company to find the cost per hour of one kilowatt of electricity. Find the number of kilowatt hours per week used by other appliances in your home. Which appliance costs the least to operate, for 1 week? Which costs the most? Find one way to save on electrical costs.

Subtraction with Unlike Denominators

A windmill is producing electricity for 150 homes. One week it operates $\frac{5}{6}$ of one day, but only $\frac{1}{3}$ of the next day.

● How much longer did it operate the first day?

 Think "How much longer" suggests subtraction.

$$\frac{5}{6} - \frac{1}{3} = \frac{?}{}$$

Step 1
Find the least common denominator. Write equivalent fractions.

$$\frac{5}{6} = \frac{5}{6}$$
$$-\frac{1}{3} = \frac{2}{6}$$

Step 2
Subtract.

$$\frac{5}{6} = \frac{5}{6}$$
$$-\frac{1}{3} = \frac{2}{6}$$
$$\frac{3}{6}$$

Step 3
Write the answer in lowest terms.

$$\frac{5}{6} = \frac{5}{6}$$
$$-\frac{1}{3} = \frac{2}{6}$$
$$\frac{3}{6} = \frac{1}{2}$$

The windmill operated $\frac{1}{2}$ **day longer** the first day.

● Subtract: $4\frac{2}{3} - 1\frac{1}{5}$.

Step 1
Write equivalent fractions.

$$4\frac{2}{3} = 4\frac{10}{15}$$
$$-1\frac{1}{5} = 1\frac{3}{15}$$

Step 2
Subtract: $\frac{10}{15} - \frac{3}{15}$.

$$4\frac{2}{3} = 4\frac{10}{15}$$
$$-1\frac{1}{5} = 1\frac{3}{15}$$
$$\frac{7}{15}$$

Step 3
Subtract: $4 - 1$.

$$4\frac{2}{3} = 4\frac{10}{15}$$
$$-1\frac{1}{5} = 1\frac{3}{15}$$
$$3\frac{7}{15}$$

PRACTICE • Subtract. Write the answers in lowest terms.

1. $\frac{7}{8}$
$-\frac{1}{2}$

2. $\frac{1}{2}$
$-\frac{3}{8}$

3. $\frac{1}{2}$
$-\frac{1}{3}$

4. $\frac{9}{10}$
$-\frac{3}{5}$

5. $\frac{4}{5}$
$-\frac{2}{3}$

6. $8\frac{3}{4}$
$-3\frac{1}{6}$

7. $2\frac{1}{2}$
-1

8. $7\frac{7}{12}$
$-5\frac{1}{3}$

9. $9\frac{3}{8}$
$-7\frac{1}{4}$

10. $8\frac{6}{7}$
$-5\frac{1}{2}$

EXERCISES • Subtract. Write the answers in lowest terms.

11. $\dfrac{7}{9}$
$-\dfrac{1}{3}$

12. $\dfrac{5}{8}$
$-\dfrac{1}{4}$

13. $\dfrac{9}{10}$
$-\dfrac{3}{5}$

14. $\dfrac{6}{7}$
$-\dfrac{2}{3}$

15. $\dfrac{4}{6}$
$-\dfrac{2}{5}$

16. $\dfrac{7}{12}$
$-\dfrac{1}{3}$

17. $\dfrac{8}{9}$
$-\dfrac{3}{4}$

18. $\dfrac{7}{8}$
$-\dfrac{3}{4}$

19. $\dfrac{8}{10}$
$-\dfrac{3}{4}$

20. $\dfrac{7}{8}$
$-\dfrac{5}{6}$

21. $9\dfrac{1}{4}$
$-8\dfrac{1}{7}$

22. $6\dfrac{3}{5}$
$-2\dfrac{3}{10}$

23. $4\dfrac{6}{9}$
$-1\dfrac{2}{5}$

24. $5\dfrac{5}{6}$
$-1\dfrac{1}{4}$

25. $8\dfrac{7}{12}$
$-3\dfrac{5}{12}$

26. $35\dfrac{1}{2}$
$-10\dfrac{3}{8}$

27. $14\dfrac{8}{16}$
$-\ 7\dfrac{4}{16}$

28. $9\dfrac{6}{7}$
$-3\dfrac{2}{4}$

29. $23\dfrac{3}{6}$
$-\ 8\dfrac{3}{8}$

30. $14\dfrac{4}{15}$
$-\ 6\dfrac{2}{15}$

31. $7\dfrac{2}{3} - 1\dfrac{5}{9} = $ ___?___

32. $5\dfrac{3}{4} - 2\dfrac{1}{16} = $ ___?___

33. $6\dfrac{1}{2} - 4\dfrac{3}{10} = $ ___?___

34. $10\dfrac{5}{8} - 4\dfrac{1}{3} = $ ___?___

35. $18\dfrac{9}{20} - 9\dfrac{3}{20} = $ ___?___

36. $8\dfrac{6}{17} - 2\dfrac{4}{17} = $ ___?___

Use − and + to make true sentences.

★ 37. $\dfrac{3}{4}$ ⬤ $\dfrac{1}{6}$ ⬤ $\dfrac{2}{8} = \dfrac{5}{6}$

★ 38. $\dfrac{2}{3}$ ⬤ $\dfrac{4}{5}$ ⬤ $\dfrac{1}{3} = 1\dfrac{2}{15}$

PROBLEM SOLVING • APPLICATIONS

39. While exploring the Artic in 1894, Fridtjof Nansen used a windmill to produce electricity. Suppose the wind blew $10\dfrac{2}{5}$ hours one day and $8\dfrac{1}{3}$ hours the next day. How many more hours of wind were there the first day?

40. For a "backyard windmill" to produce electricity, winds must reach a speed of $9\dfrac{1}{4}$ miles per hour. Winds on a certain day average $7\dfrac{1}{6}$ miles per hour. By how much must wind speed increase for the windmill to produce electricity?

PROJECT- Make a chart showing the number of hours, or fractions of hours, your family uses the following appliances each day.
a. television **b.** phonograph **c.** stove **d.** washer **e.** vacuum cleaner
What is the total number of hours each appliance is used in one week?

Subtraction with Regrouping

Burning garbage provides more energy than oil. The city of Columbus, Ohio, burns garbage to produce electricity. A truck delivers 8 tons of garbage in one day, but only $5\frac{3}{4}$ tons the next day.

● How much more garbage is delivered the first day?

Think "How much more" suggests subtraction.

$$8 - 5\frac{3}{4} = \underline{\ ?\ }$$

Step 1
Write 8 as 7 + 1.
Think: $1 = \frac{4}{4}$

$$\begin{array}{r} 8 \quad = 7\frac{4}{4} \leftarrow 7 + \frac{4}{4} \\ -5\frac{3}{4} = 5\frac{3}{4} \\ \hline \end{array}$$

Step 2
Subtract.

$$\begin{array}{r} 8 \quad = 7\frac{4}{4} \\ -5\frac{3}{4} = 5\frac{3}{4} \\ \hline 2\frac{1}{4} \end{array}$$

$2\frac{1}{4}$ tons more

● Subtract: $7\frac{1}{3} - 4\frac{2}{3}$

Step 1
$\frac{2}{3} > \frac{1}{3}$. Regroup $7\frac{1}{3}$ as $6 + 1 + \frac{1}{3}$.
Then $6 + \frac{3}{3} + \frac{1}{3} = 6 + \frac{4}{3} = 6\frac{4}{3}$.

$$\begin{array}{r} 7\frac{1}{3} = 6\frac{4}{3} \\ -4\frac{2}{3} = 4\frac{2}{3} \\ \hline \end{array}$$

Step 2
Subtract.

$$\begin{array}{r} 7\frac{1}{3} = 6\frac{4}{3} \\ -4\frac{2}{3} = 4\frac{2}{3} \\ \hline 2\frac{2}{3} \end{array}$$

PRACTICE • Subtract. Write the answers in lowest terms.

1. $\begin{array}{r} 2\frac{1}{6} \\ -1\frac{5}{6} \\ \hline \end{array}$

2. $\begin{array}{r} 3\frac{3}{12} \\ -1\frac{9}{12} \\ \hline \end{array}$

3. $\begin{array}{r} 2\frac{5}{16} \\ -1\frac{11}{16} \\ \hline \end{array}$

4. $\begin{array}{r} 4 \\ -2\frac{4}{5} \\ \hline \end{array}$

5. $\begin{array}{r} 8 \\ -6\frac{5}{8} \\ \hline \end{array}$

6. $\begin{array}{r} 5 \\ -1\frac{2}{3} \\ \hline \end{array}$

7. $\begin{array}{r} 6 \\ -4\frac{3}{5} \\ \hline \end{array}$

8. $\begin{array}{r} 4\frac{1}{4} \\ -2\frac{3}{4} \\ \hline \end{array}$

9. $\begin{array}{r} 6\frac{3}{10} \\ -3\frac{7}{10} \\ \hline \end{array}$

10. $\begin{array}{r} 5\frac{1}{8} \\ -1\frac{7}{8} \\ \hline \end{array}$

EXERCISES • Subtract. Write the answers in lowest terms.

11. 4
  $-1\frac{3}{7}$

12. 3
  $-1\frac{1}{2}$

13. $5\frac{13}{20}$
  $-2\frac{17}{20}$

14. 8
  $-5\frac{4}{9}$

15. $10\frac{2}{6}$
  $-8\frac{3}{6}$

16. $4\frac{1}{18}$
  $-1\frac{7}{18}$

17. $9\frac{3}{9}$
  $-2\frac{7}{9}$

18. $8\frac{2}{10}$
  $-5\frac{8}{10}$

19. $7\frac{1}{3}$
  $-5\frac{2}{3}$

20. 9
  $-1\frac{4}{9}$

21. 19
  $-15\frac{2}{3}$

22. $32\frac{9}{10}$
  $-7\frac{7}{10}$

23. $11\frac{3}{11}$
  $-7\frac{6}{11}$

24. 8
  $-3\frac{5}{8}$

25. $12\frac{2}{7}$
  $-6\frac{6}{7}$

26. $4\frac{5}{12} - 3\frac{7}{12} =$ _____

27. $9 - 4\frac{7}{8} =$ _____

28. $7\frac{13}{16} - 2\frac{7}{16} =$ _____

29. $8\frac{5}{11} - 2\frac{6}{11} =$ _____

30. $6 - 2\frac{1}{3} =$ _____

31. $9\frac{3}{8} - 1\frac{7}{8} =$ _____

PROBLEM SOLVING • APPLICATIONS

32. In Staten Island, N. Y., the world's largest garbage dump is used to produce gas. If the dump is $18\frac{2}{5}$ feet deep in March and $20\frac{2}{5}$ feet deep in April, how much garbage was added in one month?

33. In some places, garbage from apartment buildings is burned to provide heat. A building custodian needs at least $8\frac{1}{8}$ tons of garbage each week. If $2\frac{7}{8}$ tons are collected on Monday and $3\frac{1}{3}$ tons on Tuesday, how much more garbage is needed?

THINKER'S CORNER

Replace each □ and △ with a *different* fraction to make each sentence true.

Choose the fractions from the box at the right.

| $\frac{3}{5}$ | $\frac{4}{7}$ | $\frac{10}{21}$ |
| $\frac{5}{14}$ | $\frac{3}{4}$ | $\frac{1}{2}$ |

a. $\square + \triangle < 1$ **b.** $\square - \triangle < \frac{1}{6}$ **c.** $\square + \triangle > \frac{2}{3}$ **d.** $\square + (\square - \triangle) = \frac{17}{20}$

More Subtraction with Regrouping

Space vehicles use batteries called *fuel cells* to produce electricity. One cell produces $8\frac{1}{2}$ kilowatts of electricity. A second cell produces $5\frac{2}{3}$ kilowatts of electricity.

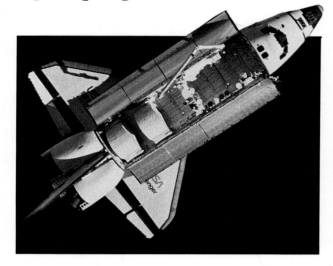

● How many more kilowatts does the first fuel cell produce?

Think: "How many more" suggests subtraction.

$$8\frac{1}{2} - 5\frac{2}{3} = ?$$

Step 1
Write equivalent fractions.

$$8\frac{1}{2} = 8\frac{3}{6}$$
$$-5\frac{2}{3} = 5\frac{4}{6}$$

Step 2
Since $\frac{4}{6} > \frac{3}{6}$, regroup $8\frac{3}{6}$ as $7\frac{9}{6}$.

$$8\frac{1}{2} = 8\frac{3}{6} = 7\frac{9}{6}$$
$$-5\frac{2}{3} = 5\frac{4}{6} = 5\frac{4}{6}$$

Step 3
Subtract.

$$8\frac{1}{2} = 8\frac{3}{6} = 7\frac{9}{6}$$
$$-5\frac{2}{3} = 5\frac{4}{6} = 5\frac{4}{6}$$
$$\overline{\phantom{-5\frac{2}{3} = 5\frac{4}{6} = }2\frac{5}{6}}$$

The second cell produces $2\frac{5}{6}$ **more kilowatts.**

EXERCISES • Subtract. Write the answers in lowest terms.

1. $5\frac{1}{6}$
   $-2\frac{2}{3}$

2. $7\frac{1}{4}$
   $-3\frac{2}{5}$

3. $3\frac{1}{10}$
   $-1\frac{4}{5}$

4. $5\frac{1}{10}$
   $-2\frac{1}{2}$

5. $5\frac{1}{3}$
   $-\frac{3}{4}$

6. $7\frac{1}{2}$
   $-1\frac{3}{5}$

7. $8\frac{1}{4}$
   $-2\frac{2}{5}$

8. $4\frac{1}{4}$
   $-1\frac{7}{12}$

9. $4\frac{1}{8}$
   $-1\frac{2}{3}$

10. $9\frac{1}{6}$
    $-3\frac{5}{9}$

EXERCISES • Subtract. Write the answers in lowest terms.

11. $4\frac{1}{8}$
    $-2\frac{3}{4}$

12. $12\frac{1}{3}$
    $-8\frac{8}{15}$

13. $2\frac{3}{8}$
    $-1\frac{2}{3}$

14. $6\frac{2}{3}$
    $-\frac{3}{4}$

15. $2\frac{1}{5}$
    $-1\frac{1}{4}$

16. $8\frac{5}{6}$
$-4\frac{8}{9}$

17. $5\frac{3}{4}$
$-3\frac{11}{12}$

18. $6\frac{1}{3}$
$-1\frac{5}{9}$

19. $2\frac{5}{8}$
$-1\frac{5}{6}$

20. $4\frac{1}{6}$
$-2\frac{3}{4}$

21. $11\frac{1}{6}$
$-10\frac{2}{3}$

22. $8\frac{3}{16}$
$-\ \frac{1}{4}$

23. $9\frac{1}{8}$
$-3\frac{7}{12}$

24. $5\frac{1}{6}$
$-2\frac{1}{3}$

25. $2\frac{3}{10}$
$-1\frac{7}{10}$

26. $18\frac{1}{6}$
$-\ 5\frac{3}{4}$

27. $20\frac{4}{5}$
$-17\frac{5}{6}$

28. $6\frac{1}{2}$
$-1\frac{3}{8}$

29. $2\frac{1}{2}$
$-1\frac{7}{8}$

30. $4\frac{1}{2}$
$-2\frac{7}{10}$

31. $5\frac{1}{6} - 3\frac{1}{2} = $ ___?___

32. $9\frac{3}{8} - 1\frac{3}{4} = $ ___?___

33. $8\frac{1}{2} - 2\frac{4}{5} = $ ___?___

34. $7\frac{2}{3} - \frac{7}{9} = $ ___?___

35. $6\frac{1}{4} - 2\frac{3}{4} = $ ___?___

★ **36.** $11\frac{1}{4} - 3\frac{7}{10} = $ ___?___

PROBLEM SOLVING • APPLICATIONS

37. Satellite weather pictures come from TV cameras powered by solar cells. During $4\frac{3}{8}$ hours of orbiting, a weather satellite sends pictures for $2\frac{1}{2}$ hours. For how many hours are no pictures available?

38. An engineer spends $12\frac{1}{4}$ hours constructing 3 panels of solar cells. One panel takes $5\frac{1}{6}$ hours to build, and a second panel takes $2\frac{1}{2}$ hours. How long does it take to build the third panel?

★ **39.** A fuel cell on a space shuttle fails $14\frac{3}{4}$ hours after launching. A mission specialist spends $2\frac{1}{6}$ hours repairing it. At $26\frac{2}{5}$ hours after launching, the fuel cell failed again. How long did it operate after being repaired?

PROBLEM SOLVING · STRATEGIES

Interpreting the Remainder

Example 1

In order to reach underground steam, a well is drilled 238 feet deep. The well pipe comes in 6–foot lengths.

● How many pieces of pipe will be needed?

Think You need to find how many 6–foot lengths of pipe (groups) there are in 238 feet. Divide.

Step 1
Divide.

```
     39 r4
6)238
   -18
     58
    -54
      4
```

Forty lengths of pipe will be needed.

Step 2
Interpret the remainder.

Think: 39 r4 means 39 pieces of 6–foot pipe are needed PLUS an additional piece of pipe 4 feet long. The pipe comes only in 6–foot lengths. To get a 4–foot length, one more 6–foot lenght will be needed.

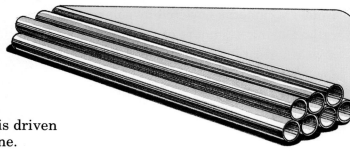

Example 2

A power company pick-up truck is driven 437 miles on 26 gallons of gasoline.

● How many miles did it travel on 1 gallon of gasoline?

Think Separate 437 miles into 26 equal parts. Divide.

Step 1
Divide.

```
      16 r21
26)437
  -26
    177
   -156
     21
```

Step 2
Interpret the remainder.

Think: The truck travels more than 16, but less than 17, miles on one gallon of gasoline. To be on the safe side, round down.

The truck travels **16 miles** on one gallon of gasoline.

PROBLEMS • Choose the sensible answer.

1. A drilling firm hires 46 men. The firm rents minivans to get them to the job site. A van holds 10 people. How many vans are needed?

    a. 4   **b.** 5   **c.** 6

2. A company produces reflective mirrors for home solar power equipment. The mirrors are packed 4 in a box. In one day they produce 39 mirrors. How many boxes did they fill?

    a. 6   **b.** 7   **c.** 9

3. A coal burning power plant requires 165 tons of coal per day. Suppose a railroad coal car holds 23 tons. Coal is available only in fully loaded cars. How many cars would be needed daily?

    a. 7   **b.** 8   **c.** 9

4. A construction company can erect one power windmill every 6 days. How many complete towers will they erect in 31 days?

    a. 5   **b.** 6   **c.** 7

Solve. Decide on the sensible answer.

5. Insulators for power lines are sold in cases of 36. An electric company needs 438 insulators. How many cases will they have to buy?

6. Air filters used in a home air conditioner are sold in packages of 3. Each package costs $5.30. How many air filters could you purchase for $23.00?

What is the question? Does your answer make sense?

---

7. A hydroelectric power plant needs to pump at least 130 gallons of water per second. A certain pump can pump 25 gallons of water each second. How many of these pumps are needed?

8. One type of propane gas tank holds 27 pounds of gas. A store has a large tank which holds 387 pounds of gas. How many smaller tanks can be filled from the large tank?

9. Pipe used for moving natural gas is sold in 24 foot lengths. A home builder needs 36 feet to finish a project. How many lengths of pipe must be bought?

10. A windmill builder can build 6 windmills in one week. He receives an order for 38 windmills. How long will it take him to build them?

The answer must be a whole number.

---

11. A company which puts out oil well fires is paid by the 24–hour day. A fire takes 56 hours to put out. What is the number of days for which they will be paid?

12. One solar heating panel can heat 450 square feet of a house. How many panels would be needed for a house which has 2,150 square feet of space?

CHAPTER REVIEW

Part 1 • VOCABULARY

For Exercises 1-7, choose from the box at the right
the word that completes the sentence.

equivalent
least
like
lowest terms
mixed numbers
opposite
regrouped

1. The fractions $\frac{5}{8}$ and $\frac{3}{8}$ have __?__ denominators.
   (Page 266)

2. You add fractions and whole numbers when adding
   __?__. (Page 266)

3. After adding or subtracting fractions, write the answer in
   __?__. (Page 266)

4. To add fractions with unlike denominators, first find the
   __?__ common denominator. (Page 268)

5. $1\frac{3}{2}$ can be __?__ as $2\frac{1}{2}$. (Page 270)

6. To work backwards, you use __?__ operations. (Page 274)

7. The first step in subtracting fractions having unlike
   denominators is to write __?__ fractions having the same
   denominator. (Page 278)

Part 2 • SKILLS

Add. Write the answers in lowest terms. (Pages 266–267)

8. $\frac{4}{6}$
   $+\frac{1}{6}$

9. $\frac{6}{10}$
   $+\frac{2}{10}$

10. $\frac{3}{15}$
    $+\frac{9}{15}$

11. $\frac{30}{36}$
    $+\frac{2}{36}$

12. $\frac{10}{50}$
    $+\frac{25}{50}$

13. $\frac{3}{15}$
    $\frac{5}{15}$
    $+\frac{2}{15}$

14. $\frac{4}{20}$
    $\frac{3}{20}$
    $+\frac{9}{20}$

15. $1\frac{3}{9}$
    $6\frac{2}{9}$
    $+4\frac{1}{9}$

16. $5\frac{2}{24}$
    $8\frac{10}{24}$
    $+7\frac{5}{24}$

17. $18\frac{4}{25}$
    $3\frac{6}{25}$
    $+15\frac{10}{25}$

18. $3\frac{5}{8} + 6\frac{2}{8} =$ __?__

19. $2\frac{3}{5} + 9\frac{1}{5} =$ __?__

20. $4\frac{2}{6} + 8\frac{2}{6} =$ __?__

Add. Write the answers in lowest terms. (Pages 268–269)

21. $\frac{1}{3}$
    $+\frac{4}{9}$

22. $\frac{2}{9}$
    $+\frac{3}{12}$

23. $4\frac{5}{10}$
    $+8\frac{2}{5}$

24. $6\frac{1}{6}$
    $+4\frac{3}{5}$

25. $9\frac{2}{9}$
    $+5\frac{3}{7}$

26. $4\frac{2}{4} + 7\frac{3}{8} =$ __?__

27. $8\frac{3}{9} + 7\frac{6}{12} =$ __?__

28. $5\frac{1}{3} + 8\frac{1}{5} =$ __?__

Add. Write the answers in lowest terms. (Pages 270–271)

29. $5\frac{1}{2}$
$+2\frac{3}{4}$

30. $6\frac{1}{4}$
$+2\frac{2}{3}$

31. $1\frac{2}{5}$
$+2\frac{3}{4}$

32. $5\frac{1}{2}$
$+2\frac{5}{6}$

33. $5\frac{5}{6} + 16\frac{2}{3} = $ ___?___

34. $36\frac{1}{2} + 13\frac{5}{8} = $ ___?___

35. $18\frac{5}{6} + \frac{2}{3} = $ ___?___

Subtract. Write the answers in lowest terms. (Pages 272–273)

36. $2\frac{3}{5}$
$-1\frac{2}{5}$

37. $9\frac{9}{10}$
$-2\frac{1}{10}$

38. $10\frac{12}{20}$
$-3\frac{2}{20}$

39. $16\frac{8}{12}$
$-9\frac{4}{12}$

40. $14\frac{17}{35}$
$-5\frac{12}{35}$

Subtract. Write the answers in lowest terms. (Pages 278–279)

41. $\frac{9}{12}$
$-\frac{2}{4}$

42. $\frac{6}{8}$
$-\frac{2}{6}$

43. $5\frac{9}{15}$
$-3\frac{2}{5}$

44. $9\frac{12}{18}$
$-7\frac{2}{6}$

45. $15\frac{4}{5}$
$-8\frac{1}{3}$

46. $5\frac{6}{8} - 2\frac{2}{4} = $ ___?___

47. $11\frac{5}{6} - 2\frac{2}{9} = $ ___?___

48. $17\frac{3}{7} - 8\frac{3}{8} = $ ___?___

Subtract. Write the answers in lowest terms. (Pages 280–281)

49. 5
$-4\frac{2}{8}$

50. $5\frac{1}{10}$
$-2\frac{6}{10}$

51. $7\frac{2}{5}$
$-3\frac{4}{5}$

52. 9
$-6\frac{6}{8}$

53. $12\frac{2}{12}$
$-5\frac{6}{12}$

54. $12\frac{1}{12} - 9\frac{8}{12} = $ ___?___

55. $10\frac{5}{9} - 3\frac{7}{9} = $ ___?___

56. $16\frac{1}{25} - 8\frac{2}{25} = $ ___?___

Subtract. Write the answers in lowest terms. (Pages 282–283)

57. $7\frac{1}{8}$
$-2\frac{1}{2}$

58. $5\frac{1}{4}$
$-3\frac{1}{2}$

59. $16\frac{1}{4}$
$-8\frac{3}{5}$

60. $5\frac{1}{6}$
$-2\frac{1}{3}$

61. $29\frac{1}{5} - 17\frac{7}{10} = $ ___?___

62. $10\frac{1}{3} - 7\frac{5}{6} = $ ___?___

63. $13\frac{5}{6} - 11\frac{9}{10} = $ ___?___

Part 3 • *PROBLEM SOLVING* • *APPLICATIONS*

64. A company produces 165 solar panels each week. Last year they produced 35 fewer panels each week. Production last year was 5 times greater than production 10 years ago. What was the production 10 years ago? (Pages 274–275)

65. A pipeline has one pumping station every 50 miles. How many stations are there in 175 miles? (Pages 284–285)

66. A car can travel 24 miles on one gallon of gasoline. The gas tank of the car holds 12 gallons. If the driver fills the tank at the start of a 325–mile trip, how many times will the tank have to be refilled? (Pages 284–285)

CHAPTER TEST

Add. Write the answers in lowest terms.

1. $\frac{2}{8}$
$+\frac{4}{8}$

2. $2\frac{6}{10}$
$+1\frac{2}{10}$

3. $\frac{1}{4}$
$+\frac{1}{2}$

4. $\frac{3}{8}$
$+\frac{1}{2}$

5. $2\frac{5}{12}$
$+1\frac{1}{3}$

6. $1\frac{1}{4}$
$+1\frac{5}{12}$

7. $3\frac{1}{8}$
$+5\frac{5}{6}$

8. $6\frac{1}{4}$
$+2\frac{1}{6}$

9. $3\frac{5}{6}$
$+2\frac{7}{8}$

10. $5\frac{3}{4}$
$+3\frac{5}{6}$

11. $1\frac{3}{4}$
$+1\frac{5}{12}$

12. $7\frac{3}{5}$
$+6\frac{2}{3}$

Subtract. Write the answers in lowest terms.

13. $\frac{3}{8}$
$-\frac{1}{8}$

14. $7\frac{7}{12}$
$-2\frac{2}{12}$

15. $\frac{7}{9}$
$-\frac{2}{3}$

16. $4\frac{3}{5}$
$-1\frac{1}{3}$

17. $5\frac{1}{6}$
$-4\frac{5}{6}$

18. 7
$-5\frac{1}{6}$

19. $8\frac{1}{4}$
$-6\frac{3}{4}$

20. $5\frac{1}{3}$
$-2\frac{2}{3}$

21. $7\frac{1}{6} - 3\frac{2}{3} = \underline{\quad?\quad}$

22. $9\frac{1}{4} - 6\frac{3}{5} = \underline{\quad?\quad}$

23. A "unit train" carries coal from the mine to the power plant. Each car carries 23 tons of coal. How many cars are needed to carry 315 tons of coal?

24. A homeowner wants to build a solar-heating unit for his pool. The unit requires 140 feet of tubing. The tubing comes 12 feet to a package. How many packages are needed?

25. In July, an electric company adds 30 trucks to its service fleet. They had tripled the number of trucks in March. They now have 120 trucks. How many trucks did they have at the end of February?

ENRICHMENT

Repeating Decimals

A power plant sends $\frac{5}{11}$ of its electricity to one city.

● Write a decimal for $\frac{5}{11}$.

Think $\frac{5}{11}$ means $5 \div 11$.

$$
\begin{array}{r}
0.4545\ldots \\
11\overline{)5.0000} \\
4\,4 \\
\hline
60 \\
55 \\
\hline
50 \\
44 \\
\hline
60 \\
55 \\
\hline
5
\end{array}
$$

Using a calculator:

 5 ÷ 11 = 0.4545454

$\frac{5}{11} = 0.4545\ldots$ ◀ **The dots show that the digits 4 and 5 continue to repeat.**

or $\frac{5}{11} = 0.\overline{45}$ ◀ **The bar shows the digits that repeat.**

EXERCISES • Write the repeating decimal for each fraction. Use a bar to show the digits that repeat.

1. $\frac{10}{33}$ **2.** $\frac{7}{3}$ **3.** $\frac{5}{9}$ **4.** $\frac{7}{11}$ **5.** $\frac{4}{99}$

6. The repeating decimal for $\frac{1}{3}$ is 0.333 . . ., or $0.\overline{3}$. Without computing, write the repeating decimal for $\frac{2}{3}$.

7. The repeating decimal for $\frac{5}{11}$ is 0.4545 . . ., or $0.\overline{45}$. Without computing, write the repeating decimal for $\frac{1}{11}$.

8. Without calculating, write the repeating decimals for $\frac{4}{3}$, $\frac{10}{3}$, and $\frac{46}{3}$.

9. Find the repeating decimal for $\frac{1}{33}$. Then, without calculating, write the repeating decimals for $\frac{2}{33}$, $\frac{5}{33}$, and $\frac{38}{33}$.

ADDITIONAL PRACTICE

SKILLS

Add. Write the answers in lowest terms. (Pages 266–267)

1. $\frac{3}{7} + \frac{2}{7} =$ ___?___

2. $4\frac{2}{10} + 3\frac{7}{10} +$ ___?___

3. $7\frac{1}{8} + 9\frac{2}{8} =$ ___?___

Add. Write the answers in lowest terms. (Pages 268–271)

4. $\frac{1}{6}$
$+\frac{2}{3}$

5. $\frac{6}{12}$
$+\frac{1}{4}$

6. $4\frac{3}{7}$
$+3\frac{3}{14}$

7. $9\frac{1}{6}$
$+1\frac{2}{5}$

8. $7\frac{3}{7}$
$+8\frac{2}{6}$

9. $4\frac{7}{8} + 2\frac{1}{4} =$ ___?___

10. $6\frac{7}{9} + 9\frac{8}{27} =$ ___?___

11. $8\frac{5}{20} + 9\frac{9}{10} =$ ___?___

Subtract. Write the answers in lowest terms. (Pages 272–273)

12. $\frac{7}{8}$
$-\frac{5}{8}$

13. $\frac{6}{9}$
$-\frac{3}{9}$

14. $\frac{17}{21}$
$-\frac{8}{21}$

15. $\frac{33}{50}$
$-\frac{18}{50}$

16. $\frac{42}{49}$
$-\frac{28}{49}$

Subtract. Write the answers in lowest terms. (Pages 278–279)

17. $\frac{3}{5}$
$-\frac{1}{6}$

18. $\frac{2}{3}$
$-\frac{1}{8}$

19. $\frac{15}{20}$
$-\frac{5}{40}$

20. $\frac{3}{9}$
$-\frac{2}{7}$

21. $\frac{4}{6}$
$-\frac{1}{12}$

Subtract. Write the answers in lowest terms. (Page 280–281)

22. 7
$-3\frac{3}{4}$

23. $9\frac{3}{5}$
$-2\frac{4}{5}$

24. $12\frac{1}{6}$
$-9\frac{5}{6}$

25. $25\frac{3}{10}$
$-7\frac{7}{10}$

Subtract. Write the answers in lowest terms. (Page 282–283)

26. $3\frac{3}{8}$
$-1\frac{8}{16}$

27. $13\frac{2}{4}$
$-9\frac{3}{5}$

28. $18\frac{2}{9}$
$-9\frac{4}{5}$

29. $29\frac{1}{3}$
$-14\frac{4}{9}$

PROBLEM SOLVING • APPLICATIONS

30. A science experiment on a space shuttle requires at least 120 volts of power. One solar electric cell provides 3.5 volts of power. How many cells will be needed?
(Pages 284–285)

31. In northern California, steam from the earth heats 99 homes. There are 3 more homes heated than last year. Last year there were 6 times as many homes heated by the steam than 10 years ago. How many homes were heated by the steam 10 years ago? (Pages 274–275)

COMPUTER APPLICATIONS

Programs: INPUT

7.5 cm

3.5 cm

You can use this program to find the area
of **any** rectangle. (**area = length × width**)
Type this program. Press **RETURN**, or **ENTER**,
or ⏎ after you type each line of the program.

10 INPUT L, W
20 PRINT "AREA ="; L∗W   **The computer displays**
30 END   **what is between the**
                              quotation marks.

Now type **RUN**. Then press **RETURN**, or **ENTER**, or ⏎. Here is the display.

RUN

Line 10 ⟶ ?

When the computer does an **INPUT** command (line 10), it displays a question
mark. This is your "cue" to type the length and width. For the rectangle above,
type **7.5, 3.5** (including the comma) after the question mark. Then press
RETURN, or **ENTER**, or ⏎. Here is the display.

RUN
? 7.5, 3.5
AREA = 26.25   ⟵———— The area is 26.25 square centimeters.
READY   ⟵———— Some computer's flash a square, ■.

The last line is the computer's "ready" symbol. You can use the program to
solve another area problem. To do this, type **RUN**. Then press **RETURN**, or
ENTER, or ⏎. The question mark will appear again. Here is the display.

RUN
?   ⟵———— Now type the length and width for the next problem.

If you turn off the computer, the program will be erased from memory.
If you do this, you will have to enter (type) the program again.

EXERCISES • RUN the program above to find the area of each rectangle.

	1.	2.	3.	4.
length	8.2 cm	620 m	76.5 cm	67.8 m
width	4.3 cm	493 m	38.6 cm	52.9 m
area	?	?	?	?

For Exercises 5–8, find the output from a RUN
of the program at the right. Use the values for
A and B that are listed.

10 INPUT A, B
20 PRINT "SUM ="; A + B
30 END

5. 66, 47   **6.** 90, 72   **7.** 14.5, 89.6   **8.** 189.7, 486.4

Mixed Practice • Choose the correct answers.

1. Write $\frac{3}{36}$ in lowest terms.

   A. $\frac{1}{36}$ B. $\frac{1}{3}$

   C. $\frac{1}{12}$ D. not here

2. Write $\frac{9}{15}$ in lowest terms.

   A. $\frac{9}{15}$ B. $\frac{3}{5}$

   C. $\frac{2}{3}$ D. not here

3. Write $\frac{16}{56}$ in lowest terms.

   A. $\frac{8}{28}$ B. $\frac{1}{1}$

   C. $\frac{8}{23}$ D. not here

4. $15 = \frac{?}{1}$

   A. 1   B. 14

   C. 15   D. not here

5. $6 = \frac{?}{1}$

   A. 6   B. 12

   C. 1   D. not here

6. Write $\frac{20}{7}$ as a mixed number.

   A. $3\frac{6}{7}$ B. $2\frac{4}{7}$

   C. $2\frac{6}{7}$ D. not here

7. Write $\frac{36}{8}$ as a mixed number.

   A. $4\frac{6}{8}$ B. $4\frac{1}{2}$

   C. $4\frac{1}{4}$ D. not here

8. Write $9\frac{1}{2}$ as an improper fraction.

   A. $\frac{19}{2}$ B. $\frac{18}{2}$

   C. $\frac{9}{2}$ D. not here

9. Write $2\frac{3}{5}$ as an improper fraction.

   A. $\frac{10}{3}$ B. $\frac{17}{5}$

   C. $\frac{13}{5}$ D. not here

10. $1 = \frac{?}{12}$

    A. 12   B. 6

    C. 1   D. not here

11. To find the area of a rectangle multiply:

    A. $w \times w$ B. $l \times w$

    C. $\frac{l}{w}$ D. not here

12. Find the perimeter.

    4 cm

    2 cm [rectangle] 2 cm

    4 cm

    A. 6 cm   B. 8 cm

    C. 12 cm   D. not here

13. On Monday Betty Milner picks $6\frac{5}{8}$ pounds of tomatoes from her garden. She picks $8\frac{3}{4}$ pounds of tomatoes on Tuesday. How many pounds did she pick both days?

    A. $14\frac{7}{8}$ pounds   B. $15\frac{1}{8}$ pounds

    C. $15\frac{3}{8}$ pounds   D. not here

14. Jeff Fisher runs $\frac{3}{5}$ mile, rests, then runs $\frac{4}{5}$ mile. How far did he run in all?

    A. $1\frac{3}{5}$ miles   B. $\frac{6}{5}$ miles

    C. $1\frac{2}{5}$ miles   D. not here

Fractions: Multiplication and Division

In August, 1876, Alexander Graham Bell received the first one-way long distance call over a line $7\frac{7}{8}$ miles long. In 1877, a Boston banker installed the first commercial telephone line. It was $3\frac{1}{5}$ miles long.

- Estimate the difference in these distances.

Eli Whitney invented the cotton gin in 1793.

Today, for every 5 bales of cotton produced in Arizona, Louisiana produces $\frac{3}{4}$ as many bales.

- What is $\frac{3}{4}$ of 5?

Multiplication

Robert Fulton, the builder of the first successful commercial steamboat, built the Nautilus, a copper-covered submarine in 1800.

The submarine design at the right shows that $\frac{1}{2}$ of the interior is machinery rooms. The control room occupies $\frac{1}{4}$ of this space.

$\frac{1}{2}$ of the interior
is machinery rooms.

$\frac{1}{4}$ of the machinery rooms
is $\frac{1}{8}$ of the interior.

● How much of the interior does the control room occupy?

Think How much is $\frac{1}{4}$ of $\frac{1}{2}$?
The word "of" suggests multiplication.

$$\frac{1}{4} \times \frac{1}{2} = \underline{\quad?\quad}$$

$$\frac{1}{4} \times \frac{1}{2} = \frac{1}{8}$$

Step 1
Multiply the numerators.

$$\frac{1}{4} \times \frac{1}{2} = \frac{1}{\quad}$$

Step 2
Multiply the denominators.

$$\frac{1}{4} \text{ of } \frac{1}{2} = \frac{1}{8}$$

The control room occupies $\frac{1}{8}$ of the interior.

PRACTICE • Use the drawings to complete the sentences.

1.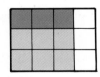

$\frac{1}{3}$ of $\frac{3}{4}$ is $\underline{\quad?\quad}$

2.

$\frac{1}{2}$ of $\frac{1}{5}$ is $\underline{\quad?\quad}$

3.

$\frac{3}{4}$ of $\frac{2}{3}$ is $\underline{\quad?\quad}$

Mental Math Multiply. Give the answers in lowest terms.

4. $\frac{1}{5} \times \frac{1}{4} = \underline{\quad?\quad}$

5. $\frac{1}{6} \times \frac{5}{8} = \underline{\quad?\quad}$

6. $\frac{2}{5} \times \frac{1}{2} = \underline{\quad?\quad}$

7. $\frac{3}{7} \times \frac{2}{5} = \underline{\quad?\quad}$

8. $\frac{1}{4} \times \frac{8}{9} = \underline{\quad?\quad}$

9. $\frac{3}{5} \times \frac{2}{9} = \underline{\quad?\quad}$

EXERCISES • Use the drawings to complete the sentences.

10.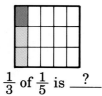

$\frac{1}{3}$ of $\frac{1}{5}$ is ___?___

11.

$\frac{2}{3}$ of $\frac{1}{5}$ is ___?___

12.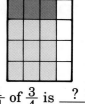

$\frac{1}{4}$ of $\frac{3}{4}$ is ___?___

13.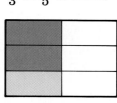

$\frac{2}{3}$ of $\frac{1}{2}$ is ___?___

14.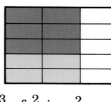

$\frac{3}{5}$ of $\frac{2}{3}$ is ___?___

15.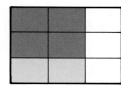

$\frac{2}{3}$ of $\frac{2}{3}$ is ___?___

Multiply. Write the answers in lowest terms.

16. $\frac{1}{2} \times \frac{6}{7} =$ ___?___

17. $\frac{1}{9} \times \frac{3}{10} =$ ___?___

18. $\frac{2}{3} \times \frac{4}{7} =$ ___?___

19. $\frac{8}{9} \times \frac{7}{11} =$ ___?___

20. $\frac{5}{6} \times \frac{8}{11} =$ ___?___

21. $\frac{1}{5} \times \frac{2}{5} =$ ___?___

22. $\frac{1}{3} \times \frac{3}{5} =$ ___?___

23. $\frac{2}{5} \times \frac{3}{5} =$ ___?___

24. $\frac{2}{3} \times \frac{1}{4} =$ ___?___

25. $\frac{2}{5} \times \frac{3}{4} =$ ___?___

26. $\frac{8}{9} \times \frac{2}{7} =$ ___?___

27. $\frac{1}{3} \times \frac{3}{4} =$ ___?___

★ **28.** $\frac{1}{2} \times \frac{2}{3} \times \frac{1}{4} =$ ___?___

★ **29.** $\frac{4}{5} \times \frac{2}{3} \times \frac{1}{8} =$ ___?___

★ **30.** $\frac{3}{4} \times \frac{5}{8} \times \frac{2}{5} =$ ___?___

PROBLEM SOLVING • APPLICATIONS

31. In 1807, Robert Fulton's steamboat, the Clermont, traveled 150 miles up the Hudson River in 32 hours. How far could the Clermont travel at the same rate in $\frac{1}{4}$ of this time?

32. In 1787, Robert Fitch demonstrated the first workable steamboat on the Delaware River. One of Fitch's boats was 60 feet long. Fulton's submarine was $\frac{7}{20}$ as long as this. How long was the submarine?

★ **33.** Fulton also built two steamboats similar to the Clermont and two ferry boats for New York harbor. A ferry in New York harbor traveled 20 miles in 35 minutes. At that rate, how far could it travel in 5 minutes?

THINKER'S CORNER

If $\frac{1}{3}$ of a number, n, equals 81, what is the value of $3 \times n$?

Multiplying Fractions and Whole Numbers

Eli Whitney invented the cotton gin in 1793. The cotton gin could clean cotton as fast as 60 persons working by hand.

The leading cotton producing states in the United States are California, Texas, Mississippi, and Arizona. For every 5 bales of cotton produced in Arizona, Louisiana produces $\frac{3}{4}$ as many bales.

● What is $\frac{3}{4}$ of 5?

Think To find $\frac{3}{4}$ of 5, multiply.

$$5 \times \frac{3}{4} = ?$$

Step 1
Write the whole number as a fraction. ⟶ $\frac{5}{1} \times \frac{3}{4} = ?$

Step 2
Multiply the numerators. ⟶ $\frac{5}{1} \times \frac{3}{4} = \frac{15}{}$

Step 3
Multiply the denominators. ⟶ $\frac{5}{1} \times \frac{3}{4} = \frac{15}{4}$

Step 4
Write a mixed number for the answer. ⟶ $\frac{5}{1} \times \frac{3}{4} = \frac{15}{4} = 3\frac{3}{4}$

For every 5 bales produced in Arizona, Louisiana produces $3\frac{3}{4}$ bales.

More Examples

$$\frac{5}{12} \times 8 = \frac{5}{12} \times \frac{8}{1} = \frac{40}{12} = 3\frac{4}{12} = 3\frac{1}{3} \qquad 12 \times \frac{5}{6} = \frac{12}{1} \times \frac{5}{6} = \frac{60}{6} = 10$$

PRACTICE • Multiply. Write the answers in lowest terms.

1. $7 \times \frac{1}{2} =$ ___?___

2. $6 \times \frac{2}{5} =$ ___?___

3. $\frac{2}{3} \times 9 =$ ___?___

4. $\frac{5}{12} \times 5 =$ ___?___

5. $4 \times \frac{1}{8} =$ ___?___

6. $\frac{4}{5} \times 8 =$ ___?___

EXERCISES • Multiply. Write the answers in lowest terms.

7. $\frac{3}{4} \times 15 = $ _____?_____

8. $8 \times \frac{5}{8} = $ _____?_____

9. $\frac{2}{3} \times 18 = $ _____?_____

10. $9 \times \frac{1}{2} = $ _____?_____

11. $16 \times \frac{2}{3} = $ _____?_____

12. $\frac{5}{8} \times 9 = $ _____?_____

13. $\frac{3}{4} \times 32 = $ _____?_____

14. $\frac{3}{8} \times 64 = $ _____?_____

15. $\frac{5}{8} \times 13 = $ _____?_____

16. $\frac{1}{20} \times 20 = $ _____?_____

17. $27 \times \frac{2}{3} = $ _____?_____

18. $\frac{5}{6} \times \frac{2}{3} = $ _____?_____

19. $\frac{2}{3} \times 15 = $ _____?_____

20. $\frac{7}{12} \times 9 = $ _____?_____

21. $\frac{4}{5} \times 10 = $ _____?_____

22. $\frac{6}{8} \times \frac{3}{4} = $ _____?_____

23. $10 \times \frac{3}{5} = $ _____?_____

24. $9 \times \frac{5}{6} = $ _____?_____

25. $\frac{2}{7} \times 14 = $ _____?_____

26. $\frac{2}{5} \times \frac{1}{2} = $ _____?_____

27. $8 \times \frac{7}{10} = $ _____?_____

28. $20 \times \frac{2}{5} \times \frac{3}{10} = $ _____?_____

★ 29. $\frac{1}{3} \times 9 \times \frac{2}{5} = $ _____?_____

★ 30. $\frac{4}{9} \times 5 \times \frac{1}{6} = $ _____?_____

PROBLEM SOLVING • APPLICATIONS

CHOOSE | • estimation • mental math • pencil and paper • calculator | SOLVE

31. As late as the 1960's, more than $\frac{1}{4}$ of the U.S. cotton crop was picked by hand. In a year in which 65 million bales of cotton were produced, how many million bales were picked by hand?

32. In an average year, a cotton farmer loses one bale out of every 8 to insect damage. How many bales would this amount to for a farm that produces 1,220 bales?

33. The world produces about 72 million bales of cotton each year. About $\frac{5}{6}$ of this amount is produced in the United States. About how many million bales are produced by the United States?

34. In 1930, a farmer worked 270 hours to produce one bale of cotton. Today, it takes $\frac{17}{200}$ of that time to produce one bale. How many hours is this?

THINKER'S CORNER

While she was on vacation, Amanda spent $\frac{1}{3}$ of the money in her purse for postcards. Then she spent $\frac{1}{3}$ of what was left for stamps. She had $5.00 left in her purse. How much did she have in her purse at the beginning?

Fractions: Multiplication and Division • 297

Multiplying Mixed Numbers

Alexander Graham Bell was a speech teacher who became interested in teaching the deaf to speak. Bell was 27 years old when he worked out the idea of transmitting sounds over electric wires.

A teacher taught for $5\frac{1}{3}$ hours on a particular day. The teacher spent $\frac{3}{8}$ of the time working with the deaf.

● How many hours were spent teaching the deaf?

 You need to find $\frac{3}{8}$ of $5\frac{1}{3}$.
The word *of* suggests multiplication.

$$\frac{3}{8} \times 5\frac{1}{3} = ?$$

Step 1 Write the mixed number as a fraction.	$\frac{3}{8} \times \frac{16}{3} = ?$
Step 2 Multiply the numerators.	$\frac{3}{8} \times \frac{16}{3} = \frac{48}{}$
Step 3 Multiply the denominators.	$\frac{3}{8} \times \frac{16}{3} = \frac{48}{24}$
Step 4 Write the answer in lowest terms.	$\frac{3}{8} \times \frac{16}{3} = \frac{48}{24} = 2$ ◀ **The teacher spent 2 hours teaching the deaf.**

More Examples

$4 \times 1\frac{2}{3} = ?$

$\frac{4}{1} \times \frac{5}{3} = ?$

$\frac{4}{1} \times \frac{5}{3} = \frac{20}{3} = \mathbf{6\frac{2}{3}}$

$2\frac{1}{2} \times 1\frac{3}{4} = ?$

$\frac{5}{2} \times \frac{7}{4} = ?$

$\frac{5}{2} \times \frac{7}{4} = \frac{35}{8} = \mathbf{4\frac{3}{8}}$

$3\frac{1}{4} \times 1\frac{1}{3} = ?$

$\frac{13}{4} \times \frac{4}{3} = ?$

$\frac{13}{4} \times \frac{4}{3} = \frac{52}{12} = 4\frac{4}{12} = \mathbf{4\frac{1}{3}}$

PRACTICE • Multiply. Write the answers in lowest terms.

1. $\frac{1}{2} \times 3\frac{1}{2} = $ ___?___

2. $5\frac{1}{3} \times 1\frac{1}{8} = $ ___?___

3. $6\frac{2}{3} \times 3\frac{1}{4} = $ ___?___

4. $2\frac{2}{5} \times \frac{7}{12} = $ ___?___

5. $\frac{4}{5} \times 3\frac{1}{4} = $ ___?___

6. $1\frac{3}{4} \times 2 = $ ___?___

7. $4\frac{1}{3} \times \frac{3}{5} = $ ___?___

8. $2\frac{5}{6} \times 8 = $ ___?___

9. $1\frac{1}{3} \times 2\frac{1}{4} = $ ___?___

EXERCISES • Multiply. Write the answers in lowest terms.

10. $3\frac{1}{2} \times 2\frac{1}{7} = $ ____?____

11. $\frac{2}{3} \times 4\frac{1}{2} = $ ____?____

12. $5 \times 1\frac{3}{4} = $ ____?____

13. $1\frac{1}{4} \times \frac{3}{5} = $ ____?____

14. $7\frac{4}{5} \times \frac{1}{3} = $ ____?____

15. $5\frac{1}{4} \times \frac{1}{7} = $ ____?____

16. $2\frac{1}{2} \times 2\frac{1}{2} = $ ____?____

17. $2\frac{1}{4} \times \frac{2}{3} = $ ____?____

18. $5\frac{3}{10} \times 1\frac{1}{4} = $ ____?____

19. $\frac{3}{4} \times 2 = $ ____?____

20. $1\frac{3}{8} \times 7 = $ ____?____

21. $\frac{1}{2} \times 1\frac{2}{5} = $ ____?____

22. $2\frac{1}{3} \times 6\frac{1}{2} = $ ____?____

23. $7\frac{1}{2} \times \frac{2}{5} = $ ____?____

24. $\frac{4}{5} \times \frac{1}{6} = $ ____?____

25. $\frac{4}{5} \times 10\frac{1}{2} = $ ____?____

26. $16 \times 8\frac{1}{2} = $ ____?____

27. $\frac{1}{3} \times 2\frac{1}{2} = $ ____?____

★ **28.** $1\frac{1}{6} \times \frac{3}{7} \times 4\frac{2}{3} = $ ____?____

★ **29.** $4 \times \frac{3}{5} \times 1\frac{3}{4} = $ ____?____

★ **30.** $\frac{3}{4} \times 6\frac{1}{7} \times 2\frac{1}{3} = $ ____?____

PROBLEM SOLVING • APPLICATIONS

31. Before he invented the telephone, Bell attempted to improve a machine which transferred sound waves to lines on a piece of smoked glass. An assistant conducted one test in $\frac{3}{4}$ of an hour. At this rate, how much time would it take to run 5 tests? *5 × 3/4*

32. Originally, Bell had hoped to invent a multiple telegraph. It would permit sending and receiving more than one message over one wire at the same time. An assistant works $4\frac{2}{3}$ hours one evening and spends $\frac{7}{8}$ of the time setting up equipment. How much time is used for setting up equipment? *7/8 × 4 2/3*

33. Bell's original telephone had the transmitter at one end of the line and the receiver at the other end. A lab assistant conducts a test using $10\frac{3}{4}$ feet of wire. The next test uses $2\frac{1}{2}$ times as much. How much more wire was needed for the second test? *10 3/4 × 2 1/2*

34. In 1907, Bell created the Aerial Experiment Association. The group pioneered early developments in aviation. Their 'Red Wing' flew for 19 seconds. Later their 'White Wing' flew $5\frac{1}{2}$ times as long. How many minutes more did the 'White Wing' fly? *19 × 5 1/2*

Using a Shortcut to Multiply Fractions

For the census of 1890, Herman Hollerith invented an electrical tabulator and sorter. The use of Hollerith's machine gave the government an unofficial count of the 1890 population only 6 weeks after the census was taken!

A punch-card operator punches $\frac{5}{6}$ of a box of cards. She stacks $\frac{4}{7}$ of these.

● What fraction of the cards are stacked?

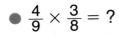   Of the box of cards, $\frac{4}{7}$ of $\frac{5}{6}$ are stacked. Multiply.

$$\frac{4}{7} \times \frac{5}{6} = ?$$

Sometimes it is easier to divide the numerator and denominator by a common factor *before* you multiply.

Step 1
Find a common factor for 4 and 6.
Divide by the common factor 2.

$$\frac{4}{7} \times \frac{5}{6} = \frac{\overset{2}{\cancel{4}}}{7} \times \frac{5}{\underset{3}{\cancel{6}}}$$

◀ $4 \div 2 = 2$
$6 \div 2 = 3$

Step 2
Multiply.

$$\frac{2}{7} \times \frac{5}{3} = \frac{10}{21}$$

◀ **The operator stacked $\frac{10}{21}$ of the cards.**

● $\frac{4}{9} \times \frac{3}{8} = ?$

Think   The common factor of 4 and 8 is 4.
The common factor of 3 and 9 is 3.

$$\frac{4}{9} \times \frac{3}{8} = \frac{\overset{1}{\cancel{4}}}{\underset{3}{\cancel{9}}} \times \frac{\overset{1}{\cancel{3}}}{\underset{2}{\cancel{8}}}$$

$$= \frac{1 \times 1}{3 \times 2} = \frac{1}{6}$$

PRACTICE • Multiply. Find the common factors before multiplying.

1. $\frac{4}{15} \times \frac{10}{28} = \underline{\ ?\ }$

2. $\frac{7}{12} \times \frac{8}{21} = \underline{\ ?\ }$

3. $\frac{9}{10} \times \frac{25}{21} = \underline{\ ?\ }$

4. $\frac{5}{12} \times \frac{3}{10} = \underline{\ ?\ }$

5. $\frac{3}{4} \times \frac{20}{27} = \underline{\ ?\ }$

6. $\frac{3}{8} \times \frac{8}{9} = \underline{\ ?\ }$

EXERCISES • Multiply. Find the common factors before multiplying.

7. $\frac{5}{8} \times \frac{6}{15} = $?____

8. $\frac{9}{15} \times \frac{7}{9} = $?____

9. $\frac{7}{8} \times \frac{12}{14} = $?____

10. $\frac{2}{3} \times \frac{5}{8} = $?____

11. $\frac{3}{5} \times \frac{7}{12} = $?____

12. $\frac{8}{5} \times \frac{9}{12} = $?____

13. $\frac{3}{8} \times \frac{4}{9} = $?____

14. $\frac{3}{4} \times \frac{5}{6} = $?____

15. $\frac{3}{5} \times 20 = $?____

16. $\frac{5}{9} \times \frac{3}{10} = $?____

17. $\frac{5}{8} \times \frac{4}{15} = $?____

18. $\frac{7}{10} \times 80 = $?____

19. $\frac{5}{6} \times \frac{12}{25} = $?____

20. $\frac{5}{9} \times \frac{3}{8} = $?____

21. $\frac{8}{9} \times \frac{21}{12} = $?____

22. $\frac{1}{3} \times 15 = $?____

23. $\frac{2}{3} \times 27 = $?____

24. $28 \times \frac{3}{7} = $?____

25. $1\frac{1}{3} \times 2\frac{1}{2} = $?____

26. $2\frac{1}{5} \times 1\frac{1}{4} = $?____

27. $9 \times 1\frac{2}{3} = $?____

28. $2\frac{2}{3} \times 1\frac{1}{4} = $?____

29. $1\frac{1}{2} \times 2\frac{2}{3} = $?____

30. $2\frac{1}{4} \times 5\frac{1}{3} = $?____

31. $3\frac{1}{4} \times 2\frac{2}{3} = $?____

32. $\frac{4}{5} \times 3\frac{3}{8} = $?____

33. $3\frac{1}{5} \times 4\frac{2}{3} = $?____

PROBLEM SOLVING • APPLICATIONS

34. The census of 1880 took $7\frac{1}{2}$ years to complete. Because of Hollerith's invention, it took $\frac{1}{3}$ of this time to complete the census of 1890. How long did it take to complete the census of 1890?

35. A computer takes $2\frac{1}{4}$ hours to complete a job. A new computer can do the job in $\frac{1}{3}$ of that time. How much time will the job take the new computer?

CALCULATOR • Multiplying Fractions

You can use a calculator to multiply fractions. The calculator gives the answer as a decimal.

$\frac{3}{5} \times \frac{7}{10} = $?

a. Multiply the denominators. Enter the product in the memory

b. Multiply the numerators. Divide by the product of the denominators.

EXERCISES

1. $\frac{6}{8} \times \frac{2}{3} = $?__

2. $\frac{5}{6} \times \frac{18}{25} = $?__

3. $\frac{9}{10} \times \frac{5}{6} = $?__

4. $\frac{30}{16} \times \frac{16}{12} \times \frac{100}{500} = $?__

5. $\frac{25}{48} \times \frac{30}{25} \times \frac{40}{50} = $?__

6. $\frac{1}{23} \times \frac{343}{49} \times \frac{161}{49} = $?__

PROBLEM SOLVING · STRATEGIES

Estimation

In August of 1876, Alexander Graham
Bell received the first one-way long
distance call. It came over a line about
$7\frac{7}{8}$ miles long.

In 1877, a Boston banker installed the
first commmercial telephone line. It
extended a distance of $3\frac{1}{5}$ miles.

● **Estimate** the difference between
these distances.

Think   Round each fraction to the nearest whole number.

> When a fraction or a fractional part of a mixed number is less than
> $\frac{1}{2}$, round down.
>
> When a fraction or a fractional part of a mixed number is $\frac{1}{2}$ or
> greater, round up.

Step 1

Round to the nearest
whole number.

$7\frac{7}{8} \longrightarrow 8$ ◄ Since $\frac{7}{8} > \frac{1}{2}$, round up.

$-3\frac{1}{5} \longrightarrow 7$ ◄ Since $\frac{1}{5} < \frac{1}{2}$, round down.

Step 2

Subtract.

$$\begin{array}{r} 8 \\ -\ 3 \\ \hline 5 \end{array}$$

The difference is about **5 miles**.

ⓔ PRACTICE • Choose the best estimate. Choose a, b, or c.

1. $1\frac{3}{4} + 5\frac{7}{8}$ **a.** $1 + 5$ **b.** $0 + 6$ **c.** $2 + 6$

2. $3\frac{1}{4} - 1\frac{3}{8}$ **a.** $3 - 1$ **b.** $3 - 2$ **c.** $2 - 2$

3. $1\frac{5}{6} \div 1\frac{3}{4}$ **a.** $0 \div 1$ **b.** $2 \div 2$ **c.** $0 \div 2$

4. $2\frac{5}{8} \times 3\frac{1}{3}$ **a.** 2×3 **b.** 3×2 **c.** 3×3

5. $2\frac{3}{4} + 4\frac{1}{6}$ **a.** 8   **b.** 10   **c.** 7

6. $3\frac{1}{8} - 1\frac{2}{3}$ **a.** 1   **b.** 2   **c.** 3

7. $1\frac{1}{10} \times 6\frac{7}{8}$ **a.** 6   **b.** 12   **c.** 7

8. $12\frac{1}{8} \div 2\frac{15}{16}$ **a.** 6   **b.** 4   **c.** 5

Ⓔ PROBLEMS

9. A steamboat burned $4\frac{3}{4}$ cords of pine logs and $7\frac{7}{8}$ cords of oak logs in one trip. Estimate how many cords this was in all.

    a. 13   **b.** 11   **c.** 12

10. An early airplane flight lasted $10\frac{1}{4}$ minutes. A later flight lasted $3\frac{1}{2}$ times as long. Estimate how long the later flight lasted.

    a. 30   **b.** 44   **c.** 40

If the fraction is $\frac{1}{2}$ or more, round up.

---

11. A glider pilot bought $12\frac{7}{8}$ yards of cloth to patch a wing. Only $3\frac{1}{3}$ yards were used. Estimate how much cloth was left over.

    a. 9   **b.** 10   **c.** 8

12. An experiment called for $5\frac{7}{8}$ yards of tin foil to use for an early phonograph cylinder. There were $1\frac{1}{5}$ yards left over. Estimate how many yards of tin foil were used.

    a. 5   **b.** 4   **c.** 3

If the fraction is less than $\frac{1}{2}$, round down.

---

13. A film developer processed $7\frac{3}{4}$ rolls of film in $2\frac{1}{6}$ hours. Estimate how many rolls of film can be processed in 1 hour at that rate.

    a. 2   **b.** 1   **c.** 4

14. A punch card operator ran $12\frac{2}{3}$ stacks of punched cards through a machine in one morning. In the afternoon, $9\frac{2}{5}$ stacks were run through the machine. Estimate the total number of stacks run that day.

    a. 19   **b.** 22   **c.** 23

PROJECT   Use your school or town library to find and list at least 5 American inventors. Record their inventions and the dates. Make a time line on a large sheet of paper or on the class bulletin board showing the information you have researched.

MID-CHAPTER REVIEW

Multiply. Write the answers in lowest terms. (Pages 294–295)

1. $\frac{1}{4}$ of $\frac{1}{2}$ is ___?___

2. $\frac{2}{6}$ of $\frac{3}{8}$ is ___?___

3. $\frac{3}{4}$ of $\frac{8}{10}$ is ___?___

4. $\frac{2}{5} \times \frac{3}{10} =$ ___?___

5. $\frac{2}{8} \times \frac{3}{4} =$ ___?___

6. $\frac{7}{12} \times \frac{2}{3} =$ ___?___

Multiply. Write the answers in lowest terms. (Pages 296–297)

7. $6 \times \frac{3}{4} =$ ___?___

8. $12 \times \frac{2}{3} =$ ___?___

9. $\frac{5}{6} \times 15 =$ ___?___

10. $\frac{3}{6} \times 10 =$ ___?___

11. $\frac{4}{7} \times 13 =$ ___?___

12. $20 \times \frac{4}{5} =$ ___?___

13. $6 \times \frac{2}{3} =$ ___?___

14. $\frac{5}{6} \times 11 =$ ___?___

15. $\frac{3}{7} \times 16 =$ ___?___

Multiply. Write the answers in lowest terms. (Pages 298–299)

16. $1\frac{1}{3} \times 2\frac{1}{4} =$ ___?___

17. $2\frac{1}{4} \times 3\frac{2}{3} =$ ___?___

18. $6\frac{1}{2} \times 1\frac{2}{4} =$ ___?___

19. $4\frac{2}{5} \times 2\frac{1}{3} =$ ___?___

20. $3\frac{1}{3} \times 2\frac{4}{5} =$ ___?___

21. $1\frac{1}{9} \times 3\frac{4}{7} =$ ___?___

22. $3\frac{1}{5} \times 4\frac{2}{3} =$ ___?___

23. $1\frac{7}{10} \times 2\frac{3}{10} =$ ___?___

24. $6\frac{1}{4} \times 2\frac{2}{5} =$ ___?___

Find the common factors. Then multiply. (Pages 300–301)

25. $\frac{3}{4} \times \frac{4}{5} =$ ___?___

26. $\frac{1}{2} \times 10 =$ ___?___

27. $\frac{1}{6} \times \frac{9}{4} =$ ___?___

28. $\frac{3}{4} \times \frac{5}{6} =$ ___?___

29. Whitney's cotton gin processed $15\frac{3}{8}$ wagon loads of cotton in $4\frac{4}{5}$ hours. Estimate how many wagon loads it processed at that rate in 1 hour. (Pages 302–303)

30. Alexander Graham Bell spent $15\frac{3}{4}$ hours preparing an experiment. The actual test took $\frac{3}{4}$ hours. Estimate the total time Bell spent on the one experiment. (Pages 302–303)

MAINTENANCE • MIXED PRACTICE

Write each fraction in lowest terms.

1. $\frac{2}{4}$

2. $\frac{5}{10}$

3. $\frac{6}{8}$

4. $\frac{20}{50}$

5. $\frac{21}{42}$

Solve.

6. $(3 \times 2) \times 4 =$ ___?___

7. $6 \times (10 \times 2) =$ ___?___

8. $(9 \times 3) \times 3 =$ ___?___

9. $(4 \times 5) + 6 =$ ___?___

10. $12 + (6 \times 8) =$ ___?___

11. $(3 \times 11) + 6 =$ ___?___

CAREER APPLICATIONS

Contractor

A contractor must calculate with measures.

EXAMPLE 1: One board is 3 feet 10 inches long. A second board is 5 feet 8 inches long.

● What is the total length?

12 in. = 1 ft
3 ft = 1 yd
16 oz = 1 lb
4 qt = 1 gal
60 min = 1 hour

Step 1 Add.

$$\begin{array}{r} 3 \text{ ft } 10 \text{ in.} \\ +5 \text{ ft } \ \ 8 \text{ in.} \\ \hline 8 \text{ ft } 18 \text{ in.} \end{array}$$

Step 2 Since 18 in. > 1 ft, regroup 18 in.

18 in. = 1 ft 6 in.

8 ft 18 in. = 8 ft + 1 ft 6 in. = 9 ft 6 in.

The total length is **9 ft 6 in.**

EXAMPLE 2:
$$\begin{array}{r} 5 \text{ ft } \ \ 8 \text{ in.} \\ -3 \text{ ft } 10 \text{ in.} \end{array}$$

Step 1 Since 8 in. < 10 in., regroup 5 ft 8 in.

5 ft = 4 ft 12 in.
So 5 ft 8 in. = 4 ft 20 in.

Step 2 Subtract.

$$\begin{array}{r} \overset{4}{\cancel{5}} \text{ ft } \overset{20}{\cancel{8}} \text{ in.} \\ -3 \text{ ft } 10 \text{ in.} \\ \hline 1 \text{ ft } 10 \text{ in.} \end{array}$$

EXERCISES • Copy and complete.

1. 13 in. = 1 ft _?_ in.
2. 26 qt = 6 gal _?_ qt
3. 18 oz = 1 lb _?_ oz
4. 71 min = 1 hr _?_ min
5. 17 ft = 5 yd _?_ ft
6. 3 ft 8 in. = 2 ft _?_ in.
7. 10 yd 2 ft = 9 yd _?_ ft
8. 7 lb 11 oz = 6 lb _?_ oz
9. 4 gal 3 qt = 3 gal _?_ qt
10. 30 hr 9 min = 29 hr _?_ min

Add or subtract. Use the table.

11.
$$\begin{array}{r} 2 \text{ ft } 6 \text{ in.} \\ +1 \text{ ft } 9 \text{ in.} \end{array}$$

12.
$$\begin{array}{r} 9 \text{ yd } 1 \text{ ft} \\ -4 \text{ yd } 2 \text{ ft} \end{array}$$

13.
$$\begin{array}{r} 5 \text{ gal } 2 \text{ qt} \\ +7 \text{ gal } 3 \text{ qt} \end{array}$$

14.
$$\begin{array}{r} 12 \text{ lb } \ \ 4 \text{ oz} \\ -7 \text{ lb } 12 \text{ oz} \end{array}$$

15. A plumber needs 6 feet 7 inches of pipe for the laundry room and 8 feet 9 inches of pipe for the kitchen. How much pipe is needed in all?

16. On Tuesday a worker delivered 7 gallons of paint. The painters used 4 gallons 3 quarts. How much paint was left over?

Division

When the product of two numbers is 1, they are **reciprocals** of each other.

$$\frac{3}{8} \times \frac{8}{3} = \frac{24}{24} = 1 \qquad\qquad \frac{1}{3} \times 3 = \frac{3}{3} = 1 \qquad\qquad \frac{9}{1} \times \frac{1}{9} = \frac{9}{9} = 1$$

To find a reciprocal of a number:

a. Write the number as a fraction ⟶ $\frac{3}{4}$ $2\frac{4}{5}$, or $\frac{14}{5}$ 6 or $\frac{6}{1}$

b. Exchange the numerator and denominator. ⟶ $\frac{4}{3}$ $\frac{5}{14}$ $\frac{1}{6}$

When Thomas Edison invented the first practical light bulb, there was no electricity available for home use. So he invented the first system to produce and distribute electricity.
A worker has 4 equal lengths of wire. It takes half a wire to make the filament (coil) for one light bulb.

● How many bulbs can be made from 4 wires?

Think   You need to find the number of halves in 4.

$$4 \div \frac{1}{2} = \,?$$

1 wire: 2 halves   2 wires: 4 halves

3 wires: 6 halves   4 wires: 8 halves

The worker can make **8** light bulbs from the wire.

$$4 \div \frac{1}{2} = 8 \qquad\qquad 4 \times \mathbf{2} = 8$$

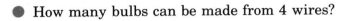 reciprocals

> To divide with fractions, multiply by the reciprocal of the divisor.

$$\frac{3}{5} \div \frac{4}{3} = \frac{3}{5} \times \frac{3}{4} = \frac{9}{20}$$

reciprocals

More examples:

$$6 \div \frac{1}{3} = 6 \times 3 = 18$$
reciprocals

$$\frac{2}{3} \div 5 = \frac{2}{3} \times \frac{1}{5} = \frac{2}{15}$$
reciprocals

$$\frac{3}{5} \div \frac{2}{7} = \frac{3}{5} \times \frac{7}{2} = \frac{21}{10} = 2\frac{1}{10}$$
reciprocals

PRACTICE • Copy and complete. Write the answers in lowest terms.

1. $\frac{1}{5} \div \frac{2}{3} = \frac{1}{5} \times \frac{3}{?} = $ _____?_____

2. $\frac{3}{4} \div \frac{1}{2} = \frac{3}{4} \times \frac{?}{1} = $ _____?_____

3. $\frac{8}{9} \div \frac{1}{3} = \frac{8}{9} \times \frac{?}{1} = $ _____?_____

4. $\frac{4}{5} \div \frac{5}{6} = \frac{4}{5} \times \frac{?}{?} = $ _____?_____

5. $\frac{5}{8} \div \frac{1}{4} = \frac{5}{8} \times \frac{?}{?} = $ _____?_____

6. $\frac{7}{8} \div \frac{3}{4} = \frac{7}{8} \times \frac{?}{?} = $ _____?_____

Divide. Write the answers in lowest terms.

7. $\frac{1}{8} \div \frac{4}{3} = $ _____?_____

8. $\frac{6}{7} \div \frac{7}{6} = $ _____?_____

9. $\frac{1}{2} \div \frac{2}{3} = $ _____?_____

EXERCISES • Divide. Write the answers in lowest terms.

10. $\frac{5}{6} \div \frac{2}{9} = $ _____?_____

11. $\frac{7}{3} \div \frac{5}{6} = $ _____?_____

12. $\frac{3}{2} \div \frac{4}{3} = $ _____?_____

13. $\frac{3}{8} \div \frac{1}{4} = $ _____?_____

14. $\frac{3}{4} \div \frac{1}{3} = $ _____?_____

15. $\frac{5}{8} \div \frac{2}{3} = $ _____?_____

16. $\frac{5}{4} \div \frac{3}{2} = $ _____?_____

17. $\frac{2}{3} \div \frac{5}{6} = $ _____?_____

18. $\frac{7}{2} \div \frac{3}{8} = $ _____?_____

19. $\frac{4}{5} \div \frac{1}{3} = $ _____?_____

20. $\frac{7}{2} \div \frac{3}{2} = $ _____?_____

21. $\frac{11}{3} \div \frac{5}{6} = $ _____?_____

22. $\frac{3}{4} \div \frac{1}{16} = $ _____?_____

23. $\frac{10}{3} \div \frac{5}{6} = $ _____?_____

24. $\frac{7}{8} \div \frac{1}{4} = $ _____?_____

25. $\frac{10}{8} \div \frac{2}{9} = $ _____?_____

26. $\frac{3}{4} \div \frac{1}{6} = $ _____?_____

27. $\frac{1}{6} \div \frac{2}{9} = $ _____?_____

★ 28. $\left(5 + \frac{1}{2}\right) \div \frac{3}{5} = $ _____?_____

★ 29. $\left(2\frac{2}{3} + \frac{1}{2}\right) \div \frac{3}{8} = $ _____?_____

★ 30. $\left(\frac{5}{8} \times \frac{3}{4}\right) \div \frac{3}{8} = $ _____?_____

PROBLEM SOLVING • APPLICATIONS

31. Edison invented the first phonograph while working on a machine to record telegraph messages. The "record" was a brass cylinder wrapped in tin foil. A worker had $\frac{7}{8}$ of a roll of tin foil. It took $\frac{1}{16}$ of a roll to make one record. How many records could be made?

32. George Eastman's flexible film made it possible for Edison to invent the first motion picture camera. The first movies were seen through a viewer. An early movie lasted $4\frac{1}{2}$ minutes. Each scene lasted $\frac{3}{4}$ of a minute. How many scenes were there?

THINKER'S CORNER

What are the next two numbers in the pattern?

a.

$\frac{1}{3}$	$\frac{1}{6}$	$\frac{1}{12}$	?	?

b.

$\frac{3}{4}$	1	$1\frac{1}{4}$	?	?

Dividing Fractions and Whole Numbers

The Wright brothers spent several years doing research before attempting to fly a power plane. They built a wind tunnel to test over 200 wing models.

A wind tunnel experiment takes $\frac{3}{4}$ of a day. The same test was repeated nine times.

● What part of the day did each test take?

Think You know how long it took for 9 tests. Divide to find how long for one test.

$$\frac{3}{4} \div 9 = ?$$

Step 1 Write the whole number as a fraction. $\longrightarrow \dfrac{3}{4} \div \dfrac{9}{1}$

Step 2 Rewrite as a multiplication problem. $\longrightarrow \dfrac{3}{4} \div \dfrac{9}{1} = \dfrac{3}{4} \times \dfrac{1}{9}$

Step 3 Multiply. $\longrightarrow \dfrac{3}{4} \div \dfrac{9}{1} = \dfrac{3}{4} \times \dfrac{1}{9} = \dfrac{3}{36}$

Step 4 Write the answer in lowest terms. $\longrightarrow \dfrac{3}{4} \div \dfrac{9}{1} = \dfrac{3}{4} \times \dfrac{1}{9} = \dfrac{3}{36} = \dfrac{1}{12}$

It took $\frac{1}{12}$ of the day for one test.

● Divide: $6 \div \dfrac{2}{3}$.

Step 1 Write the whole number as a fraction. $\longrightarrow \dfrac{6}{1} \div \dfrac{2}{3}$

Step 2 Rewrite as a multiplication problem. $\longrightarrow \dfrac{6}{1} \div \dfrac{2}{3} = \dfrac{6}{1} \times \dfrac{3}{2}$

Step 3 Multiply. $\longrightarrow \dfrac{6}{1} \div \dfrac{2}{3} = \dfrac{6}{1} \times \dfrac{3}{2} = \dfrac{18}{2}$

Step 4 Write the answer in lowest terms. $\longrightarrow \dfrac{6}{1} \div \dfrac{2}{3} = \dfrac{6}{1} \times \dfrac{3}{2} = \dfrac{18}{2} = 9$

1. $\frac{1}{10} \div 3 = $ _____?_____

2. $\frac{8}{9} \div 8 = $ _____?_____

3. $4 \div \frac{3}{5} = $ _____?_____

4. $\frac{4}{5} \div 8 = $ _____?_____

5. $9 \div \frac{3}{4} = $ _____?_____

6. $\frac{1}{5} \div 7 = $ _____?_____

EXERCISES • Divide. Write the answers in lowest terms.

7. $\frac{9}{10} \div 2 = $ _____?_____

8. $\frac{5}{6} \div 5 = $ _____?_____

9. $\frac{3}{8} \div 4 = $ _____?_____

10. $10 \div \frac{10}{9} = $ _____?_____

11. $2 \div \frac{9}{7} = $ _____?_____

12. $7 \div \frac{2}{9} = $ _____?_____

13. $\frac{3}{7} \div 8 = $ _____?_____

14. $\frac{7}{2} \div 6 = $ _____?_____

15. $\frac{4}{3} \div 2 = $ _____?_____

16. $5 \div \frac{2}{3} = $ _____?_____

17. $7 \div \frac{1}{2} = $ _____?_____

18. $\frac{1}{2} \div \frac{3}{4} = $ _____?_____

19. $\frac{2}{3} \div 4 = $ _____?_____

20. $\frac{1}{10} \div \frac{5}{6} = $ _____?_____

21. $\frac{1}{6} \div 2 = $ _____?_____

22. $6 \div \frac{3}{4} = $ _____?_____

23. $4 \div \frac{1}{3} = $ _____?_____

24. $15 \div \frac{1}{5} = $ _____?_____

25. $\frac{5}{9} \div 5 = $ _____?_____

26. $\frac{2}{5} \div 2 = $ _____?_____

27. $\frac{3}{8} \div \frac{2}{3} = $ _____?_____

PROBLEM SOLVING • APPLICATIONS

Solve. Write the answers in lowest terms.

28. The Wrights began their research with kites and gliders. They built the first practical glider and were the first skilled glider pilots. A mechanic uses $\frac{5}{8}$ of a roll of fabric to cover one glider wing. How many wings would 10 rolls of fabric cover?

29. The Wright brothers used gliders to solve many of the problems of flight control. An early glider flight covered 600 feet in $\frac{1}{6}$ of an hour. At this rate, how far could the glider fly in one hour?

30. The Wright brothers made their first power plane flights lying face down on a wing. On the first day, they made 4 flights. The last flight covered 852 feet in 59 seconds. The first flight covered about 122 feet in $\frac{1}{5}$ of a minute. At this rate, how far could the plane fly in one minute?

Dividing Fractions and Mixed Numbers

Garret A. Morgan invented the first traffic light in 1914. There were two lights, red and green, and they had to be changed by hand.

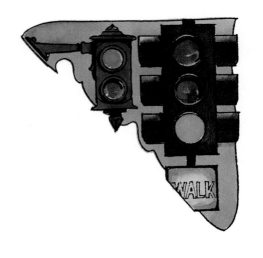

A traffic signal changes every $\frac{3}{4}$ of a minute.

● How often will it change in $3\frac{3}{4}$ minutes?

Think You need to find how many $\frac{3}{4}$ minutes there are in $3\frac{3}{4}$ minutes. Divide.

$$3\frac{3}{4} \div \frac{3}{4} = ?$$

Step 1 Write the mixed number as a fraction. $\longrightarrow$ $\frac{15}{4} \div \frac{3}{4}$

Step 2 Rewrite as a multiplication problem. $\longrightarrow$ $\frac{15}{4} \div \frac{3}{4} = \frac{15}{4} \times \frac{4}{3}$

Step 3 Multiply. $\longrightarrow$ $\frac{15}{4} \div \frac{3}{4} = \frac{15}{4} \times \frac{4}{3} = \frac{60}{12}$

Step 4 Write the answer in lowest terms. $\longrightarrow$ $\frac{15}{4} \div \frac{3}{4} = \frac{15}{4} \times \frac{4}{3} = \frac{60}{12} = 5$ ◀ **The light will change 5 times.**

● Divide: $2\frac{1}{2} \div 3\frac{1}{3}$

Step 1 Write the mixed numbers as fractions. $\longrightarrow$ $\frac{5}{2} \div \frac{10}{3}$

Step 2 Rewrite as a multiplication problem. $\longrightarrow$ $\frac{5}{2} \div \frac{10}{3} = \frac{5}{2} \times \frac{3}{10}$

Step 3 Multiply. $\longrightarrow$ $\frac{5}{2} \div \frac{10}{3} = \frac{5}{2} \times \frac{3}{10} = \frac{15}{20}$

Step 4 Write the answer in lowest terms. $\longrightarrow$ $\frac{5}{2} \div \frac{10}{3} = \frac{5}{2} \times \frac{3}{10} = \frac{15}{20} = \frac{3}{4}$

PRACTICE • Divide. Write the answers in lowest terms.

1. $2\frac{1}{3} \div \frac{3}{7} =$ ___?___

2. $\frac{2}{3} \div 3\frac{1}{5} =$ ___?___

3. $2\frac{1}{2} \div 1\frac{2}{3} =$ ___?___

4. $3\frac{1}{5} \div \frac{2}{5} =$ ___?___

5. $1\frac{1}{2} \div \frac{5}{6} =$ ___?___

6. $\frac{1}{3} \div 4\frac{1}{2} =$ ___?___

EXERCISES • Divide. Write the answers in lowest terms.

7. $2\frac{1}{7} \div \frac{2}{7} =$ ___?___

8. $4\frac{1}{3} \div \frac{2}{5} =$ ___?___

9. $\frac{4}{5} \div 3\frac{1}{2} =$ ___?___

10. $1\frac{5}{6} \div \frac{4}{5} =$ ___?___

11. $5\frac{1}{4} \div \frac{3}{10} =$ ___?___

12. $1\frac{3}{4} \div \frac{2}{9} =$ ___?___

13. $3\frac{1}{5} \div 3\frac{2}{5} =$ ___?___

14. $21 \div 2\frac{1}{3} =$ ___?___

15. $2\frac{2}{3} \div \frac{5}{9} =$ ___?___

16. $1\frac{2}{7} \div 2\frac{1}{4} =$ ___?___

17. $\frac{9}{10} \div \frac{3}{5} =$ ___?___

18. $\frac{4}{9} \div 1\frac{2}{3} =$ ___?___

19. $1\frac{1}{2} \div 3 =$ ___?___

20. $18 \div 6\frac{3}{4} =$ ___?___

21. $2\frac{1}{10} \div 1\frac{1}{5} =$ ___?___

22. $\frac{1}{2} \div \frac{1}{3} =$ ___?___

23. $1\frac{1}{3} \div 2\frac{1}{3} =$ ___?___

24. $18 \div 5\frac{1}{4} =$ ___?___

★ 25. $1\frac{1}{4} \div$ ___?___ $= \frac{1}{2}$

★ 26. $1\frac{1}{3} \div$ ___?___ $= \frac{8}{15}$

★ 27. $2\frac{2}{5} \div$ ___?___ $= \frac{3}{5}$

PROBLEM SOLVING • APPLICATIONS

Solve. Write the answers in lowest terms.

28. Garrett Morgan established a successful sewing machine repair and sales business. A worker took $1\frac{3}{4}$ hours to replace one motor. How many motors could be replaced in one $10\frac{1}{2}$ hour day?

29. A traffic light at an intersection changes every $\frac{5}{6}$ of a minute.
    a. How many times will it change in $2\frac{1}{2}$ minutes?
    b. How many times will it change in $2\frac{1}{2}$ hours?

30. A traffic light changes every $\frac{3}{4}$ of a minute from 6 A.M. to 6 P.M., and every $1\frac{1}{3}$ minutes from 6 P.M. to 6 A.M. How many times does it change in 24 hours?

Customary Units of Length

Most modern bicycles use hand brakes. The hand brake consists of two levers on the handlebars. The levers operate rubber brake pads called *shoes* that press against the wheel rims to slow down or stop the bicycle.

- The length of the handbrake is **4 inches** to the **nearest inch.**
- It is $3\frac{1}{2}$ **inches** long to the **nearest** $\frac{1}{2}$ **inch.**
- It is $3\frac{3}{4}$ **inches** long to the **nearest** $\frac{3}{4}$ **inch.**
- It is $3\frac{5}{8}$ **inches long** to the **nearest** $\frac{1}{8}$ **inch.**
- It is $3\frac{11}{16}$ **inches** long to the **nearest** $\frac{1}{16}$ **inch.**

The **foot (ft), yard (yd),** and **mile (mi)** are other customary units used to measure length. The table shows how they are related.

12 inches (in.) = 1 foot (ft)
36 inches (in.) = 1 yard (yd)
3 feet (ft) = 1 yard (yd)
5,280 feet (ft) = 1 mile (mi)
1,760 yards (yd) = 1 mile (mi)

2 ft = ? in.

Think To change larger units to smaller units, multiply.

1 ft = 12 in.
2 × 12 = 24
2 ft = 24 in.

36 in = ? ft

Think To change smaller units to larger units, divide.

12 in. = 1 ft
36 ÷ 12 = 3
36 in. = 3 ft

PRACTICE • Measure the nail to the nearest

1. inch.   **2.** $\frac{1}{2}$ inch.   **3.** $\frac{1}{4}$ inch.   **4.** $\frac{1}{8}$ inch.   **5.** $\frac{1}{16}$ inch.

Which unit of measure would you use for each? Write INCH, FOOT, YARD, or MILE.

6. the length of a clothespin   **7.** the length of a river

8. the height of a wall   **9.** the length of a fork

EXERCISES • Which unit of measure would you use for each?
Write INCH, FOOT, YARD, or MILE.

10. the length of a football field   **11.** the width of this book

12. the distance from Dallas to Miami   **13.** the width of your classroom

E Estimate the length to the nearest $\frac{1}{2}$ inch. Then measure to check your estimate.

14.   **15.**

16.

Complete.

17. 3 ft = _?_ in.

18. 2 yd = _?_ in.

19. 3 mi = _?_ yd

20. 12 ft = _?_ in.

21. 27 ft = _?_ yd

22. 72 in. = _?_ yd

23. 132 in. = _?_ ft

24. 180 in. = _?_ yd

25. 3,520 yd = _?_ mi

26. 1 ft 4 in. = _?_ in.

27. 4 yd 2 ft = _?_ ft

28. 1,946 yd = _?_ mi _?_ yd

29. 145 in. = _?_ ft _?_ in.

30. 80 ft = _?_ yd _?_ ft

★ **31.** 1 mi 92 yd = _?_ ft

32. $4\frac{1}{3}$ yd = _?_ ft

★ **33.** $1\frac{3}{8}$ mi = _?_ yd

★ **34.** $\frac{3}{8}$ mi = _?_ in.

PROBLEM SOLVING • APPLICATIONS

35. In the late 1800's, a bicycle called the *high wheeler* was invented. The front wheel of some models of this bicycle were 5 feet high.
Complete: 5 ft = _?_ yd _?_ ft

36. The most famous bicycle road race is the Tour de France. The race lasts 24 days and covers 2,400 miles.
Complete: 2,400 mi = _?_ yd

37. Bicycle track races are held on oval tracks called *velodromes*. The tracks slope inward at an angle. The distance around these tracks ranges from $\frac{1}{10}$ to $\frac{1}{3}$ of a mile. What is the range in feet?

★ **38.** Each turn of the pedals of a high wheeler (see Exercise 35) turned the large wheel around once. If the radius of the large wheel was $2\frac{1}{2}$ feet, how far did the bicycle travel on one turn of the pedals? Use $\frac{22}{7}$ for π. Round the answer to the nearest whole number.

Perimeter, Area, and Volume

You can use customary units to find perimeter, area, and volume.

In 1888, George Eastman introduced a lightweight, inexpensive box camera. It was the first camera designed for mass production.

● Find the perimeter of a side of the camera.

Think   Perimeter = length + width + length + width

$P = 5 + 4 + 5 + 4$
$P = 18$ in.   The perimeter of one side is **18 inches.**

● What is the area of the side?

Think   Area = length times width

$A = l \times w$
$A = 5 \times 4$
$A = 20$ in.^{2} The area is **20 square inches.**

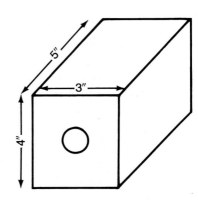

● What is the volume of the box?

Think   Volume = length times width times height

$V = l \times w \times h$
$V = 5 \times 3 \times 4$
$V = 60$ in.^{3} The volume is **60 cubic inches.**

PRACTICE • Complete.

1.

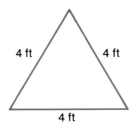

Perimeter ___?___ ft

2.

5 in.

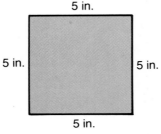

Area ___?___ in.^{2}

3.

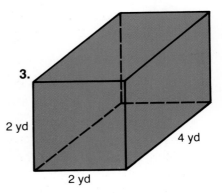

Volume ___?___ yd^3

EXERCISES • Find the perimeter and the area of each figure.

4.

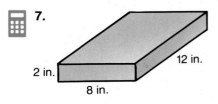

55 yd
32 yd   32 yd
55 yd

5.

12 ft
12 ft   12 ft
12 ft

★6.

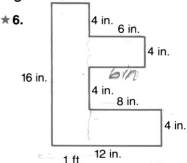

4 in.
4 in.
6 in.
4 in.
16 in.
6 in.
4 in.
8 in.
4 in.
1 ft   12 in.

Find the volume of each figure.

7.

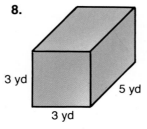

12 in.
2 in.
8 in.

8.

3 yd
5 yd
3 yd

★9.

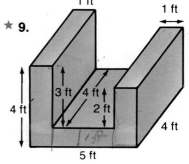

1 ft   1 ft
3 ft   4 ft
4 ft   2 ft
4 ft
5 ft

PROBLEM SOLVING • APPLICATIONS

10. The first television show took place on September 11, 1928. The picture was seen on a screen measuring 3 inches by 4 inches. What was the perimeter of the screen?

11. Before inventing an automobile starter, Charles Kettering developed a small electric motor. Modern starter motors require a space about 12 inches by 6 inches. What is the area the motor requires?

12. Oliver Evans developed a steam– powered wagon. This led to the invention of the railroad locomotive. He placed a steam engine in a wagon measuring 15 feet by 4 feet by 2 feet. What was the volume of the wagon?

13. In Exercise 12, what was the area available for the engine?

14. The first radios had two parts, a box and ear phones. The box was about 8 inches by 4 inches by 3 inches. What was the volume available for the radio parts?

Write Your Own Problem

1. Use the information in the table to write two word problems involving perimeter or area.

2. Write two multistep problems that can be answered by using the information in the table. Have the problems involve perimeter or area and the operation of subtraction.

Camera	Size of Photograph
Miniature	1 in. by $1\frac{1}{2}$ in.
Twin Lens Reflex	$2\frac{1}{4}$ in. by $2\frac{1}{4}$ in.
Instant	$3\frac{1}{4}$ in. by $4\frac{1}{4}$ in.

Customary Units of Capacity and Weight

In 1839, Charles Goodyear accidently dropped some rubber mixed with sulfur on a hot stove. This led to a process called *vulcanization*, which made rubber stronger and more resistant to heat and cold.

2 tablespoons (tbsp)	= 1 fluid ounce (1 fl. oz)
8 fluid ounces (fl. oz)	= 1 cup (c)
2 cups (c)	= 1 pint (pt)
2 pints (pt)	= 1 quart (qt)
2 quarts (qt)	= 1 half-gallon $\left(\frac{1}{2} \text{ gal}\right)$
4 quarts (qt)	= 1 gallon (gal)

● These customary units are used to measure liquid capacity.

2 tablespoons   **cup**   **saucepan 1 pint**   **pan 1 quart**   **cooking pot $\frac{1}{2}$ gallon**   **jug 1 gallon**

Rubber tires come in many sizes and weights. These customary units are used to measure weight.

16 ounces (oz) = 1 pound (lb)
1 ton (T) = 2,000 pounds (lb)

toy car tires 1 ounce   **bicycle tires 1 pound**   **earth mover tires about 1 ton**

PRACTICE • Choose the correct measure for each.

1.

1 c   1 gal

2.

30 gal   30 fl. oz

3.

1 gal   1 pt

4.

4 oz   4 lb

5.

2 lb   2 T

6.

6 lb   6 T

EXERCISES • Complete.

7. 1 pt = ___?___ fl. oz

8. 1 qt = ___?___ c

9. 2 tbsp = ___?___ fl. oz

10. 2 gal = ___?___ qt

11. $\frac{1}{2}$ gal = ___?___ qt

12. 2 pt = ___?___ c

13. 3 gal 1 qt = ___?___ qt

14. 14 pt = ___?___ gal ___?___ qt

15. 31 c = ___?___ pt ___?___ c

★ **16.** $1\frac{3}{4}$ gal = ___?___ c

★ **17.** 4 gal = ___?___ tbsp

★ **18.** $4\frac{1}{2}$ qt = ___?___ pt

Write >, <, or =.

19. 16 c ⬤ 1 gal

20. 2 qt ⬤ 8 c

21. 56 fl. oz ⬤ 7 c

22. $3\frac{1}{2}$ qt ⬤ 14 c

23. 32 tbsp ⬤ 2 pt

24. 2 qt ⬤ 5 pt

Complete.

25. 32 oz = ___?___ lb

26. 80 oz = ___?___ lb

27. 3 lb = ___?___ oz

28. 4 lb = ___?___ oz

29. 18 T = ___?___ lb

30. $\frac{1}{2}$ T = ___?___ lb

31. 46 oz = ___?___ lb ___?___ oz

32. 3 T 300 lb = ___?___ lb

33. 4,800 lb = ___?___ T ___?___ lb

★ **34.** 100 oz = ___?___ lb

★ **35.** $5\frac{3}{4}$ T = ___?___ lb

★ **36.** 8 oz = ___?___ lb

PROBLEM SOLVING • APPLICATIONS

37. Natural rubber is made from latex. Latex comes from rubber trees. One tree can produce about 20 pounds of rubber in one year. It takes about 65 pounds of rubber to make 4 automobile tires. How many trees are needed to produce this amount of rubber per year?

38. A cup is attached to each rubber tree to collect the latex. About 1 fluid ounce of latex flows into the cup each hour. How many cups of latex can be collected in one 24–hour period?

39. One acre of rubber trees can produce 1,800 pounds of latex in one year. A certain bicycle tire requires 36 ounces of rubber. How many bicycle tires can be made from the latex produced by one acre of rubber trees in one year?

40. Doctors use rubber gloves weighing about $\frac{1}{3}$ of an ounce each. A doctor purchases a box containing 24 pairs of gloves. A rubber tree can provide 1.3 ounces of latex each hour. How long will it take a rubber tree to produce enough latex to make the one box of gloves?

Claude saw these advertisements in a newspaper.

WONDER
Computers

The only choice
for the
successful
career
person!

Get more for
less with
a new
Zerotech Computer!
Save $150
(No time limit)

In order to understand what the ads really said,
Claude wrote them in "if–then" form.

CHOICE 1   If you buy a Can–do computer, then you are
buying the best computer on the market.

CHOICE 2   If you are successful in your career, then a
Wonder computer is the only choice for you.

CHOICE 3   If you buy a Zerotech computer, then you will
save $150.

MAKING A CHOICE

CHOICE 1

1. If the advertisement is true and you buy a Can–do computer, can you expect it to be the best on the market?

2. If the advertisement is true and you buy another model of computer, does this mean that you have made a poor choice?

CHOICE 2

3. If you are a successful career person and you are planning to buy a computer, should you only consider buying a Wonder computer?

4. Suppose that you buy a Wonder computer. Does that mean that you are a successful career person?

CHOICE 3

5. If the advertisement is true and you buy a Zerotech computer, how much will you pay for a computer with a regular price of $800?

6. If you buy a Zerotech computer and you have to pay the regular price, what does this say about the ad?

PROJECT   Collect 5 ads similar to the ones in this lesson from newspapers or magazines. Write the ads in "if–then" form. List one reason for, and one reason against, buying what is offered in each ad.

CHAPTER REVIEW

Part 1 • VOCABULARY

For Exercises 1–7, choose from the box at the right the words that completes the sentence.

common factor
denominators
divisor
inches
multiplication
reciprocals
width

1. To multiply fractions, you multiply the numerators and multiply the __?__. (Page 294)

2. To find $\frac{1}{4}$ of $\frac{1}{2}$, you use the operation of __?__. (Page 294)

3. When multiplying fractions, it is sometimes easier to divide the numerator and denominator by a __?__ before you multiply. (Page 300)

4. In the division problem $2 \div \frac{1}{4}$, $\frac{1}{4}$ is called the __?__. (Page 306)

5. Two fractions whose product is 1 are __?__ of each other. (Page 306)

6. One yard is equal to 36 __?__. (Page 312)

7. The area of a rectangle is equal to its length times __?__. (Page 314)

Part 2 • SKILLS

Multiply. Write the answers in lowest terms. (Pages 294–295, 300–301)

8. $\frac{1}{2} \times \frac{3}{4} = $ __?__

9. $\frac{5}{6} \times \frac{2}{5} = $ __?__

10. $\frac{8}{9} \times \frac{3}{6} = $ __?__

11. $\frac{2}{5} \times \frac{1}{3} = $ __?__

12. $\frac{5}{9} \times \frac{7}{8} = $ __?__

13. $\frac{7}{16} \times \frac{3}{15} = $ __?__

Multiply. Write the answers in lowest terms. (Pages 296–297)

14. $3 \times \frac{3}{5} = $ __?__

15. $\frac{7}{8} \times 2 = $ __?__

16. $8 \times \frac{6}{10} = $ __?__

17. $6 \times \frac{1}{5} = $ __?__

18. $21 \times \frac{5}{7} = $ __?__

19. $9 \times \frac{2}{3} = $ __?__

Multiply. Write the answers in lowest terms. (Pages 298–299)

20. $2\frac{1}{2} \times 3\frac{1}{4} = $ __?__

21. $6\frac{2}{3} \times 1\frac{4}{5} = $ __?__

22. $3\frac{1}{8} \times 1\frac{1}{2} = $ __?__

23. $3\frac{1}{7} \times 2\frac{1}{2} = $ __?__

24. $3\frac{1}{5} \times 4\frac{2}{3} = $ __?__

25. $5\frac{1}{3} \times 3\frac{3}{4} = $ __?__

Divide. Write the answers in lowest terms. (Pages 306–307)

26. $\frac{3}{4} \div \frac{6}{8} =$ __?__

27. $\frac{10}{3} \div \frac{5}{6} =$ __?__

28. $\frac{4}{5} \div \frac{3}{15} =$ __?__

29. $\frac{1}{2} \div \frac{2}{5} =$ __?__

30. $\frac{3}{8} \div \frac{1}{7} =$ __?__

31. $\frac{5}{16} \div \frac{7}{8} =$ __?__

Divide. Write the answers in lowest terms. (Pages 308–309)

32. $4 \div \frac{8}{3} =$ __?__

33. $\frac{2}{6} \div 2 =$ __?__

34. $\frac{5}{9} \div 15 =$ __?__

Divide. Write the answers in lowest terms. (Pages 310–311)

35. $5\frac{2}{4} \div 1\frac{4}{6} =$ __?__

36. $3\frac{1}{3} \div 3\frac{3}{9} =$ __?__

37. $2\frac{1}{10} \div 1\frac{2}{5} =$ __?__

38. $8\frac{3}{8} \div 3\frac{2}{7} =$ __?__

39. $2\frac{1}{8} \div 3\frac{3}{4} =$ __?__

40. $1\frac{3}{10} \div 2\frac{4}{5} =$ __?__

Complete. (Pages 312–313)

41. 144 in. = __?__ ft

42. 7,040 yd = __?__ mi

43. 85 ft = __?__ yd __?__ ft

Complete. (Pages 314–315)

44.

Perimeter = __?__

45.

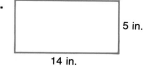

Area = __?__

46.

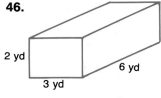

Volume = __?__

Complete. (Pages 316–317)

47. 3 gal = __?__ qt

48. 8 fl. oz = __?__ tbsp

49. 2 lb 6 oz = __?__ oz

Part 3 • *PROBLEM SOLVING* • *APPLICATIONS* (Pages 302–303)

50. A research assistant used $8\frac{3}{5}$ pounds of sulfur each week for $6\frac{1}{2}$ weeks. Estimate how many pounds of sulfur were used.

51. A glider pilot ordered $44\frac{5}{8}$ feet of lumber in order to build a glider. About $56\frac{3}{8}$ feet of lumber were needed in all. Estimate how much more lumber the pilot needed.

52. A camera technician uses $26\frac{1}{2}$ feet of film while experimenting with a motion picture camera. About $9\frac{1}{3}$ feet of film was used per experiment. Estimate the number of experiments conducted.

53. A photographer spent $5\frac{3}{4}$ hours setting up the background for a shot. It took another $2\frac{1}{5}$ hours to take the pictures. Estimate the total time spent.

CHAPTER TEST

Multiply. Write the answer in lowest terms.

1. $\frac{4}{5} \times \frac{3}{8} = $ _____?_____

2. $\frac{7}{10} \times \frac{5}{6} = $ _____?_____

3. $\frac{5}{7} \times \frac{2}{3} = $ _____?_____

4. $7 \times \frac{3}{5} = $ _____?_____

5. $9 \times \frac{1}{6} = $ _____?_____

6. $12 \times \frac{2}{3} = $ _____?_____

7. $\frac{1}{2} \times 5\frac{1}{4} = $ _____?_____

8. $9\frac{1}{3} \times 1\frac{5}{7} = $ _____?_____

9. $5\frac{2}{5} \times 4\frac{1}{3} = $ _____?_____

Divide. Write the answer in lowest terms.

10. $\frac{3}{10} \div \frac{1}{2} = $ _____?_____

11. $\frac{5}{6} \div \frac{3}{8} = $ _____?_____

12. $\frac{3}{7} \div \frac{4}{9} = $ _____?_____

13. $10 \div \frac{2}{5} = $ _____?_____

14. $6 \div \frac{2}{3} = $ _____?_____

15. $24 \div \frac{5}{6} = $ _____?_____

16. $\frac{2}{3} \div 3\frac{1}{3} = $ _____?_____

17. $4\frac{1}{2} \div 2\frac{2}{3} = $ _____?_____

18. $3\frac{5}{8} \div 1\frac{1}{2} = $ _____?_____

19. 6 gal $= $ _____?_____ qt

20. 3 lb $= $ _____?_____ oz

21. 9 yd $= $ _____?_____ ft

22. Find the area.

6 in.

11 in.

23. Find the volume.

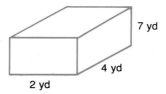

7 yd

4 yd

2 yd

Choose the best estimate.

24. An inventor used $1\frac{3}{8}$ ounces of sulfer in an experiment. For a second experiment, the inventor used $2\frac{9}{10}$ ounces more than for the first. Estimate how many ounces of sulfer were used for the second experiment.

  a. 6 oz   **b.** 4 oz   **c.** 3 oz

25. A mechanic buys a $125\frac{2}{3}$ foot roll of wire for motor repairs. The wire will be cut into $1\frac{1}{8}$ foot lengths. Estimate the number of lengths that can be cut from the roll.

  a. 63   **b.** 126   **c.** 130

ENRICHMENT

Time Zones

There are 24 time zones throughout the world.

The clocks show that when it is 10:00 A.M. in the Pacific Time Zone,
it is   11:00 A.M. in the Mountain Time Zone.
          12:00 Noon in the Central Time Zone.
          1:00 P.M. in the Eastern Time Zone.

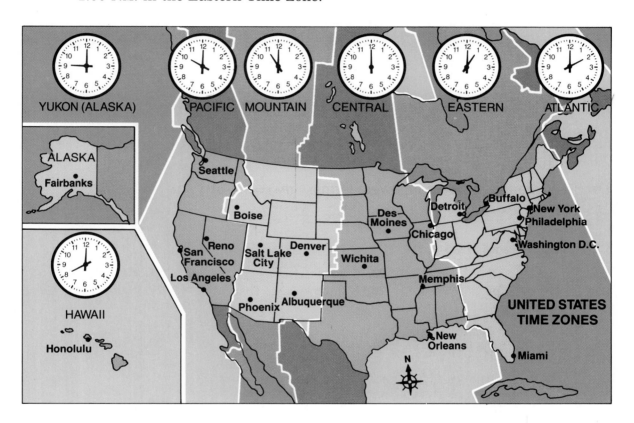

EXERCISES

It is 8:45 A.M. in Memphis. What time is it in

1. Washington, D.C.?   **2.** Boise?   **3.** New Orleans?   **4.** Reno?

It is 12:00 midnight in Albuquerque. What time is it in

5. Des Moines?   **6.** Honolulu?   **7.** Los Angeles?   **8.** Buffalo?

It is 9:15 P.M. in Washington, D.C. What time is it in

9. Wichita?   **10.** Miami?   **11.** Fairbanks?   **12.** Salt Lake City?

ADDITIONAL PRACTICE

SKILLS

Multiply. Write the answers in lowest terms.   (Pages 294–295, 300–301)

1. $\frac{2}{3} \times \frac{3}{4} = $ _?_

2. $\frac{2}{8} \times \frac{2}{3} = $ _?_

3. $\frac{3}{8} \times \frac{6}{9} = $ _?_

Multiply. Write the answers in lowest terms.   (Pages 296–297)

4. $4 \times \frac{6}{8} = $ _?_

5. $6 \times \frac{6}{9} = $ _?_

6. $\frac{3}{5} \times 10 = $ _?_

Multiply. Write the answers in lowest terms.   (Pages 298–299)

7. $3\frac{1}{2} \times 2\frac{2}{3} = $ _?_

8. $1\frac{1}{4} \times 1\frac{4}{5} = $ _?_

9. $3\frac{1}{3} \times 4\frac{1}{2} = $ _?_

10. $3\frac{1}{5} \times 4\frac{2}{3} = $ _?_

11. $3\frac{3}{4} \times 3\frac{1}{4} = $ _?_

12. $2\frac{2}{5} \times 4\frac{7}{10} = $ _?_

Divide. Write the answers in lowest terms.   (Pages 306–307, 308–309)

13. $\frac{1}{2} \div \frac{3}{2} = $ _?_

14. $\frac{3}{9} \div \frac{6}{12} = $ _?_

15. $\frac{5}{6} \div \frac{25}{30} = $ _?_

16. $3 \div \frac{9}{10} = $ _?_

17. $\frac{12}{16} \div 6 = $ _?_

18. $\frac{20}{50} \div 10 = $ _?_

Divide. Write the answers in lowest terms.   (Pages 310–311)

19. $2\frac{1}{2} \div 4\frac{2}{4} = $ _?_

20. $3\frac{1}{3} \div 1\frac{5}{6} = $ _?_

21. $5\frac{2}{4} \div 1\frac{4}{6} = $ _?_

Complete.   (Pages 312–313, 316–317)

22. 3 mi = _?_ ft

23. 6 yd = _?_ ft

24. 6 yd = _?_ in.

25. 18 c = _?_ pt

26. 8 fl. oz = _?_ tbsp

27. 8,000 lb = _?_ T

Complete.   (Pages 314–315)

28. Perimeter = _?_

29. Area = _?_

30. Volume = _?_

13 ft

13 ft

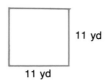

11 yd

11 yd

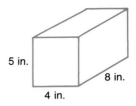

5 in.

8 in.

4 in.

PROBLEM SOLVING • APPLICATIONS   (Pages 302–303)

31. A quality control worker tests a television set for $8\frac{1}{4}$ hours one day and $9\frac{3}{8}$ hours the next day. Estimate the total time the set was tested for the two days.

32. A research worker used $35\frac{4}{5}$ feet of rubber hose to develop anti-pollution masks. The worker bought $43\frac{1}{4}$ feet of hose for the project. Estimate how many feet of rubber hose were not used.

Each of these problems contains a common error.
a. Find the correct answer.
b. Find the error.

1. Find the greatest common factor for 16 and 12.

16: 1, **2,** 4, 8, 16
12: 1, **2,** 3, 4, 6, 12

2. Find the equivalent fraction.

$\frac{2}{3} = \frac{?}{9}$

$\frac{2+6}{3+6} = \frac{8}{9}$

3. Complete.

$\frac{16}{24} = \frac{?}{12}$

$\frac{16-12}{24-12} = \frac{4}{12} = \frac{1}{3}$

4. Write $\frac{15}{45}$ in lowest terms.

$\frac{15}{45} = \frac{1}{30}$

5. Write $3\frac{5}{6}$ as a fraction.

$3\frac{5}{6} = \frac{3+5}{6} = \frac{8}{6}$

6. Add: $\frac{2}{5} + \frac{1}{5}$

$\frac{2}{5} + \frac{1}{5} = \frac{4}{10}$

7. Add: $\frac{2}{3} + \frac{1}{5}$

$$\begin{array}{r} \frac{2}{3} = \frac{2}{15} \\ +\frac{1}{5} = \frac{1}{15} \\ \hline \frac{3}{15} \end{array}$$

8. Regroup $8\frac{20}{16}$.
Write in lowest terms.

$8\frac{20}{16} = 8\frac{20 \div 4}{16 \div 4}$

$= 8\frac{5}{4}$

9. Subtract.
Write in lowest terms.

$$\begin{array}{r} \frac{7}{10} \\ -\frac{2}{10} \\ \hline \frac{5}{10} \end{array}$$

10. Subtract.
Write in lowest terms.

$$\begin{array}{r} \frac{7}{9} = \frac{7}{9} \\ -\frac{1}{3} = \frac{1}{9} \\ \hline \frac{6}{9} = \frac{2}{3} \end{array}$$

11. Subtract.

$$\begin{array}{r} 5 \\ -1\frac{2}{7} \\ \hline 4\frac{2}{7} \end{array}$$

12. Subtract.

$$\begin{array}{r} 7\frac{1}{2} = 7\frac{5}{10} \\ -3\frac{4}{5} = 3\frac{8}{10} \\ \hline 4\frac{3}{10} \end{array}$$

13. $5 \times \frac{3}{7} = \underline{\ \ ?\ \ }$

$5 \times \frac{3}{7} = \frac{1}{5} \times \frac{3}{7}$

$\qquad = \frac{3}{33}$

14. $2\frac{3}{5} \times 3\frac{1}{4} = \underline{\ \ ?\ \ }$

$2\frac{3}{5} \times 3\frac{1}{4} = 6\frac{3}{20}$

15. $\frac{2}{3} \div \frac{1}{6} = \underline{\ \ ?\ \ }$

$\frac{2}{3} \div \frac{1}{6} = \frac{3}{2} \div \frac{1}{6}$

$\qquad = \frac{3}{12}$

$\qquad = \frac{1}{4}$

CUMULATIVE REVIEW

Chapters 1 through 11

Choose the correct answer.

1. Add.

$9.45 + 26.432 = \underline{\ \ ?\ \ }$

A. 27.377
B. 0.35882
C. 35.882
D. not here

2. Subtract.

$$\begin{array}{r} 47.006 \\ -\ \ 2.341 \end{array}$$

A. 44.665
B. 0.44665
C. 45.765
D. not here

3. Divide.

$25.368 \div 100 = \underline{\ \ ?\ \ }$

A. 25.36800
B. 0.25368
C. 2536.8
D. not here

4. Multiply.

$$\begin{array}{r} 32.5 \\ \times 0.63 \end{array}$$

A. 204.75 B. 20.475
C. 1.925   D. not here

5. Divide.

$0.35\overline{)4.655}$

A. 0.133 B. 1.33
C. 13.3   D. not here

6. Which number is not a factor of 12?

A. 4   B. 3
C. 6   D. not here

7. Which number is a multiple of 6?

A. 48   B. 52
C. 44   D. not here

8. Which is a prime number?

A. 12   B. 28
C. 27   D. not here

9. Complete.

$\dfrac{3}{5} = \dfrac{12}{?}$

A. 15   B. 4
C. 20   D. not here

10. Write in lowest terms.

$\dfrac{4}{10}$

A. $\dfrac{2}{10}$ B. $\dfrac{2}{5}$
C. $\dfrac{4}{5}$ D. not here

11. Compare.

$\dfrac{3}{5}$ ● $\dfrac{5}{6}$

A. =   B. <
C. >   D. not here

12. Write as an improper fraction.

$4\dfrac{5}{6}$

A. $\dfrac{26}{6}$ B. $\dfrac{24}{6}$
C. $\dfrac{29}{6}$ D. not here

13. Jane bought 2 notebooks for $1.29 each and a pen for $0.89. How much did she spend in all?

A. $3.47   B. $4.36
C. $2.18   D. $11.48

14. Bob spends $1\dfrac{3}{4}$ hours doing his homework Monday and $2\dfrac{2}{3}$ hours on Tuesday. Estimate how much time he spent in all?

A. 2   B. 5
C. 3   D. 6

15. Divide to find the mixed number. Write in lowest terms.

$$\frac{20}{6}$$

A. $3\frac{1}{3}$ B. $3\frac{2}{6}$

C. $3\frac{1}{10}$ D. not here

16. Add. Write the answer in lowest terms.

$$5\frac{2}{9} + 6\frac{1}{9} = \underline{\ ?\ }$$

A. $11\frac{3}{9}$ B. $11\frac{3}{18}$

C. $11\frac{1}{3}$ D. not here

17. Add. Write the answer in lowest terms.

$$\frac{5}{8} + \frac{1}{2} = \underline{\ ?\ }$$

A. $1\frac{2}{16}$ B. $\frac{18}{16}$

C. $1\frac{1}{8}$ D. not here

18. Add. Write the answer in lowest terms.

$$3\frac{1}{6} + 2\frac{3}{8} = \underline{\ ?\ }$$

A. $5\frac{13}{24}$ B. $5\frac{21}{48}$

C. $6\frac{1}{3}$ D. not here

19. Subtract. Write the answer in lowest terms.

$$5\frac{4}{9} - 3\frac{1}{9} = \underline{\ ?\ }$$

A. $5\frac{5}{9}$ B. $2\frac{1}{3}$

C. $2\frac{3}{9}$ D. not here

20. Subtract. Write the answer in lowest terms.

$$5\frac{2}{5} - 1\frac{3}{5} = \underline{\ ?\ }$$

A. $3\frac{4}{5}$ B. $4\frac{1}{5}$

C. $4\frac{4}{5}$ D. not here

21. Subtract. Write the answer in lowest terms.

$$8\frac{5}{8} - 2\frac{1}{4} = \underline{\ ?\ }$$

A. $6\frac{6}{16}$ B. $6\frac{3}{8}$

C. $10\frac{3}{8}$ D. not here

22. Multiply. Write the answer in lowest terms.

$$4 \times \frac{2}{3} = \underline{\ ?\ }$$

A. $2\frac{2}{3}$ B. $\frac{8}{3}$

C. 2 D. not here

23. Multiply. Write the answer in lowest terms.

$$2\frac{1}{4} \times \frac{2}{3} = \underline{\ ?\ }$$

A. $1\frac{1}{2}$ B. $\frac{18}{12}$

C. $1\frac{6}{12}$ D. not here

24. Divide. Write the answer in lowest terms.

$$\frac{3}{8} \div \frac{2}{3} = \underline{\ ?\ }$$

A. $\frac{6}{24}$ B. $\frac{1}{4}$

C. $\frac{9}{16}$ D. not here

25. Divide. Write the answer in lowest terms.

$$6 \div \frac{3}{8} = \underline{\ ?\ }$$

A. $2\frac{1}{4}$ B. $\frac{48}{3}$

C. 16 D. not here

26. Divide. Write the answer in lowest terms.

$$\frac{2}{3} \div 4\frac{1}{2} = \underline{\ ?\ }$$

A. $\frac{18}{6}$ B. 3

C. $\frac{4}{27}$ D. not here

27. Lydia works 3 days a week. She works 4.5 hours each day. How many hours does she work each week? Choose the correct equation.

A. $3 \times 4.5 = n$ B. $3 \times n = 4.5$

C. $n \times 4.5 = 3$ D. $n \div 3 = 4.5$

28. Rick is packing books for a publisher. Each carton holds 20 books. He has 327 books. How many cartons will he need?

A. 17   B. 16 r7

C. 16   D. 20

Mixed Practice • Choose the correct answer.

1. $9 + 14 + 6 + 8 = $ __?__

   A. 47   **B.** 35
   C. 37   **D.** not here

2. $10 + 26 + 10 = $ __?__

   A. 46   **B.** 44
   C. 48   **D.** not here

3. $3 + 12 + 13 = $ __?__

   A. 27   **B.** 29
   C. 26   **D.** not here

4.   9
   $\times$ 4

   A. 38   **B.** 36
   C. 32   **D.** not here

5.   12
   $\times$ 9

   A. 108   **B.** 106
   C. 110   **D.** not here

6.   36
   $\times$ 8

   A. 288   **B.** 286
   C. 188   **D.** not here

7. Find the perimeter.

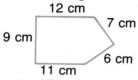

   A. 45 cm
   B. 55 cm
   C. 57 cm
   D. not here

8. Find the area.

   A. 55 mm^2
   B. 65 mm^2
   C. 75 mm^2
   D. not here

9. Find the circumference.

   A. 37.68 cm
   B. 38 cm
   C. 3,768 cm
   D. not here

10. Name the figure.

   A. rectangle
   B. triangle
   C. square
   D. not here

11. Name the figure.

   A. rectangle
   B. square
   C. triangle
   D. not here

12. Name the figure.

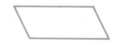

   A. square
   B. rectangle
   C. parallelogram
   D. not here

13. The distance between each of the 4 bases on a baseball field is 75 feet. How far will the batter run on hitting a home run?

   A. 225 ft   **B.** 300 ft
   C. 150 ft   **D.** not here

14. A box camera is 5 inches wide, 5 inches long, and 5 inches high. Find the volume of the camera.

   A. 25 in.^{3} **B.** 15 in.^{3}
   C. 125 in.^{3} **D.** not here

Geometry

A sundial tells time by measuring the angle of the shadow cast by the sun.

● Use the protractor to measure ∠ABC.

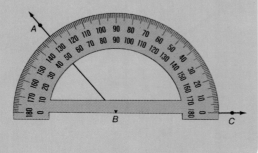

The building shown above is symmetric. You can flip the photograph along a **line of symmetry** to see a **mirror image** (a reflection) of the figure.

● Where is the line of symmetry for the figure?

329

The Vocabulary of Geometry

● A **line segment** is straight. It has two **endpoints**. A segment is named by its endpoints.

Line segment AB ($\overline{AB}$) or Line segment BA ($\overline{BA}$)

● A **line** has no endpoints. It goes on forever in both directions. A line is named by two of its points.

Line CD ($\overleftrightarrow{CD}$) or Line DC ($\overleftrightarrow{DC}$)

● A **ray** has one endpoint. It goes on forever in one direction only. Name the endpoint first.

Ray PQ ($\overrightarrow{PQ}$)

● A **plane** is a flat surface that goes on forever in all directions. Points A, B, and C all lie in the same plane.

Plane ABC

PRACTICE • Name the figures.

1.

2.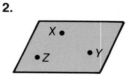

3.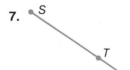

4.

5.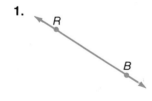

6.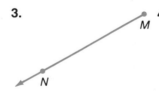

7.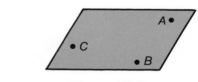

8.

9. Draw a line segment. Call it $\overline{XY}$.

10. Draw a line. Call it $\overleftrightarrow{RS}$.

11. Draw a ray. Call it $\overrightarrow{PB}$.

12. Draw a ray. Call it $\overrightarrow{BP}$.

13. Draw a line segment. Call it $\overline{PE}$.

14. Draw a line. Call it $\overleftrightarrow{AR}$.

EXERCISES • Name the figures.

Congruent line segments are the same length.
You can use a compass and a straightedge to construct a line segment
congruent to $\overline{AB}$.

Step 1
Draw $\overleftrightarrow{CD}$ to be
longer than $\overline{AB}$.

Step 2
Open the compass
to length AB.

Step 3
Put the compass point on C.
Draw a mark where the
compass meets line $\overleftrightarrow{CD}$.
Label it X.

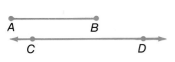

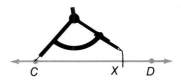

$\overline{CX}$ **is congruent to** $\overline{AB}$.

Use a compass and a straightedge to construct a line segment
congruent to each.

15. E   F

16. Q   R

17. Y   Z

18. L   M

PROBLEM SOLVING • APPLICATIONS

Use the plans for the park fountain to
answer Exercises 19–22.

19. Name 1 plane.

20. Name 4 line segments.

21. Name 3 lines.

22. Name 1 ray.

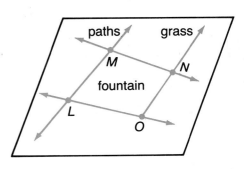

paths   grass

M   N

fountain

L

O

THINKER'S CORNER

Draw points X, Y, and Z not on the same line.

a. How many line segments can you draw using X, Y,
and Z as endpoints?

b. How many lines can you draw using points X, Y,
and Z?

c. How many lines can you draw through point Z?

Angles

The two sides of this roof meet at an *angle*. This type of roof is called a *gable* roof.

- Two rays that have the same endpoint form an **angle**.

  The endpoint is the **vertex**.

  The rays are the sides of the angle.

  The unit of measure for an angle is a **degree** (1°).

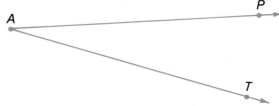

Angle *PAT* (∠*PAT*) or Angle *TAP* (∠*TAP*)

- The measure of a **right angle** is 90°.

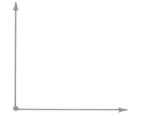

- The measure of an **acute angle** is greater than 0° and less than 90°.

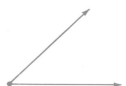

- The measure of an **obtuse angle** is greater than 90° and less than 180°.

PRACTICE • Name the angles. Then write RIGHT, ACUTE, or OBTUSE.

1.　　　　　2.　　　　　3.　　　　　4.

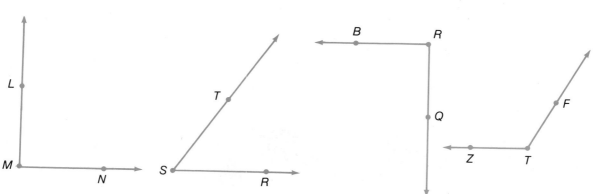

EXERCISES • Name the angles. Then write RIGHT, ACUTE, or OBTUSE.

5.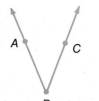

6.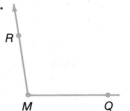

7.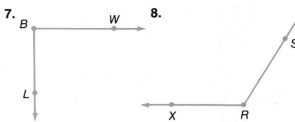

8.

9. Name the vertex of the angle.

10. Name the sides of the angle.

11. Name the angle.

12. Is the angle right, acute, or obtuse?

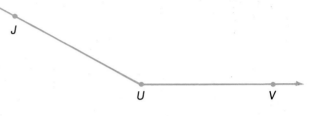

13. ∠*ABC* is an angle of the triangle. Name the other angles of the triangle.

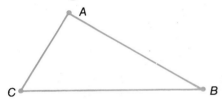

★ **14.** Name 10 angles.

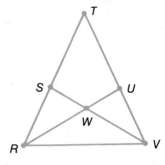

PROBLEM SOLVING • APPLICATIONS

Use the drawing of the ironing board at the right for Exercises 15–17.

15. Name two obtuse angles having *G* as the vertex.

16. Name two acute angles having *G* as the vertex.

17. Name one obtuse angle having *B* as the vertex.

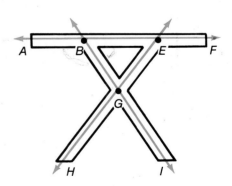

PROJECT Draw a sketch of the roofs of at least 5 buildings on your street. Use a red pencil to draw lines that show the angles made by the sides or edges of the roof with other parts of the house. Label the angles as acute, right, or obtuse.

Using a Protractor

A *sundial* tells time by measuring the angle of the shadow cast by the sun. Some people like to have a sundial in their yard or garden.

● You can use a **protractor** to measure angles.

Place the protractor so that the center mark is on the vertex of the angle and the edge is on one side of the angle. Read the scale where the other side crosses the protractor.

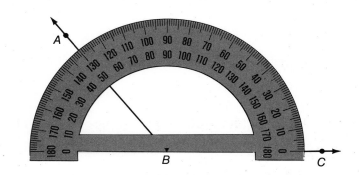

There are two numbers where the other side crosses the protractor. The numbers are 130 and 50. Since ∠ABC is obtuse, the measure of ∠ABC is 130°.

For ∠DEF, the two numbers on the scale are 110 and 70. Since ∠DEF is acute, the measure of ∠DEF is 70°.

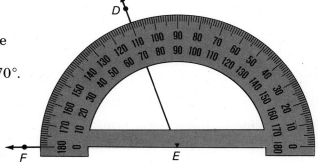

You can use a protractor to draw angles. Follow the directions.

● Draw ∠ZXY with a measure of 45°.

1. Draw $\overrightarrow{XY}$.

2. Place the protractor so that the center mark is at point X.

3. Line up the 0° mark with $\overrightarrow{XY}$.

4. Locate point Z at the 45° mark.

5. Draw $\overrightarrow{XZ}$.

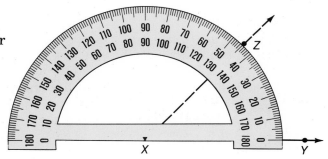

PRACTICE • Measure the angles.

1.

2.

3.

EXERCISES • Measure the angles.

4.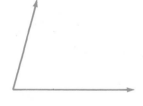

5.

6.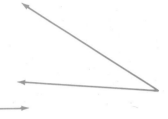

Use a protractor to draw the angles.

7. $\angle DEF$: 30°   **8.** $\angle JKL$: 150°   **9.** $\angle MNO$: 75°   **10.** $\angle PQR$: 100°

Congruent angles have the same measure.
The measure of $\angle PQR$ is 45°.
The measure of $\angle STU$ is 45°.

$\angle PQR$ is congruent to $\angle STU$.

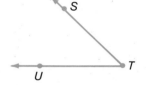

Measure each angle. Then use your protractor to draw a congruent angle for each.

11.

12.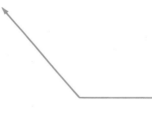

13.

PROBLEM SOLVING • **APPLICATIONS**

In this weather vane, the direction arrows meet at *P* to form four angles.

14. The measure of $\angle WPS$ is 135°, and $\angle NPE$ is congruent to $\angle WPS$. What is the measure of $\angle NPE$?

15. The measure of $\angle SPE$ is 45°, and $\angle WPN$ is congruent to $\angle SPE$. What is the measure of $\angle WPN$?

Parallel, Intersecting, and Perpendicular Lines

Decorative molding can be used
to make a small room seem
larger.

Parallel strips of molding can
make a narrow space seem
wider.

● **Parallel lines** are lines that
are always the same distance
apart. They will never meet.

$\overset{\leftrightarrow}{AB} \parallel \overset{\leftrightarrow}{CD}$

Intersecting strips of molding in
corners appear to make more
space.

● **Intersecting lines** are lines
that meet or cross each
other. They meet at a point.

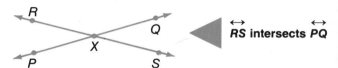

$\overset{\leftrightarrow}{RS}$ intersects $\overset{\leftrightarrow}{PQ}$

Molding which is perpendicular
to the ceiling makes the ceiling
seem higher.

● **Perpendicular lines** are
lines that intersect to form
right angles.

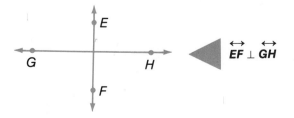

$\overset{\leftrightarrow}{EF} \perp \overset{\leftrightarrow}{GH}$

PRACTICE • Write PARALLEL, INTERSECTING, or PERPENDICULAR.

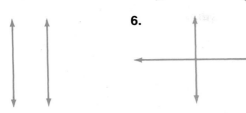
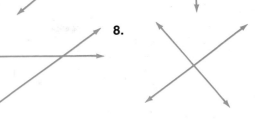

1.   **2.**   **3.**   **4.**

5.   **6.**   **7.**   **8.**

EXERCISES • Study the figure.

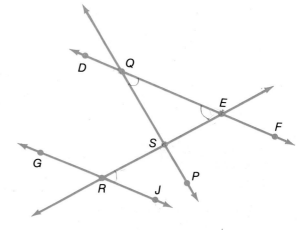

9. Name a pair of parallel lines.

10. Name 3 pairs of intersecting lines.

11. Name a pair of perpendicular lines.

12. Name 4 right angles.

13. Name 3 acute angles.

14. Name 3 obtuse angles.

15. Will $\overleftrightarrow{QP}$ intersect $\overleftrightarrow{GJ}$?

Lines that are not parallel and do not intersect are called **skew lines**.

Are they skew lines? Write YES or NO.

★ **16.** $\overleftrightarrow{AB}$ and $\overleftrightarrow{FG}$ ★ **17.** $\overleftrightarrow{DC}$ and $\overleftrightarrow{CB}$

★ **18.** $\overrightarrow{DA}$ and $\overrightarrow{BG}$ ★ **19.** $\overleftrightarrow{DE}$ and $\overleftrightarrow{CF}$

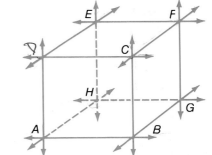

PROBLEM SOLVING • APPLICATIONS

Use the picture frames to answer Exercises 20–22.

20. Which line segments are parallel?

21. Which line segments intersect $\overline{QR}$?

22. Which line segments are perpendicular to $\overline{CD}$?

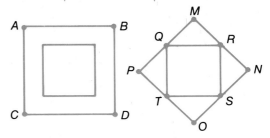

PROJECT   Photographers use lines when taking pictures. Find out how they do this. Bring to class pictures which illustrate the use of lines in photography.

PROBLEM SOLVING · STRATEGIES

Using Logical Reasoning

Example

George, Sam, Amanda and Sue each own a different vehicle: a dump truck, a pickup truck, a sports car, and a jeep. George does not own a car or a jeep. Amanda went to the beach with the owner of the sports car. Sam owns a dump truck.

● Which vehicle does Sue own?

You can use a chart to organize your conclusions.

Think Each person owns 1 vehicle.
There can be only one yes in each column and row.

Step 1

	Sports Car	Jeep	Pickup Truck	Dump Truck
Amanda				No
Sue				No
Sam	No	No	No	Yes
George	No	No		No

Step 2

	Sports Car	Jeep	Pickup Truck	Dump Truck
Amanda			**No**	No
Sue			**No**	No
Sam	No	No	No	Yes
George	No	No	**Yes**	No

Step 3

	Sports Car	Jeep	Pickup Truck	Dump Truck
Amanda	**No**	**Yes**	No	No
Sue	**Yes**	**No**	No	No
Sam	No	No	No	Yes
George	No	No	Yes	No

◀ Sam owns a dump truck.
George does not own a car or jeep.

◀ Since George doesn't own the car, jeep, or dump truck, he must own the pickup truck.

◀ Since Amanda does not own the sports car, she must own the jeep.

◀ Sue must own the sports car.

PROBLEMS

Choose the correct conclusion.

Eric owns a ten–speed or five–speed bike. He does not own a five–speed bike.

a. Eric owns a ten–speed bike.
b. Eric owns a five–speed bike.

2. All cats have whiskers. Sandy has a cat.

a. Sandy's cat does not have whiskers.
b. Sandy's cat does have whiskers.

3. Some buildings in Leewood have fire escapes. The Crocker building is in Leewood.

a. The Crocker building has fire escapes.
b. The Crocker building may, or may not, have fire escapes.

What information are you given?

4. Some architects are carpenters. Jane Smalley is a carpenter.

a. Jane Smalley may, or may not, be an architect.
b. Jane Smalley is an architect.

5. All angles have a vertex. Angle *A* is a right angle.

a. Angle *A* has a vertex.
b. Angle *A* may, or may not, have a vertex.

Solve the problems. Use a chart to organize your conclusions.

6. Armondo, Carol, Ida, and Louis have different job titles: architect, carpenter, interior designer, and landscaper. No person's name begins with the same first letter as that person's profession. Armondo cannot work with outdoor plants. Ida works with nails all day. What is each person's profession?

What conclusions can you make?

7. Fran, Harold, Susan, and Ted each sketched a design for one building: a fire station, a house, a school, and a theater. No person's name begins with the same first letter as the building. Fran designed the theater. Susan did not design the house. Which design did each person sketch?

8. Betty, Jim, Manuel, and Rosa won the first four prizes in a design contest. Jim won second prize. Manuel did not win third prize. Rosa won fourth prize. What prize did Betty win?

MID-CHAPTER REVIEW

Name the figures. (Pages 330-331)

1.

2.

3.

4.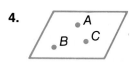

5. Draw a line.
Call it $\overleftrightarrow{GH}$.

6. Draw a line segment.
Call it $\overline{IJ}$.

7. Draw a ray.
Call it $\overrightarrow{KL}$.

Name the angles. Then write RIGHT, ACUTE, or OBTUSE. (Pages 332-333)

8.

9.

10.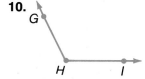

11.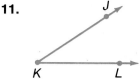

Measure the angles. Use a protractor to draw a congruent angle for each.
(Pages 334-335)

12.

13.

14.

Write PARALLEL, INTERSECTING, or PERPENDICULAR. (Pages 336-337)

15.

16.

17.

18.

Choose the correct conclusions. (Pages 338–339)

19. All two-story homes have stairs.
Maxim's house has two stories.

   a. Maxim's house has stairs.
   b. Maxim's house may, or may not have two stories.

20. Some architects design shopping centers. Josh McGuire is an architect.

   a. Josh McGuire designs shopping centers.
   b. Josh McGuire may, or may not, design shopping centers.

MAINTENANCE • MIXED PRACTICE

Add.

1. $2\frac{1}{8} + 8\frac{4}{8} = $ ____?____

2. $3\frac{3}{4} + 5\frac{1}{2} = $ ____?____

3. $15\frac{7}{8} + 22\frac{5}{6} = $ ____?____

Subtract.

4. $9\frac{4}{5} - 3\frac{1}{5} = $ ____?____

5. $5\frac{7}{10} - 2\frac{3}{5} = $ ____?____

6. $5\frac{5}{6} - 3\frac{1}{4} = $ ____?____

Interior Designer

Interior designers suggest which paint and wallpaper you should use in your home.

To find the amount of wallpaper needed for a room, an interior designer can use a table. First, the designer must answer the **hidden question:**

"How much must be subtracted for the doors and windows?"

CEILING HEIGHT	8 Feet	9 Feet	10 Feet
Size of Room in Feet	NUMBER OF SINGLE ROLLS		
8 × 10	9	10	11
10 × 10	10	11	13
10 × 12	11	12	14
10 × 14	12	14	15
12 × 12	12	14	15
12 × 14	13	15	16

NOTE: Subtract 1 roll for every door. Subtract 1 roll for every two windows.

EXAMPLE: A room is $9\frac{1}{2}$ feet wide and $11\frac{3}{4}$ feet long. The ceiling is 8 feet high. The room has 2 doors and 3 windows. How many single rolls of wallpaper are needed?

$\boxed{1}$ Round $9\frac{1}{2}$ and $11\frac{3}{4}$ up to the next foot $\longrightarrow$ **10 × 12**

$\boxed{2}$ Use the table to find the number of rolls $\longrightarrow$ **11**

$\boxed{3}$ Calculate the allowance for windows and doors.

2 doors	2	rolls
3 windows	$1\frac{1}{2}$	rolls
Total Allowance	$3\frac{1}{2}$	rolls

◀ **See the note in the table**

$\boxed{4}$ Subtract $11 - 3\frac{1}{2} = 7\frac{1}{2}$

Number of rolls needed: **8** ◀ **Round up to the next whole number.**

EXERCISES • Find the number of single rolls of wallpaper needed for each room.

	Room	Length	Width	Ceiling Height	Number of Doors	Number of Windows
1.	Den	$9\frac{1}{2}$ft	$9\frac{1}{2}$ft	8 ft	2	4
2.	Kitchen	$7\frac{3}{4}$ft	$9\frac{1}{2}$ft	9 ft	1	5
3.	Living Room	$11\frac{1}{2}$ft	12 ft	10 ft	3	4
4.	Bedroom	$9\frac{1}{2}$ft	$13\frac{1}{2}$ft	8 ft	2	3

PROJECT Make a plan to wallpaper a room in your home. Measure the room. Select the wallpaper. Find the cost.

Polygons

Landscape architects plan the use of land. Sometimes they use wooden decks to create attractive and useful outdoor areas. In this deck design, all of the various shapes are **polygons.**

● The sides of a **polygon** are line segments. The sides meet to form angles.

Names are given to polygons according to the number of sides and the number of angles they have.

● **Triangles** are polygons that have three sides. Some triangles have special names.

Equilateral
There are three congruent sides.

Isosceles
There are at least two congruent sides.

Scalene
There are no congruent sides.

● **Quadrilaterals** are polygons that have four sides. Some quadrilaterals have special names.

Parallelogram
A quadrilateral whose opposite sides are parallel and congruent

Rhombus
A parallelogram with four congruent sides

Rectangle
A parallelogram with four right angles

Square
A rectangle with four congruent sides

Trapezoid
A quadrilateral with two and only two sides parallel

● These polygons are also named according to the number of sides and angles.

Pentagon
5 sides
5 angles

Hexagon
6 sides
6 angles

Octagon
8 sides
8 angles

Decagon
10 sides
10 angles

PRACTICE • Name the polygons.

1.
2.
3.
4.

EXERCISES • Name the polygons.

5.
6.
7.
8.

Which polygons below are

9. quadrilaterals?
10. rectangles?
11. squares?

12. rhombuses?
13. parallelograms?
14. trapezoids?

a.
b.
c.
d.
e.
f.

A **diagonal** is a line segment that joins vertices of a polygon but is not a side.

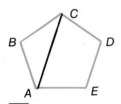

$\overline{AC}$ is a diagonal.

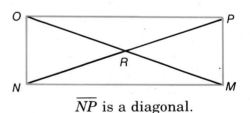

$\overline{NP}$ is a diagonal.

15. Name the triangles formed by the diagonals in the rectangle.

16. Trace pentagon *ABCDE*. Draw the other diagonals. Name them.

PROBLEM SOLVING • APPLICATIONS

17. In this landscaping plan, name the polygon each letter identifies.

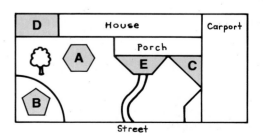

Congruent Polygons

Tim's parents are laying square tiles on their kitchen floor. Each tile is exactly the same size and shape.

● Polygons which have the same size and shape are **congruent.**

Trace triangle *STU*.
Place the tracing over triangle *MNO*.
The tracing fits exactly.
Triangle *STU* **is congruent to** triangle *MNO*.

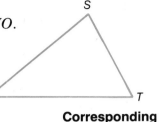
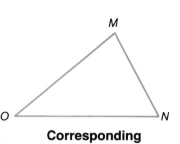

The parts that fit together are called **corresponding parts.** If the polygons are congruent, then their corresponding parts are also congruent. The symbol ↔ means "corresponds to."

Corresponding sides	Corresponding angles
$\overline{ST} \leftrightarrow \overline{MN}$	$\angle S \leftrightarrow \angle M$
$\overline{TU} \leftrightarrow \overline{NO}$	$\angle T \leftrightarrow \angle N$
$\overline{US} \leftrightarrow \overline{OM}$	$\angle U \leftrightarrow \angle O$

PRACTICE • Are they congruent? Write YES or NO. Use a tracing to help you.

1.

2.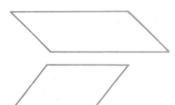

3.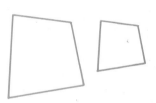

Triangles *EFG* and *QRS* are congruent. Name the corresponding parts.

4. $\overline{EF} \leftrightarrow$ ___?___

5. $\angle E \leftrightarrow$ ___?___

6. $\overline{FG} \leftrightarrow$ ___?___

7. $\angle F \leftrightarrow$ ___?___

8. $\overline{GE} \leftrightarrow$ ___?___

9. $\angle G \leftrightarrow$ ___?___

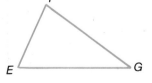

EXERCISES • Are they congruent? Write YES or NO.

10.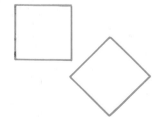

11.

12.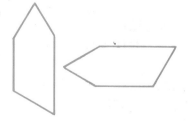

Quadrilaterals *JKLM* and *WXYZ* are congruent. Name the corresponding parts.

13. $\overline{JK}$ ↔ ___?___

14. ∠*J* ↔ ___?___

15. $\overline{KL}$ ↔ ___?___

16. ∠*K* ↔ ___?___

17. $\overline{LM}$ ↔ ___?___

18. ∠*L* ↔ ___?___

19. $\overline{MJ}$ ↔ ___?___

20. ∠*M* ↔ ___?___

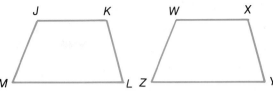

21. Find two pairs of congruent polygons. Use a tracing to help you.
    Then name the corresponding parts of the congruent polygons.

a.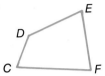
b.
c.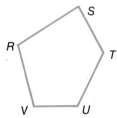
d.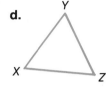

e.
f.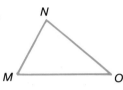
g.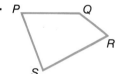
h.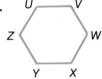

You must use three letters to name an angle when two angles have the same vertex.

∠*D* could be ∠*EDH*, ∠*GDF*, or ∠*EDF*.

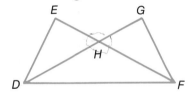

★ 22. Name two pairs of congruent triangles.

★ 23. List their corresponding sides and angles.

PROBLEM SOLVING • APPLICATIONS

Rebecca cuts a piece of wood to make a
brace for this gate. The brace, $\overline{AC}$, forms
two congruent triangles with sides *AB*,
BC, *CD*, and *DA*. Triangle *ABC* is
congruent to triangle *CDA*.

24. Name the corresponding congruent
    sides of the triangles.

★ 25. Name the corresponding congruent
    angles.

Circles

A landscape architect designs a lawn sprinkler system. She uses a compass to draw circles to show how far each sprinkler will reach.

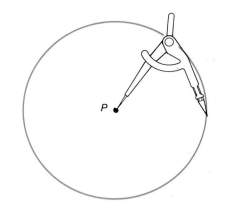

- Point *P* is the **center** of the circle. This circle is called circle *P*.

- A **radius** of the circle is a segment that joins the center and a point on the circle. All radii of the same circle have the same length.

$\overline{PB}$ and $\overline{PA}$ are radii of circle *P*. The length of $\overline{PB}$ is 3 centimeters.

A **chord** is a segment that joins two points on the circle.

$\overline{DE}$ is a chord.

A **diameter** is a chord that passes through the center of the circle. It is twice as long as the length of a radius.

$\overline{BC}$ is a diameter. The length of $\overline{BC}$ is 6 centimeters.

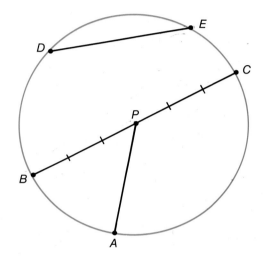

PRACTICE • Study the figure.

1. What is the name of this circle?

2. Name two chords of this circle.

3. How long is radius *BR*?

4. How long is radius *BQ*?

5. If you drew another radius for this circle, how long would it be?

6. How long is diameter *PR*?

7. How is the length of diameter *PR* related to the length of radius *PB*?

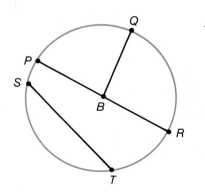

EXERCISES • Study the figure.

8. Name the circle.
9. Name three radii.
10. Name three chords.
11. Name a diameter.
12. Name an obtuse angle.
13. Name an acute angle.

In each circle, point *M* is the center.
Name the segments that are radii.

14.
15.
16.
17.

In each circle point *L* is the center.
Name the segments that are diameters.

18.
19.
20.
21.

Complete.

	22.	23.	24.	25.	26.	27.	★ 28.	★ 29.
Radius	8 cm	?	13 km	?	9.8 m	?	?	?
Diameter	?	124 mm	?	264 m	?	32.4 cm	5.52 m	1.06 m

Draw segments with the lengths given.
Use each as a radius to construct a circle.

30. 4 cm   31. 6 cm   32. 2.5 cm   33. 6.5 cm   34. 30 mm

PROBLEM SOLVING • APPLICATIONS

35. The Tuckers put lamps along one edge of their driveway. Each light provides a radius of 2 feet of illumination. How many lights will they need?

Driveway

←————— 20 ft —————→

36. A landscape architect designs a circular tulip garden having a radius of 5.85 meters. Estimate the circumference of the garden.

   a. 18 m   **b.** 30 m   **c.** 36 m

Symmetry and Reflections

The drawing at the right shows an architect's design for an airport terminal building.

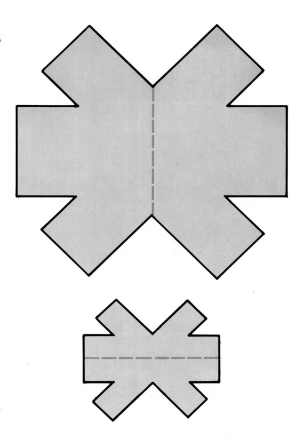

Trace the design and the dotted line. Cut it out. Fold along the dotted line. Do the halves match?

● The figure is **symmetric.**

● The dotted line is a **line of symmetry.**

Unfold the figure. Now fold it along the line shown in the small picture.

How many lines of symmetry have you found for this figure?

Are there other lines of symmetry for this figure?

There are only two lines of symmetry.

Trace the parallelogram and cut it out.

How many lines of symmetry does this figure have?
The figure has no lines of symmetry.

You can **flip** a figure along a line of symmetry to see a **mirror image** (or **reflection image**) of the figure.

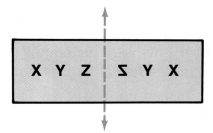

PRACTICE • Is the dotted line a line of symmetry for the figure? Write YES or NO.

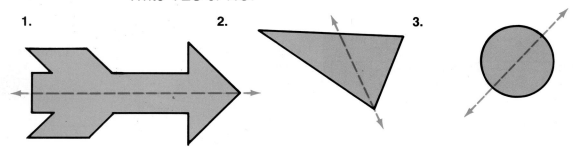

1.   **2.**   **3.**

EXERCISES • Trace the figures. Draw the lines of symmetry.

4.

5.

6.

Do the pictures show mirror images? Write YES or NO.

7.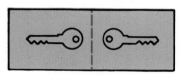

8.

9.

Trace the drawings. Then complete them to make figures that are symmetric.

10.

11.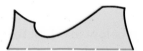

12.

★ **13.** Make your own snowflake.

Draw a circle.
Cut it out.

Fold it in half.

Fold again into thirds.

Cut out a pattern.
Unfold a snowflake.

PROBLEM SOLVING • APPLICATIONS

14. Matt wants to hang a picture on each side of his fireplace. The fireplace is in the exact center of the wall. He hangs one picture 1 meter down from the ceiling and 1 meter to the right of the fireplace. To keep the symmetry of the fireplace and the pictures, where should Matt hang the other picture?

15. Carol is hanging new drapes on a window 48 inches wide. The rod is 58 inches long. Draw a sketch to show the measurements Carol must use to place the rod so that the drapes will hang symmetrically over the window.

THINKER'S CORNER

Sophie brings home a round of cheese. Her father asks her if she can cut it into 8 congruent pieces with only three cuts. How can she do it?

Solid Figures

Architects design lofts to create more floor space. This loft bed is built on top of a closet. The closet is an example of a **cube.**

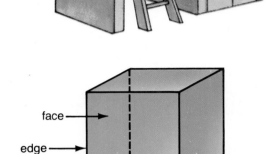

- A cube is a solid figure. Each flat surface of a cube is a face. A cube has six faces.

- The shape of each face is a **square.**

- Two faces meet at an **edge.**

- Edges meet at a **vertex.**

- The cube rests on its **base.**

face ⟶
edge ⟶
base
vertex ⟶

- The cube and the solid figures below are **prisms**. The shape of the base is used to name the prism. What is the shape of each of the other faces?

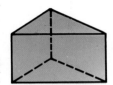

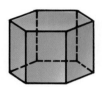

Triangular Prism   Rectangular Prism   Hexagonal Prism

The shape of the other faces is a rectangle. The top face of each prism is the same shape as the base.

- These solid figures are **pyramids**. The shape of the base is used to name the pyramid. What is the shape of each of the other faces?

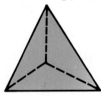
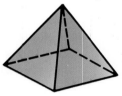
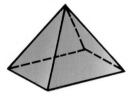

Triangular Pyramid   Square Pyramid   Rectangular Pyramid   Hexagonal Pyramid

The shape of each of the other faces is a triangle.

These are some other special solid figures.   Cylinder   Cone   Sphere

PRACTICE • Name the shapes.

1.

2.

3.

4.

EXERCISES • Name the shapes.

5.

6.

7.

8.

Complete.

	Figure	Number of Faces	Number of Edges	Number of Vertices
9.	Cube	6	?	?
10.	Triangular pyramid	?	?	?
11.	Hexagonal pyramid	?	?	?
12.	Rectangular prism	?	?	?
13.	Triangular prism	?	?	?
14.	Hexagonal prism	?	?	?
15.	Square pyramid	?	?	?

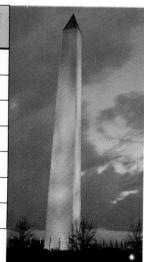

PROBLEM SOLVING • APPLICATIONS

Each of these patterns can be folded to make a solid figure.
Name the figures.

16.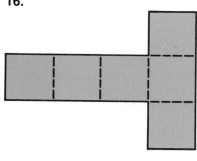

17.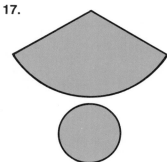

18.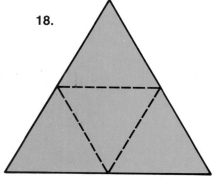

PROBLEM SOLVING · STRATEGIES

Patterns

Sometimes you must find a pattern in order to solve a problem.
Geometric figures can be used to make patterns.

Example 1

A park landscaper used this
pattern for the design of the
park markers.

● What figures will be used for the next three markers?

Think   There are three different figures.
They are arranged in a certain order.
The order repeats itself.

The next three figures would look like this:

Example 2

● What is the next figure in this pattern?

Think   There is one figure.
It changes its position.

The next figure would be:

More Examples

Change of size and figure

Same figure, adding line segments

PROBLEMS • Complete the pattern.

1. △ □ ⬠ ⬡ __?__ __?__

2. □ ○ ◯ □ __?__ __?__

3. ◻ ◻ ◻ __?__

4. ⊤ ⊥ ⊤ __?__

How are the figures related?

5. △ ◁▷ △△ __?__

6. ◉ ◉ ◉ __?__

7. ▯△▫ ▯△ __?__

8. □ ▣ □ __?__

9. □ ■ □ □ ■ __?__ __?__ __?__

10. □ ◁ ◹ __?__ __?__

11. ◔ ◑ ◕ __?__

12. ∩ ⊃ ∪ __?__

13. ⬡ ⬡ ⬡ __?__

How are the first two figures related?
Choose the correct answer.

14. △ is to ▲ as □ is to?

a. b. c. d.

15. △ is to □ as ▲ is to?

a. b. c. d.

How does the second figure change?

16. △ is to □ as ⬠ is to?

a. b. c. d.

17. ⌐ is to ⌐ as ◔ is to?

a. b. c. d.

18. ∃ is to E as ⊤ is to?

a. b. c. d.

CHAPTER REVIEW

Part 1 • VOCABULARY

For Exercises 1–8, choose from the box at
the right the word that completes the sentence.

1. A __?__ goes on forever in both directions.   (Page 330)

2. A flat surface that goes on forever
   in all directions is a __?__.   (Page 330)

3. Two rays that have the same vertex
   form an __?__.   (Page 336)

4. Lines that meet to form right angles
   are __?__ lines.   (Page 336)

5. A figure made from line segments which meet
   to form angles is called a __?__.   (Page 342)

6. Quadrilaterals that have the same size and shape
   are called __?__ quadrilaterals.   (Page 344)

7. A diameter of a circle is twice the
   length of the __?__.   (Page 346)

8. When the two halves of a figure fit exactly on
   each other, the figure is __?__.   (Page 348)

angle
congruent
line
perpendicular
plane
polygon
radius
symmetric

Part 2 • SKILLS

Name the figures.   (Pages 330–331)

9.

10.

11.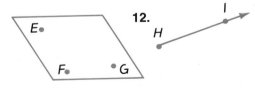

12.

Name the angles. Then write RIGHT, ACUTE, or OBTUSE.   (Pages 332–333)

13.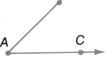

14.

15.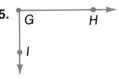

16.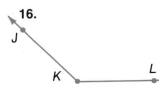

Measure the angles.   (Pages 334–335)

17.

18.

19.

Write PARALLEL, INTERSECTING, or PERPENDICULAR.   (Pages 336–337)

20.

21.

22.

23.

Name the polygons.   (Pages 342–343)

24.

25.

26.

27.

Triangles *ABC* and *XYZ* are congruent. Name the corresponding parts. (Pages 344–345)

28. $\overrightarrow{AB} \leftrightarrow$ _?_

29. $\overrightarrow{BC} \leftrightarrow$ _?_

30. $\angle C \leftrightarrow$ _?_ .

31. $\angle A \leftrightarrow$ _?_

Use the circle to find the answers.   (Pages 346–347)

32. Name the circle.

33. Name a diameter.

34. Name a radius.

35. Name a chord.

Trace the figures. Draw the lines of symmetry.   (Pages 348–349)

36.

37.

38.

Name the figures.   (Pages 350–351)

39.

40.

41.

42.

Part 3 • *PROBLEM SOLVING* • *APPLICATIONS*

43. Choose the correct conclusion.

All giraffes have long necks.
Biki is a giraffe.

a. Biki's neck is long.
b. Biki's neck is short.

(Pages 338–339)

44. Complete the pattern:
(Pages 352–353)

a. **b.** **c.**

CHAPTER TEST

Name the figures.

1.

2.

3.

4.

Write PARALLEL, INTERSECTING, or PERPENDICULAR.

5.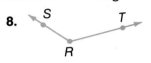

6.

7.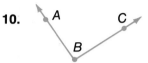

Measure the angles. Write ACUTE, RIGHT, or OBTUSE.

8.

9.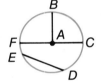

10.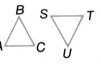

Name the polygons.

11.

12.

13.

14. Name the circle.
15. Name a radius.
16. Name the diameter.
17. Name a chord.

18. Triangles ABC and SUT are congruent. Name the corresponding sides.

Is the dashed line a line of symmetry for the figure. Write YES or NO.

19.

20.

Name the shapes. Complete.

21. ___?___ edges

22. ___?___ vertices

23. ___?___ faces

Complete the pattern.

24. F ⊓ ⊣ ⊔ F ___?___

25. A hotel has four meeting rooms: the Citrus, the Orange, the Gulf, and the Seacoast. The carpet in each room is a different color: gold, red, beige, or brown. The Gulf Room is the largest. The Citrus Room has gold carpeting. The colors of the carpet in the Orange and Gulf Rooms begin with the same letter. The largest room does not have beige carpeting. Which room has the beige carpet?

ENRICHMENT

Translations

As you learned in Chapter 5, you can use an ordered pair of numbers to locate points on a grid.

Study parallelogram *ABCD*. Point *A* is located at (8, 5). Name the locations of points *B*, *C*, and *D*.

Suppose you wanted to slide parallelogram *ABCD* to a new position—4 units to the right and 5 units up.

Follow these steps:

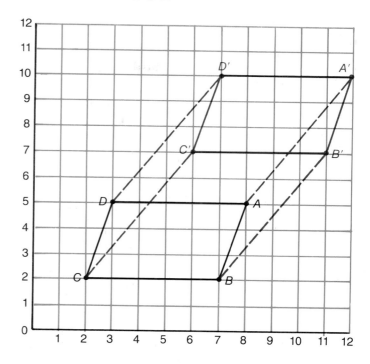

Step 1 Mark point *A'* (read: *A* prime) at (12, 10), the point that is 4 units to the right and 5 units up from Point *A*.

Step 2 Mark point *B'* at (11, 7), the point that is 4 units to the right and 5 units up from point *B*.

Step 3 Mark point *C'* at (6, 7), the point that is 4 units to the right and 5 units up from point *C*.

Step 4 Mark point *D'* at (7, 10), the point that is 4 units to the right and 5 units up from point *D*.

Step 5 Connect points *A'*, *B'*, *C'*, and *D'* in order.

● The new parallelogram, *A' B' C' D'*, is called a **slide image** or **translation image** of parallelogram *ABCD*. Are parallelograms *ABCD* and *A' B' C' D'* congruent? How can you prove your answer?

EXERCISES

On a piece of graph paper, make three copies of the grid and parallelogram *ABCD*. Then make three translation images, sliding the parallelogram to these new positions.

1. 7 units up   **2.** 2 units to the right and 3 units up

3. 1 unit to the left and 2 units down

ADDITIONAL PRACTICE

SKILLS

Name the figures. (Pages 330–331)

1.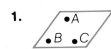
2.
3.
4.

Measure the angles. Use a protractor to draw a congruent angle for each.
(Pages 334–335)

5.
6.
7.
8.

Write PARALLEL, INTERSECTING, or PERPENDICULAR. (Pages 336–337)

9.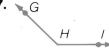
10.
11.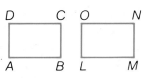
12.

Name the polygons. (Pages 342–343)

13.
14.
15.
16.

Quadrilaterals *ABCD* and *LMNO* are congruent. Name
the corresponding parts. (Pages 344–345)

17. $\overline{DA} \leftrightarrow$ ___?___

18. $\overline{AB} \leftrightarrow$ ___?___

19. $\angle B \leftrightarrow$ ___?___

20. $\angle C \leftrightarrow$ ___?___

Use the circle to find the answers. (Pages 346–347)

21. Name the circle.

22. Name a diameter.

23. Name a radius.

24. Name a chord.

Name the shapes. (Pages 350–351)

25. **26.** **27.** **28.**

PROBLEM SOLVING • APPLICATIONS

29. Choose the correct conclusion.

Some pools are rectangular. The
Smyths have a pool.

a. The Smyth's pool is rectangular.
b. The Smyth's pool may, or may
not be rectangular.
(Pages 338–339)

30. Complete the pattern.
(Pages 352–353)

⨆⨆⨆ ___?___

a. ⨆ **b.** ⨆ **c.** ⨆

PROBLEM SOLVING MAINTENANCE
Chapters 10 through 12

1. Carol is making a dress. She needs 14 yards of lace to trim the dress. Lace comes in 5 yard rolls. How many rolls of lace will she need to buy? (Page 284)

2. The sixth grade students at Southville School are going on a trip. Each bus seats 30 people. There are 115 students. How many buses will they need? (Page 284)

Work backward to solve Exercise 3.

3. Rick shelves books for the library. On Friday he shelved 450 books. On Wednesday he shelved twice as many books as he did on Monday. On Friday he had shelved 50 more books than he shelved on Wednesday. How many books did he shelve on Monday? (Page 274)

4. Beth is wrapping a present. She needs $2\frac{1}{3}$ feet of ribbon to go around the box and $3\frac{3}{4}$ feet of ribbon to make a bow. Estimate how many feet of ribbon she will need. (Page 302)

   a. 6 ft   b. 5 ft   c. 7 ft

5. Steve is building a book shelf. It will be $6\frac{2}{9}$ feet long. He has a board $8\frac{7}{8}$ feet long. Estimate how much of the board will be left over. (Page 302)

   a. 5 ft   b. 3 ft   c. 2 ft

Choose the correct conclusion.

6. All the houses in Greenville have brown roofs. Brian lives in Greenville. (Page 338)

   a. Brian's house has a brown roof.
   b. Brian's house does not have a brown roof.

7. Some students like math. Rita is a student. (Page 338)

   a. Rita likes math.
   b. Rita may, or may not, like math.

8. Complete the pattern. (Page 352)

Write an equation. Solve.

9. Marisa works 5 days a week. She works $6\frac{1}{2}$ hours a day. How many hours a week does she work? (Page 240)

10. Sol, Beatrice, Maria and Corliss live in different kinds of homes. One lives in a condiminium, one lives in a house, one lives in an apartment and one lives in a mobile home. Corliss does not like apartment living. Beatrice bought her own condominium. Maria likes to take her home with her when she moves. Where does each one live? (Page 338)

Mixed Practice • Choose the correct answers.

1. What part is blue?

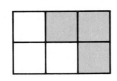

 A. $\frac{2}{6}$ B. $\frac{6}{3}$
 C. $\frac{3}{6}$ D. not here

2. $\frac{3}{4} = \frac{?}{28}$

 A. 18   B. 7
 C. 21   D. not here

3. $\frac{5}{13} = \frac{20}{?}$

 A. 52   B. 28
 C. 4   D. not here

4. $\frac{12}{50} = \frac{?}{100}$

 A. 12   B. 26
 C. 14   D. not here

5. 2×6 ⬤ 3×4

 A. =   B. <
 C. >   D. not here

6. 3×7 ⬤ 4×6

 A. =   B. >
 C. <   D. not here

7. Write 0.67 as a fraction.

 A. $6\frac{7}{10}$ B. $\frac{1}{67}$
 C. $6\frac{7}{100}$ D. not here

8. Write $\frac{86}{100}$ as a decimal.

 A. 86.00   B. 8.6
 C. 0.86   D. not here

9. Write $\frac{3}{10}$ as a decimal.

 A. 0.3   B. 0.03
 C. 3   D. not here

10. Write 0.25 as a fraction.

 A. $\frac{1}{2}$ B. $\frac{1}{5}$
 C. $\frac{1}{4}$ D. not here

11. $\frac{1}{2}$ of 36 = _____

 A. 18   B. 72
 C. 16   D. not here

12. $\frac{2}{3}$ of 90 = _____

 A. 135   B. 60
 C. 324   D. not here

13. Sophie spent $2.00 for 5 combs. What is the price of 1 comb?

 A. $0.40   B. $0.50
 C. $0.30   D. not here

14. Mr. Barker earns $1,785 each month. He spends about $\frac{1}{3}$ of his pay for rent. Estimate how much he will pay each month for rent.

 A. $900   B. $250
 C. $600   D. not here

Ratio and Percent

Rosemary's hobby is photography. This photo and its enlargement have the same shape but not the same size.

● Complete: The polygons are _?_ .

● Complete: The ratios of the lengths of the corresponding sides of the polygons are _?_ .

Ted's hobby is reading about the history of our country. He learned that by 1818, the U.S. flag had 20 stars for 20 states. Within 3 years, there were 15% more stars.

● How many stars were added in 3 years?

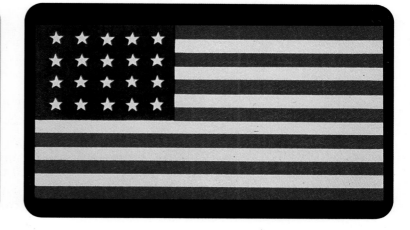

361

Ratio

People take part in recreational activities for enjoyment and relaxation. Many people enjoy outdoor forms of recreation.

This picture shows 4 baseball bats and 3 catcher's mitts.
The *ratio* of bats to mitts is **4 to 3.**

Here are three ways to show the ratio.

4 to 3   **4:3** $\frac{4}{3}$

● A **ratio** is a way of comparing numbers.

● Find each ratio.

a. mitts to bats   **b.** bats to mitts plus bats

a. **Think**   Mitts: 3   Bats: 4   **b.** **Think**   Bats: 4   Bats + mitts: 7

Ratio: $\frac{3}{4}$ ⟵ **Number of mitts**
                  ⟵ **Number of bats**

Ratio: $\frac{4}{7}$ ⟵ **Number of bats**
                  ⟵ **Bats + mitts**

PRACTICE • **Mental Math** Name a fraction for each ratio.

1. roller skates to ice skates

2. ice skates to roller skates

3. roller skates to all the skates

4. 3 to 8

5. 7 to 4

6. 10 to 1

7. 2 to 9

8. 14:3

9. 25:100

10. 45:23

11. 26:50

12. baseballs to mitts

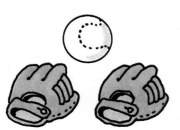

13. hats to whistles

14. hockey sticks to golf clubs

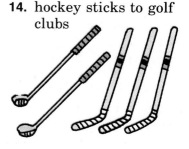

15. golf balls to tees

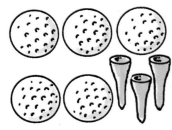

16. tennis rackets to bats and rackets

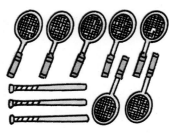

17. skis to boots

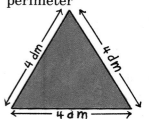

18. length to width

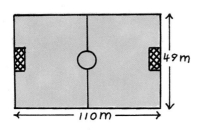

19. length of the base to height

★ 20. length of a side to perimeter

21. 2 to 5	**22.** 7 to 13	**23.** 9 to 4	**24.** 17 to 32
25. 6 to 1	**26.** 4 to 7	**27.** 8 to 21	**28.** 5 to 92
29. 225 : 48	**30.** 15 : 19	**31.** 72 : 10	**32.** 47 : 100

PROBLEM SOLVING • APPLICATIONS

33. Mavis is putting away 3 helmets and 4 hats. What is the ratio of hats to helmets?

34. In the basement Sally found 1 baseball in a mitt. What is the ratio of baseballs to mitts?

★ 35. Jane and Angela have 2 pairs of yellow shoelaces, 3 pairs of orange shoelaces, and 2 pairs of skates. What is the ratio of pairs of orange shoelaces to pairs of skates? What information was not needed to answer the question?

★ 36. There are 2 wooden hockey sticks, 3 wooden baseball bats, and 4 metal tennis rackets in the garage. What is the ratio of wooden objects to metal objects?

Ratio and Proportion

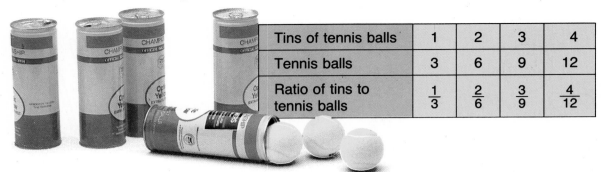

Tins of tennis balls	1	2	3	4
Tennis balls	3	6	9	12
Ratio of tins to tennis balls	$\frac{1}{3}$	$\frac{2}{6}$	$\frac{3}{9}$	$\frac{4}{12}$

Each tin contains 3 tennis balls.
No matter how many tins you buy, the ratio of tins to tennis balls remains the same.

$$\frac{1}{3} = \frac{2}{6} = \frac{3}{9} = \frac{4}{12}$$ ◀ **Equal ratios**

● A **proportion** is a statement that two ratios are equal.

Number of tins ⟶ $\dfrac{2}{6} = \dfrac{3}{9}$ ⟵ Number of tins
Number of tennis balls ⟶ $\phantom{\dfrac{2}{6} = \dfrac{3}{9}}$ ⟵ Number of tennis balls

● You can use **cross products** to test a proportion.
If the cross products are equal, then the proportion is true.
The ratios are equal.

● Is the proportion $\frac{2}{6} = \frac{7}{21}$ true?

Think Use cross products.

$$\frac{2}{6} \overset{?}{=} \frac{7}{21}$$

2×21 ● 7×6 ⟵ Cross products ⟶
42 ● 42
$=$

Yes, the proportion is **true.**
The ratios are equal.

● Is the proportion $\frac{11}{31} = \frac{3}{9}$ true?

Think Use cross products.

$$\frac{11}{31} \overset{?}{=} \frac{3}{9}$$

11×9 ● 3×31
99 ● 93
$\neq$

No, the proportion is **not true.**
The ratios are not equal.

● You can also use cross products to solve proportions.

● Solve for n: $\frac{3}{72} = \frac{n}{120}$

Think Use cross products.

$$\frac{3}{72} = \frac{n}{120}$$
$$72 \times n = 3 \times 120$$
$$72 \times n = 360$$
$$n = 360 \div 72$$
$$n = 5$$

Since the cross products are equal, the ratios are equal when $n = 5$.

Mental Math Is the proportion true? Compare the cross products.

1. $\dfrac{4}{5} = \dfrac{16}{20}$ 2. $\dfrac{2}{3} = \dfrac{20}{40}$ 3. $\dfrac{3}{4} = \dfrac{18}{24}$ 4. $\dfrac{1}{2} = \dfrac{4}{6}$

Write = or ≠.

5. $\dfrac{1}{8}$ ⬤ $\dfrac{3}{24}$ 6. $\dfrac{4}{7}$ ⬤ $\dfrac{2}{3}$ 7. $\dfrac{5}{9}$ ⬤ $\dfrac{4}{7}$ 8. $\dfrac{6}{20}$ ⬤ $\dfrac{3}{10}$

EXERCISES • Is the proportion true? Compare the cross products. Then write YES or NO.

9. $\dfrac{2}{5} = \dfrac{10}{25}$ 10. $\dfrac{2}{9} = \dfrac{14}{64}$ 11. $\dfrac{3}{8} = \dfrac{9}{24}$ 12. $\dfrac{7}{10} = \dfrac{18}{25}$

13. $\dfrac{4}{15} = \dfrac{6}{22}$ 14. $\dfrac{7}{8} = \dfrac{28}{32}$ 15. $\dfrac{9}{3} = \dfrac{3}{1}$ 16. $\dfrac{5}{6} = \dfrac{3}{4}$

Write = or ≠.

17. $\dfrac{5}{8}$ ⬤ $\dfrac{15}{24}$ 18. $\dfrac{1}{4}$ ⬤ $\dfrac{1}{3}$ 19. $\dfrac{2}{7}$ ⬤ $\dfrac{5}{28}$ 20. $\dfrac{10}{4}$ ⬤ $\dfrac{5}{2}$

21. $\dfrac{3}{14}$ ⬤ $\dfrac{5}{12}$ 22. $\dfrac{35}{40}$ ⬤ $\dfrac{7}{8}$ 23. $\dfrac{4}{9}$ ⬤ $\dfrac{12}{27}$ 24. $\dfrac{3}{5}$ ⬤ $\dfrac{4}{6}$

Solve each proportion.

25. $\dfrac{6}{8} = \dfrac{n}{12}$ 26. $\dfrac{9}{15} = \dfrac{n}{10}$ 27. $\dfrac{3}{9} = \dfrac{n}{21}$ 28. $\dfrac{12}{9} = \dfrac{n}{12}$

29. $\dfrac{15}{20} = \dfrac{n}{16}$ 30. $\dfrac{14}{4} = \dfrac{n}{12}$ 31. $\dfrac{12}{8} = \dfrac{n}{18}$ 32. $\dfrac{12}{30} = \dfrac{n}{15}$

★ 33. $\dfrac{0.9}{1.8} = \dfrac{n}{2.4}$ ★ 34. $\dfrac{1.6}{2.8} = \dfrac{4}{n}$ ★ 35. $\dfrac{2.5}{4} = \dfrac{n}{6}$ ★ 36. $\dfrac{0.99}{5} = \dfrac{5.94}{n}$

PROBLEM SOLVING • APPLICATIONS

Complete the proportion. Then solve for *n*.

37. The ratio of packages to golf balls is 1 to 6. How many golf balls will 9 packages contain?
$$\dfrac{1}{?} = \dfrac{9}{n}$$

38. The ratio of tennis balls to packages is 6 to 1. How many tennis balls will 7 packages contain?
$$\dfrac{6}{?} = \dfrac{n}{7}$$

39. One croquet set has 4 mallets and 2 balls. How many mallets and balls will a dozen sets have?

40. A tennis set contains 3 balls and 2 rackets. Can 24 balls and 18 rackets be made into complete sets with no pieces left over?

Scale Drawings

For some people, visiting museums or attending the theater
is a favorite form of recreation.

● The drawing below is a **scale drawing** of a museum.   Scale: 1 cm = 8 m

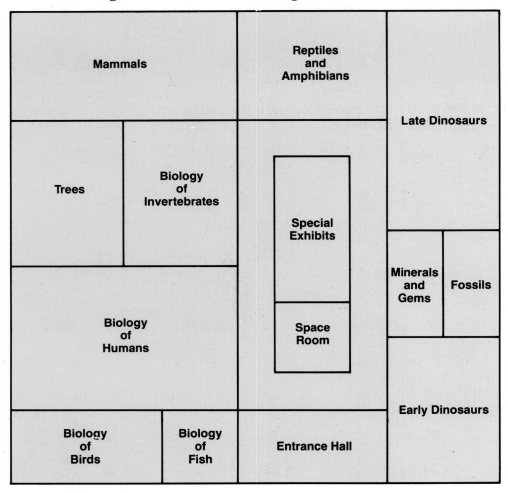

Each centimeter in the scale drawing
represents 8 meters in the museum.
The scale can be written as the ratio, 1:8.

$\dfrac{1}{8}$ ⟵———— **centimeters**
         ⟵———— **meters**

In the drawing, the length of the entrance hall is 4 centimeters.

● What is the actual length?

Think	Length on drawing ⟶	$\dfrac{1}{8} = \dfrac{4}{n}$ ⟵	Length on drawing
	Actual length ⟶		Actual length

Solve the proportion. $\dfrac{1}{8} = \dfrac{4}{n}$
Use cross products.

$$1 \times n = 8 \times 4$$
$$1 \times n = 32$$
$$n = 32 \div 1, \text{ or } \mathbf{32}$$

◄ **Actual length:
32 meters**

On the scale drawing, the width of the entrance hall is 2 centimeters.

● Find the actual width.

Think　Length on drawing ⟶　　　$\dfrac{1}{8} = \dfrac{2}{n}$ ⟵ Length on drawing
　　　　　Actual length ⟶　　　　　　　 ⟵ Actual length

Solve the proportion.　　　$1 \times n = 8 \times 2$
Use cross products.　　　　$1 \times n = 16$
　　　　　　　　　　　　　$n = 16 \div 1,$ or $\mathbf{16}$　◀　**Actual width: 16 meters**

The dimensions of the entrance hall are **32 meters by 16 meters.**

PRACTICE • Measure the drawing. Find the dimensions of the rooms.

1. Trees

2. Biology of Fish

3. Space Room

EXERCISES • Measure the drawing. Find the dimensions of the rooms.

4. Special Exhibits

5. Biology of Humans

6. Late Dinosaurs

7. Biology of Birds

★ **8.** Minerals and Gems

★ **9.** Fossils

★ **10.** Find the actual dimensions of the entire museum.

PROBLEM SOLVING • APPLICATIONS

11. The museum is going to add a new wing. On a scale drawing, the new wing measures 13 centimeters by 6 centimeters. On the drawing each centimeter represents 6 meters. What are the actual dimensions of the new wing?

12. An excavation site is in the shape of a square. In a scale drawing, one side of the excavation is 26 centimeters. On the drawing each centimeter represents 3 meters. What is the perimeter of the site?

The museum is building a model of the Great Pyramid. In the model 1 centimeter represents 3 meters.

★ **13.** The pyramid was 147 meters high when it was first built. What will the height be in the model?

★ **14.** The grand gallery of the pyramid was 47 meters long and 8.5 meters high. What will these dimensions be in the model? (Round to the nearest hundredth.)

PROJECT　Make a scale drawing of a room in your home. Be sure to mark the scale you use on the drawing.

Ratio and Similar Polygons

Hobbies are an important recreation for some people. Rosemary's hobby is photography. This photo that she took while on vacation and its enlargement have the same shape.

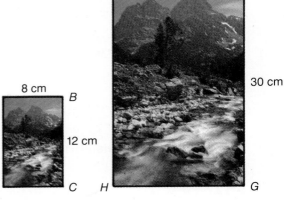

● They are **similar** polygons.

Side *AB* corresponds to side *EF*.
Side *BC* corresponds to side *FG*.
Side *CD* corresponds to side *GH*.
Side *DA* corresponds to side *HE*.

● The ratios of the lengths of the **corresponding sides** are equal.

● Write a proportion to show how these lengths are related.

Compare the cross products to show that the proportion is true.

Think

$$\text{side } AB \longrightarrow \frac{8}{20} = \frac{12}{30} \longleftarrow \text{side } BC$$
$$\text{side } EF \longrightarrow \frac{8}{20} = \frac{12}{30} \longleftarrow \text{side } FG$$

$$8 \times 30 = 12 \times 20$$
$$240 = 240 \qquad \text{The proportion is } \textbf{true.}$$

These triangles are similar.

Side *MN* corresponds to side *PQ*.
Side *NO* corresponds to side *QR*.
Side *OM* corresponds to side *RP*.

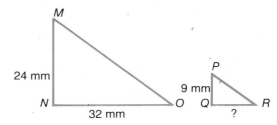

● Use cross products to find the length of side *QR*.

Think

$$\text{side } MN \longrightarrow \frac{24}{9} = \frac{32}{n} \longleftarrow \text{side } NO$$
$$\text{side } PQ \longrightarrow \frac{24}{9} = \frac{32}{n} \longleftarrow \text{side } QR$$

$$24 \times n = 32 \times 9$$
$$24 \times n = 288$$
$$n = 288 \div 24$$
$$n = 12$$

The length of $\overline{QR}$ is **12 millimeters.**

PRACTICE • Rectangles *JKLM* and *WXYZ* are similar.
Name the side that corresponds to

1. side *JK*.   **2.** side *KL*.

3. side *WZ*.   **4.** side *ZY*.

Find the missing measures.

5. $\overline{JK}$ = 4 cm
$\overline{KL}$ = 5 cm
$\overline{WX}$ = 16 cm
$\overline{XY}$ = ___?___

6. $\overline{JK}$ = 6 mm
$\overline{KL}$ = 14 mm
$\overline{WX}$ = 24 mm
$\overline{XY}$ = ___?___

EXERCISES • Triangles EFG and RST are similar.
Name the side that corresponds to

7. side EF.
8. side FG.
9. side GE.

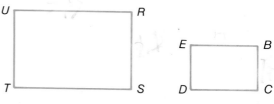

Find the missing measures.

10. $\overline{EF}$ = 3 cm
$\overline{FG}$ = 4 cm
$\overline{RS}$ = 9 cm
$\overline{ST}$ = ___?___

11. $\overline{EF}$ = 5 mm
$\overline{FG}$ = 8 mm
$\overline{RS}$ = 40 mm
$\overline{ST}$ = ___?___

Rectangles *RSTU* and *BCDE* are similar.
Name the side that corresponds to

12. side RS.
13. side RU.

14. side DC.
15. side ED.

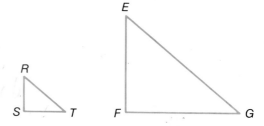

Find the missing measures.

16. $\overline{RS}$ = 8 cm
$\overline{RU}$ = 32 cm
$\overline{BC}$ = 12 cm
$\overline{BE}$ = ___?___

17. $\overline{RS}$ = 10 mm
$\overline{RU}$ = 15 mm
$\overline{BC}$ = 28 mm
$\overline{BE}$ = ___?___

★ **18.** $\overline{RS}$ = 2.1 cm
$\overline{RU}$ = 2.8 cm
$\overline{BC}$ = 1.8 cm
$\overline{BE}$ = ___?___

PROBLEM SOLVING • APPLICATIONS

19. Rosemary is making wooden frames for some of her pictures. Side *LM* of her larger frame is 50 centimeters. Side *MN* is 35 centimeters. The two frames are similar. For the smaller picture frame, side *EF* is 30 centimeters. What is the length of side *FG*?

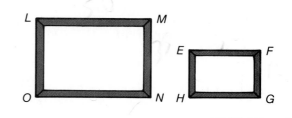

20. Rosemary is mailing pictures to her friends. She uses similar envelopes. One envelope is 20 centimeters long and 8 centimeters wide. The other envelope is 30 centimeters long. How wide is it?

Ratio and Probability

Some people enjoy playing board games for recreation. Many board games use a spinner such as this one.

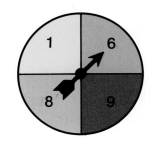

- On a spin of the pointer, there are four possible **outcomes.** That is, the spinner could stop on 1, 6, 8, or 9.

- Since the spinner has 4 sections of equal size, the outcomes are **equally likely.** The chances, or **probability,** of spinning a 1 is the ratio, $\frac{1}{4}$.

- What is the probability (P) of spinning a 9?

Think   There are 4 possible outcomes.
There is only one 9 on the spinner.

$$P(\text{spinning a 9}) = \frac{\text{number of ways of spinning a 9 (}\textbf{favorable outcome}\text{)}}{\text{total number of outcomes}}$$

$$= \frac{1}{4}$$

- What is the probability of spinning a number divisible by 2?

Think   Both 6 and 8 are divisible by 2.

$$P(\text{spinning a number divisible by 2}) = \frac{\text{number of favorable outcomes}}{\text{total number of outcomes}}$$

$$= \frac{2}{4} \longleftarrow \textbf{Two numbers are divisible by 2.}$$
$$\phantom{= \frac{2}{4}} \longleftarrow \textbf{There are 4 possible outcomes.}$$

$$= \frac{1}{2} \longleftarrow \textbf{Lowest terms}$$

- What is the probability of spinning a number greater than 1?

Think   Favorable outcomes: 6, 8, and 9

$$P(\text{number greater than 1}) = \frac{\text{number of favorable outcomes}}{\text{total number of outcomes}}$$

$$= \frac{3}{4}$$

- If an event will **always** happen, the probability is 1.

- If an event will **never** happen, the probability is 0.

PRACTICE • Find each probability. Refer to the spinner.

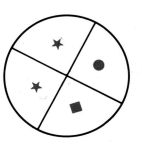

1. P(spinning a circle)

2. P(spinning a star)

3. P(spinning a star or a square)

4. P(spinning a star, a circle, or a square)

EXERCISES

Complete.

	Experiment	Outcomes	Probability
5.	Toss a coin once.	Heads (H) or Tails (T)	P(H) = ___?___ P(T) = ___?___
6.	Draw one card without looking. 5 7 12 15 9	5 7 9 12 15	P(getting an odd number) = ___?___
7.	Draw a marble from 3 green, 2 red, and 4 yellow marbles.	○ ● ○	P(drawing a yellow marble) = ___?___

PROBLEM SOLVING • APPLICATIONS

There are 7 red, 5 green, and 3 blue marbles in a jar. You pick a marble without looking. What is the probability of picking a marble that is

8. red?   9. green?   10. blue?

A number cube has faces numbered 2, 4, 6, 8, 10, and 12.

11. What is the probability of tossing an even number?

12. What is the probability of tossing an odd number?

13. What is the probability of tossing a number less than 13?

★ 14. What is the probability of tossing an odd number greater than 5?

You toss a coin twice.
The tree diagram shows the four possible outcomes.

15. What is the total number of outcomes?

16. What is the probability of getting two heads?

17. What is the probability of getting two tails?

18. What is the probability of getting TH?

TOSSING TWO COINS

First Toss	Second Toss	Outcomes
H	H	HH
	T	HT
T	H	TH
	T	TT

Probability/Prediction/Expected Numbers

Tad's favorite recreation is playing the board game, Twin Luck. He has played the game 30 times and has won 20 games.

● What is the probability that Tad will win the next game?

Think Number of favorable outcomes: 20
Total number of outcomes: 30

$$P(\text{winning the next game}) = \frac{20}{30} = \frac{2}{3}$$

● Predict whether Tad is more likely to win or lose the next game.

Think Compare Tad's chances of winning with his chances of losing.

$$P(\text{winning}) = \frac{2}{3} \qquad P(\text{losing}) = 1 - \frac{2}{3} = \frac{1}{3}$$

Since $\frac{2}{3} > \frac{1}{3}$, Tad is **more likely to win.**

Tad plans to play the game of Twin Luck once every day for ninety days.

● How many games can he expect to win?

Think You know Tad's probability of winning one game.
To find how many of the 90 games he can expect to win,
multiply $\frac{2}{3}$ and 90.

$$\frac{2}{\cancel{3}} \times \overset{30}{90} = 2 \times 30 = 60$$

Tad can expect to win **60** of the 90 games.

PRACTICE • Mental Math

a. Find the probability of getting a star in one spin.
b. Find the probability of getting a star in 30 spins.

1.   2.   3.   4.

EXERCISES • Mental Math How many stars can you expect to get

5. in 6 spins?

6. in 12 spins?

7. in 18 spins?

8. in 24 spins?

9. in 4 spins?

10. in 8 spins?

11. in 12 spins?

12. in 16 spins?

PROBLEM SOLVING • APPLICATIONS

13. Based on the records for the last 5 years, Washington Junior High's probability of winning its next soccer game is $\frac{3}{5}$.

  a. Is Washington Junior High's soccer team more likely to have a winning or a losing season this year?

  b. How many of its next 10 games can it expect to win?

14. The probability of rain on any day in April for a certain city is $\frac{1}{3}$. How many rainy days can the residents of the city expect in the month of April?

16. Maria has won 4 of her last 6 races.

  a. Based on this record, is she more likely to win or lose her next race?

  b. Based on this record, how many of her next 3 races can Maria expect to win?

15. A weather reporter anounces that the probability for good weather for the last World Series game is $\frac{1}{7}$. What is the probability that the game will be rained out?

17. Jane Silverfoot correctly predicted the outcome of the Superbowl in 3 of the last 5 years. What is the probability that her next prediction will be in incorrect?

PROBLEM SOLVING · STRATEGIES

Using Proportions to Solve Problems

Because faster ways of transportation are constantly being developed, travel as a favorite form of recreation is becoming more and more commonplace.

Example 1

The first airplane traveled 120 feet in 12 seconds.

- At this rate, how far will it travel in 60 seconds?

 Think Use a proportion.

Step 1 Write a proportion.
Let n = number of feet traveled in 60 sec.

seconds $\longrightarrow$ $\dfrac{12}{120} = \dfrac{60}{n}$ $\longleftarrow$ seconds
feet $\longrightarrow$ $\qquad\qquad$ $\longleftarrow$ feet

Step 2 Solve the proportion. Use cross products.

$$12 \times n = 120 \times 60$$
$$12 \times n = 7{,}200$$
$$n = 7{,}200 \div 12$$
$$n = 600 \qquad \blacktriangleleft \quad \textbf{600 feet}$$

Example 2

The average speed of the Metroliner is 130 kilometers per hour.

- At this rate, how long will it take the Metroliner to travel 715 kilometers?

Think Use a proportion.

Step 1 Write a proportion.

hours $\longrightarrow$ $\dfrac{1}{130} = \dfrac{n}{715}$ $\longleftarrow$ kilometers
kilometers $\longrightarrow$ $\qquad\qquad$ $\longleftarrow$ hours

Step 2 Solve the proportion. Use cross products.

$$130 \times n = 1 \times 715$$
$$130 \times n = 715$$
$$n = 715 \div 130$$
$$n = 5.5$$

The Metroliner will take **5.5**, or $5\frac{1}{2}$ **hours.**

PROBLEMS

Choose the correct proportion.
Choose a or b.

1. The fastest crossing of the Pacific Ocean by a boat was made by the Sea–Land Commerce. In 3 hours, the boat traveled 114 miles. At this rate, how far could it travel in 24 hours?

   a. $\dfrac{3}{114} = \dfrac{24}{n}$ **b.** $\dfrac{3}{114} = \dfrac{n}{24}$

2. An *air cushion vehicle* (ACV) can travel on land or on water. One ACV travels 480 kilometers in 3 hours. At this rate, how long will it take the ACV to travel 240 kilometers?

   a. $\dfrac{480}{3} = \dfrac{n}{240}$ **b.** $\dfrac{3}{480} = \dfrac{n}{240}$

Write a proportion. Let *n* represent what you want to find.

3. A *hydrofoil* is a boat that rides above the surface of the water on foils, or skis. A trip of 42 miles takes 28 minutes. How many miles is this per hour?

   a. $\dfrac{n}{60} = \dfrac{28}{42}$ **b.** $\dfrac{28}{42} = \dfrac{60}{n}$

4. A *houseboat* is any kind of floating home. One houseboat travels 47.5 kilometers in 2.5 hours. At this rate, how far can it travel in 8 hours?

   a. $\dfrac{2.5}{47.5} = \dfrac{n}{8}$ **b.** $\dfrac{2.5}{47.5} = \dfrac{8}{n}$

Write a proportion. Solve.

5. The world's fastest aircraft traveled 146 miles in 4 seconds. At this rate, how far could it travel in 30 seconds?

Use cross products to solve proportions.

6. A *supersonic jet* (SST) traveled 7,482 kilometers in 3 hours. At this rate, how long will it take the SST to travel 6,235 kilometers?

7. During a 15–minute speed trial, the world's fastest submarine traveled 12 miles. How many miles per hour is this?

8. The fastest helicopter speed record is for a distance of 178 miles in 30 minutes. At this rate, how many minutes would it take the helicopter to travel 89 miles?

9. The French National Railroad operates a train that can travel at a speed of 158 miles per hour. At this rate, how many minutes will it take the train to reach its first stop after traveling 79 miles?

10. On a test run of a new high–speed passenger train called a *magnetic levitation vehicle,* the train traveled 160 kilometers in 20 minutes. At this rate, how far could the train travel in $1\frac{1}{2}$ hours?

Write Your Own Problem

Use the information in this table to write four problems that can be solved by using proportions. Two of the problems should contain a hidden question.

Average Speeds	
Walking	3.5 mph
Bicycle	10 mph
Intercity bus	52 mph
Ocean liner	33 mph

MID-CHAPTER REVIEW

Write a fraction for each ratio. (Pages 362–363)

1. 3 to 5   **2.** 4 to 9   **3.** 6 to 85   **4.** 30:52   **5.** 215:65

Solve. (Pages 364–365)

6. $\dfrac{5}{6} = \dfrac{10}{n}$ **7.** $\dfrac{3}{4} = \dfrac{n}{12}$ **8.** $\dfrac{10}{n} = \dfrac{20}{40}$ **9.** $\dfrac{n}{9} = \dfrac{30}{45}$ **10.** $\dfrac{3}{14} = \dfrac{n}{42}$

Write = or ≠. (Pages 364–365)

11. $\dfrac{3}{4}$ ● $\dfrac{9}{12}$ **12.** $\dfrac{2}{5}$ ● $\dfrac{5}{15}$ **13.** $\dfrac{12}{8}$ ● $\dfrac{36}{24}$ **14.** $\dfrac{8}{1}$ ● $\dfrac{16}{4}$ **15.** $\dfrac{13}{14}$ ● $\dfrac{26}{28}$

Rectangles *ABCD* and *EFGH* are similar. Name the corresponding sides.
(Pages 368–369)

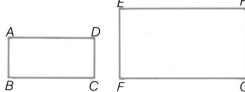

16. side *EF*.   **17.** side *EH*.

18. side *FG*.   **19.** side *HG*.

Find the missing measure. (Pages 368–369)

20. $\overline{EF}$ = 6 mm $\overline{EH}$ = 8 mm $\overline{AB}$ = 3 mm $\overline{AD}$ = _____?_____

How many stars can you expect? (Pages 370–373)

21. in 4 spins?   **22.** in 8 spins?   **23.** in 12 spins?

24. To build a model ship, Mae used a scale of 1 meter for every 15 meters. The actual length of the ship is 22.5 meters. What is the length of the model?
(Pages 366–367)

25. A diving bell descends 7 meters in 5 seconds. At this rate, how far can the diving bell descend in 11.5 seconds? (Pages 374–375)

MAINTENANCE • MIXED PRACTICE

Multiply.

1. $54 \times 68 =$ _____?_____   **2.** $128 \times 49 =$ _____?_____   **3.** $456 \times 820 =$ _____?_____

4. $207 \times 43 =$ _____?_____   **5.** $699 \times 427 =$ _____?_____   **6.** $525 \times 178 =$ _____?_____

7. $3\frac{1}{2} \times 2 =$ _____?_____   **8.** $4\frac{2}{3} \times 5\frac{1}{6} =$ _____?_____   **9.** $1\frac{1}{2} \times 1\frac{5}{9} =$ _____?_____

Divide.

10. $6\frac{1}{3} \div 1\frac{1}{3} =$ _____?_____   **11.** $5\frac{2}{3} \div 1\frac{3}{4} =$ _____?_____   **12.** $3\frac{1}{2} \div \frac{1}{4} =$ _____?_____

News Photographer

News photographer Cindy Clayton takes a picture of a training ship. The picture is 12 centimeters long and 8 centimeters wide. She must reduce it to fit a space 7 centimeters long.

● What will be the width of the reduced picture?

Write a word rule.

$$\frac{\text{Length of Original}}{\text{Width of Original}} = \frac{\text{Length of Copy}}{\text{Width of Copy}}$$

 ◀ **Use cross products.**

$12 \times n = 8 \times 7$

$12n = 56$ ⟵ Find n. Use either paper and pencil or a calculator.

      ◀ $n = 4.6666666$

Rounded to the nearest tenth, the width is about **4.7 centimeters.**

EXERCISES • For Exercise 1–6, complete the table. Round each answer to the nearest tenth.

	Length of Original	Width of Original	Length of Copy	Width of Copy
1.	12 cm	8 cm	6 cm	?
2.	15 cm	7 cm	12 cm	?
3.	16 cm	8 cm	?	4 cm
4.	27 cm	15 cm	11 cm	?
5.	30 cm	12 cm	?	10 cm
6.	60 cm	55 cm	12 cm	?

7. A photograph 15 centimeters long and 12 centimeters wide has to be reduced to fit in a space 10 centimeters long. Find the width of the reduced photograph.

8. A picture 25 centimeters long and 20 centimeters wide has to be enlarged to fit in a frame 30 centimeters long. Find the width of the enlarged photograph.

Percent

● Another way to show a ratio is to use *percent*. **Percent** means per hundred. The symbol for percent is %.

● Use a percent to show the ratio of blue blocks to all 100 blocks.

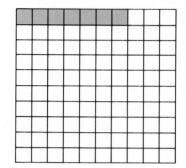 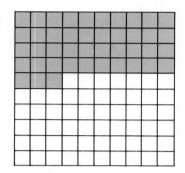 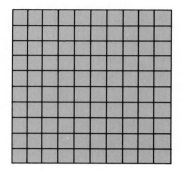

Think	7 out of 100	43 out of 100	100 out of 100
Ratio	$\frac{7}{100}$	$\frac{43}{100}$	$\frac{100}{100}$
Decimal	0.07	0.43	1.00
Percent	7%	43%	100%

PRACTICE • **Mental Math**   Name the percent that tells what part is shaded.

1.   2.   3.   4.

Name the percent for each ratio.

5. 9 out of 100   **6.** 58 out of 100   **7.** 77 out of 100

8. $\frac{6}{100}$ **9.** $\frac{17}{100}$ **10.** $\frac{42}{100}$ **11.** $\frac{1}{100}$ **12.** $\frac{25}{100}$ **13.** $\frac{13}{100}$

Write the percents for the decimals.

14. 0.87   **15.** 0.65   **16.** 0.45   **17.** 0.15   **18.** 0.99   **19.** 0.37

EXERCISES • `Mental Math` Name the percent that tells what part is shaded.

20. 21. 22. 23.

Name the percent for each ratio.

24. 3 out of 100   **25.** 8 out of 100   **26.** 36 out of 100

27. 50 out of 100   **28.** 66 out of 100   **29.** 89 out of 100

30. 5 per 100   **31.** 49 per 100   **32.** 93 per 100

33. $\frac{4}{100}$ **34.** $\frac{39}{100}$ **35.** $\frac{19}{100}$ **36.** $\frac{23}{100}$ **37.** $\frac{11}{100}$ **38.** $\frac{31}{100}$

39. $\frac{27}{100}$ **40.** $\frac{90}{100}$ **41.** $\frac{63}{100}$ **42.** $\frac{29}{100}$ **43.** $\frac{52}{100}$ **44.** $\frac{74}{100}$

Write the percents for the decimals.

45. 0.34   **46.** 0.22   **47.** 0.02   **48.** 0.88   **49.** 1.00   **50.** 0.67

51. 0.75   **52.** 0.28   **53.** 0.97   **54.** 0.61   **55.** 0.56   **56.** 0.35

57. 0.01   **58.** 0.72   ★**59.** 0.8   ★**60.** 0.6   ★**61.** 0.1   ★**62.** 0.9

PROBLEM SOLVING • APPLICATIONS

Collecting coins is a favorite hobby of many people.

63. In a collector's catalog, 70 out of 100 pages show coins. What percent of the pages show coins?

64. Out of 100 coins, 54 are in an album. What percent of the coins are in an album?

65. Flip 100 pennies. Of these, 48 land on heads. What percent land on heads?

66. There are 100 coins. Of these, 23 are copper. What percent are copper?

★**67.** There are 100 coins. Of these, 74 are silver. What percent are not silver?

★**68.** There are 100 coins. Of these, 56 are nickels. What percent are not nickels?

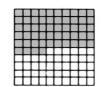
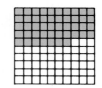

Ratio and Percent • **379**

Decimals and Fractions for Percents

Bicycling is a recreational activity that appeals to people of all ages.

Forty-one of the 100 bicycles are red. This is 41% of the bicycles.

● Write the decimal for 41%.

Think 41% is 41 hundredths.

41% = **0.41**

● Thirty-two of the bicycles are blue.

This is 32% of the bicycles.

● Write the fraction for 32%.

Think 32% is 32 hundredths.

Step 1 Write a fraction. $\longrightarrow \dfrac{32}{100}$

Step 2 Write the fraction in lowest terms. $\longrightarrow \dfrac{8}{25}$

$32\% = \dfrac{8}{25}$

PRACTICE • Mental Math Name the decimal for each percent.

1. 33%   **2.** 48%   **3.** 6%   **4.** 80%   **5.** 30%   **6.** 12%

Write the fraction for each percent. Write each answer in lowest terms.

7. 25%   **8.** 50%   **9.** 20%   **10.** 30%   **11.** 28%   **12.** 55%

EXERCISES • Mental Math Name the decimal for each percent.

13. 11%   **14.** 8%   **15.** 54%   **16.** 35%   **17.** 75%   **18.** 70%

19. 29%   **20.** 42%   **21.** 38%   **22.** 96%   **23.** 99%   **24.** 86%

25. 7%   **26.** 16%   **27.** 65%   **28.** 13%   **29.** 83%   **30.** 77%

31. 93%   **32.** 23%   **33.** 58%   **34.** 25%   **35.** 67%   **36.** 59%

Write the fraction for each percent. Write each answer in lowest terms.

37. 37%   **38.** 44%   **39.** 13%   **40.** 40%   **41.** 21%   **42.** 16%

43. 81%   **44.** 66%   **45.** 98%   **46.** 85%   **47.** 71%   **48.** 90%

49. 4%   **50.** 75%   **51.** 56%   **52.** 64%   **53.** 15%   **54.** 48%

55. 70%   **56.** 45%   **57.** 68%   **58.** 83%   **59.** 95%   **60.** 72%

The manager at Pohanka Cycle sets a sales goal of 100 bikes per year for each salesperson.

Last year Clare sold 136 bikes.
The ratio of bikes sold to the sales goal is $\frac{136}{100}$.

bikes sold $\longrightarrow$ $\frac{136}{100} = 136\%$
sales goal $\longrightarrow$

Clare sold **136%** of the goal.

Write the percent for each ratio.

★ **61.** 125 to 100   ★ **62.** 360 to 100   ★ **63.** 500 to 100   ★ **64.** 256 to 100

PROBLEM SOLVING • APPLICATIONS

65. Sal orders 100 new bikes for his shop. Of these, 65% are dirt bikes. What fraction of the bikes are dirt bikes?

66. Of the bikes Sal orders, 36% are imported. Write the decimal to show the percent of imported bikes that Sal orders.

67. A shipment of 100 bikes arrives. Of these, 72% are ten-speed. How many bikes in the shipment are not ten-speed?

★ **68.** Sal sends in an order for 50 bikes. Of these, 16% are five-speed. The rest are three-speed. How many three-speed bikes does he order?

Percents for Fractions

The most popular form of recreation is watching television. Many people enjoy programs that show how people live in other countries, such as Iceland.

Iceland is an island nation close to the Arctic Circle. Because $\frac{3}{4}$ of the country is glaciers, lakes, and desert, almost all Icelanders live on $\frac{1}{4}$ of the island.

● What percent of the island is glaciers, lakes, and desert?

Think Write a ratio with 100 as the denominator: $\frac{n}{100}$

Step 1
Write a proportion.

$$\frac{3}{4} = \frac{n}{100}$$

Step 2
Solve. Use cross products.

$$3 \times 100 = 4 \times n$$
$$300 = 4 \times n$$
$$300 \div 4 = n$$
$$75 = n$$

Glaciers, lakes, and desert make up **75%** of Iceland.

● You can also divide to find the percent for $\frac{2}{5}$. Carry out the division to the hundredths place.

Step 1 Divide.

$$\begin{array}{r} 0.40 \\ 5\overline{)2.00} \\ -2\ 0\downarrow \\ \hline 00 \\ -\ 0 \\ \hline 0 \end{array}$$

Step 2 Write the decimal as a percent.

$$0.40 = 40\%$$

● Find the percent for $\frac{4}{7}$.

Think Divide 4 by 7. Carry out the division to the hundredths place.

Step 1 Divide.

$$\begin{array}{r} 0.57\frac{1}{7} \\ 7\overline{)4.00} \\ -3\ 5\downarrow \\ \hline 50 \\ -49 \\ \hline 1 \end{array}$$

Step 2 Write the quotient as a percent.

$$0.57\frac{1}{7} = 57\frac{1}{7}\%$$

PRACTICE • Write the percents for the fractions.

1. $\frac{1}{2}$ 2. $\frac{1}{4}$ 3. $\frac{3}{4}$ 4. $\frac{7}{10}$ 5. $\frac{1}{10}$ 6. $\frac{5}{10}$

EXERCISES • Write the percent for each fraction.

7. $\frac{3}{8}$ 8. $\frac{2}{3}$ 9. $\frac{5}{6}$ 10. $\frac{4}{9}$ 11. $\frac{5}{8}$ 12. $\frac{3}{7}$

13. $\frac{3}{20}$ 14. $\frac{1}{5}$ 15. $\frac{8}{10}$ 16. $\frac{6}{25}$ 17. $\frac{17}{20}$ 18. $\frac{9}{50}$

19. $\frac{4}{5}$ 20. $\frac{9}{20}$ 21. $\frac{23}{25}$ 22. $\frac{13}{50}$ 23. $\frac{27}{50}$ 24. $\frac{3}{10}$

25. $\frac{1}{3}$ 26. $\frac{7}{9}$ 27. $\frac{5}{12}$ 28. $\frac{2}{7}$ 29. $\frac{7}{8}$ 30. $\frac{1}{6}$

31. $\frac{4}{15}$ 32. $\frac{6}{13}$ 33. $\frac{13}{15}$ 34. $\frac{11}{24}$ 35. $\frac{5}{13}$ 36. $\frac{7}{11}$

37. $\frac{7}{15}$ 38. $\frac{8}{11}$ 39. $\frac{17}{24}$ ★ 40. $\frac{50}{39}$ ★ 41. $\frac{35}{6}$ ★ 42. $\frac{46}{15}$

Complete.

	Fraction	Decimal	Percent
43.	$\frac{1}{4}$	?	?
44.	?	0.8	?
45.	?	?	75%
46.	$\frac{4}{25}$	?	?
47.	?	0.29	?

PROBLEM SOLVING • APPLICATIONS

48. In Brazil, 9 out of 10 citizens live on a narrow belt of land along the Atlantic coast. What percent of the population lives on the coast?

49. The coast of Brazil that holds most of the population includes only $\frac{1}{3}$ of Brazil's land. What percent of the land is this?

★ 50. About $\frac{3}{4}$ of the land of Japan is covered by mountains and hills and cannot be farmed. What percent of Japanese land can be used as farmland?

★ 51. There are 2000 islands included in the nation of Greece, but only 169 of them are inhabited. What percent of the Greek islands are uninhabited?

THINKER'S CORNER

Write a decimal and a percent for each fraction.

a. $\frac{\frac{1}{2}}{100}$ b. $\frac{\frac{1}{4}}{100}$

c. $\frac{\frac{1}{10}}{100}$ d. $\frac{\frac{1}{8}}{100}$

Percent of a Number

Some people use their leisure to find out more about a subject that interests them. The study of American history is one of these subjects.

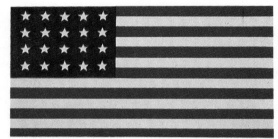

By 1818, the U. S. flag had 20 stars for 20 states. Within 3 years there were 15% more stars.

● How many stars were added in three years?

15% of 20 = ___?___

Think You can write 15% as $\frac{15}{100}$ or 0.15.

There are two ways you can solve the problem.

Method 1
Use a fraction to name the percent. Then multiply.

$$15\% = \frac{15}{100}, \text{ or } \frac{3}{20}$$

$$\frac{3}{20} \times \frac{20}{1} = \frac{60}{20}$$

$$= 3$$

There were **3 stars** added in three years.

Method 2
Use a decimal to name the percent. Then multiply.

$$15\% = 0.15$$

$$
\begin{array}{r}
20 \\
\times 0.15 \\
\hline
1\ 00 \\
2\ 00 \\
\hline
3.00
\end{array}
$$

PRACTICE • Use fractions to find the answers.

1. 50% of 42 = ___?___

2. 25% of 24 = ___?___

3. 75% of 12 = ___?___

Use decimals to find the answers.

4. 32% of 74 = ___?___

5. 16% of 28 = ___?___

6. 55% of 72 = ___?___

EXERCISES • Find the answers.

7. 20% of 55 = ___?___

8. 45% of 500 = ___?___

9. 94% of 46 = ___?___

10. 15% of 400 = ___?___

11. 16% of 48 = ___?___

12. 25% of 140 = ___?___

13. 2% of 350 = ___?___

14. 50% of 94 = ___?___

15. 5% of 860 = ___?___

16. 30% of 40 = ___?___

17. 45% of 330 = ___?___

18. 78% of 120 = ___?___

● What percent of 20 is 3?

? % of 20 = 3

Think: $\frac{3}{20} = \frac{n}{100}$

$3 \times 100 = n \times 20$

$300 = n \times 20$

$300 \div 20 = n$

$15 = n$

15% of 20 is 3.

● What percent of 90 is 45?

? % of 90 = 45

Think: $\frac{45}{90} = \frac{n}{100}$

$45 \times 100 = n \times 90$

$4500 = n \times 90$

$4500 \div 90 = n$

$50 = n$

50% of 90 is 45.

Find the answers.

★ **19.** __?__ % of 30 = 6

★ **20.** __?__ % of 8 = 4

★ **21.** __?__ % of 25 = 15

★ **22.** __?__ % of 50 = 33

★ **23.** __?__ % of 10 = 1

★ **24.** __?__ % of 80 = 60

PROBLEM SOLVING • APPLICATIONS CHOOSE ● mental math ● pencil and paper ● calculator SOLVE

25. There are 25 national flags which are white and one other color. Of these, 8% are green and white. How many nations have a green-and-white flag?

26. There are 20 two-color flags that include red. Of these, 30% are either red and yellow or are red and green. How many nations fly red-and-yellow or red-and-green flags?

27. From 1791 to 1844, 11 stars were added to the United States flag. From 1844 to 1863, another 8 stars were added. Of the 50 states, what percent of states joined the United States between 1791 and 1863?

★ **28.** In 1790, there were 13 stars on the United States flag. Use the information in Exercise 27 to find what percent of all the stars on the flag in 1844 were added after 1790. Round the answer to the nearest whole number.

CALCULATOR ● Finding Percents

Use a calculator to find 54% of 24.

Think: Use the key.

Press: ② ④ ⓧ ⑤ ④ ⑨ⓞ ⑤ 12.96

EXERCISES • Use a calculator to find each answer.

1. 22% of 42.9   **2.** 78% of 1.26   **3.** 1.8% of 96   **4.** 4.7% of 237.5

Circle Graphs

Jim has a part-time job at a service station. Because he wants to use his money wisely, he plans how much he can spend on such items as recreation and food by making a *budget*. A **budget** is a plan for using money.

Jim earns more some weekends than others. By using percents he can tell how to use the money he earns each week. Jim shows his budget on a **circle graph.**

One week, Jim earns $25.00.

● How much should he spend for recreation?

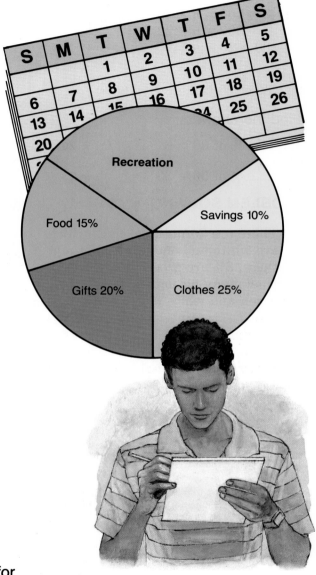

Think   The circle graph shows that he can spend 30% of his earnings for recreation.

30% of $25 = ?

$$\begin{array}{r} \$25.00 \\ \times\quad 0.30 \\ \hline \$7.5000 \end{array}$$

Jim can spend **$7.50** on recreation

PRACTICE • Use Jim's circle graph to answer the questions.

1. What is the sum of the percents shown on the graph?

2. On which item does Jim spend the most money?

3. For which item does he budget the least money?

What percent of Jim's earnings is used for

4. savings?   5. food?   6. gifts?   7. clothes?

If Jim earns $40.00, how much is budgeted for

8. recreation?   9. food?   10. gifts?   11. clothes?

12. Last week, Jim earned $32.80. How much would he budget for each item?

EXERCISES • Use Eric's circle graph to answer the questions.

13. What is the sum of the percents shown on the graph?

Eric's yearly income is $18,000. How much money does he spend on

14. housing?   **15.** food?

16. taxes?   **17.** clothing?

18. How much more does he spend on medical care than on transportation?

19. For which item does Eric budget $1,620?

20. For which item does Eric budget $1,080?

21. Suppose Eric's yearly income is $26,500. List how it is budgeted according to the graph.

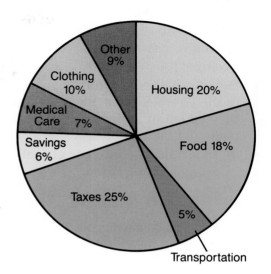

ERIC STANTON'S ANNUAL EXPENSES

Other 9%
Clothing 10%
Medical Care 7%
Savings 6%
Taxes 25%
Housing 20%
Food 18%
5%
Transportation

PROBLEM SOLVING • **APPLICATIONS**

Gary works at Fred's sport shop. He gets a 15% employee discount. A **discount** is an amount that is subtracted from the original cost. Use the percent to find how much the discount will be.

Gary buys a tennis racket that sells for $65.00. How much is his discount?

15% of $65.00 = ?

$$\begin{array}{r} \$65.00 \\ \times\ \ 0.15 \\ \hline \$\ 9.75 \end{array}$$

Gary gets a discount of **$9.75.**

How much does the tennis racket cost Gary?
Original cost − discount = new cost

$$\begin{array}{r} \$65.00 \\ -\ \ 9.75 \\ \hline \$55.25 \end{array}$$

The racket costs Gary **$55.25.**

Find the discount.

22. original cost: $18.75
discount: 40%

23. original cost: $172.60
discount: 10%

24. original cost: $14.76
discount: 25%

What is the discount and the new cost of each item?

25. 20% discount on a football jersey that sells for $15.95

26. 18% discount on golf clubs that sell for $175.00

Ratio and Percent • **387**

PROBLEM SOLVING · STRATEGIES

Estimating Percents

To estimate a percent of a number, you can sometimes round the number only. It may also be helpful to write the percent as a fraction.

Example 1

During the Dunn family's vacation tour of the Great Barrier Reef in Australia, they sailed to 20% of the 289 nearby reefs and islands.

● **Estimate** the number of reefs and islands they visited.

Think $20\% = \frac{20}{100} = \frac{1}{5}$

Step 1 Round the number.   289 is about 300.

Step 2 Multiply. $\frac{1}{\cancel{5}} \times \cancel{300}^{\,60} = 60$

The Dunns visited about **60** reefs and islands.

Sometimes you can use **compatible numbers** to round to a convenient percent.

Example 2

The Dunns spent 12% of the $2,150 budgeted for their ski trip to rmany's Bavarian Alps for skiing costs.

● **Estimate** the amount spent.

Step 1 Choose a compatible percent.

Think $10\% = \frac{10}{100} = \frac{1}{10}$

Step 2 Multiply.

$\frac{1}{10} \times 2{,}150 = 215$

The Dunns spent **$215** for skiing costs.

Ⓔ PRACTICE

Estimate by rounding the number. Choose a, b, or c.

1. 10% of $29.95   **a.** 10% of $20   **b.** 10% of $25   **c.** 10% of $30

2. 60% of $71.80   **a.** 60% of $70   **b.** 60% of $80   **c.** 60% of $60

3. 40% of $179.55   **a.** $68   **b.** $72   **c.** $80

4. 75% of $101.25   **a.** $75   **b.** $90   **c.** $60

Estimate by rounding the percent. Choose a, b, or c.

5. 21% of $150   **a.** 30% of $150   **b.** 25% of $150   **c.** 20% of $150

6. 31% of $90   **a.** 30% of $90   **b.** 35% of $90   **c.** 40% of $90

7. 19% of $80   **a.** $8   **b.** $16   **c.** $20

8. 41% of $1,600   **a.** $800   **b.** $480   **c.** $640

E **PROBLEMS** • Estimate each answer. Choose a, b, or c.

9. While visiting the Great Pyramid in Egypt, the Dunns learned that it originally stood 147 meters tall. At the present time, it is about 90% of its original height. Estimate the present height.

   a. 90 m   **b.** 135 m   **c.** 180 m

10. During one vacation, the Dunns visited 2% of the 904 museums and art galleries in Great Britain. Estimate the number of museums and art galleries they visited.

   a. 18   **b.** 9   **c.** 45

Write a decimal or a fraction for the percent—whichever is easier to use.

---

11. The Dunns want to attend the Monaco Grand Prix auto race. They know that rain is expected in Monaco on 17% of the days of the year. Estimate how many days this is.

   a. 100   **b.** 80   **c.** 73

12. The Dunns calculated that their car would use about 447 gallons of fuel during their vacation in Canada. After returning home, they found that the car actually used 80% of the expected amount of fuel. Estimate the number of gallons of fuel actually used.

   a. 320   **b.** 360   **c.** 400

13. While attending the French Open tennis tournament, Mr. Dunn saw warm-up suits offered for $138. After bargaining with the owner of the shop, he bought a warm-up suit at a 25% discount. Estimate the discount.

   a. $45   **b.** $25   **c.** $35

Round to the nearest convenient number.

---

14. The Dunns passed through the small country of Liechtenstein on their European tour. They learned that 69% of the 6,720 urban residents in the country live in Vaduz, the capital. Estimate how many people live in Vaduz.

   a. 4,704   **b.** 4,900   **c.** 4,032

CHAPTER REVIEW

Part 1 • VOCABULARY

For Exercises 1-8, choose from the box at the right the word(s) that completes the sentence.

1. The statements 2 to 3, 2:3, and $\frac{2}{3}$ are examples of __?__.   (Page 362)

2. A word that means per hundred is __?__.   (Page 378)

3. If the ratios of the lengths of corresponding sides of a polygon are equal, the polygons are __?__.   (Page 368)

4. The ratios $\frac{1}{2}$, $\frac{2}{4}$, $\frac{3}{6}$, and $\frac{4}{8}$ are __?__ ratios.   (Page 364)

5. On a __?__, the scale compares distance on a drawing to actual distance.   (Page 366)

6. A statement which says two ratios are equal is called a __?__.   (Page 364)

7. A number from 0 to 1 that tells how likely it is that an event will happen is called a __?__.   (Page 372)

8. You can test a proportion by using __?__.   (Page 364)

cross products
equal
percent
probability
proportion
ratios
scale drawing
similar

Part 2 • SKILLS

Write a fraction for each ratio.   (Pages 362–363)

9. 2 to 7   10. 5 to 10   11. 3 to 42   12. 16:32   13. 150:50

Solve.   (Pages 364–365)

14. $\frac{3}{4} = \frac{9}{n}$ 15. $\frac{6}{8} = \frac{n}{16}$ 16. $\frac{10}{n} = \frac{30}{90}$ 17. $\frac{n}{9} = \frac{35}{45}$ 18. $\frac{2}{5} = \frac{n}{40}$

Write = or ≠.   (Pages 364–365)

19. $\frac{3}{5} \bullet \frac{9}{15}$ 20. $\frac{3}{6} \bullet \frac{9}{12}$ 21. $\frac{16}{3} \bullet \frac{32}{9}$ 22. $\frac{5}{1} \bullet \frac{20}{4}$ 23. $\frac{13}{39} \bullet \frac{1}{3}$

Rectangles *ABCD* and *EFGH* are similar. Find the missing measures.
(Pages 368–369)

24. $\overline{AB}$ = 8 m
    $\overline{AD}$ = 12 m
    $\overline{EF}$ = 4 m
    $\overline{EH}$ = __?__ m

25. $\overline{AB}$ = 9 cm
    $\overline{BC}$ = 12 cm
    $\overline{EF}$ = 3 cm
    $\overline{FG}$ = __?__ cm

You spin this spinner once.   (Pages 370–373)

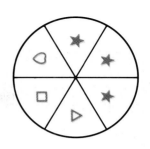

26. On which shape is the spinner most likely to stop?

27. P(getting a star) = ____?____

28. How many stars can you expect to get in 12 spins?

Write the percents.   (Pages 378–379, 382–383)

29. 5 out of 100   **30.** 75 out of 100   **31.** $\frac{3}{100}$ **32.** $\frac{62}{100}$

33. 0.25   **34.** 0.75   **35.** 0.43   **36.** 1.00   **37.** 0.03

38. $\frac{1}{2}$ **39.** $\frac{3}{4}$ **40.** $\frac{9}{10}$ **41.** $\frac{1}{3}$ **42.** $\frac{17}{25}$

Write a decimal for each percent.   (Pages 380–381)

43. 50%   **44.** 80%   **45.** 21%   **46.** 99%   **47.** 4%

Write a fraction for each percent. Write the fraction in lowest terms.
(Pages 380–381)

48. 25%   **49.** 60%   **50.** 75%   **51.** 5%   **52.** 42%

Complete.   (Pages 384–385)

53. 30% of 70 = ____?____   **54.** 6% of 34 = ____?____   **55.** 50% of 86 = ____?____

Use the circle graph for Exercises 56–58.   (Pages 386–387)

Last week, Clarence earned $200.80. How much of this is budgeted for

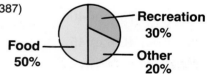

56. food?   **57.** recreation?   **58.** other?

Part 3 • PROBLEM SOLVING • APPLICATIONS

59. A stamp collector pastes a stamp and an enlargement of the stamp in an album. The stamp is 3 centimeters long and 2 centimeters wide. The enlargement is 9 centimeters long. How wide is it?   (Pages 366–367)

60. In 1927, Charles Lindberg flew the Spirit of St. Louis about 3,600 miles from New York to Paris. The flight took 34 hours. At that rate, how far could the plane travel in 51 hours?   (Pages 374–375)

61. The regular price of a tennis racket is $49.95. It is on sale at a 40% discount. Estimate how much it would cost.   (Pages 386–389)

62. While on vacation, the Yokiri family camped near a forest that covered 170 acres. A forest ranger told them that 22% of the forest had been cut for lumber. Estimate the number of acres that were <u>not</u> cut.   (Pages 388–389)

CHAPTER TEST

Solve.

1. $\frac{3}{4} = \frac{n}{24}$

2. $\frac{16}{18} = \frac{8}{n}$

3. $\frac{11}{12} = \frac{n}{144}$

Write = or ≠.

4. $\frac{5}{6}$ ● $\frac{25}{30}$

5. $\frac{7}{15}$ ● $\frac{56}{150}$

6. $\frac{5}{9}$ ● $\frac{22}{25}$

You spin this spinner once. Find each probability.

7. P(getting a circle)

8. P(getting a triangle)

9. How many stars can you expect to get in 15 spins?

Write the fraction for the percent.

10. 27%

11. 2%

Write the decimal for the percent.

12. 65%

13. 8%

Write the percent for each decimal.

14. 0.91

15. 0.05

Write the percent for each fraction.

16. $\frac{4}{25}$

17. $\frac{19}{50}$

18. Find 75% of 400.

19. Find 15% of 80.

20. Find 40% of 45.

21. Find 10% of 165.

Solve.

22. Lauren made a scale drawing of her room. In the drawing, the length of the room is 2 centimeters and the width is 2 centimeters. Each centimeter represents 2 meters. What are the actual dimensions of Lauren's room?

23. The first solor-powered plane traveled 6 miles in 20 minutes. At this rate, how many minutes would it take to travel 24 miles?

Choose the best estimate. Choose a, b, or c.

24. Rain is expected in a certain city 19% of the days of the year. Estimate how many days this is.

   a. 50   **b.** 60   **c.** 73

25. Manchu sees a record album for $8.95. He gets a $9\frac{1}{2}$% discount on the album. Estimate how much he pays.

   a. $8.00   **b.** $6.00   **c.** $5.50

ENRICHMENT

Experimental Probability

Toss a coin.

The probability that it will land heads is 1 out of 2, or $\frac{1}{2}$.

About how many times can you expect it to land heads if you toss it 2 times? 4 times? 6 times?

Complete the prediction table.

Now toss a coin and complete the results table.

- ● Compare the results with your prediction.

Prediction

Tosses	2	4	6	8	10
Heads	1	?	?	?	?

Results

Tosses	2	4	6	8	10
Heads	?	?	?	?	?

A number cube has faces numbered 1, 2, 3, 4, 5, and 6.

Toss the number cube. The probability of tossing a 4 or a 5 is 2 out of 6, or $\frac{2}{6}$.

Make a prediction table.

Now toss the number cube and complete the results table.

- ● Compare the results with your prediction.

Prediction

Tosses	6	12	18	24	30	36
4 or 5	2	?	?	?	?	?

Results

Tosses	6	12	18	24	30	36
4 or 5	?	?	?	?	?	?

Look at a book.

The probability that the letter *e* will appear in 1,000 letters is about 1 out of 13, or $\frac{1}{13}$.

Complete the prediction table.

Look at your book. Use it to complete the results chart.

- ● Compare the results with your prediction.

Prediction

Letters	13	26	39	52	65
e	1	?	?	?	?

Results

Letters	13	26	39	52	65
e	?	?	?	?	?

ADDITIONAL PRACTICE

SKILLS

Write a fraction for each ratio.   (Pages 362–363)

1. 7 to 10   **2.** 2 to 6   **3.** 20 to 45   **4.** 15 to 25

Solve.   (Pages 364–365)

5. $\frac{5}{6} = \frac{n}{12}$ **6.** $\frac{3}{4} = \frac{12}{n}$ **7.** $\frac{2}{n} = \frac{6}{15}$ **8.** $\frac{n}{8} = \frac{21}{42}$ **9.** $\frac{7}{9} = \frac{n}{36}$

Write = or ≠ .   (Pages 364–365)

10. $\frac{3}{4}$ ⬤ $\frac{9}{12}$ **11.** $\frac{2}{5}$ ⬤ $\frac{4}{10}$ **12.** $\frac{3}{7}$ ⬤ $\frac{9}{14}$ **13.** $\frac{6}{1}$ ⬤ $\frac{24}{6}$ **14.** $\frac{3}{9}$ ⬤ $\frac{27}{81}$

How many stars can you expect?   (Pages 370–373)

15. in 6 spins   **16.** in 12 spins   **17.** in 18 spins

Write the percents for the decimals and fractions.   (Pages 378–383)

18. 0.50   **19.** 0.20   **20.** 1.00   **21.** $\frac{3}{5}$ **22.** $\frac{7}{20}$

Write the decimals for the percents.   (Pages 380–381)

23. 25%   **24.** 33%   **25.** 6%   **26.** 100%   **27.** 40%

Write the fractions for the percents. Write the answers in lowest terms.
(Pages 380–381)

28. 50%   **29.** 20%   **30.** 8%   **31.** 90%   **32.** 64%

Complete.   (Pages 384–385)

33. 20% of 60 = ___?___   **34.** 5% of 46 = ___?___   **35.** 50% of 90 = ___?___

PROBLEM SOLVING • APPLICATIONS

36. On a scale drawing, each centimeter represents 6 meters. The dimensions of a room on the drawing are 25 cm by 19 cm. What are the actual dimensions?   (Pages 366–367)

37. A train traveled 960 kilometers in 2 hours. At this rate, how far can it travel in 5 hours?   (Pages 374–375)

38. Sonia budgets 25% each week for food. Last week she earned $178.20. Estimate how much she could spend for food.   (Pages 386–389)

39. Steve buys a basketball that sells for $21.50. He gets a 39% discount. Estimate the amount of the discount.   (Pages 386–389)

COMPUTER APPLICATIONS

Programs and Problem Solving

A baseball player's batting average is defined as a ratio.

$$\frac{\textbf{number of hits}}{\textbf{number of times-at-bat}}$$

PROBLEM: Write a program that computes a players batting average.

Solution: There are four logical steps for solving this problem.

① Write a formula for finding the batting average.

   Batting Average = Number of Hits ÷ Times-at-Bat

② Use letters to stand for the words in the formula.

   A = Batting Average
   H = Number of Hits
   B = Number of Times-at-Bat

③ Write a program.

   10 INPUT H, B
   20 PRINT "A=";H/B ⟵——— **A = H ÷ B**
   30 END

④ Check the program by using numbers for H and B. For example, let H = 81 and B = 360.
   Type the program. Press **RETURN**, or **ENTER**, or ⟵——⏎ after you type each line of the program. Then type **RUN**. Here is the display.

   RUN
   ? 81,360   ◀ The INPUT displays a question mark.
   A=.225   This is your "cue" to type 81,360.
   READY   ◀ The computer's "ready" symbol tells you to
                  type RUN to find another batting average.

EXERCISES • Run the program above to find each batting average.

1. H = 21, B = 40   **2.** H = 78, B = 400   **3.** H = 315, B = 840   **4.** H = 75, B = 200

5. Write a program that computes a worker's weekly pay. Use this formula.

   Pay = Hours Worked × Rate per Hour

   Find Jim's pay if he worked 35 hours and earned $5.25 per hour.

★ **6.** Write a program that computes the volume of a rectangular prism.

   Volume = Length × Width × Height

   Find the volume of a box where L = 32 cm, W = 20 cm, and H = 18 cm.

MIXED PRACTICE • Choose the correct answers.

1. Estimate the sum.

$989 + 101$

- **A.** 1,000
- **B.** 1,100
- **C.** 1,200
- **D.** not here

2. Estimate the difference.

$9\frac{1}{8} - 3\frac{3}{4}$

- **A.** 5
- **B.** 6
- **C.** 7
- **D.** not here

3. Estimate the product.

18.98×0.9

- **A.** 20
- **B.** 19
- **C.** 10
- **D.** not here

---

4. $39 - 14$ 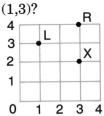 $85 - 60$

- **A.** >
- **B.** =
- **C.** <
- **D.** not here

5. 9×12 ● 8×19

- **A.** >
- **B.** =
- **C.** <
- **D.** not here

6. $\frac{2}{3} + \frac{1}{2}$ ● $1\frac{1}{8}$

- **A.** >
- **B.** =
- **C.** <
- **D.** not here

---

7. Which shows the inverse of

$31 - 19 = ?$

- **A.** $31 = ? \div 2$
- **B.** $16 + ? = 31$
- **C.** $19 + ? = 31$
- **D.** not here

8. Which shows the inverse of

$52 + 19 = ?$

- **A.** $52 = ? - 19$
- **B.** $19 + ? = 52$
- **C.** $73 = 52 - ?$
- **D.** not here

9. Which shows the inverse of

$18 + ? = 72$

- **A.** $54 - 18 = ?$
- **B.** $18 = 72 - ?$
- **C.** $18 + 72 = ?$
- **D.** not here

---

10. What letter is located at point (1,3)?

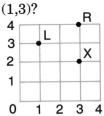

- **A.** R
- **B.** X
- **C.** L
- **D.** not here

11. What is the ordered pair for point C?

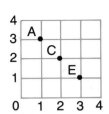

- **A.** (2,2)
- **B.** (3,4)
- **C.** (1,4)
- **D.** not here

12. What is the temperature?

- **A.** 0°
- **B.** +1°
- **C.** −1°
- **D.** not here

---

13. Pam earned $8 babysitting. She spent $3 for earrings. How much does she have left?

- **A.** $8
- **B.** $5
- **C.** $3
- **D.** not here

14. Mr. Walters lost 8 pounds last month and lost 7 pounds this month. What is his total loss?

- **A.** 15 pounds
- **B.** 1 pound
- **C.** 7 pounds
- **D.** not here

Integers

An atomic scientist studies an atom with an electrical charge of ⁻11. The scientist removes four negative charges.

● What is the charge now?

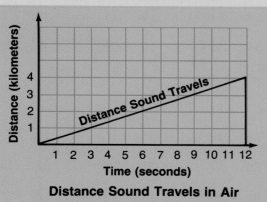

Distance (kilometers)

4
3
2
1

Distance Sound Travels

1 2 3 4 5 6 7 8 9 10 11 12

Time (seconds)

Distance Sound Travels in Air

A farmer noticed that a flash of lightning is followed 4 seconds later by a clap of thunder. A second flash of lightning is followed 6 seconds later by thunder.

● Use the graph to find about how far the storm has moved.

397

Opposites • Mental Math

Kara Martin is a swimming and diving coach. Her students dive from a board 2 meters above the surface of the water. The bottom of the diving well is 3 meters below the surface of the water.

- You can use **positive numbers** and **negative numbers** to show **opposites**.

- Use positive and negative numbers to show:
  a. the height of the board.
  b. the depth of the diving well.

Think Measure from the surface of the water. The surface of the water is the starting point, 0.

Height of the diving board ⟶ $^+2$ Read: positive two

Depth of the water ⟶ $^-3$ Read: negative three

A positive number that can describe 5 blocks to the right: $^+5$
- What negative number can describe 5 blocks to the left?

Think Find the opposite of $^+5$.

Five blocks to the left: $^-5$

PRACTICE • What is the opposite?

1. North   **2.** Down   **3.** West   **4.** Stop

Name the opposite numbers.

5. $^+7$ **6.** $^-5$ **7.** $^-16$ **8.** $^+24$ **9.** $^+54$ **10.** $^-73$

11. $^-127$ **12.** $^+450$ **13.** $^+777$ **14.** $^-813$ **15.** $^+690$ **16.** $^-907$

EXERCISES • Name the opposite numbers.

17. $^+3$ **18.** $^-3$ **19.** $^+5$ **20.** $^-4$ **21.** $^-8$ **22.** $^+7$

23. $^+16$ **24.** $^+18$ **25.** $^-12$ **26.** $^-17$ **27.** $^+15$ **28.** $^-11$

29. $^+42$ **30.** $^-36$ **31.** $^+50$ **32.** $^-28$ **33.** $^-92$ **34.** $^+76$

35. ⁻35	**36.** ⁺72	**37.** ⁺96	**38.** ⁻45	**39.** ⁻67	**40.** ⁻83
41. ⁺126	**42.** ⁻328	**43.** ⁻240	**44.** ⁺163	**45.** ⁺238	**46.** ⁻333
47. ⁻216	**48.** ⁺512	**49.** ⁺380	**50.** ⁻741	**51.** ⁻652	**52.** ⁺491
53. ⁺632	**54.** ⁻809	**55.** ⁺555	**56.** ⁻199	**57.** ⁺817	**58.** ⁻902

Name the opposites.

★ **59.** 55 meters above sea level

★ **60.** 20 kilometers southeast

★ **61.** 18 revolutions faster

★ **62.** 2 hours before

★ **63.** earn 14 dollars

★ **64.** 145 kilograms heavier

PROBLEM SOLVING • APPLICATIONS

65. Tim's football team gains 10 yards. This is shown by ⁺10. What number would show a loss of 10 yards?

66. You get on an elevator and go up 23 floors. This is shown by ⁺23. What number would show going down 23 floors?

67. Death Valley, California, is 85 meters below sea level. This is shown by ⁻85. What number would show 85 meters above sea level?

68. Ingrid spends 12 dollars. This is shown by ⁻12. What number would show earning 12 dollars?

69. The countdown for a rocket blastoff is at minus 8 seconds. This is shown by ⁻8. What number would show 8 seconds after blastoff?

70. It is 2 hours before the airplane departure. This is shown by ⁻2. What number would show 2 hours after departure?

THINKER'S CORNER

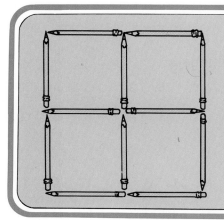

Use pencils or paperclips to make a design like this.

1. Remove 4 clips, leaving only 1 square.

2. Start with the original design. Remove 4 clips, leaving exactly 2 squares.

3. Start with the original design. Remove 2 clips, leaving exactly 3 squares.

4. Start with the original design. Remove 2 clips, leaving exactly 2 squares.

Integers

NASA flight engineers use integers to count the seconds to lift-off.

● **Integers** can be shown on the number line. Those to the right of 0 are **positive integers.** Those to the left of 0 are **negative integers.** 0 is an integer, but it is neither positive nor negative.

$^+5$ and $^-5$ are the same distance from 0.
$^+5$ and $^-5$ are opposite integers.

Move your finger along the number line from left to right. Notice that the numbers become greater.

$^+6$ is greater than $^+5$. $^+6 > {^+5}$
$^+4$ is greater than $^-4$. $^+4 > {^-4}$
$^-3$ is greater than $^-5$. $^-3 > {^-5}$

● Which is greater, $^+6$ or $^-6$?

Think $^+6$ is to the right of $^-6$ on the number line. So $^+6 > {^-6}$.

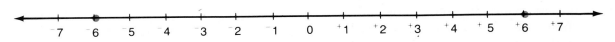

● Which is greater, $^-7$ or $^-5$?

Think $^-5$ is to the right of $^-7$. So $^-5 > {^-7}$.

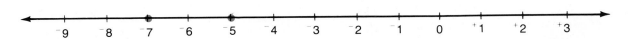

PRACTICE • **Mental Math**   Name the opposite integers.

1. $^+6$ 2. $^-4$ 3. $^+9$ 4. $^-10$ 5. $^+2$ 6. $^+3$

7. $^-12$ 8. $^+7$ 9. $^+38$ 10. $^-17$ 11. $^+52$ 12. $^+93$

Which is greater?

13. $^+8, {^+9}$ 14. $^-6, {^-5}$ 15. $^+2, {^-2}$ 16. $^+1, {^-8}$ 17. $^-7, {^+3}$

18. $^+6, {^-4}$ 19. $^-12, {^+12}$ 20. $^-8, {^+6}$ 21. $^+4, {^-9}$ 22. $^-11, {^-16}$

EXERCISES • Mental Math Name the opposite integers.

23. $^+10$ **24.** $^-9$ **25.** $^+1$ **26.** $^-7$ **27.** $^-16$ **28.** $^+20$

29. $^-26$ **30.** $^+42$ **31.** $^+25$ **32.** $^-64$ **33.** $^+22$ **34.** $^-5$

Which is greater?

35. $^+1, ^+4$ **36.** $^-1, ^-4$ **37.** $0, ^-6$ **38.** $^+2, ^+20$ **39.** $^-2, ^-20$

40. $^+5, ^-5$ **41.** $^+10, ^-3$ **42.** $^-10, ^+3$ **43.** $^-9, ^+4$ **44.** $^+9, ^-4$

Write > or <.

45. $^+8$ ● $^+3$ **46.** $^+2$ ● $^+7$ **47.** $^-2$ ● $^+7$

48. $^-9$ ● $^-4$ **49.** $^-3$ ● $^-6$ **50.** $^-6$ ● $^+2$

51. $^+12$ ● $^-15$ **52.** $^-12$ ● $^+15$ **53.** $^-26$ ● $^+13$

Write in order from least to greatest.

54. $^+3, ^-4, 0, ^-6, ^+6$ **55.** $^-8, ^-3, ^-1, ^+7, ^-7$

56. $^+6, ^+4, 0, ^-5, ^-7$ **57.** $^-19, ^+78, ^-45, ^+23, ^-89$

PROBLEM SOLVING • APPLICATIONS

58. On one mission, electrical system A is to be checked at $^-9$ seconds. Computer system A is to be checked at $^+2$ seconds. Which check will happen later?

59. A communications check is scheduled at $^-15$ seconds. A fuel check is scheduled at $^-8$ seconds. Which check will happen first?

60. A data check is scheduled for $^+8$ seconds. It will take 3 seconds to complete. When will the data check be completed?

61. A back-up system check must be complete at the time of ignition (0 seconds.) This check takes 9 seconds to complete. When should this back-up check be started?

Adding with Like Signs

Melinda Carter is a stockbroker. She buys and sells shares of stock. On Monday, her Gibson stock gained 3 points. On Tuesday, the stock gained 7 points.

● What was the total gain for the two days?

You can use a number line to help you add integers.

Think

3 point gain $\longrightarrow$ $^+3$
7 point gain $\longrightarrow$ $^+7$

$^+3$ and $^+7 = ?$

Step 1 Graph the first addend.

Step 2 From this point, draw an arrow to the right for the second addend.

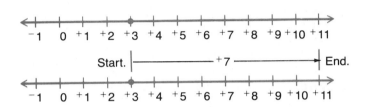

Step 3 Read the coordinate of the point where the arrow ends. $\longrightarrow$ $^+10$

$$^+3 + {}^+7 = {}^+10$$

The Gibson stock gained **10 points.**

Federal stock lost 3 points on Monday and 7 points on Tuesday.

● What was the total gain or loss?

$$^-3 + {}^-7 = ?$$

Think

3 point loss $\longrightarrow$ $^-3$
7 point loss $\longrightarrow$ $^-7$

Step 1 Graph the first addend.

Step 2 From this point, draw an arrow to the left for the second addend.

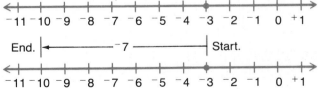

Step 3 Read the coordinate of the point where the arrow ends. $\longrightarrow$ $^-10$

$$^-3 + {}^-7 = {}^-10$$

Federal stock lost a total of **10 points.**

1. $^+2 + {}^+5 =$ ___?___

2. $^-2 + {}^-5 =$ ___?___

3. $^+3 + {}^+5 =$ ___?___

4. $^-3 + {}^-5 =$ ___?___

5. $0 + {}^-3 =$ ___?___

6. $^+5 + 0 =$ ___?___

EXERCISES • Add.

7. $^+5 + {}^+2 =$ ___?___

8. $^-5 + {}^-2 =$ ___?___

9. $^+3 + {}^+4 =$ ___?___

10. $^-3 + {}^-4 =$ ___?___

11. $^+4 + {}^+3 =$ ___?___

12. $^-4 + {}^-3 =$ ___?___

13. $^+6 + 0 =$ ___?___

14. $^-6 + 0 =$ ___?___

15. $^-1 + {}^-3 =$ ___?___

16. $^+1 + {}^+3 =$ ___?___

17. $^+9 + {}^+8 =$ ___?___

18. $^-9 + {}^-8 =$ ___?___

19. $^+5 + {}^+7 =$ ___?___

20. $^-7 + {}^-5 =$ ___?___

21. $0 + {}^+8 =$ ___?___

22. $^-8 + 0 =$ ___?___

23. $^-2 + {}^-3 =$ ___?___

24. $^-5 + {}^-1 =$ ___?___

25. $^+7 + {}^+2 =$ ___?___

26. $^-4 + {}^-6 =$ ___?___

27. $^+7 + {}^+1 =$ ___?___

★ 28. $0 +$ ___?___ $= {}^-4$

★ 29. $^-8 +$ ___?___ $= {}^-10$

★ 30. ___?___ $+ {}^+5 = 10$

★ 31. $^+8 +$ ___?___ $= {}^+15$

★ 32. ___?___ $+ {}^-6 = {}^-6$

★ 33. $^-9 +$ ___?___ $= {}^-12$

PROBLEM SOLVING • APPLICATIONS

Use integers to write the number sentences. Then solve.

34. TLP stock lost 2 points on Monday. It lost 4 points on Tuesday. What was the total gain or loss?

35. Silva stock gained 14 points on Wednesday. It gained 3 points on Thursday. What was the total gain or loss?

36. Melinda's trades made a profit of $900 on Monday. She made a profit of $200 on Tuesday. What was her total profit or loss?

37. Melinda's trades gave her a loss of $500 on Wednesday. She had a loss of $300 on Thursday. What was her total profit or loss for these two days?

38. Between 9 A.M. and 1 P.M., INK stock gained 9 points. Between 1 P.M. and 2 P.M., INK stock gained 3 points. Between 2 P.M. and the end of the day, INK stock gained 2 points. What was the total gain or loss for the day?

★ 39. Melinda's favorite stock, ALPHA, had an opening price of $10 on Monday. During Monday's trading, ALPHA gained 5 points. On Tuesday, ALPHA gained 3 points. What was the price of ALPHA stock at the close of trading Tuesday?

Adding with Unlike Signs

Eric Dorand, a running back for the Manatees, gains 6 yards on one play. He is tackled for a 4–yard loss on the next play.

● What was his total gain or loss for these two plays?

Think "Total" suggests addition.

$$^+6 + {}^-4 = ?$$

Step 1 Graph the first addend.

Step 2 From this point, draw an arrow to the left for the second addend.

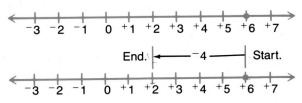

Step 3 Read the coordinate of the point where the arrow ends. ⟶ $^+2$

$$^+6 + {}^-4 = {}^+2$$

Eric Dorand **gained 2 yards** on the two plays.

● What is the total of an 8 yard loss and a 3 yard gain?

Think "Total" suggests addition.

$$^-8 + {}^+3 = ?$$

Step 1 Graph the first addend.

Step 2 From this point, draw an arrow to the right for the second addend.

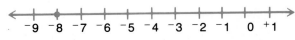

Step 3 Read the coordinate of the point where the arrow ends. ⟶ $^-5$

$$^-8 + {}^+3 = {}^-5$$

The total is a **5–yard loss.**

PRACTICE • Add.

1. $^+5 + {}^-2 = $ _____?_____

2. $^-5 + {}^+2 = $ _____?_____

3. $^+5 + {}^-5 = $ _____?_____

4. $^+4 + {}^-5 = $ _____?_____

5. $^-4 + {}^+5 = $ _____?_____

6. $^-5 + {}^+4 = $ _____?_____

EXERCISES • Add.

7. $^+3 + {}^-5 = $ _?_

8. $^-3 + {}^+5 = $ _?_

9. $^-4 + {}^-4 = $ _?_

10. $^-4 + {}^+4 = $ _?_

11. $^+8 + {}^-3 = $ _?_

12. $^-8 + {}^+3 = $ _?_

13. $^-3 + {}^+4 = $ _?_

14. $^+4 + {}^-3 = $ _?_

15. $^+3 + {}^-4 = $ _?_

16. $^-4 + {}^+3 = $ _?_

17. $^+11 + {}^-3 = $ _?_

18. $^+3 + {}^-11 = $ _?_

19. $^-9 + {}^+2 = $ _?_

20. $^+2 + {}^-9 = $ _?_

21. $^-3 + {}^+3 = $ _?_

22. $^+6 + {}^-7 = $ _?_

23. $^+12 + {}^-5 = $ _?_

24. $^-14 + {}^+8 = $ _?_

25. $^+3 + {}^+6 = $ _?_

26. $^-4 + {}^-2 = $ _?_

27. $^-6 + {}^-4 = $ _?_

 ★ **28.** $^+7 + {}^+3 + {}^+10 = $ _?_

★ **29.** $^-7 + {}^-5 + {}^-6 = $ _?_

★ **30.** $^+9 + {}^-2 + {}^+4 = $ _?_

★ **31.** $^-2 + {}^+8 + {}^-7 = $ _?_

PROBLEM SOLVING • APPLICATIONS

Use integers to write the number sentences. Then solve.

32. On his first carry, Dorand gained 6 yards. On the next carry, he lost 2 yards. What was his total for the two carries?

33. The Manatees lost 11 yards on one play. They gained 5 yards on the next play. What was their total for the two plays?

CALCULATOR • Adding Integers

You can use a calculator to add integers.

$$^+225 + {}^-58 + {}^+47 = ?$$

To enter a negative integer into a calculator, press the ⨤ key after entering the negative integer.

Press: ② ② ⑤ ⊕ ⑤ ⑧ ± ⊕ ④ ⑦ ⊜ [214]

EXERCISES • Add. Use the calculator.

1. $^+436 + {}^-318 + {}^+39 = $ _?_ **2.** $^+667 + {}^-442 + {}^-34 = $ _?_ **3.** $^-559 + {}^+334 + {}^-221 = $ _?_

PROBLEM SOLVING · STRATEGIES

Graphs and Estimation

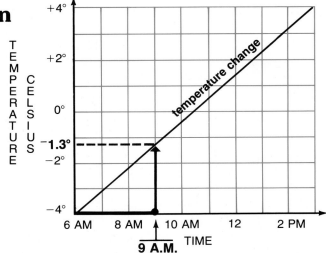

Example

You can use a graph to estimate an answer to a problem.

The graph shows the temperature change from 6 A.M. to 2 P.M.

● **Estimate** the temperature at 9 A.M.

Step 1 Locate 9 A.M. on the horizontal scale.

Step 2 Locate the point where 9 A.M. intersects the temperature change line.

Step 3 Read the approximate temperature from the vertical scale.

The point on the vertical scale is between ⁻1° C and ⁻2° C.
The temperature is **about ⁻1.3° C.**

Ⓔ PROBLEMS

Estimate the answer. Use the graph above.

1. Estimate the temperature at 12 noon.

2. At what time was the temperature about ⁻2.2° C?

3. About how many degrees did the temperature change between 6 A.M. and 1 P.M.?

4. About how much time did it take for the temperature to change from ⁻2° C to ⁺2° C?

Use the Moped Sales Graph to estimate the answers for Problems 5 through 7.

5. Estimate the difference in sales between Mizer Mite and Zumi for 1984.

6. Lazer mopeds are not selling well. Estimate the difference in sales between 1980 and 1986?

7. About how many more mopeds did Mizer Mite sell than Zumi between 1983 and 1986?

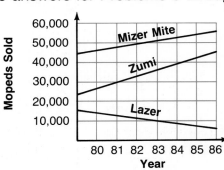

Moped Sales: 1980–85

You can estimate your distance from a storm by counting the seconds between the lightning and the thunder.
Use the Distance/Sound Graph to answer Problems 8–11.

8. A sailor is checking on an approaching thunderstorm. The sailor counts 6 seconds between the flash of lightning and the sound of thunder. About how far away is the storm?

9. A farmer is rushing to put equipment away before a thunderstorm arrives. The storm is about 2.5 kilometers away. How many seconds are there between the lightning and the thunder?

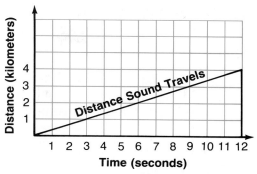

Distance Sound Travels in Air

10. A golfer is trying to finish playing the last hole. A thunderstorm is moving toward the golf course. There are 4 seconds between the lightning and the thunder. About how far away is the storm?

11. A flash of lightning is followed 4 seconds later by the clap of thunder. A second flash of lightning is followed 6 seconds later by thunder. About how far has the storm moved?

Write Your Own Problem

A commercial jet travels at 550 mph. Use this fact and the table of ordered pairs given to make a time/distance graph.

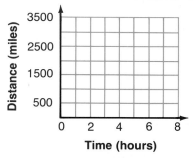

Ordered Pairs (Time, Distance)
(1 hour, 550 miles)
(2 hours, 1,100 miles)
(3 hours, 1,650 miles)
(4 hours, 2,200 miles)
(5 hours, 2,750 miles)
(6 hours, 3,300 miles)

Use the time-distance graph you made to write two problems as described below.

a. **Given:** Number of hours   **Estimate:** Number of miles

b. **Given:** Number of miles   **Estimate:** Number of hours

MID-CHAPTER REVIEW

Name the opposite numbers.   (Pages 398–399)

1. $^+5$ **2.** $^-9$ **3.** $^+12$ **4.** $^-75$ **5.** $^+29$

Write < or >.   (Pages 400–401)

6. $^+5$ ● $^+2$ **7.** $^-3$ ● $^-2$ **8.** $^+12$ ● $^-4$ **9.** $^-6$ ● $^+3$ **10.** $^-40$ ● $^+5$

Write in order from least to greatest.   (Pages 400–401)

11. $^+2, ^-3, 0\ ^-1, ^+5$ **12.** $^+12, ^-8, ^+1, ^+8, ^-4$ **13.** $^+6, ^-6, ^+9, ^-9, ^-3$

Add.   (Pages 402–403)

14. $^+6 + ^+3 = $ __?__   **15.** $^-8 + ^-5 = $ __?__   **16.** $^-7 + ^-8 = $ __?__

17. $^+8 + ^+9 = $ __?__   **18.** $^-7 + ^-7 = $ __?__   **19.** $^-9 + ^-6 = $ __?__

20. $0 + ^-9 = $ __?__   **21.** $^+3 + ^+8 = $ __?__   **22.** $^-7 + ^-3 = $ __?__

Add.   (Pages 404–405)

23. $^-7 + ^+3 = $ __?__   **24.** $^+8 + ^-3 = $ __?__   **25.** $^-10 + ^+8 = $ __?__

26. $^+6 + ^-6 = $ __?__   **27.** $^-1 + ^+10 = $ __?__   **28.** $^+9 + ^-5 = $ __?__

29. $^-6 + ^+4 = $ __?__   **30.** $^-2 + ^+7 = $ __?__   **31.** $^+10 + ^-8 = $ __?__

Use the graph to solve each problem.

32. Estimate the fuel used for a 200–mile trip.   (Page 406–407)

33. Estimate how many miles can be traveled on 450 gallons of fuel.   (Page 406–407)

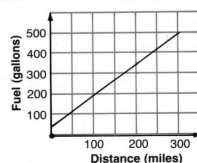

MAINTENANCE • MIXED PRACTICE

Add.

1. 456
$+398$

2. 709
$+387$

3. 3,067
$+5,944$

4. 18,595
$+29,606$

5. 254,326
$+594,684$

Complete.

6. $6 + $ __?__ $= 13$ **7.** __?__ $+ 7 = 16$ **8.** $4 + $ __?__ $= 11$

Subtract.

9. 502
-469

10. 692
-397

11. 6,008
$-4,257$

12. 32,421
$-18,909$

13. 600,253
$-499,496$

CAREER APPLICATIONS

Meteorologist

Meteorologists use averages to predict weather. One of these is the average amount of rainfall for a given month. When the rainfall is below the average, a negative number is used. This is called a **deficiency.** When the rainfall is above the average, a positive number is used. This is called an **excess.** The **net excess** or **deficiency** of rainfall for a 6–month period is the sum of the excesses and the deficiencies for the 6 months.

EXAMPLE: Find the net excess or deficiency of rainfall.

Sept.	Oct.	Nov.	Dec.	Jan.	Feb.
$^+3$ cm	$^-1$ cm	$^-3$ cm	$^-3$ cm	$^+2$ cm	$^+4$ cm

Step 1 Add the negative numbers. $\longrightarrow$ $^-1 + {^-3} + {^-3} = {^-7}$

Step 2 Add the positive numbers. $\longrightarrow$ $^+3 + {^+2} + {^+4} = {^+9}$

Step 3 Add the results. $\longrightarrow$ $^+9 + {^-7} = {^+}\mathbf{2}$

There was an **excess of 2 centimeters** of rainfall.

EXERCISES • Find the net excess or deficiency of rainfall.

1.

Jan.	Feb.	March	April	May	June
$^+1.2$ cm	$^+2.3$ cm	$^-0.6$ cm	$^+1.2$ cm	$^-1.5$ cm	$^-0.9$ cm

2.

July	Aug.	Sept.	Oct.	Nov.	Dec.
$^-1.5$ cm	$^-0.2$ cm	$^+1.1$ cm	$^+1.4$ cm	$^-2.7$ cm	$^+3.3$ cm

3.

April	May	June	July	Aug.	Sept.
$^+0.8$ cm	$^-1.5$ cm	$^+2.3$ cm	$^+1.2$ cm	$^-3.5$ cm	$^+0.4$ cm

4.

Oct.	Nov.	Dec.	Jan.	Feb.	March
$^-2.5$ cm	$^+1.8$ cm	$^-0.7$ cm	$^-1.3$ cm	$^+1.6$ cm	$^-2.6$ cm

PROJECT   Find the average temperature for May in your part of the country. Compare it with the average daily temperature for a seven–day period. Record the difference as a positive or a negative number. Was the temperature above or below average for the seven–day period?

Subtracting with Like Signs

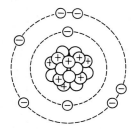

An atomic scientist studies an atom with an electrical charge of ⁻11. The scientist removes 4 negative charges.

Think Addition and subtraction are related.
You can think of subtraction as finding a missing addend.

$^-11 - {}^-4 = ?$ ⟶ $^-11 = {}^-4 + ?$

 Rewrite as an addition problem.

Step 1 Use the addition problem. Graph ⁻4.

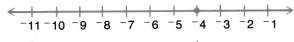

Step 2 You want to reach ⁻11. Draw an arrow from ⁻4 to ⁻11.

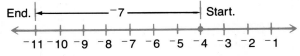

Step 3 Count the number of units. Since you moved 7 units to the left, the result is ⁻7.

$$^-11 - {}^-4 = {}^-\mathbf{7}$$

An atom has an electrical charge of ⁺6. The scientist takes away ⁺8 electrical charges.

● What is the charge now?

Think "Takes away" suggests subtraction.

$^+6 - {}^+8 = ?$ ⟶ $^+6 = {}^+8 + ?$

Rewrite as an addition problem.

Step 1 Use the addition problem. Graph ⁺8.

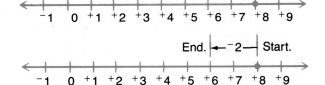

Step 2 You want to reach ⁺6. Draw an arrow from ⁺8 to ⁺6.

Step 3 Count the number of units. Since you moved 2 units to the left, the result is ⁻2.

$$^+6 - {}^+8 = {}^-\mathbf{2}$$

PRACTICE • Find the missing addends.

1. $^+3 + \underline{\ \ ?\ \ } = {}^+7$

2. $^-4 + \underline{\ \ ?\ \ } = {}^-6$

3. $^-5 + \underline{\ \ ?\ \ } = {}^-2$

Subtract.

4. $^+8 - {}^+4 = \underline{\ \ ?\ \ }$

5. $^-6 - {}^-2 = \underline{\ \ ?\ \ }$

6. $^-2 - {}^-7 = \underline{\ \ ?\ \ }$

EXERCISES • Subtract.

7. $^-4 - {}^-1 = \underline{\quad?\quad}$

8. $^+4 - {}^+1 = \underline{\quad?\quad}$

9. $^+5 - {}^+2 = \underline{\quad?\quad}$

10. $^-5 - {}^-2 = \underline{\quad?\quad}$

11. $^+3 - {}^+4 = \underline{\quad?\quad}$

12. $^-3 - {}^-4 = \underline{\quad?\quad}$

13. $^-9 - {}^-2 = \underline{\quad?\quad}$

14. $^+9 - {}^+2 = \underline{\quad?\quad}$

15. $^-3 - {}^-8 = \underline{\quad?\quad}$

16. $^+11 - {}^+7 = \underline{\quad?\quad}$

17. $^+3 - {}^+10 = \underline{\quad?\quad}$

18. $^-3 - {}^-10 = \underline{\quad?\quad}$

19. $^+6 - {}^+5 = \underline{\quad?\quad}$

20. $^-6 - {}^-5 = \underline{\quad?\quad}$

21. $^-6 - {}^-7 = \underline{\quad?\quad}$

22. $^+6 - {}^+7 = \underline{\quad?\quad}$

23. $^+4 - {}^+6 = \underline{\quad?\quad}$

24. $^-4 - {}^-6 = \underline{\quad?\quad}$

25. $^+13 - {}^+3 = \underline{\quad?\quad}$

26. $^-13 - {}^-3 = \underline{\quad?\quad}$

27. $^+2 - {}^+8 = \underline{\quad?\quad}$

28. $^-2 - {}^-8 = \underline{\quad?\quad}$

29. $^+10 - {}^+7 = \underline{\quad?\quad}$

30. $^-10 - {}^-7 = \underline{\quad?\quad}$

31. $^+8 - {}^+9 = \underline{\quad?\quad}$

32. $^-8 - {}^-9 = \underline{\quad?\quad}$

33. $^-3 - {}^-3 = \underline{\quad?\quad}$

★ 34. $^+3 - \underline{\quad?\quad} = 0$

★ 35. $\underline{\quad?\quad} - {}^-6 = {}^+6$

★ 36. $^+3 - \underline{\quad?\quad} = {}^-3$

PROBLEM SOLVING • APPLICATIONS

Use integers to write the number sentences. Then solve.

37. An atom has an electrical charge of $^-9$. Six of the negative charges are removed. What is the charge on the atom now?

38. An atom has an electrical charge of $^-2$. Then 7 negative charges are removed. What is the new charge on the atom?

★ 39. At the beginning of an experiment, the electrical charge on an atom was $^-2$. Three more negative charges were added. Then 4 negative charges were removed. What was the charge on the atom at the end of the experiment?

★ 40. The electrical charge on an atom was $^-6$. During the experiment, charges were removed. At the end of the experiment, the charge on the atom was $^-1$. What charges were removed?

PROJECT Find examples of integers in your local newspaper. Write three word problems using the examples you find. Exchange your problems with your classmates.

Subtracting with Unlike Signs

A meteorologist uses integers to report weather conditions. At 8 A.M. today the temperature was $^+8°C$. Yesterday at 8:00 A.M. the temperature was $^-3°C$.

● What was the temperature change for this 24-hour period?

Think Subtract to find the amount of change.

$^+8 - ^-3 = ?$ $^+8 = ^-3 + ?$ ◀ **Rewrite as an addition problem.**

Step 1 Use the addition problem. Graph $^-3$.

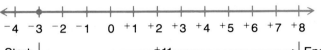

Step 2 You want to reach $^+8$. Draw an arrow from $^-3$ to $^+8$.

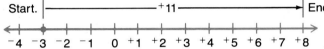

Step 3 Count the number of units. Since you moved 11 units **to the right,** the result is $^+11$.

$$^+8 - ^-3 = ^+11$$

● Subtract: $^-7 - ^+5 = ?$

Think Write an addition problem.

$^-7 - ^+5 = ?$ $^-7 = ^+5 + ?$

Step 1 Use the addition problem. Graph $^+5$.

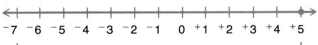

Step 2 You want to reach $^-7$. Draw an arrow from $^+5$ to $^-7$.

Step 3 Count the number of units. Since you moved 12 units **to the left,** the result is -12.

$$^-7 - ^+5 = ^-12$$

PRACTICE • Find the missing addends.

1. $^-4 + \underline{\quad ? \quad} = ^+3$

2. $^+5 + \underline{\quad ? \quad} = ^-2$

3. $^-6 + \underline{\quad ? \quad} = ^+10$

EXERCISES • Subtract.

4. $^+7 - ^-3 = \underline{\quad ? \quad}$

5. $^-4 - ^+1 = \underline{\quad ? \quad}$

6. $^-6 - ^+2 = \underline{\quad ? \quad}$

7. $^+8 - {}^-3 = $ ___?___

8. $^-8 - {}^+3 = $ ___?___

9. $^-9 - {}^+6 = $ ___?___

10. $^+9 - {}^-6 = $ ___?___

11. $^-11 - {}^+4 = $ ___?___

12. $^+11 - {}^-4 = $ ___?___

13. $^+10 - {}^-3 = $ ___?___

14. $^-10 - {}^+3 = $ ___?___

15. $^+6 - {}^-5 = $ ___?___

16. $^-6 - {}^+5 = $ ___?___

17. $^-5 - {}^+5 = $ ___?___

18. $^+5 - {}^-5 = $ ___?___

19. $^+4 - {}^-6 = $ ___?___

20. $^-4 - {}^+6 = $ ___?___

21. $^-7 - {}^+10 = $ ___?___

22. $^+7 - {}^-10 = $ ___?___

23. $^+2 - {}^-8 = $ ___?___

24. $^-2 - {}^+8 = $ ___?___

25. $^-8 - {}^+6 = $ ___?___

26. $^-8 - {}^-6 = $ ___?___

27. $^+6 - {}^+13 = $ ___?___

28. $^+6 - {}^-13 = $ ___?___

29. $^+2 - {}^-10 = $ ___?___

30. $^-2 - {}^+10 = $ ___?___

31. $^+15 - {}^+6 = $ ___?___

32. $^-15 - {}^+6 = $ ___?___

33. $^-9 - {}^-15 = $ ___?___

Write + and − to make a true sentence.

★ 34. $^+6$ ⬤ $^-3$ ⬤ $^+4 = {}^-1$ ★ 35. $^+5$ ⬤ $^-2$ ⬤ $^+8 = {}^+15$ ★ 36. $^+2$ ⬤ $^+7$ ⬤ $^-5 = {}^+14$

Complete the table. The first one is done for you.

The temperature is $^+4°C$. It was $^-2°C$ an hour ago. The temperature changed $^+6°$.

	Now	Before	Change
37.	$^+4°C$	$^-2°C$	$^+6°$
38.	$^+8°C$	$^-3°C$	?
39.	$^-4°C$	$^+2°C$	?
40.	$^-8°C$	$^+3°C$	?
41.	$^-6°C$	$^+6°C$	?
42.	$^+3°C$	$^-5°C$	?

PROBLEM SOLVING • APPLICATIONS

CHOOSE   • mental math • pencil and paper • calculator   SOLVE

Use integers to write the number sentences. Then solve.

43. Last winter, the high temperature in Phoenix was 7°C. The low that day in Flagstaff was $^-8°C$. What was the difference between these Arizona temperatures?

44. A national high temperature of 30°C was reported in Corpus Christi, Texas. On the same day, the national low temperature of $^-27°C$ was reported in West Yellowstone, Montana. What was the difference between the national high and low temperatures for that day?

45. Before a storm, the temperature was 9°C. After the storm passed, the temperature was $^-3°C$. What was the change in temperature?

Integers • 413

Graphing Ordered Pairs of Integers

Lester Ray manages school buses. He receives a computer printout listing all students who take the bus. Pick-up points are coded by ordered pairs. Lester uses a grid to graph the ordered pairs.

The ordered pair ($^-$4, $^+$3) locates pick up point D. The ordered pair ($^-$4, $^+$3) means to start at 0, move 4 spaces to the left, then move 3 spaces up.

The ordered pair ($^+$3, $^-$4) locates point F. Point F is 3 spaces to the right, then 4 spaces down.

The ordered pair (0, $^+$3) locates point G. G is 0 spaces to the left or the right and 3 spaces up.

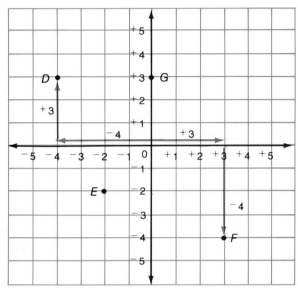

PRACTICE • What letter is at the point?

1. ($^+$5, $^-$3)   **2.** ($^-$2, $^-$2)   **3.** ($^+$3, $^-$5)

4. ($^+$1, $^-$1)   **5.** ($^+$4, $^+$1)   **6.** ($^+$4, $^-$2)

Give the ordered pair for the point.

7. K   **8.** N   **9.** P

10. Q   **11.** S   **12.** U

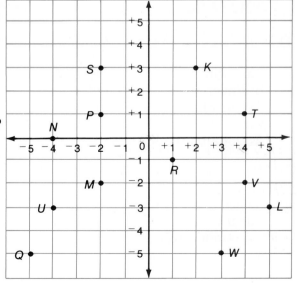

EXERCISES • What letter is at the point?

13. $(^+3, ^-3)$ **14.** $(^-6, ^-2)$

15. $(^-5, 0)$ **16.** $(^-1, ^+5)$

17. $(^+1, ^-2)$ **18.** $(^-3, ^-2)$

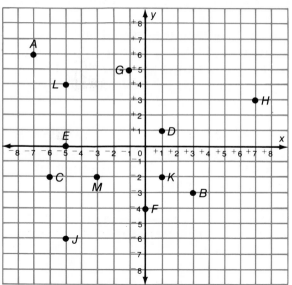

Give the ordered pair for the point.

19. A   **20.** D

21. F   **22.** H

23. J   **24.** L

PROBLEM SOLVING • APPLICATIONS

Make a grid like Lester's
on a sheet of graph paper.
Locate the ordered pairs.
Draw a dot at each point.
Label the dots with the letter.

Connect the dots to form a picture.

25.

Point	Ordered Pair
S	$(^+2, ^+5)$
T	$(^+2, ^-3)$
U	$(^-3, ^-5)$
V	$(^-3, ^+3)$
S	$(^+2, ^+5)$

26.

Point	Ordered Pair
A	$(^+4, ^-4)$
B	$(^+4, ^-1)$
C	$(^+3, ^-2)$
D	$(0, ^+3)$
E	$(^-2, ^+1)$
F	$(^+2, ^-3)$
G	$(^+1, ^-4)$
A	$(^+4, ^-4)$

Follow the rule. Complete
the table. Use the ordered
pairs (INPUT, OUTPUT) to
locate the points on a grid.

Draw a line through the points.

★ **27. Subtract** $^-4$.

INPUT	OUTPUT
$^-3$	$^+1$
$^-2$	?
$^-1$	?
0	?
$^+1$	?
$^+2$	?
$^+3$	?

★ **28. Add** $^-2$.

INPUT	OUTPUT
$^-3$	$^-5$
$^-2$	?
$^-1$	?
0	?
$^+1$	?
$^+2$	?
$^+3$	?

NON-ROUTINE PROBLEM SOLVING

Ramon likes to play golf during the 8 weeks of his summer vacation. He talked with his parents about buying a season pass, paying regular fees, or using a permit. This list shows the possible choices.

CHOICE 1

A season pass costs $95.

CHOICE 2

The regular fee is $5.75 per game.

CHOICE 3

A permit costs $30 paid in advance. There is an additional fee of $3.75 per game.

FIND THE COST

Ramon decided to make a table to show the total cost of each choice when playing once, twice, three times, or four times a week.

	Times Played per Week	Cost		
		Choice 1	Choice 2	Choice 3
1.	1	?	?	?
2.	2	?	?	?
3.	3	?	?	?
4.	4	?	?	?

5. What is the greatest number of games Ramon can play paying regular fees before the total cost is greater than the cost of a season pass?

6. What is the greatest number of games Ramon can play with a permit before the total cost is greater than the cost of a season pass?

MAKING A CHOICE

7. What is the least expensive choice for the golfer who plays once a week?

8. What do the table and the results of Exercises 5 and 6 show about the cost of the 3 choices for the golfer who plays twice a week?

9. What does the table show about the cost of the three choices for the golfer who plays more than twice a week?

10. Ramon decided he would play twice a week. He selected Choice 1. Give one advantage to this choice.

11. Rebecca also plans to play golf about twice a week. She selected Choice 3. Give one advantage to this choice.

12. Suppose you were Ramon and that you play golf 2 or 3 times a week. Which choice would you make? Give reasons for your choice.

CHAPTER REVIEW

Part 1 • VOCABULARY

For Exercises 1–6, choose from the box at the right the word(s) that completes the sentence.

1. The number $^-16$ is called a __?__ number.   (Page 398)

2. The number $^+7$ is called a __?__ number.   (Page 398)

3. The numbers used to locate points on a grid are called __?__.   (Page 414)

4. The numbers to the right of 0 on a number line are __?__ integers.   (Page 400)

5. You can tell whether a number is positive or negative by looking at its __?__.   (Page 398)

6. The integers $^+5$ and $^-5$ are __?__ integers.   (Page 398)

integers

negative

opposite

ordered pairs

positive

sign

Part 2 • SKILLS

Name the opposite numbers.   (Pages 398–399)

7. $^+7$
8. $^-3$
9. $^+14$
10. $^-39$
11. $^+96$

Write < or >.   (Pages 400–401)

12. $^+4$ ⬤ $^-4$
13. $^-3$ ⬤ $^-4$
14. $^+12$ ⬤ $^-13$
15. $^-7$ ⬤ $^+5$
16. $^-36$ ⬤ 0

Write in order from least to greatest   (Pages 400–401)

17. $^-3, ^-4, ^+4, ^+3, ^+1$
18. $0, ^-12, ^-13, ^+8, ^+3$
19. $^+4, ^+2, ^-2, ^+11, ^-11$

Add.   (Pages 402–403)

20. $^+5 + ^+4 = $ __?__
21. $^-7 + ^-3 = $ __?__
22. $^-9 + ^-4 = $ __?__

23. $^+6 + ^+9 = $ __?__
24. $^-8 + ^-8 = $ __?__
25. $^-3 + ^-9 = $ __?__

26. $^+10 + ^+7 = $ __?__
27. $^-3 + ^-11 = $ __?__
28. $^-16 + ^-4 = $ __?__

29. $^-5 + ^-9 = $ __?__
30. $^+4 + ^+9 = $ __?__
31. $^-6 + ^-2 = $ __?__

Add.   (Pages 404–405)

32. $^-8 + ^+9 = $ __?__
33. $^+6 + ^-6 = $ __?__
34. $^+10 + ^-5 = $ __?__

35. $^-2 + {}^+6 = $ ___?___

36. $^+4 + {}^-5 = $ ___?___

37. $^-9 + {}^+9 = $ ___?___

38. $^-7 + {}^+7 = $ ___?___

39. $^-2 + {}^+7 = $ ___?___

40. $^+2 + {}^-8 = $ ___?___

41. $^-12 + {}^+6 = $ ___?___

42. $^+11 + {}^-5 = $ ___?___

43. $^-9 + {}^+7 = $ ___?___

Subtract. (Pages 410–411)

44. $^-4 - {}^-3 = $ ___?___

45. $^+6 - {}^+10 = $ ___?___

46. $^-13 - {}^-3 = $ ___?___

47. $^+8 - {}^+8 = $ ___?___

48. $^-10 - {}^-4 = $ ___?___

49. $^-9 - {}^-9 = $ ___?___

50. $^+6 - {}^+3 = $ ___?___

51. $^-10 - {}^-6 = $ ___?___

52. $^-12 - {}^-7 = $ ___?___

53. $^+3 - {}^+3 = $ ___?___

54. $^+7 - {}^+2 = $ ___?___

55. $^-10 - {}^-10 = $ ___?___

Subtract. (Pages 412–413)

56. $^+7 - {}^-4 = $ ___?___

57. $^+4 - {}^-10 = $ ___?___

58. $^-5 - {}^+9 = $ ___?___

59. $^+6 - {}^-13 = $ ___?___

60. $^-2 - {}^+3 = $ ___?___

61. $^-8 - {}^+10 = $ ___?___

62. $^+10 - {}^-3 = $ ___?___

63. $^-7 - {}^+3 = $ ___?___

64. $^-14 - {}^+7 = $ ___?___

65. $^-9 - {}^+6 = $ ___?___

66. $^-4 - {}^+10 = $ ___?___

67. $^+1 - {}^-13 = $ ___?___

Use the grid. What letter is at the point? (Pages 414–415)

68. $(^+1, {}^-2)$

69. $(^+2, {}^-2)$

70. $(^+3, 0)$

71. $(^-2, {}^-3)$

Use the grid. Give the ordered pair for the point.

72. B

73. E

74. G

75. D

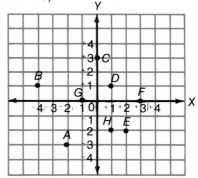

Part 3 • PROBLEM SOLVING • APPLICATIONS

Use the graph to solve each problem. (pages 406–407)

76. Estimate the kg of rubber latex produced on 40 acres of trees.

77. Estimate the number of acres required to produce 45,000 kg of rubber latex.

78. Estimate how much more latex can be produced on 100 acres than 20 acres of rubber trees.

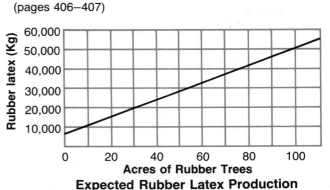

Expected Rubber Latex Production

CHAPTER TEST

Name the opposite integers.

1. $^+5$

2. $^-12$

3. $^+39$

Write > or <.

4. $^+2$ 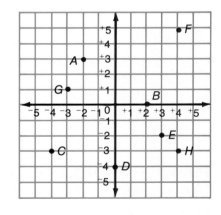 $^+9$

5. $^-5$ $^-7$

6. $^+12$ $^-14$

Add.

7. $^+7 + {}^+6 = \underline{\quad?\quad}$

8. $^-2 + {}^-2 = \underline{\quad?\quad}$

9. $^-4 + {}^-3 = \underline{\quad?\quad}$

10. $^+3 + {}^-6 = \underline{\quad?\quad}$

11. $^-6 + 0 = \underline{\quad?\quad}$

12. $^-10 + {}^+9 = \underline{\quad?\quad}$

Subtract.

13. $^+8 - {}^+7 = \underline{\quad?\quad}$

14. $^-10 - {}^-6 = \underline{\quad?\quad}$

15. $^+14 - {}^+6 = \underline{\quad?\quad}$

16. $^+5 - {}^-1 = \underline{\quad?\quad}$

17. $^-2 - {}^+1 = \underline{\quad?\quad}$

18. $^+4 - {}^-7 = \underline{\quad?\quad}$

What letter is at the point?

19. $(^-2, {}^+3)$

20. $(^+4, {}^-3)$

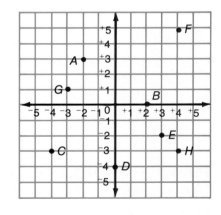

Give the ordered pair for the point.

21. C

22. B

Use the line graph to estimate the answer.

23. About how many more bicycles than Abello did Dumas export in 1980?

24. About how many bicycles were exported by all three companies in 1976?

25. About how many more bicycles did Dumas export in 1982 than in 1976?

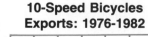

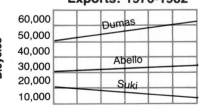

ENRICHMENT

Square Root

To find the number of tiles that are needed to cover this square, multiply the number of rows by the number in each row.

$4 \times 4 = 16$

When the two factors are the same, the product is the **square** of the factor. The factor is the **square root** of the product. The symbol for square root is $\sqrt{}$ and is read "the square root of."

Since $4 \times 4 = 16$, $\sqrt{16} = 4$.
The square of 4 is 16.
The square root of 16 is 4.

Since $3 \times 3 = 9$, $\sqrt{9} = 3$.
The square of 3 is 9.
The square root of 9 is 3.

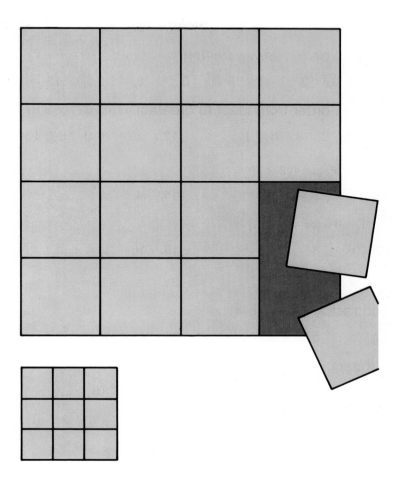

EXERCISES • Copy and complete the table.

					1.	2.	3.	4.	5.	6.
Number	1	2	3	4	5	6	7	8	9	10
Square	1	4	9	16	?	?	?	?	?	?

Use the table to find the square roots.

7. $\sqrt{16}$ **8.** $\sqrt{9}$ **9.** $\sqrt{49}$ **10.** $\sqrt{4}$ **11.** $\sqrt{81}$

12. $\sqrt{1}$ **13.** $\sqrt{25}$ **14.** $\sqrt{100}$ **15.** $\sqrt{36}$ **16.** $\sqrt{64}$

ADDITIONAL PRACTICE

SKILLS

Name the opposite numbers. (Pages 398–399)

1. $^+3$ **2.** $^-9$ **3.** $^+10$ **4.** $^-47$ **5.** $^+85$

Write < or >. (Pages 400–401)

6. $^-3$ ⬤ $^+2$ **7.** $^-5$ ⬤ $^+5$ **8.** $^+14$ ⬤ $^-13$ **9.** 0 ⬤ $^-8$ **10.** $^+1$ ⬤ $^-2$

Write in order from least to greatest. (Pages 400-401)

11. $^-2, ^+2, ^+4, ^-3, ^+1$ **12.** $^-12, ^+3, 0, ^+6, ^-13$ **13.** $^+1, ^+2, ^-1, ^+3, ^-5$

Add. (Pages 402–403)

14. $^+7 + ^+8 = $ _?_   **15.** $^-4 + ^-4 = $ _?_   **16.** $^-9 + ^-9 = $ _?_

Add. (Pages 404–405)

17. $^-6 + ^+8 = $ _?_   **18.** $^+9 + ^-2 = $ _?_   **19.** $^-3 + ^+6 = $ _?_

20. $^-7 + ^+8 = $ _?_   **21.** $^+4 + ^-10 = $ _?_   **22.** $^-9 + ^+12 = $ _?_

Subtract. (Pages 410–411)

23. $^-8 - ^-5 = $ _?_   **24.** $^+3 - ^+8 - $ _?_   **25.** $^-9 - ^-9 = $ _?_

Subtract. (Pages 412–413)

26. $^+9 - ^-6$ _?_   **27.** $^-4 - ^+10 = $ _?_   **28.** $^+7 - ^-8 = $ _?_

29. $^-2 - ^+8 = $ _?_   **30.** $^+8 - ^-6 = $ _?_   **31.** $^-10 - ^+3 = $ _?_

Use the grid. What letter is at the point?
(Pages 414–415)

32. $(^-3, ^+2)$ **33.** $(^-2, ^-1)$ **34.** $(^+2, ^-2)$

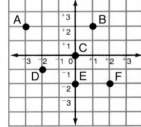

Use the grid. Give the ordered pair for
the point. (Pages 414–415)

35. B   **36.** C   **37.** E

PROBLEM SOLVING APPLICATIONS

Use the graph.

38. Estimate how much water would
be required if there were 60 hotel
guests. (Pages 406–407)

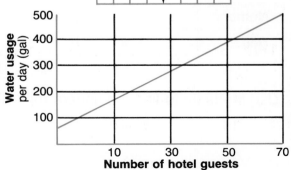

COMMON ERRORS

Each of these problems contains a common error.

a. Find the correct answer.
b. Find the error.

1. Name the angle

$\angle EFD$

2. Name the figure.

line

3. Name the figure.

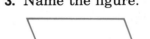

rectangle

4. Name the diameter.

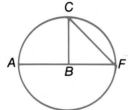

$\overline{BF}$ = **diameter**

5. Find the equal ratio.

$\dfrac{2}{7} = \dfrac{?}{14}$

$\dfrac{2}{7} + \dfrac{7}{7} = \dfrac{9}{14}$

6. Write = or ≠.

$\dfrac{2}{5}$ ● $\dfrac{6}{15}$ → $\dfrac{12}{75}$

$\dfrac{2}{5} \neq \dfrac{6}{15}$

7. Write a fraction for 65%

$\dfrac{65}{1,000}$

8. Write a percent for $\frac{3}{5}$.

$\begin{array}{r} 1.66 \\ 3\overline{)5.00} \\ 3 \\ \overline{2}\,0 \\ 1\,8 \\ \overline{20} \\ 18 \\ \overline{2} \end{array}$ $\dfrac{2}{3} = 1.66\dfrac{2}{3}\%$

9. Complete.

5% of 60 = $\underline{\ ?\ }$.

$\begin{array}{r} 60 \\ \times\ 5 \\ \hline 300 \end{array}$

10. Write 13% as a decimal.

13% = **1.3**

11. Add.

$^-6 + {}^-4 = \underline{\ ?\ }$

$^-6 + {}^-4 = 2$

12. Add.

$^-8 + {}^+3 = \underline{\ ?\ }$

$^-8 + {}^+3 = {}^-11$

13. Subtract.

$^+9 - {}^+5 = \underline{\ ?\ }$

$^+9 - {}^+5 = {}^-14$

14. Subtract.

$^+4 - {}^-3 = \underline{\ ?\ }$

$^+4 - {}^-3 = {}^-7$

15. Name the lines.

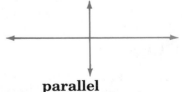

parallel

CUMULATIVE REVIEW

Chapters 1 through 14

Choose the correct answer

1. Divide.

$25\overline{)3553}$

A. 142 r 3   **B.** 1423
C. 14 r 3   **D.** not here

2. What digit is in the thousandths place?

49632.705

A. 9   **B.** 5
C. 4   **D.** not here

3. Add.

$24.63 + 4.8 + 326.5 = ?$

A. 3.5593   **B.** 355.93
C. 0.5776   **D.** not here

---

4. Compare.

$\frac{5}{7}$ ● $\frac{2}{3}$

A. <
B. >
C. =
D. not here

5. Name the angle.

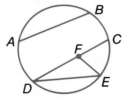

A. right
B. acute
C. obtuse
D. not here

6. Name the lines.

A. parallel
B. perpendicular
C. intersecting
D. not here

---

7. How many faces are there in this solid figure?

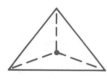

A. 3

B. 6

C. 4

D. not here

8. Name the 3 radii of the circle.

A. BA, EF, DE

B. CF, EF, DF

C. BA, DE, CD

D. not here

9. Write a fraction for the ratio.

2:7

A. $\frac{2}{7}$

B. $\frac{7}{2}$

C. $\frac{4}{7}$

D. not here

---

10. Joan played tennis $2\frac{1}{2}$ hours on Tuesday and $1\frac{3}{5}$ hours on Friday. How many hours did she play in all?

A. 3 hours   **B.** 4 hours
C. 5 hours   **D.** not here

11. On Saturday morning, the temperature was ⁻4°C. By 2 P.M. the temperature had risen 7°C. What was the temperature at 2 P.M.?

A. ⁺11°C   **B.** ⁻3°C
C. ⁺3°C   **D.** not here

12. Find the equal ratio.

$$\frac{16}{24} = \frac{n}{3}$$

A. 8   **B.** 6
C. 2   **D.** not here

13. Solve the proportion.

$$\frac{3}{5} = \frac{n}{125}$$

A. 75   **B.** 375
C. 15   **D.** not here

14. Solve the proportion.

$$\frac{3}{8} = \frac{6}{n}$$

A. 16   **B.** 18
C. 24   **D.** not here

15. How many stars can you expect to get in 9 spins?

A. 9   **B.** 6
C. 3   **D.** not here

16. Write the decimal for 59%.

A. 0.059

B. 0.59

C. 5.9

D. not here

17. Write the fraction for 35%.
Write the answer in lowest terms.

A. $\frac{35}{100}$

B. $\frac{7}{20}$

C. $\frac{3}{10}$

D. not here

18. Write $\frac{4}{5}$ as a percent.

A. 8%   **B.** 20%
C. 80%   **D.** not here

19. Use a fraction to find the percent.

75% of 300 = ___?___

A. 225   **B.** $\frac{900}{4}$
C. 900   **D.** not here

20. Use a decimal to find the percent.

25% of 80 = ___?___

A. 40   **B.** 60
C. 20   **D.** not here

21. What percent of 60 is 12?

A. 30%   **B.** 20%
C. 12%   **D.** not here

22. Compare.

$^-3 \bullet {}^-7$

A. >   **B.** <
C. =   **D.** not here

23. Add.

$^-3 + {}^-4 =$ ___?___

A. 7   **B.** 1
C. 1   **D.** not here

24. Add.

$^-6 + {}^+8 =$ ___?___

A. $^-2$ **B.** $^+2$
C. $^-14$ **D.** not here

25. Subtract.

$^-6 - {}^-5 =$ ___?___

A. $^-1$ **B.** $^+13$
C. $^+1$ **D.** not here

26. Subtract.

$^+7 - {}^-2 =$ ___?___

A. $^-5$ **B.** $^+5$
C. $^+9$ **D.** not here

27. Brian bought a record album marked $12.95 at a 20% discount. Estimate the amount of discount.

A. $8.00   **B.** $2.00
C. $5.00   **D.** not here

28. Ralph walks 8 miles in 2 hours. Use a proportion to find how far he will walk in 12 hours at that rate.

A. 16 miles   **B.** 3 miles
C. 48 miles   **D.** not here

TABLE OF MEASURES

Metric

United States Customary

Length

10 millimeters (mm) = 1 centimeter (cm)
10 centimeters = 1 decimeter (dm)
10 decimeters = 1 meter (m)
1,000 meters = 1 kilometer (km)

12 inches (in.) = 1 foot (ft)
36 inches ⎫
3 feet ⎬ = 1 yard (yd)
5,280 feet ⎫
1,760 yards ⎬ = 1 mile (mi)

Area

100 square millimeters (mm^2) = 1 square centimeter (cm^2)
10,000 square centimeters = 1 square meter (m^2)

144 square inches (in.^{2}) = 1 square foot (ft^2)
9 square feet = 1 square yard (yd^2)

Volume

1,000 cubic millimeters (mm^3) = 1 cubic centimeter (cm^3)
1,000,000 cubic centimeters = 1 cubic meter (m^3)

1,728 cubic inches (in.^{3}) = 1 cubic foot (ft^3)
27 cubic feet = 1 cubic yard (yd^3)

Capacity

1,000 milliliters (mL) = 1 liter (L)
1,000 liters = 1 kiloliter (kL)

1 cup (c) = 8 fluid ounces (fl. oz)
2 cups = 1 pint (pt)
2 pints = 1 quart (qt)
4 quarts = 1 gallon (gal)

Mass/Weight

1,000 milligrams (mg) = 1 gram (g)
1,000 grams = 1 kilogram (kg)

16 ounces (oz) = 1 pound (lb)
2,000 pounds = 1 ton (T)

Time

60 seconds (s) = 1 minute (min)
60 minutes = 1 hour (h)
24 hours = 1 day (d)
7 days = 1 week (wk)
28 to 31 days = 1 month (mo)
12 months ⎫
52 weeks ⎬ = 1 year (yr)
100 years = 1 century (cen)

TABLE OF SYMBOLS

$+$	plus
$-$	minus
$\times$	times
$\div$	divided by
$=$	equals or is equal to
$\neq$	is not equal to
$>$	is greater than
$<$	is less than
$\approx$	is approximately equal to
$\sim$	is similar to
$\cong$	is congruent to
. . .	pattern continues without end
7 r4	seven remainder four
14.3	decimal point: fourteen and three tenths
$0.\overline{27}$	repeating decimal: 0.272727 . . .
30%	percent: thirty percent
4:3	ratio: four to three
8^2	eight to the second power or eight squared
$\sqrt{64}$	square root: square root of sixty-four
$+3$	positive three
-3	negative three
(1,4)	ordered pair: ($x = 1$, $y = 4$)
$\llcorner$	right angle
$\angle ABC$	angle ABC
$\circ$	degree (angle or temperature)
$\bullet A$	point A
$\overline{AB}$	line segment with endpoints A and B
$\overrightarrow{AB}$	ray AB with endpoint A
$\overleftrightarrow{AB}$	line through points A and B
$\parallel$	is parallel to
$\perp$	is perpendicular to
$\triangle ABC$	triangle ABC
π	pi (approximately 3.14 or $\frac{22}{7}$)
P(E)	probability of event E

GLOSSARY

Acute angle   An angle whose measure is greater than 0° and less than 90°. (p. 332)

Addend   A number that is added. (p. 24)
Example: 8 + 7 = 15 The addends are 8 and 7.

Addition (+)   An operation on two numbers resulting in their sum. (p. 24)
Example: 9 + 8 = 17   9 and 8 are addends. 17 is the sum.

Angle   Two rays with the same endpoint. The endpoint is the vertex of the angle. (p. 332)
Example:

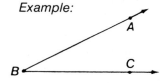

Point *B* is the vertex of ∠*ABC*.

Area   The number of square units needed to cover a surface. (p. 198)
Examples: Some formulas to find area are:
rectangle	$A = l \times w$
parallelogram	$A = b \times h$
triangle	$A = \frac{1}{2} \times b \times h$
circle	$A = \pi \times r^2$

Associative property of addition   The way in which addends are grouped does not change the sum. (p. 24)
Example: (7 + 5) + 6 = 7 + (5 + 6).

Associative property of multiplication   The way in which factors are grouped does not change the product. (p. 50)
Example: (3 × 4) × 5 = 3 × (4 × 5)

Average (mean)   The quotient found by dividing a sum by the number of addends. (p. 82)
Example: The average of 2, 3, and 7 is 4 because 2 + 3 + 7 = 12 and 12 ÷ 3 = 4.

Bar graph   A graph with bars (rectangles) of different heights to show and compare information. (p. 112)

Capacity   The amount a container will hold when filled. (p. 210)

Chord   A line segment with endpoints on a circle. (p. 346)

Circle   A closed curve with all points an equal distance from a center point. (p. 346)

Circumference   The distance around a circle. (p. 196)

Common denominator   A common multiple of the denominators of two or more fractions. (p. 250)
Example: 18 is a common denominator for $\frac{5}{6}$ and $\frac{2}{3}$.

Common factor   A factor of two or more numbers. (p. 236)
Example: 1, 2, 3, and 6 are the common factors of 6 and 12.

Commutative property of addition   The order in which addends are added does not change the sum. (p. 24)
Example: 6 + 4 = 4 + 6

Commutative property of multiplication   The order in which factors are multiplied does not change the product. (p. 50)
Example: 5 × 7 = 7 × 5

Composite number   A whole number greater than 1 that has more than two factors. (p. 232)
Example: 8 is a composite number since its factors are 1, 2, 4, 8.

Cone   A solid with one circular face and one vertex. (p. 350)

Congruent angles   Angles that have the same measure. (p. 335)

Congruent polygons   Polygons that have the same size and shape. (p. 344)

Coordinate graph   A drawing of numbered lines that cross at right angles and are used to name the positions of points. (p. 414)

Cube   A rectangular prism with six congruent square faces. (p. 350)
   Example:

Customary measurement system   A measurement system that uses inches, feet, yards, and miles as units of length; cups, pints, quarts, and gallons for liquid capacity; ounces, pounds, and tons as units of weight; and degrees Fahrenheit as units of temperature. (p. 312)

Cylinder   A solid with two bases that are congruent circles. (p. 350)

Decagon   A polygon with ten sides. (p. 342)

Decimal   A number that uses place value and a decimal point to show tenths, hundredths, thousandths, and so on. (p. 130)
   Example: 3.85   Read as three and eighty-five hundredths.

Degree (°)   A standard unit for measuring angles. (p. 332)

Degree Celsius (°C)   A standard unit for measuring temperature in the metric system. (p. 214)
   Example: Water freezes at 0°C and boils at 100°C.

Degree Fahrenheit (°F)   A standard unit for measuring temperature in the customary

   Example: Water freezes at 32°F and boils at 212°F.

Denominator   The number below the bar in a fraction. (p. 244)
   Example: $\frac{3}{4}$ The denominator is 4.

Diameter   A line segment through the center of a circle with endpoints on the circle. (p. 346)

Difference   The answer to a subtraction problem. (p. 24)
   Example: $14 - 9 = 5$ The difference is 5.

Digit   Any one of the ten symbols 0, 1, 2, 3, 4, 5, 6, 7, 8, or 9. (p. 2)

Distributive property of multiplication over addition   The product of a number and the sum of two numbers equals the sum of the two products. (p. 52)
   Example: $3 \times (4 + 2) = (3 \times 4) + (3 \times 2)$

Dividend   The number that is divided in a division problem. (p. 74)
   Example: $12 \div 4$ 12 is the dividend.

Divisible   A number is divisible by another number if the quotient is a whole number and the remainder is 0. (p. 230)
   Example: 18 is divisible by 6.

Division ($\overline{)}$ or $\div$)   An operation on two numbers that results in a quotient and a remainder. (p. 74)

Divisor   The number by which the dividend is divided. (p. 74)
   Example: $7\overline{)45}$ 6r3   The divisor is 7.

Edge   The line segment where two faces of a solid meet. (p. 350)
   Example:

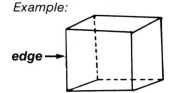

edge →

Endpoint   A point at the end of a line segment or ray. (p. 330)

Equal ratios   Ratios that show the same comparison. (p. 364)
Example: $\frac{1}{3}$, $\frac{2}{6}$, and $\frac{3}{9}$ are equivalent ratios.

Equation   A number sentence that uses the symbol $=$. (p. 148)
Examples: $5 \times 4 = 20$; $8 + n = 13$

Equilateral triangle   A triangle with three equal sides. Each angle measures 60°. (p. 342)

Equivalent fractions   Fractions that name the same number. (p. 246)
Example: $\frac{3}{4}$ and $\frac{6}{8}$ are equivalent.

Even number   A whole number that is a multiple of 2. An even number has 0, 2, 4, 6, or 8 in the ones place. (p. 230)
Examples: 4, 16, 28, 120 are even numbers.

Expanded form   A way to show a number as a sum of multiples of ten. (p. 2)
Example: $387 = 3 \times 100 + 8 \times 10 + 7 \times 1$.

Exponent   A number that tells how many times the base is used as a factor. (p. 12)
Example: ┌──**exponent**
$3^2 = 3 \times 3$ or 9.
└──**base**

Face   A flat surface of a solid. (p. 350)

Factor   A factor of a number is a whole number that divides it exactly. (p. 232)
Example: 1, 2, 3, and 6 are factors of 6.

Factor tree   The prime factors of a number can be found by making a factor tree. (p. 234)
Example:

```
        20
       /  \
      2  ×  10
           /  \
   2  ×  2  ×  5
```

$20 = 2^2 \times 5$

Fraction   The quotient of two whole numbers: $a \div b = \frac{a}{b}$. In the fraction $\frac{a}{b}$, a is called the numerator and b is called the denominator. (p. 244)

Graph   A drawing used to show and compare information. Some types of graphs are bar graphs, circle graphs, line graphs, and picture graphs. (p. 110)

Greatest common factor   (GCF) The greatest factor that two or more numbers have in common. (p. 236)
Example: 7 is the GCF of 14 and 21.

Hexagon   A polygon with six sides. (p. 342)

Integers   The whole numbers and their opposites.
$\ldots, ^-3, ^-2, ^-1, 0, ^+1, ^+2, ^+3, \ldots$
$^-2$ is a negative integer, $^+2$ or 2 is a positive integer. (p. 400)

Intersecting lines   Lines that meet or cross. Intersecting lines have only one point in common. (p. 336)

Inverse operations   Operations that undo each other. Addition and subtraction as well as multiplication and division are inverse operations. (p. 75)
Examples:
$29 - 13 = 16$ and $16 + 13 = 29$
$15 \div 3 = 5$ and $5 \times 3 = 15$.

Isosceles triangle   A triangle with two equal sides and two equal angles. (p. 342)

Least common denominator (LCD)   The least common multiple of the denominators of two or more fractions. (p. 250)
Example: 12 is the LCD for $\frac{1}{4}$ and $\frac{5}{6}$.

Least common multiple (LCM) The smallest nonzero multiple that two or more numbers have in common. (p. 238)
Example: The LCM of 6 and 9 is 18.

Line A straight path extending in both directions with no endpoints. (p. 330)

Line graph A graph in which a line is used to show a change. (p. 114)

Line of symmetry A line that divides a figure into two congruent parts. (p. 348)

Line segment Part of a line with two endpoints. (p. 330)

Lowest terms A fraction is in lowest terms when the numerator and the denominator have no common factor greater than one. (p. 248)

Median The middle score in a distribution. (p. 89)

Metric system A measurement system that uses centimeters, meters, and kilometers as units of length; milliliters and liters as units of capacity; grams and kilograms as units of mass; and degrees Celsius as units of temperature. (p. 190)

Mixed number The sum of a whole number and a fraction. (p. 252)
Example: $3\frac{1}{2} = 3 + \frac{1}{2}$.

Mode The score with the highest frequency in a group of scores. (p. 89)
Example: 3 is the mode of 2, 3, 3, 4, 5.

Multiple A number that is the product of a given number and a whole number (p. 238)
Example: Multiples of 3: 3, 6, 9, 12, 15, . . .

Multiplication ($\times$) An operation on two numbers, called factors, which results in a product. (p. 50)
Example: $8 \times 9 = 72$
The factors are 8 and 9.
The product is 72.

Negative number A number less than zero. (p. 398)

Number line A line with equally spaced points named by numbers. (p. 400)
Example:

$$\xleftarrow{\quad} \overset{\bullet}{\underset{^-3}{}} \; \overset{\bullet}{\underset{^-2}{}} \; \overset{\bullet}{\underset{^-1}{}} \; \overset{\bullet}{\underset{0}{}} \; \overset{\bullet}{\underset{1}{}} \; \overset{\bullet}{\underset{2}{}} \; \overset{\bullet}{\underset{3}{}} \xrightarrow{\quad}$$

Numerator The number above the bar in a fraction. (p. 244)
Example: $\frac{2}{5}$ The numerator is 2.

Obtuse angle An angle whose measure is greater than 90° and less than 180°. (p. 332)

Octagon A polygon with eight sides. (p. 342)

Odd number A whole number that is not a multiple of 2. An odd number ends in 1, 3, 5, 7, or 9. (p. 230)
Examples: 3, 17, 29, 235 are odd numbers.

Opposite numbers Two numbers whose points on the number line are the same distance from 0, but in opposite directions. (p. 398)
Examples: 4 and $^-4$ are opposites.
$^-\frac{2}{3}$ and $\frac{2}{3}$ are opposites.

Ordered pair A pair of numbers, (x, y), arranged in order so that x is first and y is second. (p. 116)

Outcome Each possible result in a probability experiment. (p. 370)

Parallel lines Lines in the same plane that do not intersect. Parallel lines have no points in common. (p. 336)

Parallelogram A quadrilateral with opposite sides parallel and congruent. (p. 342)

Pentagon   A polygon with five sides. (p. 342)

Percent (%)   Percent means per hundred.
P% = $\frac{P}{100}$. (p. 378)
   Example: $\frac{2}{5} = \frac{40}{100} = 40\%$

Perimeter   The sum of the lengths of the
sides of a polygon. (p. 194)
   Examples: Some formulas to find
   perimeter are:
   rectangle P = 2 × (ℓ + w)
   square   P = 4 × s

Period   A group of three digits set off by a
comma in a number. (p. 6)
   Example: Three million, four hundred
   twenty thousand, seventy-one is written:
   3,420,071.

Perpendicular lines   Two lines that intersect
to form right angles. (p. 336)

Pi (π)   The number that is the ratio of the
circumference of any circle to the length of
a diameter of that circle. Approximations for
π are 3.14 and $\frac{22}{7}$. (p. 196)

Pictograph   A visual representation used to
make comparisons. A key always appears
at the bottom of a pictograph or picture
graph showing how many each object
represents. (p. 110)

Place value   In a decimal number, each
place for a digit has a value ten times the
value of the place at its right. (pp. 4 and 130)
   Example: 8,763 = 8 × 1,000 + 7 × 100
   + 6 × 10 + 3 × 1.

Point   An exact location. A dot is often drawn
to represent a point. (p. 330)

Polygon   A closed plane figure formed by
three or more line segments joined at the
endpoints. (p. 342)

Positive number   A number that is greater
than zero. (p. 398)

Prime factorization   Any composite number
can be factored as a product of primes. This
product is called the prime factorization of
that number. (p. 234)

Examples: 24 = 2 × 2 × 2 × 3 or 2^3 × 3.
   45 = 3 × 3 × 5   or 3^2 × 5.
   60 = 2 × 2 × 3 × 5 or 2^2 × 3
   × 5.

Prime number   A whole number greater than
1 that has only two factors, 1 and itself.
(p. 232)
   Examples: 2, 3, 5, 7, 11, 13, 17, 19 are
   all prime numbers.

Probability   A number from 0 to 1 that tells
how likely it is that an event will take place.
(p. 370)

Product   The answer to a multiplication
problem. (p. 50)

Property of one for multiplication   When
one of the two factors is 1, the product
equals the other factor. (p. 50)
   Examples: a × 1 = a; 6 × 1 = 6.

Proportion   An equality of two ratios. Cross
products are often used to test a
proportion. If $\frac{a}{b} = \frac{c}{d}$ then a × d = b × c.
(p. 364)
   Example: $\frac{5}{8} = \frac{15}{24}$ since 5 × 24 = 8 × 15.

Protractor   An instrument used to measure
angles. (p. 334)

Pyramid   A solid with one face that is a
polygon and three or more faces that are
triangles with a common vertex. (p. 350)
   Example:

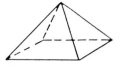

Quadrilateral   A polygon with four sides.
(p. 342)

Quotient   The answer to a division problem.

Radius (pl. radii)   A line segment with one
endpoint at the center of a circle and the
other endpoint on the circle. All radii of a
circle are equal. (p. 346)

Ratio A comparison of two numbers. (p. 362)

Example: The ratio of two to five can be written as 2 to 5, 2:5, or $\frac{2}{5}$.

Ray A part of a line that has one endpoint and extends forever in only one direction. (p. 330)

Reciprocals Two numbers whose product is one. (p. 306)

Examples: $\frac{3}{5}$ and $\frac{5}{3}$ are reciprocals.

8 and $\frac{1}{8}$ are reciprocals.

Rectangle A parallelogram with four right angles. (p. 342)

Remainder The number left over in a division problem. The remainder must be less than the divisor. (p. 74)

Example:

$$4\overline{)39} \quad \begin{array}{c} 9 \ r3 \end{array}$$ The remainder is 3.

Rhombus A parallelogram with four congruent sides. (p. 342)

Right angle An angle that measures 90°. (p. 332)

Right triangle A triangle with one right angle. (p. 332)

Roman numerals Symbols used by the Romans to name numbers. Roman numeration does not use place value. (p. 19)

Examples:

I	V	X	L	C	D	M
1	5	10	50	100	500	1,000

Rounding Expressing a number to the nearest thousandth, hundredth, tenth, one, ten, hundred, thousand. (p. 10)

Example: 37.85 rounded to the nearest tenth is 37.9.

Scale drawing A drawing that is the same shape as an actual object, but not the same size. The scale gives the ratio of the size in the drawing to the size of the actual object. (p. 366)

Scalene triangle A triangle with three unequal sides. (p. 342)

Scientific notation Writing a number as the product of two factors. The first factor is between 1 and 10. The second factor is a power of 10. (p. 185)

Example: $32,000 = 3.2 \times 10^4$

$0.035 = 3.5 \times 10^{-2}$

Similar polygons Polygons that have the same shape. Corresponding sides of similar polygons are in proportion. Corresponding angles are congruent. (p. 368)

Sphere A solid with all points an equal distance from the center. (p. 350)

Square A rectangle with 4 congruent sides. (p. 342)

Square number The product of a number and itself. (p. 421)

Example: $5^2 = 5 \times 5 = 25$ The square of 5 is 25.

Square root One of the two equal factors of a number. (p. 421)

Example: $\sqrt{25} = 5$ because $5^2 = 25$

Subtraction (−) An operation on two numbers resulting in a difference. (p. 24)

Example:

$$\begin{array}{rl} 25 & \text{minuend} \\ -\ 8 & \text{subtrahend} \\ \hline 17 & \text{difference} \end{array}$$

Sum The answer to an addition problem. (p. 24)

Surface area The sum of the areas of all the surfaces of a solid. (p. 206)

Symmetry (line) A figure has line symmetry if it can be folded about a line so that the two halves of the figure are congruent. The fold line is the line of symmetry. (p. 348)

Trapezoid   A quadrilateral with one pair of parallel sides. (p. 342)
> *Example:*

Triangle   A polygon with three sides (p. 342)

Unit price   The ratio of the total cost to the number of units. (p. 169)

Unlike fractions   Fractions with different denominators. (p. 268)
> *Example:* $\frac{2}{3}$ and $\frac{3}{4}$ are unlike fractions.

Venn diagram   A useful diagram showing relationships. (p. 45)
> *Example:* Some numbers divisible by 3 are odd numbers.

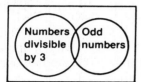

Vertex (pl. vertices)   The point at which two rays of an angle, two sides of a polygon, or three or more edges of a solid meet. (p. 332)

Volume   The number of cubic units needed to fill a solid. (p. 208)
> *Example:* Volume of a rectangular solid is $V = \ell \times w \times h$.

Zero property for addition   When 0 is added to any addend, the sum equals the addend. (p. 24)
> *Examples:* $9 + 0 = 9$; $0 + 12 = 12$.

Zero property for multiplication   If 0 is a factor, the product is always 0. (p. 50)
> *Examples:* $13 \times 0 = 0$; $0 \times 7 = 0$.

Zero property for subtraction   When 0 is subtracted from a number, the answer is the number. (p. 36)
> *Example:* $8 - 0 = 8$.

INDEX

similar, and ratio, 368–369
Positive integers, 400–401
Positive numbers, to show opposites, 398–399, 432
Pound, 316–317
Powers, 12–13, 185
Prediction, and probability, 372–373, 393
Pricing, unit, 169
Prime factorization, 234–235, 432
Prime factors, 234–235
Prime Number Sieve, 233
Prime numbers, 232–233, 432
twin, 233
Prisms, 350–351
rectangular. *See* Rectangular prism
Probability, 432
and prediction, 372–373, 393
and ratio, 370–371
Problem Formulation, 15, 65, 87, 101, 149, 167, 219, 257, 315, 375, 407
Problem solving applications
addition and subtraction, 25, 27, 29, 35, 37, 39
decimals: adding and subtracting, 131, 133, 135, 137, 139, 145, 147
decimals: multiplication and division, 159, 161, 163, 165, 171, 173, 175, 177, 179
division, 75, 77, 79, 81, 83, 85, 91, 93, 95, 97, 99
fractions: addition and subtraction, 267, 269, 271, 273, 279, 281, 283
fractions: multiplication and division, 295, 297, 299, 301, 307, 309, 311, 313, 315, 317
geometry, 331, 333, 335, 337, 343, 345, 347, 349, 351
graphing, 111, 113, 115, 117
integers, 399, 401, 403, 405, 411, 413, 415
measurement, 191, 193, 195, 197, 199, 201, 203, 207, 209, 211, 213, 215, 217
multiplication, 51, 53, 55, 57, 63

number theory and fractions, 231, 233, 235, 237, 239, 245, 247, 249, 251, 253, 255
numeration, 3, 5, 7, 9, 11, 13
ratio and percent, 363, 365, 367, 369, 371, 373, 379, 381, 383, 385, 387
Problem Solving Maintenance, 71, 155, 263, 359
Problem solving strategies
add, subtract, multiply, or divide, 100–101
choosing a strategy, 71, 155, 263, 359
equations, 148–149, 240–241
estimation, 58–59, 218–219, 302–303, 388–389, 406–407
guess and check, 64–65
interpret the remainder, 284–285
logical reasoning, 338–339
making a drawing, 256–257
missing information, 86–87
multistep, 166–167
non–routine, 40–41, 180–81, 318–319, 416–417
patterns, 140–141, 352–353
reading maps, 30–31
too much information, 86–87
using equations, 148–149, 240–241
using line graphs, 118–119
using a table, 14–15
using proportions, 374–375
working backwards, 274–275
write your own question, *See* Problem formulation
Products, 13, 50, 432
cross, 247, 364–365, 374–375
estimating, with decimals, 158–159
writing in lowest terms, 300–301
zeros in, with decimals, 162–163
Projects, 7, 19, 39, 61, 97, 143, 147, 173, 181, 205, 243, 277, 279, 303, 319, 333, 337, 341, 367, 409, 411
Properties

of addition, 24, 428, 434
of multiplication, 50, 428, 429, 432, 434
Proportion(s), 432
ratio and, 364–365
solving, 374–375
Protractor, 334–335, 432
Pyramids, 350–351, 432

Quadrilaterals, 342–343, 432
Quart, 316–317
Quotients, 74, 432
two-digit, 76–77, 94–95
zero(s) in, 80–81
using a calculator, 99

Radius, 346–347, 432
Range, 119
Ratio(s), 362–363, 433 *See also* Percent
equal, 364
fractions for, 362–363
and probability, 370–371
and proportion, 364–365
scale drawing, 366–367
and similar polygons, 368–369
Rays, 330–331, 332, 433
Reciprocals, 306, 433
Rectangles, 342–343, 433
area of, customary units of, 314–315
area of, metric units of, 198–199
Rectangular prism, 350–351
surface area of, 206–207
volume of, 208–209
Rectangular pyramid, 350–351
Regrouping
addition with, 28–29
subtraction with, 34–35
Remainder, interpreting the, 284–285, 433
Reviews, 16–17, 42–43, 66–67, 102–103, 120–121, 150–151, 182–183, 220–221, 258–259, 286–287, 320–321, 354–355, 390–391, 418–419
Rhombus, 342–343, 433
Right angle, 332–333, 433
Roman numerals, 19, 433

Picture credits continued

Researchers; 211, Bob McKeever/Tom Stack & Associates; 215 (t), Mitchell Funk/The Image Bank; 215 (b), John Bryson/The Image Bank; 216, Alan Manley/Shostal Associates; 217, Spencer Swanger/Tom Stack & Associates; 218, Kevin Schafer/Tom Stack & Associates; 229 (t), Larry Lefever/Grant Heilman; 229 (b), Grant Heilman/Grant Heilman; 231, Grant Heilman/Grant Heilman; 232, Alan Pitcairn/Grant Heilman; 234, Grant Heilman/Grant Heilman; 234, Grant Heilman; 236 (t), Larry Lefever/Grant Heilman; 236 (b), John Aikins/UNIPHOTO; 238, John Colwell/Grant Heilman; 239, HBJ Photo/b.b. Steel; 240, HBJ Photo/b.b. Steel; 241 (t), HBJ Photo/b.b. Steel; 241 (b), HBJ Photo, Beverly Brosius; 248, Ed Cooper/H. Armstrong Roberts; 249, John Colwell/Grant Heilman; 250, R. Hamilton Smith; 254, Missouri Historical Society; 255, The Granger Collection; 257, HBJ Photo/Rodney Jones; 260, Larry Lefever/Grant Heilman; 265 (tr), Gerald Corsi/Tom Stack & Associates; 265 (bl), Robert Frerck/Woodfin Camp & Associates; 266 (t), Robert Frerck/Woodfin Camp & Associates; 266 (b), NASA; 268, Peter Silvia/PHOTOUNIQUE; 270, Nawrocki Stock Photo; 272, Phil Degginger; 274, Robert Frerck/Woodfin Camp & Associates; 275 (t), Ted Cordingley/Nawrocki Stock Photo; 275 (b), W. Wright/H. Armstrong Roberts; 277, HBJ Photo/Rodney Jones; 278, Robert V. Eckert, Jr./The Picture Cube; 281, HBJ Photo/Marion Bernstein; 282, NASA; 283, TRW, Inc.; 284, Gerald Corsi/Tom Stack & Associates; 285, Merrell Wood/The Image Bank; 289, Marc Romanelli/The Image Bank; 293 (tl), A.T.&T.; 293 (br), Culver Pictures, Inc.; 296 (t), The Bettmann Archive; 296 (b), Culver Pictures, Inc.; 298, Wide World Photos; 300, Courtesy of I.B.M.; 302 (t), A.T.&T.; 302 (b), A.T.&T.; 306, The Bettmann Archive; 309, The Granger Collection; 312, John Coletti/The Picture Cube; 313, Roy Morsch; 314, The Bettmann Archive; 329 (bl), Shostal Associates; 329 (tr), Mitchell Funk/The Image Bank; 332, H. Armstrong Roberts; 334, Shostal Associates; 335, HBJ Photo/Erik Arnesen; 338 (t), ARTSTREET; 338 (c), ARTSTREET; 338 (b), Stanley Rosenthal/Leo de Wys; 339, Rhoda Sidney/Leo de Wys; 351 Bob Glander/Shostal Associates; 361, The Granger Collection; 362, Michael Heron; 364, Michael Heron; 368, Shostal Associates; 372, Terry McKoy/The Picture Cube; 373, George Ancona/International Stock Photography; 374 (t), Keith Skelton/PHOTOUNIQUE; 374 (b), Milt and Joan Mann/Cameramann Int'l.; 379, Roy Morsch; 381, John Marmaras/Woodfin Camp Associates; 382, ARTSTREET; 383, The Photosource, Inc.; 384, The Granger Collection; 388 (t), The Photosource, Inc.; 388 (b), E. Streichan/The Photosource, Inc.; 393, Roy Morsch; 397 E.R. Degginger; 400 (t), NASA; 400, (inset), Comstock, Inc./T. Grill; 401, NASA; 402, Sepp Seitz/Woodfin Camp & Associates; 403, Comstock, Inc./T. Grill; 404, Focus on Sports; 405, Focus on Sports; 410, E.R. Degginger; 411, E.R. Degginger; 412, Phil Degginger.

6
B 7
C 8
D 9
E 0
F 1
G 2
H 3
I 4
J 5